# ICH/美国临床试验法规选编

陈 东 主编

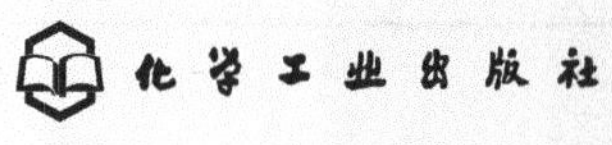


·北 京·

本书以中英文对照的形式对 ICH GCP（E6_R2）以及美国联邦法规 21CFR 和 45CFR 有关临床试验相关章节进行翻译、汇编，中英文对照方便读者学习、查阅。本书适用于制药企业、新药研发机构、临床试验机构、CRO 公司、SMO 公司的从业人员，也可供相关管理部门参考。

**图书在版编目（CIP）数据**

ICH/美国临床试验法规选编：汉英对照/陈东主编. —北京：化学工业出版社，2018.11（2023.1 重印）

ISBN 978-7-122-32884-7

Ⅰ.①I… Ⅱ.①陈… Ⅲ.①临床药学-药效试验-卫生法-美国-汉、英 Ⅳ.①D971.221

中国版本图书馆 CIP 数据核字（2018）第 198775 号

---

责任编辑：邱飞婵　　装帧设计：关　飞

责任校对：王素芹

---

出版发行：化学工业出版社（北京市东城区青年湖南街 13 号　邮政编码 100011）

印　　装：涿州市般润文化传播有限公司

850mm×1168mm　1/32　印张 16¼　字数 471 千字

2023 年 1 月北京第 1 版第 4 次印刷

---

购书咨询：010-64518888　　售后服务：010-64518899

网　　址：http://www.cip.com.cn

凡购买本书，如有缺损质量问题，本社销售中心负责调换。

---

定　　价：80.00 元

版权所有　违者必究

# 编写人员名单

主　编　陈　东

编　者　陈　东　颜　湘　祝勇梅　孙　洁　胡　涛

# 前　言

2017 年 6 月，中国成为国际人用药品注册技术协调会正式成员，我国真正融入国际药品监管体系。近些年来在海外开展临床试验的中国境内药企不再是凤毛麟角，国内开展的临床试验也逐步向国际标准看齐，越来越多药物研发从业人员加入学习、实践临床试验国际化标准的队伍。顺应时势需要，我们就临床试验中经常涉及的问题选择翻译了 ICH GCP（E6_R2），美国联邦法案 21CFR 中关于电子记录/电子签名、保护人类受试者、临床研究者财务公开、机构审查委员会、研究新药申请、研究器械豁免以及美国联邦法规 45CFR 中关于保护人类受试者部分，以供有志于中国临床试验发展的同行们共同学习。翻译过程中难免出现错误疏忽之处，敬请指正。后附英文原文，以便大家对照学习。

特别致谢：中南大学湘雅二医院内分泌科颜湘医生与浙江大学附属第一医院血液科孙洁医生在繁重的医疗工作中抽出时间对翻译稿进行校正。

声明：本书中文译文非 ICH 和 FDA 官方认可的翻译文件。

**陈　东**

**2018 年 6 月**

# 目 录

## 国际人用药品注册技术协调会（ICH）
## ——临床试验质量管理规范指导原则（E6_R2）

## 美国联邦法案

# ICH GUIDELINE FOR GOOD CLINICAL PRACTICE (GCP) (E6_R2)

Current Step 4 version dated 9 November 2016

## CODE OF FEDERAL REGULATIONS

[2016 年 11 月 9 日版本]

# 国际人用药品注册技术协调会
# （ICH）

## ——临床试验质量管理规范指导原则
## （E6_R2）

## E6（R1）
## 文件历史

| 首次编码 | 历史 | 日期 | 新编码 2005年11月 |
| --- | --- | --- | --- |
| E6 | 第2阶段经指导委员会批准，公布以征求公众意见 | 1995年4月27日 | E6 |
| E6 | 在第4阶段经指导委员会批准，推荐ICH三方监管机构采用 | 1996年5月1日 | E6 |

## E6（R1）第4阶段版本

| | | | |
| --- | --- | --- | --- |
| E6 | 由指导委员会批准第4阶段后编辑校订 | 1996年6月10日 | E6（R1） |

## 现行E6（R2）第4阶段版本的增补

| 编码 | 历史 | 日期 |
| --- | --- | --- |
| E6（R2） | 第4阶段被ICH监管成员采纳<br>增补内容已整合到ICH E6（R1）文件中，增补内容直接整合到以前版本指导原则的以下章节中：引言，1.63，1.64，1.65，2.10，2.13，4.2.5，4.2.6，4.9.0，5.0，5.0.1，5.0.2，5.0.3，5.0.4，5.0.5，5.0.6，5.0.7，5.2.2，5.5.3（a），5.5.3（b），5.5.3（h），5.18.3，5.18.6（e），5.18.7，5.20.1，8.1 | 2016年11月9日 |

**法律公告：**本指导原则中的所有内容均受版权保护，在承认ICH对本文件版权所有的前提下，可使用、复制本文件、也可将其嵌入到其他文件中，进行改编、修正、翻译或分发。如果对本文件进行改编、修正或翻译，必须采取合理步骤，清晰标记、指出或者用其他方式识别哪些是基于原文件，哪些对原文件有所更改。在对原文件进行改编、修正或翻译时，必须避免产生任何对原文件的改编、修正或翻译是由ICH支持或赞助的错误印象。

本文件提供的文件是“按原样”的文件，不提供任何形式的授权。ICH或者本原文件的作者不承担任何因使用本文件而产生的索赔、损失或者其他责任。

上述权限不适用于由第三方提供的内容。因此，当使用归属于第三方版权的文件时，复制文件必须获取版权所有人的许可。

# 引　言

临床试验质量管理规范（GCP）是针对涉及人类受试者参加试验的设计、实施、记录和报告而制定的国际性伦理和科学质量标准。遵循此标准为受试者的权利、安全和福祉提供了公共保障。此标准与源自赫尔辛基宣言的原则保持一致，并为临床试验数据的可信性提供保证。

ICH GCP 指导原则的目的是为欧盟、日本和美国提供统一的标准，促进这些管辖地区的管理当局相互接受临床试验数据。

本指导原则是在参考欧盟、日本、美国以及澳大利亚、加拿大、北欧等国家和世界卫生组织（WHO）现行的临床试验质量管理规范后形成的。

在产生拟提交给管理当局的临床试验数据时应当遵循本指导原则。

本文中确立的指导原则也适用于可影响人类受试者安全和福祉的其他临床研究。

**增补**

自从制定 ICH GCP 以来，临床试验的规模、复杂性和成本在不断增加。技术的发展和风险管理操作规程的发展，为提高临床试验效率和聚焦于重要活动带来新的发展机遇。在制定 ICH E6（R1）时，大部分临床试验还在使用基于纸质流程的操作程序。使用电子数据记录及报告的技术发展促生了新的临床试验方法。例如，如今对大规模临床试验使用中心化监查方式较传统模式更有优势。因此，对本指导原则进行修订，在继续确保受试者得到保护以及试验结果可靠的基础上，鼓励在临床试验的设计、实施、监督、记录及报告中采用更先进、更有效的方法。同时更新了电子记录和核心文件的标准，以提高临床试验的质量和效率。

本指导原则应当结合与临床试验实施相关的其他ICH指导原则一起阅读，如E2A（临床安全性数据管理）、E3（临床研究报告）、E7（老年人群）、E8（临床试验一般考虑）、E9（统计原则）和E11（儿科人群）。

本ICH GCP完整增补版指导原则为欧盟、日本、美国、加拿大和瑞士提供了统一标准，以促进上述管理当局在其管辖范围内相互认可彼此提供的临床数据。当E6（R1）内容和E6（R2）增补内容出现冲突时，以E6（R2）内容为优先考虑。

# 1 术 语

## 1.1 药品不良反应（ADR）

对于仍处于上市前临床研究的新药品或药品新用途，尤其在其治疗剂量尚未确定前，所有与任何剂量药品有关的有害的和非预期的反应都应被考虑为药品不良反应（ADR）。药品不良反应意味着在药品与不良事件之间存在因果关系，或其中的关联至少存在合理的可能，即不能排除因果关系。

对已上市药品，药品不良反应是指在用于预防、诊断或治疗疾病或改善生理功能时，使用正常剂量的药品对人产生的有害和非预期反应（参见“ICH临床安全性数据管理指导原则：快速报告的定义和标准”）。

## 1.2 不良事件（AE）

在使用药品的患者或临床研究受试者中发生的任何不适医学事件，不一定与此治疗有因果关系。因此，不良事件（AE）可以是与使用试验用药在时间上相关的任何不适和非预期的体征（包括异常实验室发现）、症状或疾病，而不管此事件是否与试验用药相关（参见“ICH临床安全性数据管理指导原则：快速报告的定义和标准”）。

## 1.3 增补（试验方案）

见“试验方案增补”。

### 1.4 适用管理法规

任何阐述实施试验用药临床试验的相关法律和法规。

### 1.5 批准（与机构审查委员会相关）

机构审查委员会表示赞成的决定：指对临床试验已经经过审评，可在机构审查委员会、研究机构、GCP和适用管理法规的约束下，在研究机构处实施临床试验。

### 1.6 稽查

对试验相关活动和文件进行的系统性和独立的检查，以判定临床试验的实施和数据的记录、分析与报告是否符合试验方案、申办者标准操作规程（SOP）、临床试验质量管理规范（GCP）以及适用的管理法规。

### 1.7 稽查证书

稽查员确认已进行稽查的声明。

### 1.8 稽查报告

申办者的稽查人员提供的关于稽查结果的书面评估。

### 1.9 稽查轨迹

允许重构事件过程的文件。

### 1.10 设盲

使参与试验的一方或多方人员对治疗分配保持未知的程序。单盲通常指受试者对试验治疗未知；双盲通常指受试者、研究者、监查员，以及在某些情况下数据分析人员也不知道治疗分配情况。

### 1.11 病例报告表（CRF）

印刷、光学或电子文件，设计用来记录试验方案所要求的、需向申办者报告的每一例受试者的全部试验信息。

### 1.12 临床试验/研究

任何涉及人类受试者的研究，旨在发现或证实试验用药的临床、药理学和/或药效学作用，和/或确定试验用药的任何不良反应，和/或研究试验用药的吸收、分布、代谢和排泄，以确定药物的安全性和/或有效性。临床试验和临床研究为同义词。

### 1.13 临床试验/研究报告

对在人类受试者身上进行的任何治疗、预防或诊断制剂试验/研究的书面描述。将临床和统计学描述、说明和分析全部综合为一份报告（参见“ICH 临床试验报告的结构和内容指导原则”）。

### 1.14 对照品（产品）

临床试验中用做参照对比的试验产品或市售产品（即阳性对照）或安慰剂。

### 1.15 依从性（与试验相关）

遵从所有与试验相关的要求、临床试验质量管理规范（GCP）要求和适用管理法规要求。

### 1.16 保密

不得向未经授权的个人泄漏申办者的专利信息或受试者身份信息。

### 1.17 合同

由参与的双方或多方签署的书面协议（注明日期），其中规定了任务、责任和财务（如适用）的授权和分工安排。试验方案可以作为合同的基础。

### 1.18 协调委员会

申办者组织的协调实施多中心试验的委员会。

### 1.19 协调研究者

负责协调各中心参加多中心临床试验工作的研究者。

### 1.20 合同研究组织（CRO）

与申办者签订契约，完成一个或多个申办者的试验职责和职能的个人或组织（商业性的、学术性的或其他性质的）。

### 1.21 直接查阅

允许直接检查、分析、核对和复制对于评价临床试验有重要意义的记录和报告。进行直接查阅的任何一方（如国内和国外管理当局、申办者监查员和稽查员）应当遵从适用管理法规的要求，采取一切合理的预防措施来保证受试者身份和申办者专利信息不被泄露。

### 1.22 文件

描述或记录试验方法、实施和/或试验结果、影响试验因素，以及采取措施等任何形式的记录（包括但不限于书面、电子、磁性和光学记录，以及扫描、X线和心电图）。

### 1.23 核心文件

可分别及综合地对研究执行情况和所得到数据的质量进行评估的文件（参见“8 实施临床试验的核心文件”）。

### 1.24 临床试验质量管理规范（GCP）

临床试验的设计、实施、执行、监查、稽查、记录、分析和报告的标准，为试验数据和报告结果的可信性和准确性提供保证，并保护受试者的权利、健全和隐私。

### 1.25 独立数据监查委员会（IDMC）（数据和安全监查委员会、监查委员会、数据监查委员会）

由申办者设立的独立数据监查委员会，定期对研究进展、安全性数据和重要疗效终点进行评估，向申办者建议是否继续、调整或终止试验。

### 1.26 公正见证人

独立于临床试验、不受试验参与者不公正影响的个人。如果受试者或受试者法定授权代表不能阅读，公正见证人将参与知情同意过程，并为受试者宣读提供给受试者的知情同意书和其他书面信息。

### 1.27 独立伦理委员会（IEC）

由医学专业人士和非医学专业人士组成的独立机构（研究机构，地区、国家或跨国的审评机构或委员会)，其职责是通过对试验方案、研究者资格、试验设施以及获得和记录受试者知情同意的方法和知情同意书进行审评和批准/提供赞成意见，保护受试者的权利、安全和福祉，并对此保护提供公众保证。

在不同的国家，独立伦理委员会的法律地位、组成、职责、运作及适用管理法规可能不同，但是应当依照本指导原则，允许独立伦理委员会按 GCP 的规定行使职责。

### 1.28 知情同意

告知受试者所有可能影响其做出是否参与试验决定的相关信息后，受试者自愿确认他/她参加试验意愿的过程。知情同意通过由受试者签署并注明日期的书面知情同意书来记录。

### 1.29 视察

在研究中心、申办者和/或 CRO 或管理当局认为合适的其他场所，管理当局对其认为与临床试验相关的文档、设备、记录和其他资源进行的官方审查活动。

### 1.30 （医学）研究机构

任何实施临床试验的公共或私人实体、代理机构、医学或牙科诊所。

### 1.31 机构审查委员会（IRB）

由医学、科学和非科学成员组成的独立机构，其职责是通过对试验方案及其增补、获得并签署受试者知情同意的方法和其他信息进行审评、批准和持续审评，确保参加试验受试者的权利、安全和福祉得到保护。

### 1.32 临床试验/研究中期报告

根据试验进行过程中所做的分析而写出的中期结果和评估报告。

### 1.33 试验用药

在临床试验中供试验或作为对照的、含活性成分的药物制剂或安慰剂。当已批准上市的药品在临床试验中的用法或包装与已批准的形式不同（制剂或包装），或将之用于未经批准的适应证，或用来获得已批准用法的更多信息时，试验用药也包括已批准上市的药品。

### 1.34 研究者

在研究中心负责实施临床试验的人员。如果在研究中心是由一组人员实施试验，研究者是指该组人员中的负责人，也称为主要研究者。亦见“协助研究者”。

### 1.35 研究者/研究机构

指“符合适用管理法规要求的研究者和/或研究机构”。

### 1.36 研究者手册

试验用药的临床和非临床数据汇编，与该试验用药在人类受试者的研究相关（参见“7 研究者手册”）。

### 1.37 法定授权代表

在适用法律授权下代表可能的受试者同意参加临床试验的个人、法人或其他团体。

### 1.38 监查

监督临床试验的进展，保证临床试验依照试验方案、标准操作规程（SOP）、临床试验质量管理规范（GCP）和适用管理法规实施、记录和报告的行为。

### 1.39 监查报告

监查员在每次现场访视和/或其他与试验有关的沟通交流后，根据申办者的SOP写给申办者的书面报告。

### 1.40 多中心试验

按照同一试验方案，在一个以上研究中心实施，由一名以上研究者完成的临床试验。

### 1.41 非临床研究

不在人类受试者身上进行的生物医学研究。

### 1.42 意见（与独立伦理委员会相关）

由独立伦理委员会（IEC）提供的判断和/或建议。

### 1.43 原始医学记录

见“原始文件”。

### 1.44 试验方案

描述试验目的、设计、方法学、统计学考虑和试验组织的文件。试验方案通常也提供试验的背景和理论基础，但这些内容也可由其他方案参考文件提供。在ICH GCP中，试验方案这一术语泛指试验方案和试验方案增补。

### 1.45 试验方案增补

对试验方案的变更或对试验方案进行正式澄清的书面描述。

### 1.46 质量保证（QA）

为保证试验的执行和数据产生、记录及报告都符合临床试验质量管理规范（GCP）和适用管理法规要求而采取的有计划的、系统的行动。

### 1.47 质量控制（QC）

在质量保证系统范围内执行的操作技术和活动，以核实试验相关活动是否符合质量要求。

### 1.48 随机化

为了减少偏倚，采用按照概率进行分配的方法，将受试者分配至治疗组或对照组的过程。

### 1.49 管理当局

有权进行管理的实体。在ICH GCP指导原则中，管理当局一词包括有权审评提交的临床数据和有权实施视察的机构（见1.29）。这些实体有时被称为主管当局。

### 1.50 严重不良事件（SAE）或严重药品不良反应（Serious ADR）

任何剂量下发生的任何未预期的医疗事件：

—导致死亡；

—危及生命；

—需要住院治疗或延长住院时间；

—导致永久或严重残疾/丧失能力；

—或先天畸形/出生缺陷。

（参见“ICH临床安全性数据管理指导原则：快速报告的定义和标准”）

### 1.51 原始数据

重构和评估临床试验所必需的临床发现、观察或其他活动的原始记录及其核证副本的全部信息。原始数据包含在原始文件中（原始记录或核证副本）。

### 1.52 原始文件

原始文件、数据和记录（如住院记录、门诊记录、实验报告、备忘录、受试者日记或评估表、药房发药记录、自动仪器记录数据、核证副本或誊抄件、微缩胶片、照相负片、缩微胶卷或磁性介质、X线片、受试者文件，以及保存在药房、实验室和参与临床试验医技部门的记录)。

**1.53 申办者**

负责启动、管理和/或资助临床试验的个人、公司、机构或组织。

**1.54 申办-研究者**

启动并且实施临床试验的个人，单独或与他人合作。在他（们）的直接指示下，给受试者施用、分发或由受试者使用试验用药。该术语并不包括除个体以外的其他组织（例如，不包括公司或代理机构）。申办-研究者同时兼负申办者和研究者的责任。

**1.55 标准操作规程（SOP）**

为具体职能部门达成统一绩效而制定的详细书面说明。

**1.56 协助研究者**

在研究中心，主要研究者指定和督导的临床试验团队中执行重要的试验相关操作和/或做出重要的试验相关决定的任何成员（如助理、住院医生、研究员）。亦见“研究者”。

**1.57 受试者/试验受试者**

参加临床试验，接受试验用药或对照药的个人。

**1.58 受试者识别编码**

研究者为每位受试者指定的独特的识别号码，以保护受试者的身份，在研究者报告不良事件和/或其他试验相关数据时代替受试者姓名。

**1.59 研究中心**

实际开展临床试验相关活动的场所。

**1.60 非预期的药品不良反应**

发生的不良反应，其性质或严重程度与现有产品信息［例如，研究者手册（未批准试验用药），或产品说明书或产品性能概要（已批准产品)］不一致的不良反应（参见“ICH临床安全性数据管理指导原则：快速报告的定义和标准”）。

### 1.61 弱势受试者

可能因受到不当影响而成为临床试验志愿者的人：如可能因为期望得到利益（无论正当与否）而参与试验，或者因为害怕拒绝参加试验而受到等级体系中高级成员的报复而参与试验。如在等级制度下的团体成员：医学、药学、牙科或护理专业的学生，附属医院和实验室人员，制药公司雇员，军人，以及被监禁的人。其他弱势受试者包括难以救治的患者，住在敬老院/养老院的人，失业者或穷人，危重病患者，少数民族，无家可归者，流浪者，未成年人和无能力给出知情同意的人。

### 1.62 （试验受试者的）福祉

参加临床试验受试者体格上和精神上的健全。

**增补**

### 1.63 核证副本

与原始记录核实过（如通过签名并注明日期或通过可验证程序而产生）的副本（无论使用何种类型媒介），与原始记录有相同信息，包含描述背景知识、内容和结构的数据。

### 1.64 监查计划

描述监查临床试验的策略、方法、职责和要求的文件。

### 1.65 计算机系统验证

建立并记录计算机系统符合规定要求的过程，该计算机系统需要持续满足设计要求，直至系统退役或过渡至新的系统中。验证方法需要基于风险评估，考虑到计算机系统的预期用途以及计算机系统影响受试者的保护和试验结果可靠性的潜在可能。

## 2 ICH GCP 的原则

**2.1** 临床试验的实施应依照源于赫尔辛基宣言的伦理原则，并符合临床试验质量管理规范（GCP）和适用管理法规。

**2.2** 在开始试验之前，应当权衡对受试者和对社会的可预期风险、不便和预期受益。只有当预期受益大于预期风险时，才能启动和继续临床试验。

**2.3** 受试者的权利、安全和福祉是最重要的考量，应当胜过科学和社会的利益。

**2.4** 试验用药的现有非临床和临床信息应足以支持拟议的临床试验。

**2.5** 临床试验应当有坚实的科学基础，在试验方案中有明确、详细的描述。

**2.6** 临床试验应当依从机构审查委员会（IRB）/独立伦理委员会（IEC）已批准/赞成的方案实施。

**2.7** 为受试者提供医疗保障、为受试者做出医学决定始终是合格医生/牙医的职责。

**2.8** 参与实施临床试验的人员均应在教育、培训和经验方面具有相应资格以完成各自任务。

**2.9** 参加临床试验前，应获得每位受试者自愿签署的知情同意书。

**2.10** 应妥善地记录、处理和保存所有临床试验相关信息，以确保能对相关信息准确报告、解释和核对。

**增补**

本原则适用于 ICH GCP 中所指的所有记录，无论记录使用何种类型媒介。

**2.11** 遵从适用管理法规中尊重隐私和保密的规定，应对可能识别受试者身份的保密性记录进行保护。

**2.12** 试验用药应按照适用的药品生产质量管理规范（GMP）进行生产、管理和储存。应根据已获批准的方案来使用试验用药。

**2.13** 应当建立相应的操作系统来保证试验各方面质量。

**增补**

确保受试者受到保护以及试验结果的可靠性对临床试验至关重要，应是质量管理系统关注的重点。

# 3 机构审查委员会/独立伦理委员会（IRB/IEC）

## 3.1 职责

3.1.1 IRB/IEC应当保护所有受试者的权利、安全和福祉。应当特别注意可能涉及弱势受试者参与的试验。

3.1.2 IRB/IEC应当得到以下文件：

试验方案/增补，研究者用于试验的书面知情同意书及其更新件，受试者招募程序（例如广告），提供给受试者的书面信息，研究者手册（IB），已知安全性信息，有关给予受试者酬劳和补偿的信息，研究者最新简历/或其他资格证明文件，以及IRB/IEC履行其职责所要求的任何其他文件。

IRB/IEC应当在合理的时限内审查拟议临床研究，给出书面审评意见，清楚确认试验名称、已审评文件和日期：

—批准/赞成意见；

—批准/赞成之前所需要进行的修改；

—不批准/反对意见；

—终止/暂停先前的批准/赞成意见。

3.1.3 IRB/IEC应当参照最新简历和/或IRB/IEC要求的其他相关文件来考虑拟议试验的研究者资格。

3.1.4 IRB/IEC应当根据试验对人类受试者的危害程度，定期对正在进行的试验持续审评，至少每年一次。

3.1.5 当IRB/IEC判断需补充信息以保护受试者的权利、安全和/或福祉时，IRB/IEC可要求给受试者提供除4.8.10所要求的更多信息。

3.1.6 当非治疗性试验是由受试者法定授权代表给出知情同意时（见4.8.12，4.8.14），IRB/IEC应当确认方案和/或其他文件已经充分说明了相关伦理学考虑，并符合这类试验的适用管理法规。

3.1.7 试验方案指出受试者或其法定授权代表不可能事先给出知情同意时（见4.8.15），IRB/IEC应当确认拟进行方案和/或其他文件充分说明了伦理方面的考虑，并符合这类试验的适用管理法规（例如在紧急情况下）。

3.1.8 IRB/IEC应审评支付给受试者款项的数额和方式，确认不存在对受试者胁迫或不当影响。给受试者的支付款项应当按比例分配，不应完全以受试者完成试验作为获取款项的前提条件。

3.1.9 IRB/IEC应当保证，给受试者的支付（包括支付方式、数额和支付给受试者的时间表）已列在知情同意书以及提供给受试者的其他书面信息上，并详细注明按比例支付的方式。

## 3.2 组成、职责和运作

3.2.1 IRB/IEC应由合理人数的成员组成。这个由不同成员组成的集体有资格和经验对拟进行试验的科学、医学及伦理方面进行审阅和评估。建议IRB/IEC应包括：

(a) 至少5名成员。

(b) 至少1名成员的主要关注领域为非科学领域。

(c) 至少1名成员不属于研究机构/研究中心。

只有与该试验研究者和申办者无关的IRB/IEC成员才能对试验相关事项进行投票/提出意见。

应当保留IRB/IEC成员名单和其资格证明。

3.2.2 IRB/IEC应按照书面操作规程执行其功能，应当保存其活动的书面记录和会议记录，并应遵守GCP和适用管理法规的要求。

3.2.3 IRB/IEC应在达到其书面操作规程中规定法定人数的正式会议上做出决定。

3.2.4 只有参加审评和讨论的IRB/IEC成员才能投票，提出他们的意见和/或建议。

3.2.5 研究者可提供试验各方面的信息，但不得参加IRB/IEC的审议或IRB/IEC的投票/意见。

3.2.6 IRB/IEC可邀请在特殊领域有专门知识的非伦理委员会成员进行协助。

## 3.3 程序

IRB/IEC应当建立并书面记录操作规程，并遵循此程序，操作规程应包括：

3.3.1 确定 IRB/IEC 的组成（成员姓名和资格）和其相应的授权。

3.3.2 安排、通知成员并召开会议。

3.3.3 对试验进行初次审评和持续审评。

3.3.4 确定适当的持续审评频率。

3.3.5 依照适用管理法规，对 IRB/IEC 已批准/赞成的试验在执行过程中进行微小更改提供快速审评和批准/赞成意见。

3.3.6 指明在 IRB/IEC 书面签署对试验的批准/赞成意见之前，不得入选受试者进入试验。

3.3.7 指明在方案增补获得 IRB/IEC 书面批准/赞成之前，不能偏离或改变试验方案，除非为了消除对受试者的紧急危害，或方案变更仅涉及试验行政或管理方面（例如更换监查员，更改电话号码）（参见 4.5.2）。

3.3.8 指明如出现下列情况，研究者应当立即报告 IRB/IEC：

(a) 偏离或改变方案以消除对受试者的紧急危害（参见 3.3.7，4.5.2，4.5.4）。

(b) 受试者风险的增加和/或明显影响试验进行的改变（参见 4.10.2）。

(c) 所有严重的和非预期的药品不良反应（ADR）。

(d) 可能对试验的实施或受试者安全产生不利影响的新信息。

3.3.9 确保 IRB/IEC 迅速书面通知研究者/研究机构的事项：

(a) 与该试验有关的决定/意见。

(b) IRB/IEC 决定/意见的理由。

(c) 对 IRB/IEC 决定/意见的申述程序。

### 3.4 记录

IRB/IEC 应当保留全部试验相关记录（如书面程序，成员名单，成员职业/所属机构，呈送文件，会议记录以及往来信件）至试验完成后至少 3 年，并在管理当局要求时可以提供。

研究者、申办者及管理当局可向 IRB/IEC 要求提供其书面的操作程序和成员名单。

# 4 研究者

## 4.1 研究者的资格和协议

4.1.1 研究者应当在受教育、培训和经验方面有资格承担实施临床试验的责任，应当符合适用管理法规所明确的所有条件，并应当提供最新个人简历和/或申办者、IRB/IEC和/或管理当局要求的其他相关文件证明其研究资格。

4.1.2 通过参阅试验方案、研究者手册、产品信息以及申办者提供的其他信息，研究者应当充分熟悉试验用药的正确使用方法。

4.1.3 研究者应当了解并遵循GCP和适用管理法规。

4.1.4 研究者/研究机构应当允许申办者进行监查和稽查，允许相关管理当局进行视察。

4.1.5 研究者应当保存已将试验相关任务授权给合格研究者的研究人员名单。

## 4.2 足够的资源

4.2.1 研究者应证明（如参考回顾性数据）能在协议约定期限内入组足够数量的合格受试者。

4.2.2 研究者在协议约定试验期内应当有足够的时间实施和完成试验。

4.2.3 在可预见试验期内，研究者应当有足够的合格研究者和充足的试验设备，正确、安全地实施试验。

4.2.4 研究者应当保证所有试验辅助人员都充分了解试验方案、试验用药，和每人在试验中的相关责任和职能。

**增补**

4.2.5 研究者负责监督其授权的个人和团体在研究中心履行试验相关职责和职能。

4.2.6 如果研究者/研究机构授权个人或团体履行试验相关的职责和职能，授权研究者应当保证被授权的个人或团体有资格履行试验相关的职责和职能，并建立和实施相应的操作规程，确保正确执行试验相关职责和职能以及所有试验数据的完整性。

### 4.3 受试者的医疗保健

4.3.1 作为研究者或协助研究者的合格医生（或牙医），应当对所有试验相关的医疗（牙科）决策负责。

4.3.2 在受试者参加试验期间或其后，研究者/研究机构应当保证为受试者发生的任何不良事件（包括与试验相关的有临床意义的实验室异常测定值）提供适当的医疗救助。当研究者发现需要对并发疾病进行治疗时，研究者/研究机构应当通知受试者。

4.3.3 如果受试者有保健医生并且受试者同意让保健医生知晓时，建议研究者将受试者参加试验的事实通知受试者的保健医生。

4.3.4 尽管受试者不需要给出他/她中途退出试验的理由，研究者仍应当在充分尊重受试者权利的同时，尽量确认其退出的理由。

### 4.4 与 IRB/IEC 沟通

4.4.1 试验开始前，研究者/研究机构应当获得 IRB/IEC 对试验方案、知情同意书、知情同意书更新、受试者招募程序（如广告），以及提供给受试者的其他书面信息的书面批准/赞成意见，且注明日期。

4.4.2 研究者/研究机构向 IRB/IEC 书面申请时，应当向 IRB/IEC 提供研究者手册的最新版本。如果研究者手册在试验期间更新，研究者/研究机构应当向 IRB/IEC 提供更新版的研究者手册。

4.4.3 试验期间，研究者/研究机构应当向 IRB/IEC 提供全部供审评的文件。

### 4.5 依从试验方案

4.5.1 研究者/研究机构应当依从已获得申办者和管理当局（如有必要）许可、并得到 IRB/IEC 批准/赞成的方案，实施试验。研究者/研究机构和申办者应当在方案上或另立的合同上签字，确认同意方案。

4.5.2 研究者未取得申办者同意且事先未得到 IRB/IEC 对于方案增补审评的书面批准/赞成时，不应偏离或改变试验方案，除非需要消除对受试者的紧急危害，或对方案的更改只涉及试验行政或管理方面（如更换监查员、更改电话号码等）。

4.5.3 研究者或研究者指定人员应当记录和解释对已批准试验方案的任何偏离。

4.5.4 为了消除对受试者的紧急伤害，研究者可以在无 IRB/IEC 事先批准/赞成意见的情况下偏离或更改方案。所实施的偏离或更改、更改的原因，以及提议的方案增补应尽快提交给：

(a) IRB/IEC，以进行审评并得到批准/赞成意见。

(b) 申办者，以得到同意。

(c) 管理当局（如果需要）。

## 4.6 试验用药

4.6.1 在研究中心，对试验用药计数的责任属于研究者/研究机构。

4.6.2 只要允许/需要，研究者/研究机构可以/应当将研究中心/机构对试验用药计数的部分或全部责任分配给在研究者/研究机构监督下的合适的药师或其他适当人员。

4.6.3 研究者/研究机构和/或其指定的药师或其他适当人员，应当保存试验用药发送至研究中心的记录、研究中心库存清单、每位受试者使用记录，和未使用药品交还给申办者或另行处置的记录。这些记录应包含日期、数量、批号/序列号、失效期（如有）、分配给试验用药和受试者的专用编码。研究者应保存按方案说明给予受试者规定剂量的用药记录，并与从申办者处收到的试验用药总数一致。

4.6.4 试验用药应按申办者的说明进行储存（见 5.13.2 和 5.14.3)，并符合适用管理法规。

4.6.5 研究者应当保证仅按已批准的方案使用试验用药。

4.6.6 研究者或研究者/研究机构指定人员，应当向每位受试者解释试验用药的正确用法，并应在试验期间定期检查每位受试者是否完全遵照使用说明用药。

## 4.7 随机化程序和破盲

研究者应当遵循试验的随机化程序（如果有)，并应保证仅依照方案规定打开随机号码。如果试验采用盲法，研究者应当立即记录并向申办者解释试验用药提前破盲的情况（如意外破盲、因严重不良事件而破盲)。

### 4.8 受试者的知情同意

4.8.1 在获得和记录知情同意过程中，研究者应当遵循适用管理法规，符合 GCP 和源自赫尔辛基宣言的伦理学原则。在开始试验前，研究者应当获取 IRB/IEC 对于知情同意书和提供给受试者其他文字信息的书面批准/赞成意见。

4.8.2 当得到可能对受试者是否同意参加临床试验产生影响的新信息后，提供给受试者的知情同意书和其他文字信息都应当进行增补。增补后的知情同意书和其他文字信息在使用前都应当获得 IRB/IEC 的批准/赞成意见。如果得到有可能影响受试者继续参加试验意愿的新信息时，应及时通知受试者和受试者法定授权代表。对有关信息进行的通知应当记录在案。

4.8.3 无论研究者本人还是试验相关人员，都不应胁迫或不当影响受试者做出参加或继续参加试验的决定。

4.8.4 关于试验的口述或书面信息，包括知情同意书，都不应包含可引起受试者或受试者法定授权代表放弃或看似放弃其合法权利的语言；或者免除或看似免除研究者、机构、申办者或其代表过失责任的语言。

4.8.5 研究者或由研究者指定的人员，应当充分告知受试者或受试者法定授权代表（如受试者不能提供知情同意书时）所有试验相关信息，包括 IRB/IEC 的批准/赞成意见及文字信息。

4.8.6 关于试验的口述和书面信息，包括知情同意书中所用的语言应当是非专业用语，容易被受试者或其法定授权代表或公正见证人理解。

4.8.7 在获得知情同意之前，研究者或研究者指定人员应当给受试者或其法定授权代表充足时间和机会以便询问关于试验的细节并决定是否参加试验。受试者或其法定授权代表提出的所有试验相关问题均应得到满意的答复。

4.8.8 在受试者参加试验之前，受试者或其法定授权代表以及负责知情同意讨论的人员应签署书面知情同意书并各自注明日期。

4.8.9 如果受试者或其法定授权代表不能阅读，则在整个知情同意讨论期间应有公正见证人在场。经过向受试者或其法定授权代表宣读并解释知情同意书和所有其他提交给受试者的书面信息，受试者或其法定授权代表已经口头同意受试者参加试验后，如果有能力，他们应在知情同意书上签名并注明日期，见证人也应在知情同意书上签名并注明日期。见证人通过签署知情同意书证明知情同意书和所有其他文字信息已被准确地向受试者或其法定授权代表作了解释，受试者或其法定授权代表显然理解所表述的内容，知情同意是受试者或其法定授权代表自愿给出的。

4.8.10　知情同意讨论和提供给受试者的书面知情同意书以及所有其他书面信息应当包括对以下问题的解释：

(a) 试验涉及研究。

(b) 试验目的。

(c) 试验治疗和随机分配到每一治疗组的可能性。

(d) 应遵守的试验步骤，包括所有创伤性操作。

(e) 受试者的责任。

(f) 试验的探索性内容。

(g) 带给受试者，可能时带给胚胎、胎儿或哺乳婴儿的可合理预见的危险或不便。

(h) 可合理预见的受益。当不存在对受试者预期临床受益时，应告知受试者。

(i) 可供受试者选择的可替代治疗手段或疗程及其重要潜在受益和风险。

(j) 当发生与试验相关的伤害事件时受试者可获得的补偿和/或治疗。

(k) 预计支付给受试者参加试验的费用（如果有），此费用是随试验流程按比例支付的。

(l) 预计受试者因参加试验需要付出的花费（如果有）。

(m) 受试者参加试验应是自愿的，受试者可以拒绝参加试验，或在任何时候退出试验而不会受到惩罚或损失其应得利益。

(n) 在不侵犯受试者隐私的前提下，在适用法律与规定准许的范围内，允许监查员、稽查员、IRB/IEC和管理当局直接查阅受试者的原始医学记录以核查试验程序和/或数据，受试者或其法定授权代表通过签署书面知情同意书授权这种查阅。

（o）在适用法律和/或规定允许的范围，有关受试者身份识别的记录应保密，不得公开这些记录。即使公开发表试验结果，受试者身份仍然是保密的。

（p）如果得到可能影响受试者继续参加试验意愿的相关信息，将及时通知受试者或其法定授权代表。

（q）需要进一步了解有关试验和受试者权益相关信息时的联系人信息，以及发生与试验相关伤害时的联系人信息。

（r）预期受试者可能被终止参加试验的情形和/或理由。

（s）预计受试者参加试验的时间期限。

（t）参加试验受试者的大约人数。

4.8.11 在参加试验前，应将已签署并注明日期的知情同意书和提供给受试者的所有其他书面信息的复印件交给受试者或其法定授权代表。受试者参加试验期间，应将已签署并注明日期的知情同意书的更新文本和提供给受试者的所有书面信息增补交给受试者或其法定授权代表。

4.8.12 当临床试验（治疗性的或非治疗性的）包含只能由受试者法定授权代表同意才能入组试验的受试者时（如未成年人，或严重痴呆患者），应当按照受试者可理解程度告知受试者试验相关信息。如可能，受试者应当亲自签署知情同意书并注明日期。

4.8.13 非治疗性试验（如预估对受试者无直接临床获益的试验）应当在本人同意并在知情同意书上签名和签注日期的受试者中进行。4.8.14 描述的情形除外。

4.8.14 只要符合下列条件，非治疗性试验可以在经法定授权代表同意的受试者中进行：

（a）不能通过受试者本人能给出知情同意的常规试验达到试验目的。

（b）对受试者的预期风险低。

（c）对受试者健康的不良影响被减小和降低。

（d）法律不禁止进行该种试验。

（e）明确征求 IRB/IEC 对入选这类受试者的批准/赞成意见；且获得书面批准/赞成意见，同意入选这些受试者。

除特殊情况外，这类试验应当在患有适用试验用药的疾病或症状的患者中进行。这类试验中，受试者应当受到特殊的密切监测，且一旦发现对受试者造成过度痛苦，即让受试者退出试验。

4.8.15　在紧急情况下，当不可能事先获得受试者知情同意时，应该寻求受试者法定授权代表的同意（如果在场）。当不可能事先获得受试者知情同意，且受试者法定授权代表不在时，为保护受试者的权利、安全和福祉，并遵从适用管理法规的要求，入选受试者应根据已获得 IRB/IEC 书面批准/赞成意见的方案和/或其他文件描述的方法进行。应尽快告知受试者或其法定授权代表有关试验的情况，并应征得其是否继续参加试验和对其他事项（见 4.8.10）的同意。

## 4.9　记录和报告

**增补**

4.9.0　研究者/研究机构应当保留足够的、准确的原始文件和试验记录，包括研究中心对每位试验受试者的全部相关观察记录。原始数据应该具有可归因性、易读性、同时性、原始性、准确性和完整性。原始数据的更改应该是有追踪痕迹的，不得遮掩最初的记录，必要时应进行解释（例如：通过稽查轨迹）。

4.9.1　研究者应当保证提供给申办者的病例报告表（CRF）及所有要求的报告中数据的准确性、完整性、可读性和及时性。

4.9.2　CRF 中来源于原始文件的数据应当与原始文件一致，如有不一致，应加以解释。

4.9.3　对 CRF 中数据的任何更改或更正，应当注明日期、姓名首字母和说明（如有必要），并应依然可见原来的记录（即应保留稽查轨迹）；这种要求同样适用于对书面的和电子信息的更改或更正［见 5.18.4(n)］。申办者应当向研究者和/或研究者指定代表提供关于如何进行更正的指南。申办者应写出操作规程以保证指定代表在 CRF 中做出的更改或更正：已记录在案；是有必要的；且得到研究者的认可。研究者应当保留对这些更改或更正的记录。

4.9.4　研究者/研究机构应当按“8　实施临床试验的核心文件”所述和适用管理法规要求保存试验文件。研究者/研究机构应当采取措施防止核心文件意外或提前销毁。

4.9.5 在ICH地区内，核心文件应当保留到最近一次上市申请获批后至少2年，同时没有还未完成的或仍在考虑的上市申请，或试验用药的临床研究正式终止后至少已过去2年。但是，如果适用管理法规要求或与申办者签署的协议有要求，则这些文件应当被保存至更长的时间。当不需要再保存这些文件时，申办者有责任通知研究者/研究机构（见5.5.12）。

4.9.6 应在申办者与研究者/研究机构的协议书中说明试验财务方面的事宜。

4.9.7 根据监查员、稽查员、IRB/IEC或管理当局的要求，研究者/研究机构应允许其直接查阅所要求的全部试验相关记录。

## 4.10 进展报告

4.10.1 研究者应当每年一次，或按IRB/IEC要求的频度，向IRB/IEC提交书面的试验进展总结。

4.10.2 当出现任何可能显著影响试验实施和/或增加受试者风险的情况时，研究者应当迅速向申办者、IRB/IEC（见3.3.8）和研究机构（如果需要）提供书面报告。

## 4.11 安全性报告

4.11.1 除了试验方案或其他文件（如研究者手册）规定的无需即时报告的严重不良事件（SAE）以外，所有SAE都应当立即向申办者报告。即时报告之后应尽快提供详细的书面报告。即时和随访报告中对受试者身份应当采用分配给受试者的专用编码，而不应使用受试者姓名、个人身份号码和/或地址。研究者还应遵从适用管理法规向管理当局和IRB/IEC报告非预期的药品严重不良反应。

4.11.2 根据申办者在方案中规定的报告要求和报告时限，应将可能对安全性评价非常重要的不良事件和/或实验室异常值向申办者报告。

4.11.3 报告死亡事件时，研究者应当向申办者和IRB/IEC提供所要求的全部附加信息（如尸检报告和最终医疗报告）。

## 4.12 试验的终止或暂停

如果试验无论因何种原因提前终止或暂停，研究者/研究机构应当迅速通知受试者，应当保证受试者得到适当治疗和随访。适用管理法规有要求时，应当通知管理当局。另外：

4.12.1 如果研究者未事先征得申办者同意便终止或暂停试验，研究者应当通知研究机构；研究者/研究机构应当立即通知申办者和IRB/IEC，并提供终止或暂停试验的详细书面解释。

4.12.2 如果申办者终止或暂停试验（见5.21），研究者应当立即通知研究机构，研究者/研究机构应立即通知IRB/IEC并向IRB/IEC提供终止和暂停的详细书面解释。

4.12.3 如果IRB/IEC终止或暂停其对试验的批准/赞成意见（见3.1.2和3.3.9），研究者应当通知研究机构，研究者/研究机构应当立即通报申办者并提供终止或暂停原因的详细书面解释。

### 4.13 研究者的最终报告

在试验完成后，研究者应当通知研究机构，研究者/研究机构应当向IRB/IEC提供试验结果的总结，向管理当局提供所要求的所有报告。

# 5 申办者

**增补**

### 5.0 质量管理

申办者应该建立质量管理体系，在试验过程的所有阶段对试验的质量进行管理。

申办者应该关注于确保受试者得到保护和试验结果可靠的核心试验活动。质量管理包括设计有效的临床试验方案、工具和流程，收集及处理数据，以及收集对做出决策特别重要的信息。

临床试验质量保证和质量控制的方法应该与试验内在风险和收集信息的重要性相称。申办者应该确保试验的所有方面都是可操作的，应该避免不必要的复杂化，避免不必要的步骤和收集不必要的数据。方案、病例报告表和其他操作文件应该清晰、简洁、前后一致。

质量管理体系应该采用基于风险的方法，如下所述。

5.0.1 识别关键流程和关键数据

在方案制定过程中，申办者应该识别出对保证受试者得到保护和试验结果可靠特别重要的流程和数据。

5.0.2 风险识别

申办者应该识别出对关键流程和关键数据的风险。申办者需要在两个层面考虑风险：系统层面（如标准操作规程、计算机系统、人员）和临床试验层面（如试验设计、数据收集、知情同意过程）。

5.0.3 风险评估

申办者应该评估已经识别的风险，对照现有的风险控制措施，考虑：

(a) 错误发生的可能性。

(b) 错误可被察觉的程度。

(c) 错误对受试者保护和试验结果可靠性的影响。

5.0.4 风险控制

申办者应该决定哪些风险需要降低，哪些风险可被接受。将风险降低至可接受程度的方法应该与风险的重要性相称。降低风险的措施应该嵌入方案设计及实施、监查计划、定义双（多）方角色和责任的协议、确保遵守标准操作规程的系统性安全措施，以及对操作流程和程序的培训中。

应预先设定质量容许限度，考虑到变量的医学和统计学特征以及试验的统计设计，发现能影响受试者安全和试验结果可靠性的系统性问题。一旦发现偏离预先设定的质量容许限度，应引发对风险的评估，以确定是否需要采取措施。

5.0.5 风险沟通

申办者应该记录质量管理活动。申办者应该与相关人员或受活动影响人员沟通质量管埋活动，促进在临床试验执行过程中对风险进行审核和不断改进质量。

5.0.6 风险审核

申办者应该定期审核风险控制措施来确定考虑到新出现的知识和经验，目前所实施的质量管理活动是否依然有效及相关。

5.0.7 风险报告

申办者应该在临床试验报告中描述试验中实施的质量管理方法，总结严重偏离预先设定质量容许限度的事件及其补救措施（ICH E3，9.6 数据质量保证）。

## 5.1 质量保证和质量控制

5.1.1 申办者负责按照书面SOP执行和维持质量保证及质量控制系统，确保试验的实施和数据的产生、记录、报告均能符合方案、GCP，及适用管理法规的要求。

5.1.2 申办者负责与试验所涉各方达成协议，保证申办者进行监查和稽查时或国内外药品监督管理当局视察时，可以直接检查各研究中心，查阅原始数据/文件及试验报告（见1.21）。

5.1.3 在数据处理各阶段均应采用质量控制，以保证所有数据真实可信，并处理得当。

5.1.4 申办者和研究者/研究机构以及参加临床试验的其他各方签订的协议应该是书面的，可作为方案的一部分，或另立独立协议。

## 5.2 合同研究组织（CRO）

5.2.1 申办者可以将试验相关责任和任务部分或全部移交给CRO，但试验数据的质量和完整性的最终责任始终在申办者。CRO应当落实质量保证和实施质量控制。

5.2.2 对任何移交给CRO承担的试验相关责任和职能均应进行书面说明。

**增补**

申办者应该确保监督任何试验相关责任和职能，包括由CRO外包给第三方的试验相关责任和职能。

5.2.3 任何没有明确移交给CRO的试验相关责任和职能仍然由申办者承担。

5.2.4 本指导原则中涉及申办者的条款也适用于受委托的CRO，适用限度由CRO在试验中所承担的责任和职能而定。

## 5.3 医学专家

申办者应指定有相应资格的医学人士，他们能及时对试验相关医学疑问或问题提出建议。必要时，可以聘请外部顾问。

### 5.4 试验设计

5.4.1 在试验进行的各个阶段，从试验方案和 CRF 的设计、分析计划，到临床试验中期及最终总结报告的分析和准备，申办者应当任用有合适资质的人员（如生物统计学专家、临床药理学家和医师）来进行。

5.4.2 进一步的指导原则见“6 临床试验方案和方案增补”，“ICH 临床试验报告的结构和内容指导原则”和其他关于试验设计、方案和实施的 ICH 指导原则。

### 5.5 试验管理、数据处理与记录保存

5.5.1 申办者应当任用有相应资格的人员来监督试验的全面实施、处理数据、核对数据，进行统计分析和准备试验报告。

5.5.2 申办者应考虑建立独立数据监查委员会（IDMC），定期评价临床试验进展，包括安全性数据及关键性疗效终点情况，以向申办者建议是否继续、修改或终止试验。IDMC 应当有书面操作规程并保存所有会议记录。

5.5.3 应用电子试验数据处理和/或远程电子试验数据系统时，申办者应当做到以下方面：

(a) 确保并证明电子数据处理系统符合申办者对于完整性、准确性、可靠性和预期结果一致性（如数据确认）的既定要求。

**增补**

申办者应该根据所进行的风险评估进行系统验证，期间需要考虑到系统的使用目的和系统影响受试者保护和试验结果可靠性的可能性。

(b) 维护使用这些系统的 SOP。

**增补**

SOP 应该包含系统设置、安装和使用。SOP 应该描述系统验证、功能测试、数据收集和处理、系统维护、系统安全措施、变更控制、数据备份、数据恢复、应急计划和系统退役。使用计算

机系统的申办者、研究者和其他人员的职责应该清晰，使用前应当为用户提供相关培训。

(c) 保证系统的设计能允许按如下方式进行数据更改：数据更改必须提供文件证明，不应删除已经录入的数据（即：保留稽查轨迹、数据轨迹和编辑轨迹）。

(d) 维护可阻止未经授权查阅数据的安全系统。

(e) 保存经授权可以修改数据的人员名单（见 4.1.5 和 4.9.3）。

(f) 保存足够的数据备份。

(g) 如采用盲法，保护盲法安全（例如，在数据输入和处理期间维持盲法）。

**增补**

(h) 确保数据的完整性，包括任何描述背景、内容和结构的数据。保证数据的完整性特别重要，尤其是当计算机系统需要进行变更时，如软件升级或数据转移时。

5.5.4 如果在处理过程中进行了数据转换，应当将原始数据与处理后的观测值进行比较。

5.5.5 申办者应当使用明确的受试者识别编码（见 1.58），以识别每一位受试者的所有数据。

5.5.6 申办者或其他数据拥有者，应当保留与试验相关的申办者专属的所有核心文件（见“8 实施临床试验的核心文件”）。

5.5.7 在产品已上市和/或准备报批的国家，申办者应当保留所有申办者专属、符合该国适用管理法规的核心文件。

5.5.8 如果申办者终止试验用药的临床开发（如针对某一或全部适应证、给药途径或剂型的研究），申办者应当维护所有申办者专属核心文件，直至试验正式终止后至少 2 年，或与适用管理法规相一致。

5.5.9 如果申办者终止试验用药的临床开发，申办者应当通报所有试验研究者/研究机构和所有管理当局。

5.5.10 任何数据所有权的转让均应按适用管理法规向相应管理当局报告。

5.5.11 申办者专属核心文件应当保留至最近一次在ICH地区获得批准上市后至少2年，同时直至在ICH地区无未完成的或仍在考虑的上市许可申请，或试验用药的临床研究正式终止后至少过去2年。但如果适用管理法规要求或申办者需要，核心文件应当保留更长时间。

5.5.12 申办者应当书面通知研究者/研究机构关于记录保存的要求，当不再需要试验相关记录时，应书面通告研究者/研究机构。

### 5.6 研究者的选择

5.6.1 申办者有责任选择研究者/研究机构。每位入选的研究者应当接受过培训且具备资格和经验，应当有足够的资源以妥善实施试验（见4.1，4.2）。如果在多中心试验中采用协调委员会组织和/或选择协助研究者，则该协调委员会的组织和/或协调研究者的选择也是申办者的责任。

5.6.2 在与研究者/研究机构签署临床试验协议之前，申办者应当向研究者/研究机构提供试验方案和最新的研究者手册，并应当提供足够的时间以便研究者/研究机构审议方案和所提供的信息。

5.6.3 申办者应当获得研究者/研究机构的同意：

(a) 按照GCP、适用管理法规（见4.1.3）和经申办者同意、IRB/IEC批准/赞成的方案（见4.5.1）实施临床试验。

(b) 遵从数据记录/报告规程。

(c) 允许监查、稽查和视察（见4.1.4）。

(d) 保存与试验相关的核心文件，直至申办者通知研究者/研究机构不再需要这些文件（见4.9.4和5.5.12）。

申办者和研究者/研究机构应当共同签署方案或替代文件以确认达成协议。

### 5.7 责任的分配

在开始试验前，申办者应当确定、建立和分配试验相关的所有责任和职能。

### 5.8 对受试者和研究者的补偿

5.8.1 如果适用管理法规要求，申办者应当为研究者/研究机构提供因试验目的而要求的保险或适当补偿（法律和财务范围），但因治疗不当和/或过失引起的索赔要求除外。

5.8.2 申办者的保险单和保险程序应当依照适用管理法规，说明发生试验相关伤害时对受试者的治疗费用。

5.8.3 受试者接受补偿时，其补偿的方式方法应当符合适用管理法规的要求。

### 5.9 财务

试验财务方面的内容应当列入申办者和研究者/研究机构之间的协议中。

### 5.10 通知/申报管理当局

在开始临床试验前，申办者（或根据适用管理法规要求，申办者和研究者）应当向相应的管理当局提交申请表，以供审评、接受和/或许可（如适用管理法规要求）而开始试验。任何通报/提交的信息均应注明日期，并有足够的信息以标识试验方案。

### 5.11 IRB/IEC 审评和确认

5.11.1 申办者应当从研究者/研究机构方得到：

(a) 研究者/研究机构的 IRB/IEC 成员的姓名和地址。

(b) IRB/IEC 关于 IRB/IEC 组织和操作符合 GCP 和适用法规的声明。

(c) IRB/IEC 的书面批准/赞成意见文件，以及如果申办者要求，最新的试验方案、知情同意书和所有其他提供给受试者的书面信息复印件，受试者招募程序，受试者可能得到的报酬和补偿的相关文件，和 IRB/IEC 要求的所有其他文件。

5.11.2 如果 IRB/IEC 提供批准/赞成意见的前提条件是对试验的某个方面进行修改，如修改试验方案、知情同意书、其他任何提供给受试者的书面信息和/或其他程序，申办者应当从研究者/研究机构处得到已作修改的修改版副本和 IRB/IEC 给出批准/赞成意见的日期。

5.11.3 申办者应当从研究者/研究机构处得到所有 IRB/IEC 给出再批准/再审评的赞成意见，以及撤销或暂停批准/赞成意见的文件和日期。

## 5.12 有关试验用药信息

5.12.1 计划试验时，申办者应当保证有足够的从非临床研究和/或临床研究中获得的安全性和有效性数据，以支持按照给药途径、剂量和用药时间在受试者人群中进行研究。

5.12.2 当有重要的新信息时，申办者应当更新研究者手册（见“7 研究者手册”）。

## 5.13 试验用药的生产、包装、标签和编码

5.13.1 申办者应当保证试验用药（包括阳性对照品和安慰剂）的特征符合产品开发阶段，按照相关 GMP 生产，以保护盲法的方式编码和进行标签。此外，标签应当符合适用管理法规要求。

5.13.2 申办者应当确定试验用药的允许储存温度、储存条件（如避光）、储存时间、静脉给药时的配液溶媒和程序，以及输注方法。申办者应当将这些规定通知所有有关各方（如监查员、研究者、药剂师、储存管理人员）。

5.13.3 试验用药的包装应当能在其运输和储存期间防止污染和防止出现不可接受的变质。

5.13.4 在盲法试验中，试验用药的编码系统应当包括在医学紧急情况下允许迅速识别药品的机制，但不允许出现已经破盲、而破盲的事实却不被发现的情形。

5.13.5 在临床开发过程中，如果试验用药或对照品的配方有显著变化，在新制剂用于临床试验之前需评估新制剂的全部附加研究结果（如稳定性、溶出速率、生物利用度），评价这些变化是否显著改变药物的药代动力学模式。

## 5.14 试验用药的供应和管理

5.14.1 申办者负责向研究者/研究机构提供试验用药。

5.14.2 申办者在得到所要求的全部文件之前（如：IRB/IEC 和管理当局的批准/赞成意见），不得向研究者/研究机构提供试验用药。

5.14.3 申办者应当确保书面操作规程包含研究者/研究机构应遵循的关于试验用药处理和储存的指导以及其他文件。操作规程应当说明正确并安全地接收、处理、储存、分发、回收受试者未使用药品以及将未使用的试验用药返还给申办者的方法（或经申办者授权并遵

照适用管理法规进行销毁）。

5.14.4　申办者应当：

(a) 确保按时将试验用药送达至研究者。

(b) 保存证明试验用药的运输、接收、分发、回收和销毁的记录（见“8　实施临床试验的核心文件”）。

(c) 维持回收试验用药的系统并记录这种回收过程（如召回有缺陷的产品、试验完成后药品的回收、对过期药品的回收）。

(d) 维持对未使用试验用药进行处置的系统，并将此种处置措施记录下来。

5.14.5　申办者应当：

(a) 采取措施以保证试验用药在整个使用期内的稳定性。

(b) 维持足够数量的试验用药并确认其规格，如需要，保存同批次样品的分析检验报告。在产品稳定性允许的范围内，应当保留样品直至完成试验数据分析或适用管理法规要求的时间，取两者中较长者的保留期限。

## 5.15　记录查阅

5.15.1　申办者应当确保在试验方案中或其他书面协议中已声明：研究者/研究机构应提供可直接查阅的原始数据或文件，供试验相关的监查、稽查、IRB/IEC 审核和管理当局视察。

5.15.2　申办者应当核实，每位受试者已书面同意：在进行试验相关的监查、稽查、IRB/IEC 审评和管理当局视察时，可以直接查阅他/她的原始医疗记录。

## 5.16　安全性信息

5.16.1　申办者负责对试验用药进行持续的安全性评价。

5.16.2　发现可能对受试者安全造成不良影响、或影响试验进行、或 IRB/IEC 可能因此将不再批准试验继续进行时，申办者应当立即通知所有相关研究者/研究机构和管理当局。

## 5.17　药品不良反应报告

5.17.1　申办者应当迅速向所有相关研究者/研究机构、IRB/IEC、管理当局（如果需要）报告所有严重的且非预期的药品不良反应。

5.17.2　这种快速报告应当符合适用管理法规和“ICH 临床安全性数据管理指导原则：快速报告的定义和标准”。

5.17.3　申办者应当根据适用管理法规要求向管理当局提交所有更新的安全性报告和定期的安全性报告。

## 5.18　监查

5.18.1　目的

试验监查的目的是核实：

(a) 受试者的权利和福祉得到保护。

(b) 所报告试验数据准确、完整，并能从原始文件中得到证实。

(c) 试验的实施符合最新批准的方案/方案增补，符合 GCP 和适用管理法规。

5.18.2　监查员的选择和资格

(a) 监查员应当由申办者指定。

(b) 监查员应当受过相应的培训，应当有足够的监查试验所需的科学或临床知识。应当记录监查员的资格。

(c) 监查员应当透彻了解试验用药、研究方案、知情同意书和任何其他提供给受试者的书面信息、申办者的 SOP、GCP 和适用管理法规。

5.18.3　监查的范围和性质

申办者应当保证试验得到适当的监查。申办者应当决定监查的合适范围和性质。监查的范围和性质应当根据试验目标、目的、设计、复杂性、盲法、样本量和试验终点而确定。通常要求在试验前、试验期间和试验后进行现场监查。但是在特别的场合，申办者可以决定将某些步骤（如研究者培训和研究者会议）合在一起进行中央监查。全面的书面指导原则可以保证试验依从 GCP 原则合理实施。可接受采取统计抽样控制的方法选择需要核对的数据。

**增补**

申办者应当建立系统化的、优化的、基于风险的方法来监查临床试验。本节描述的监查范围和内容的灵活性目的是允许采用不同的方式来改善监查的效力和效率。申办者可以选择现场监查的方法，现场监查与中心化监查相结合的方法，或在有充分理由的情形下，只采用中心化监查的方法。申办者应该记录选择监查策略的依据（例如，在监查计划中写明）。

现场监查是在临床试验实施的研究中心进行。中心化监查是对收集的数据进行远程评估，及时由具有相应资质并接受过培训的人员来完成（例如：数据管理者、生物统计师）。

中心化监查的操作规程提供了额外的监查资源，能对现场监查进行补充，能减少现场监查的范围和/或频率，并能帮助区分可靠数据与潜在不可靠数据。

对中心化监查的累积数据集进行审核（也可能包括统计分析）可用于：

(a) 发现丢失数据、不一致数据、离群值数据、非预期变异性缺失、方案偏离。

(b) 检查同一研究中心内和不同研究中心间的数据趋势，如数据的范围、一致性和变异性。

(c) 评估同一研究中心内或者不同研究中心间收集和报告的数据有无系统性或显著性误差，或有无潜在的操纵数据或数据完整性方面的问题。

(d) 分析研究中心特征和绩效指标。

(e) 选择研究中心和/或流程进行有针对性的现场监查。

5.18.4 监查员的责任

按照申办者的要求，试验和研究中心相关监查员在必要时应当通过采取下列行动以保证试验的正确实施和妥善记录：

(a) 作为申办者和研究者沟通的主要联系渠道。

(b) 核实研究者有足够的资格和资源（见 4.1，4.2，5.6），包括实验室、仪器和职员的整体资源足以保障安全和正确地实施试验，并且在整个试验期间一直有足够资源。

(c) 对于试验用药，需核实：

(i) 储存时间和条件是可接受的，在试验期间供应充足。

(ii) 试验用药只提供给合格的受试者，并按试验方案规定的剂量给药。

(iii) 向受试者提供正确使用、处理、储存和归还试验用药的必要指导。

(iv) 在研究中心，试验用药的接收、使用和归还应严格管理和记录。

(v) 研究中心对未使用的试验用药的处置符合管理法规和申办者的要求。

(d) 核实研究者遵循已批准的研究方案和所有已批准的增补。

(e) 核实每位受试者在参加试验前已经签署知情同意书。

(f) 确保研究者收到最新的研究者手册、所有的文件和正确实施试验并符合适用管理法规的全部试验所需物料。

(g) 保证研究者及研究成员对试验有充分的了解。

(h) 核实研究者及研究成员按照方案和申办者与研究者/研究机构签署的其他书面协议，正确行使其指定的试验职能，而未将这些职能委托给未经授权的人。

(i) 确保研究者只招募合格的受试者。

(j) 报告受试者招募速度。

(k) 核实原始文件和其他试验记录准确、完整、保持更新并被保存。

(l) 核实研究者提供所有要求的报告、通知、申请和递交文件，并且这些文件均准确、完整、及时、清晰易读、注明日期，并确认属于该试验。

(m) 核对 CRF 的录入与原始文件和其他试验相关记录的准确性及完整性。监查员尤其应当监查：

(i) 试验方案所要求的数据在 CRF 上有准确记录，并与原始文件一致。

(ii) 每位受试者的用药剂量和/或治疗调整均妥当记录。

(iii) 不良事件、伴随用药和试验过程中发生的并发症均按试验方案要求记录在 CRF 上。

(iv) 受试者未进行的试验随访、未进行的检验、未完成的检查在 CRF 上清楚如实记录。

(v) 已入选受试者退出试验或中途退出，已在 CRF 上报告并做出解释。

(n) 通知研究者所有 CRF 上的填写错误、遗漏或字迹不清。监查员应当确保研究者或经研究者授权修改 CRF 的研究成员正确更改、增加或删减 CRF 内容，并注明日期、加以解释（如有必要），签上研究成员姓名首字母。授权应当有文件记录。

(o) 确定是否所有不良事件（AE）在GCP、试验方案、IRB/IEC、申办者和适用管理法规所要求的期限内进行了适当的报告。

(p) 确定研究者是否保存核心文件（“见8　实施临床试验的核心文件”）。

(q) 通知研究者关于对试验方案、SOP、GCP和适用管理法规要求的偏离，并采取适当措施以防止再次发生上述偏离。

5.18.5　监查规程

监查员应当遵循申办者制订的各种书面SOP以及申办者为监查某项具体试验而特别制订的操作规程。

5.18.6　监查报告

(a) 每次对研究中心现场监查或进行与试验相关的沟通后，监查员应当向申办者递交书面报告。

(b) 报告应当包括日期、地点、监查员姓名、研究者或其他接触人员的姓名。

(c) 报告还应包括监查员监查内容的概要，监查员对有关重大发现/事实、偏离和不足、结论、已采取的或将采取的措施、和/或为保证依从性推荐采取行动的陈述。

(d) 申办者对监查报告进行的审评和跟进措施应当由申办者指定代表进行记录。

**增补**

(e) 现场监查或中心化监查报告应当及时递交给申办者（包括负责试验和研究中心的相关管理者和雇员），供审评和跟进。监查活动的结果应当有足够详细的记录，以便确认是否遵守监查计划。应定期报告中心化监查活动，可独立于现场监查。

**增补**

5.18.7　监查计划

申办者应当根据试验特有的受试者保护和数据完整性的风险定制监查计划。监查计划应当描述监查策略，所有涉及人员的监查责任，采用不同的监查方式及其理由。监查计划应当强调对关键数据和关键过程的监查，应特别关注于非常规临床实践和要求额外培训的那些方面。监查计划应当参考适用的策略和规程。

### 5.19 稽查

作为实现质量保证的一部分，当申办者进行稽查时应当考虑：

5.19.1 目的

申办者进行的稽查为独立的审查、不同于常规监查或质量控制，其目的是评价试验的实施和对试验方案、SOP、GCP和适用管理法规的依从性。

5.19.2 稽查员的选择和资格

(a) 申办者应当指定独立于临床试验/系统的人员实施稽查。

(b) 申办者应当保证稽查员是培训合格并有经验正确实施稽查的人员。稽查员的资格应备案。

5.19.3 稽查程序

(a) 申办者应当确保对临床试验/系统的稽查是按照申办者关于稽查内容、稽查方法、稽查频度、稽查报告格式及内容的书面操作规程进行。

(b) 申办者对某一项试验进行稽查的稽查计划和操作规程应当根据向管理当局提交试验的重要性、试验中受试者数量、试验类型和复杂性、对受试者的危险程度和可能出现的任何特定问题而定。

(c) 稽查的观察信息和发现应进行记录。

(d) 为保证稽查工作的独立性和价值，管理当局不应例行公事地要求提供稽查报告。当有证据显示严重违反GCP时，或在法律诉讼期间，管理当局可根据具体情况设法获得试验稽查报告。

(e) 如适用法律或法规要求，申办者应当提供稽查证书。

### 5.20 不依从

5.20.1 研究者/研究机构或申办者的职员对于试验方案、SOP、GCP和/或适用管理法规不依从时，申办者应立即采取措施以保证试验的依从性。

**增补**

如果发现的不依从已显著影响或可能显著影响对人类受试者的保护或试验结果的可靠性时，申办者应当进行根本原因分析，采取适当的纠正和预防措施。

5.20.2 如果监查和/或稽查认定研究机构的某一部门出现严重和/或持续的不依从，申办者应当终止研究者/研究机构参与临床试验。当研究者/研究机构因为不依从而被终止参加试验时，申办者应当立即通报管理当局。

### 5.21 提前终止或暂停试验

如果提前终止或暂停试验，申办者应当立即通知各研究者/研究机构以及管理当局终止或暂停事宜及其理由。根据适用管理法规的说明，申办者或研究者/研究机构还应当立即通知 IRB/IEC，并提供终止或暂停的理由。

### 5.22 临床试验/研究报告

无论临床试验是已经完成或提前终止，申办者都应确保按照适用管理法规要求准备临床试验报告，并提供给管理当局。申办者还应当确保上市申请的临床试验报告符合“ICH 临床试验报告的结构和内容指导原则”的标准（注：“ICH 临床试验报告的结构和内容指导原则”明确说明在某些情况下可接受简要的试验报告）。

### 5.23 多中心试验

对于多中心试验，申办者应当保证：

5.23.1 实施试验的所有研究者严格遵循申办者同意的、并得到 IRB/IEC 批准/赞成意见的试验方案（必要时经管理当局同意）。

5.23.2 在多中心研究中，设计病例报告表（CRF）用来记录所要求的试验数据。对于收集额外数据的研究者，应向他们提供设计用来收集额外数据的补充 CRF。

5.23.3 协助研究者及其他参加试验研究者的职责需在试验开始之前进行记录。

5.23.4 向所有研究者提供关于遵从试验方案、按统一标准评价临床和实验室发现并完成 CRF 的操作指导。

5.23.5 促进研究者之间的交流。

# 6 临床试验方案和方案增补

试验方案的内容通常应当包括以下主题。但是研究中心的特别信息可在分开的方案页提供，或写在单独的协议中，下列某些信息可记录于方案的其他参考文件中，如研究者手册中。

## 6.1 一般信息

6.1.1 试验方案的题目、方案编号和日期。任何增补均应有版本号和日期。

6.1.2 申办者和监查员（如与申办者非同一个人）的姓名和地址。

6.1.3 被授权为申办者签署试验方案和方案增补人员的姓名和职称。

6.1.4 申办者的医学专家（或牙医）的姓名、职称、地址和电话号码。

6.1.5 负责实施试验研究者的姓名和职称，以及研究中心的地址和电话号码。

6.1.6 负责研究中心所有医学（或牙科）决策的合格医生（或牙医）（如与研究者不是同一人）的姓名、职称、地址及电话号码。

6.1.7 临床实验室和其他医学和/或技术部门、和/或参与试验机构的名称和地址。

## 6.2 背景信息

6.2.1 试验用药的名称和描述。

6.2.2 非临床研究中有潜在临床意义的发现和临床试验中与试验有关的发现概述。

6.2.3 对人类受试者已知的和潜在的风险和利益（如有）概述。

6.2.4 对给药途径、剂量、剂量方案和治疗周期的描述和理由。

6.2.5 说明试验将遵从方案、GCP和适用管理法规进行。

6.2.6 对试验人群的描述。

6.2.7 与试验相关，并提供试验背景信息的参考文献和数据。

## 6.3 试验目标和目的

详细描述试验的目标和目的。

## 6.4 试验设计

临床试验的科学完整性和试验数据的真实可信性主要取决于试验设计。对试验设计的描述应当包括以下几方面：

6.4.1 试验期间要测量的主要终点和次要终点（如有）的具体说明。

6.4.2 对所实施试验的类型/设计的描述（如双盲、安慰剂对照、平行设计），和试验设计流程图、操作步骤及试验阶段示意图。

6.4.3 为减少/避免偏倚所采取措施的描述，包括：

(a) 随机化。

(b) 设盲。

6.4.4 对试验治疗和试验用药的剂量及给药方案的描述，还包括对试验用药的剂型、包装及标签的描述。

6.4.5 受试者参加试验的预估持续时间，以及对试验流程的说明，包括随访（如有）。

6.4.6 对受试者个人、部分试验和全部试验的“停止规则”或“终止标准”的描述。

6.4.7 试验用药（包括安慰剂和对照药品）的计数程序。

6.4.8 保持试验治疗随机编码和破盲规程。

6.4.9 指出直接记录在CRF上（即事先未书面记录或以电子记录数据），且将其视为原始数据的任何数据。

## 6.5 受试者的选择和退出

6.5.1 受试者的入选标准。

6.5.2 受试者的排除标准。

6.5.3 受试者的退出标准（即终止试验用药治疗/试验治疗）和步骤说明：

(a) 何时和如何终止受试者的试验/试验用药治疗。

(b) 收集退出受试者数据的类型和时间。

(c) 是否和如何替换受试者。

(d) 对退出试验用药治疗/试验治疗受试者的随访。

## 6.6 受试者的治疗

6.6.1 试验中包括随访期所给予的治疗，包括每个试验用药治疗组/试验治疗组的受试者所使用的所有药物的名称、剂量、给药方案、给药途径/方法和治疗周期。

6.6.2 在试验开始前和/或试验期间允许和不允许使用的药物/治疗（包括急救药物）。

6.6.3 监查受试者依从性的规程。

## 6.7 有效性评价

6.7.1 疗效指标的说明。

6.7.2 评价、记录和分析疗效指标的方法和时间。

## 6.8 安全性评价

6.8.1 安全性指标的说明。

6.8.2 评价、记录和分析安全性指标的方法和时间。

6.8.3 记录和报告不良事件与并发疾病的程序。

6.8.4 发生不良事件后对受试者随访的方式和持续时间。

## 6.9 统计

6.9.1 描述所采用的统计方法，包括计划进行中期分析的时间。

6.9.2 计划招募的受试者数目。如为多中心试验，应当确定每个试验中心计划招募的受试者人数。阐明选择样本数量的理由，包括考虑（或估算）试验的统计学强度和临床方面的理由。

6.9.3 所采用的显著性水平。

6.9.4 终止试验的标准。

6.9.5 处理缺失数据、无用数据和离群数据的规程。

6.9.6 所有偏离原定统计计划的报告程序（对原定统计计划的任何偏离均应在方案和/或最终报告中描述并说明理由）。

6.9.7 统计分析应包括受试者选择的方法（如：所有随机受试者、所有用药受试者、所有合格受试者及可评价受试者）。

## 6.10 直接查阅原始数据/文件

申办者应当确保在试验方案中或在其他书面协议中规定研究者/研究机构将允许对试验相关的监查、稽查、IRB/IEC审查和管理当局的视察，并可直接查阅原始数据/文件。

### 6.11　质量控制和质量保证

### 6.12　伦理学

描述与试验有关的伦理学考虑。

### 6.13　数据处理与记录保存

### 6.14　财务和保险

未在另行单独协议书中提到的财务和保险。

### 6.15　出版策略

未在另行单独协议书中提到的出版策略。

### 6.16　补充

（注：由于试验方案与临床试验/研究报告密切相关，在《ICH临床试验报告的结构和内容指导原则》中可找到进一步的相关信息。）

## 7　研究者手册

### 7.1　引言

研究者手册（IB）是对涉及人类受试者的临床试验中有关试验用药的临床信息和非临床信息的汇编。研究者手册的目的是向研究者和参与试验的其他人员提供信息，帮助他们理解方案很多关键特性的设计依据，如剂量、用药频率/间隔、给药途径和安全性监测程序，从而促进他们对临床试验的依从性。研究者手册也可在临床试验期间对受试者的临床处理提供思路。手册中的信息应当简明、简单、客观、公正、不带任何促销宣传性质，使临床医生或潜在研究者正确理解手册内容，对拟进行试验的合理性做出公正的风险/受益评估。因此，研究者手册的编写通常需要合格的医学人士参与，但是研究者手册内容应当得到产生所述数据的专业人士确认。

本指导原则描述的是在研究者手册中应当包括的最低限度的信息，同时对其结构提出建议。可以预料，可得到的信息类型和范围将随试验用药的开发阶段而有所不同。如果试验用药已上市且它的药理学已被医生广泛了解，则不要求全面详尽的研究者手册。若管理当局批准，基本产品信息手册、产品说明书或产品标签可作为合适的替代方式，提供对研究者较为重要的试验用药的最新、综合、详细的全面信息。如果研究已上市产品的新用途（即新适应证），应当特别准备一本关于该新用途的研究者手册。研究者手册至少应当每年审评一次，必要时按照申办者的操作规程进行修改。根据新药开发阶段以及获取的新信息，研究者手册可能需要进行更为频繁的修正。依照GCP要求，有关新信息可能极为重要，在将其列入增补的研究者手册之前应该通知研究者、IRB/IEC和/或管理当局。通常，申办者负责保证向研究者提供最新的研究者手册，研究者有责任将最新的研究者手册提供给相关的IRB/IEC。在研究者申办的试验中，申办-研究者应当明确是否可从制造商处获得研究者手册。如果由申办-研究者提供试验用药，那么他/她应当向研究人员提供有关该药的必要信息。当不可能准备一本正规的研究者手册时，作为替代，申办-研究者应当在试验方案中扩增背景信息的内容，包含本指导原则中所述的最低要求的最新信息。

## 7.2 总论

研究者手册应当包含：

7.2.1 扉页

扉页应当提供申办者姓名，每一个试验用药的识别特征（如：新药研究代码、化学名或已批准的通用名、申办者希望使用的合法商品名），以及发布日期。建议列出版本号和批准日期。示例见附录1。

7.2.2 保密声明

申办者可在研究者手册中包含一项声明，指导研究者/收件人将研究者手册作为机密文件进行处理，仅供研究者小组成员和IRB/IEC使用。

## 7.3 研究者手册的内容

研究者手册应当包括下列各节，每节附相应的参考文献：

7.3.1 目录

目录示例见附录2。

7.3.2 概要

应当有简短概要（最好不超过 2 页），重点是试验用药在不同临床开发阶段得到的重要资料，包括物理、化学、药学、药理学、毒理学、药代动力学、代谢和临床信息。

7.3.3 引言

应当有简短的引言，说明试验用药的化学名（批准时的通用名和商品名），所有活性成分，试验用药的药理学分类和它在该类中的预期地位（如优势），试验用药正在进行研究的基本原理，预期的预防、治疗或诊断适应证。最后，引言应当提供评价试验用药的一般方法。

7.3.4 物理、化学和药学特性及处方

应提供关于试验用药的描述（包括化学式和/或结构式），以及其物理、化学和药学特性的概述。为在试验过程中采取适当的安全措施，如有临床相关性，应当提供对所用配方的描述（包括辅料），以及配方理由。还应给出制剂储存和处置说明。应当写清楚药品与任何其他已知化合物在结构上的相似之处。

7.3.5 临床前研究

引言：

应当以概要形式提供所有有关非临床的药理学、毒理学、药代动力学和试验用药代谢研究结果。概要应当说明所采用的试验方法和结果，并对研究中治疗作用相关发现和可能对人体不利及非预期影响进行讨论。

如果已知道/得到，应适当提供下列信息：

- 试验动物的种属；
- 每组动物的数目和性别；
- 剂量单位［如：毫克/千克(mg/kg)］；
- 给药时间间隔；
- 给药途径；
- 给药持续时间；
- 全身分布的信息；
- 给药后观察期限；
- 结果，包括下列方面：
  - 药理学或毒理学作用的性质和发生率；
  - 药理学或毒理学作用的严重性或强度；

- 开始作用时间；
- 作用的可逆转性；
- 作用持续时间；
- 量效关系。

如有可能，应采用表格/列表形式使表述更清晰。

随后的章节应当讨论研究的最重要发现，包括所观察到的作用量效关系、与人类的相关性，以及在人体研究中涉及的各个方面。如有可能，应当对在同一动物种属的有效剂量和非毒性剂量发现进行比较（即：应当讨论治疗指数）。应当说明这一信息与人用推荐剂量的相关性。如有可能，应基于药物血液/组织水平而非基于 mg/kg 进行比较。

(a) 非临床药理学

应当包括试验用药的药理学总结，如有可能，还应包括该药品在动物体内的重要代谢研究概要。此总结应当包含评价潜在治疗活性的研究（如：有效性模型、受体结合和特异性）以及评价安全性的研究（如：评价预期治疗作用以外的其他药理学作用的特殊研究）。

(b) 在动物体内进行的药代动力学和药物代谢

应当给出试验用药在所研究种属动物中的药代动力学、生物转化以及分布的研究总结。对研究发现的讨论应当说明试验用药及其代谢产物在动物体内的吸收和局部及全身的生物利用度，以及它们与该种属动物中的药理学和毒理学发现之间的关系。

(c) 毒理学

对在不同动物种属中进行相关研究发现的毒理作用进行总结时应包含以下部分：

- 单剂量给药；
- 重复剂量给药；
- 致癌性；
- 特殊毒理研究（如刺激性和致敏性）；
- 生殖毒性；
- 遗传毒性（致突变性）。

7.3.6　人体作用

引言：

研究者手册应当提供试验用药对人体产生的已知反应的详尽讨论，包括关于药物药代动力学、代谢、药效动力学、量效关系、安全性、有效性和其他药理学活性。如可能，应当提供每个已完成的临床试验的总结。还应当提供试验用药在临床试验以外的用途而得到的结果，如上市后取得的经验。

(a) 试验用药在人体中的药代动力学和代谢

应提供试验用药的药代动力学信息总结，如有可能，包括以下方面：

- 药代动力学（包括代谢、吸收、血浆蛋白结合、分布和排泄）；
- 研究用药使用参考剂量时的生物利用度（如可能，绝对和/或相对生物利用度）；
- 人群亚组（如性别、年龄和脏器功能受损者）；
- 相互作用（如药物之间相互作用和药物与食物的相互作用）；
- 其他药代动力学数据（如在临床试验中进行的人群研究结果）。

(b) 安全性和有效性

应当提供先前人体试验（健康志愿者和/或患者）中得到的试验用药（必要时包含其代谢产物）安全性、药效学、有效性和量效关系的资料综述，并讨论这些信息的影响。如果已经完成一定数量的临床试验，采用在多个研究中按适应证亚组所做安全性和有效性的总结可清楚地展示有关数据。可用表格汇总所有临床试验的药品不良反应（包括所有已研究的适应证）。应当对出现在不同适应证或不同亚组之间药品不良反应类型/发生率的重大差异进行讨论。

在研究者手册中应该基于试验用药及其相关产品在以往的研究中所得出的经验，对使用试验用药可能出现的危险及药品不良反应进行描述。同时也应提供在试验用药的研究应用中所应采取的预防措施和特殊监护手段的描述。

（c）上市后经验

研究者手册应当明确指出试验用药已经上市或已获批准的国家。应对从上市后应用中得到的所有重要信息进行总结（如配方、剂量、给药途径和药品不良反应）。研究者手册也应当指出试验用药还没有得到批准/注册上市的国家或撤销其上市/注册的所有国家。

7.3.7 给研究者的数据总结和指南

本部分应当对所有非临床和临床数据进行全面讨论，如有可能，对各种来源的试验用药各方面信息进行总结。由此，研究者可以得到对现有数据最翔实的阐述，以及对这些信息对于将来临床试验的意义进行的评估。

如有必要，应对有关上市产品已发表的报告进行讨论。这将有助于研究者预测临床试验中可能出现的药品不良反应或其他问题。

本部分主要目的是帮助研究者明确理解试验用药可能出现的危险和不良反应，以及临床试验中可能需要的特殊检查、观察和防范措施。这种理解是以已知研究用药物理、化学、药学、药理、毒理和临床信息为基础的。根据以往对研究用药的临床药理学经验，还应向临床研究者提供识别和处理可能发生的药物过量及药品不良反应的指导。

## 7.4 附录1

**研究者手册扉页（示例）**

**申办者名称**

**药品：**

**研究编号：**

**名称：**化学名，通用名（如已批准）

商品名（如合法并且申办者希望采用）

**研究者手册**

版本号：

发布日期：

被替代的前版本号：

日期：

## 7.5 附录 2

**研究者手册目录（示例）**

— 保密声明（可选择）

— 签字页（可选择）

1 目录

2 概要

3 引言

4 物理、化学、药学特性和处方

5 临床前研究

5.1 非临床药理学

5.2 动物体内药代动力学和药物代谢

5.3 毒理学

6 人体作用

6.1 人体药代动力学和药物代谢

6.2 安全性和有效性

6.3 上市后经验

7 数据综述和研究者指南

注：参考资料：1. 公开出版物；2. 报告

参考资料应在每章结尾列出

附录（若有）

# 8　实施临床试验的核心文件

## 8.1　引言

核心文件是指可单独和集合起来用以评价试验的实施及所产生数据质量的文件。这些文件用来表明研究者、申办者和监查员对 GCP 和所有现行管理法规的依从性。

核心文件也用于其他用途。在研究者/研究机构和申办者处将这些核心文件及时归档，非常有助于研究者、申办者和监查员对试验进行成功管理。在确认试验实施的有效性和收集数据完整性过程中，这些文件通常会被申办者委派的独立稽查部门稽查，并被管理当局视察。

下面列出最低限度要求的核心文件。根据产生文件的不同试验阶段，可将各种文件分为以下三个部分：临床试验开始之前；临床试验进行期间；完成或终止临床试验后。列表中对每个文件都有其目的说明，以及是否将该文件列入研究者/研究机构或申办者或双方的档案中。如果每个文件都易被识别，可以将这些文件合并。

试验开始时，在研究者/研究机构及申办者办公室都应建立试验总档案。只有当监查员审核了研究者/研究机构及申办者双方的文档，并确定所有必要的文件都妥善归档后，试验才能最后结束。

本指导原则内提及的任何或所有文件均应提交，并可能受到申办者稽查员的稽查和管理当局的视察。

**增补**

申办者和研究者/研究机构应当保留一份关于各自核心文件存档地点的记录，包括原始文件。试验过程中用来存档的存储系统应当提供文档标识、版本历史、搜索和检索（无论文档使用何种媒介类型）。

临床试验核心文件应当可以根据具体文件对试验的重要性和关联性进行适当增补或缩减（在试验启动前进行调整）。

申办者应当确保研究者可以监管并能持续查阅报告给申办者的 CRF 数据。申办者不应当独自管控这些数据。

当要求使用副本来代替原始文件时（如原始文件、CRF），副本应该满足“核证副本”的要求。

在试验开始之前、试验进行期间和试验完成后，研究者/研究机构应当管控所有由其产生的核心文件和记录。

## 8.2 临床试验开始之前

在试验计划阶段，应产生下列文件并在试验正式开始之前归档（表1）。

**表1 临床试验开始前**

| | 文件名称 | 目的 | 归档在 | |
|---|---|---|---|---|
| | | | 研究者/研究机构 | 申办者 |
| 8.2.1 | 研究者手册 | 记录向研究者提供有关试验用药的最新科学信息 | × | × |
| 8.2.2 | 已签署的试验方案和方案增补（若有）和病例报告表（CRF）样本 | 记录研究者和申办者同意试验方案/方案增补和CRF | × | × |
| 8.2.3 | 给受试者的相关信息 | | | |
| | — 知情同意书（包括所有适用译文） | 记录知情同意 | × | × |
| | — 任何其他书面信息 | 记录受试者获得恰当的书面信息（内容及措辞），以支持其能够给出充分知情同意 | × | × |
| | — 受试者招募广告（如使用） | 记录招募方法是适当的且无胁迫嫌疑 | × | |
| 8.2.4 | 试验的财务状况 | 记录研究者/研究机构与申办者就试验财务方面所达成的协议 | × | × |
| 8.2.5 | 保险声明（必要时） | 记录当受试者遭受与试验相关伤害时将得到的补偿 | × | × |

续表

| | 文件名称 | 目的 | 归档在 | |
|---|---|---|---|---|
| | | | 研究者/研究机构 | 申办者 |
| 8.2.6 | 参与试验各方之间签署的协议，例如：<br>一研究者/研究机构和申办者<br>一研究者/研究机构和CRO<br>一申办者和CRO<br>一研究者/研究机构和管理当局（必要时） | 记录协议内容 | <br><br>×<br>×<br>× | <br><br>×<br>×（必要时）<br>×<br>× |
| 8.2.7 | IRB/IEC对下列文件的批准/赞成意见并注明日期<br>一试验方案和任何增补<br>一CRF（如适用）<br>一知情同意书<br>一向受试者提供的所有其他书面信息<br>一志愿者招募广告（若有）<br>一对受试者的赔偿（若有）<br>一所有其他获得批准/赞成意见的文件 | 记录试验已经过IRB/IEC审评并获得批准/赞成意见。确认文件的版本编号及日期 | × | × |
| 8.2.8 | IRB/IEC的组成 | 记录IRB/IEC的组成符合GCP要求 | × | ×（必要时） |
| 8.2.9 | 管理当局对试验方案的认可/批准/通知（必要时） | 记录在试验开始前已按照管理法规获取管理当局相应的认可/批准/通知 | ×（必要时） | ×（必要时） |
| 8.2.10 | 研究者和协助研究者简历和/或证明其资格的其他相关文件 | 记录研究者有资格并适合执行试验和/或对受试者进行医学监管 | × | × |
| 8.2.11 | 试验方案中涉及的医学/实验室/技术操作和/或检验的正常值/正常范围 | 记录各项检测的正常值和/或正常范围 | × | × |

续表

| | 文件名称 | 目的 | 归档在 | |
|---|---|---|---|---|
| | | | 研究者/研究机构 | 申办者 |
| 8.2.12 | 医学/实验室/技术操作/检验<br>—资格证明，<br>—或认证，<br>—或已建立的质量控制和/或外部质量评估，<br>—或其他验证（必要时） | 记录相应设备具备所要求的检测能力，支持研究结果的可靠性 | ×<br>（必要时） | × |
| 8.2.13 | 试验用药容器上的标签样本 | 记录标签符合有关法规要求，并向受试者提供了相应的指导说明 | | × |
| 8.2.14 | 试验用药及试验相关物品管理指导（如在试验方案或研究者手册中未提及） | 记录为确保试验用药和试验相关物品得到正确储存、包装、分发和处置所需要的指导 | × | × |
| 8.2.15 | 试验用药及试验相关物品的运送单 | 记录试验用药及试验相关物品的运送日期、批号和运送方法。允许追踪药品批号、审核运输条件及计数 | × | × |
| 8.2.16 | 所运送试验用药的药检报告 | 记录试验用药的成分、纯度和规格 | | × |
| 8.2.17 | 盲法试验的破盲规程 | 记录在紧急状况下，如何将设盲的试验用药揭盲而对其余受试者的治疗维持盲态 | × | ×<br>（第三方，如适用） |
| 8.2.18 | 总随机表 | 记录受试人群的随机化方法 | | ×<br>（第三方，如适用） |
| 8.2.19 | 试验前监查报告 | 记录研究中心适合开展临床试验（可与8.2.20合并） | | × |
| 8.2.20 | 试验启动监查报告 | 证明研究者及研究小组成员已审阅了试验规程（可与8.2.19合并） | × | × |

## 8.3 临床试验进行期间

除了表1中的文件应归档外，在试验进行过程中，表2中的文件也应添加到档案中以证明所有新的相关信息都记录在案。

**表 2　临床试验进行期间**

| | 文件名称 | 目的 | 归档在 | |
|---|---|---|---|---|
| | | | 研究者/研究机构 | 申办者 |
| 8.3.1 | 更新的研究者手册 | 记录一旦获得新的相关信息即及时通知给研究者 | × | × |
| 8.3.2 | 所有对下列文件的更改：<br>一试验方案/方案增补和 CRF<br>一知情同意书<br>一任何其他提供给受试者的书面信息<br>一受试者招募广告（如使用） | 记录试验期间生效的试验相关文件修订 | × | × |
| 8.3.3 | IRB/IEC 对下列文件的书面批准/赞成意见（注明日期）<br>一试验方案增补<br>一下列文件的修订<br>• 知情同意书<br>• 所有向受试者提供的其他书面信息<br>• 志愿者招募广告（如使用）<br>一任何其他获得批准/赞成意见的文件<br>一对试验的持续审评（必要时） | 记录所有增补和/修订文件都经过 IRB/IEC 的审评并获得批准/赞成意见。确认文件的版本号和日期 | × | × |
| 8.3.4 | 必要时管理当局对下列内容的认可/批准/通报<br>一 试验方案增补及其他文件 | 记录符合适用管理法规要求 | ×<br>（必要时） | × |
| 8.3.5 | 新研究者和/或协助研究者履历 | （见 8.2.10） | × | × |
| 8.3.6 | 试验方案中涉及的医学/实验室/技术操作/检验的正常值/正常范围更新 | 记录在试验期间对正常值和正常范围的修改（见 8.2.11） | × | × |
| 8.3.7 | 医学/实验室/技术操作/检验的更新<br>一资格证明，<br>一或认证，<br>一或已建立的质量控制和/或外部质量评估，<br>一或其他验证（必要时） | 记录在整个试验期间各项检验都符合要求（见 8.2.12） | ×<br>（必要时） | × |

续表

| | 文件名称 | 目的 | 归档在 | |
|---|---|---|---|---|
| | | | 研究者/研究机构 | 申办者 |
| 8.3.8 | 试验用药及试验相关物品的记录 | （见 8.2.15） | × | × |
| 8.3.9 | 新批次试验用药的药检报告 | （见 8.2.16） | | × |
| 8.3.10 | 监查员访视报告 | 记录监查员对研究中心的访视和发现 | | × |
| 8.3.11 | 中心访视以外的相关通信联络<br>—信件<br>—会议记录<br>—电话记录 | 记录关于试验管理、违背试验方案、试验实施、不良事件（AE）报告等方面的所有协议或重要讨论 | × | × |
| 8.3.12 | 已签署的知情同意书 | 记录每位受试者均按照GCP和试验方案要求，在参加研究之前签署知情同意，同时记录受试者对直接查阅其数据的许可（见 8.2.3） | × | |
| 8.3.13 | 原始文件 | 记录受试者的客观状态，以及试验中所收集数据的完整性，包括与试验和医学治疗相关的原始文件及受试者的病史记录 | × | |
| 8.3.14 | 已签名、注明日期且完整的病例报告表（CRF） | 记录研究者或授权的研究小组成员确认所记录的观测值 | ×<br>（复印件） | ×<br>（原件） |
| 8.3.15 | CRF 更正记录 | 记录对 CRF 初始数据记录的所有修改、补充或更正 | ×<br>（复印件） | ×<br>（原件） |
| 8.3.16 | 发现严重不良事件的研究者向申办者通报严重不良事件的初始报告 | 发现严重不良事件的研究者根据 4.11 向申办者通报严重不良事件的初始报告 | × | × |
| 8.3.17 | 申办者和/或研究者向管理当局和 IRB/IEC 提交的非预期的严重药品不良反应及其他安全性信息 | 申办者和/或研究者向管理当局和 IRB/IEC 通报非预期的严重药品不良反应（根据 5.17 和 4.11.1）及其他安全性信息（根据 5.16.2 和 4.11.2） | ×<br>（必要时） | × |

续表

| | 文件名称 | 目的 | 归档在 | |
|---|---|---|---|---|
| | | | 研究者/研究机构 | 申办者 |
| 8.3.18 | 申办者向研究者报告的安全性信息 | 申办者根据5.16.2向研究者报告安全性信息 | × | × |
| 8.3.19 | 向IRB/IEC和管理当局提交的中期报告或年度报告 | 根据4.10向IRB/IEC和根据5.17.3向管理当局提交中期报告或年度报告 | × | ×(必要时) |
| 8.3.20 | 受试者筛选表 | 记录所有进入试验前筛选程序的受试者身份确认 | × | ×(必要时) |
| 8.3.21 | 受试者身份确认编码表 | 研究者/研究机构保存的一份保密名单表，记录了受招募进入试验并获得试验编码的所有受试者姓名。允许研究者/研究机构确认受试者的身份 | × | |
| 8.3.22 | 受试者入选表 | 记录按试验编号按时间顺序入选受试者 | × | |
| 8.3.23 | 研究中心试验用药计数 | 记录试验用药按照试验方案使用 | × | × |
| 8.3.24 | 签字页 | 记录所有经授权填写和/或改正CRF的人员签名及姓名首字母 | × | × |
| 8.3.25 | 体液/组织样本的保存记录(若有) | 记录如果需重复分析时保留样本的存放地点和标识 | × | × |

## 8.4 临床试验完成或终止之后

在试验完成或终止之后，所有8.2节及8.3节所列文件应与表3中的文件一起归档。

**表3 临床试验完成或终止后**

| | 文件名称 | 目的 | 归档在 | |
|---|---|---|---|---|
| | | | 研究者/研究机构 | 申办者 |
| 8.4.1 | 研究中心试验用药计数 | 记录试验用药根据试验方案使用。记录研究中心收到、发放给受试者、受试者交还以及返还给申办者的试验用药数量 | × | × |

续表

| | 文件名称 | 目的 | 归档在 | |
|---|---|---|---|---|
| | | | 研究者/研究机构 | 申办者 |
| 8.4.2 | 试验用药销毁记录 | 记录未被使用的试验用药由申办者或在研究中心销毁的情况 | ×（若在研究中心销毁） | × |
| 8.4.3 | 完整的受试者身份确认编码表 | 在要求随访时允许确认被招募进入试验的所有受试者身份。编码表需保密并保存至协议约定时间 | × | |
| 8.4.4 | 稽查证明（如要求） | 记录已进行过稽查 | | × |
| 8.4.5 | 试验结束监查报告 | 记录所有试验结束所需步骤均已完成，所有核心文件的副本均妥善归档 | | × |
| 8.4.6 | 治疗分配表及解码记录 | 返还给申办者以证明所有已发生的解码 | | × |
| 8.4.7 | 研究者向IRB/IEC（如要求）及向管理当局（如适用）提交的总结报告 | 记录试验完成 | × | |
| 8.4.8 | 临床研究报告 | 记录试验的结果及意义 | × | × |

# 美国联邦法案

[2016年4月1日修改]

# 21CFR 第11部分 电子记录/电子签名

## 子部分A 总则

### 11.1 适用范围

(a) 本部分法规建立电子记录、电子签名以及从手写签名转换成电子记录的标准。按此标准制成的电子记录，美国食品药品管理局（FDA）认为其可信可靠，且这种电子记录可等同于纸质记录，这种电子签名可等同于手写签名。

(b) 本部分法规适用于所有符合FDA规定要求，以电子形式创建、修改、维护、归档、检索或发送的记录。本部分法规同样适用于按照《联邦食品、药品和化妆品法案》以及《公众卫生服务法》要求呈送给FDA的电子记录。本条款不适用于目前正在和已经以电子形式发送的纸质记录。

(c) 一旦电子签名和相关电子记录符合本部分法规要求，FDA认可电子签名等同于手写签名、缩写签名和其他FDA要求的一般签名。自1997年8月20日（含）之后生效的法案明确对此不予认可的情形除外。

(d) 依照条款11.2，除非有需要使用纸质记录的特殊要求，符合本部分法规要求的电子记录可以代替纸质记录。

(e) 本部分法规下维护的计算机系统（包括硬件和软件）、系统管控和随附文件应随时准备接受FDA视察。

(f)-(o)（略）

### 11.2 履行

(a) 对于需要保存、但不提交给FDA的记录，如果符合本部分法规要求，可以全部或部分使用电子记录代替纸质记录或用电子签名代替传统签名。

(b) 对于提交给 FDA 的记录，如果满足以下条件，可以使用全部或部分电子记录代替纸质记录或以电子签名代替传统签名（手写签名）：

(1) 符合本部分法规的要求；

(2) 需提交的文件或文件的一部分，已在编号为 92S-0251 的公共记事表上标明其为 FDA 认可的以电子形式提交的文件。这个记事表会具体标明在无纸质记录的情况下，什么类型的文件或文件的部分可以电子形式提交，并告知应该向 FDA 的哪个接收部门（例如，特定的中心、办公室、部门、分支机构）提交。如果提交给接收部门的文件未在公共记事表上明确列出，那么以电子形式呈交给 FDA 的文件将不被认为是正式文件。在这种情况下，纸质文件将被认为是正式文件，因此，任何电子记录必须伴有纸质记录。相关人员应该就如何提交文件的细节（例如，传递的方式、媒介、文件格式和技术规程）以及是否需要以电子形式提交等向 FDA 相应接收部门咨询。

## 11.3 定义

(a) 本法案第 201 部分中术语的定义和解释适用于本部分法规中使用的术语。

(b) 下列术语的定义也适用于本部分法规：

(1) **法案** 指《联邦食品、药品和化妆品法案》。

(2) **机构** 指美国食品药品管理局（FDA）。

(3) **生物测定** 指基于对个体身体特征或重复行为的测量（这些特征和/或行为对于个体来说既是唯一的，也是可测量的）来核实个体身份的方法。

(4) **封闭系统** 指一种环境，在此环境中，登录系统受电子记录系统负责人控制。

(5) **数字签名** 指电子签名，通过对发送人身份认证并加密，使用一套规则和一系列参数进行计算，达到核实签名者身份和数据真实性的目的。

(6) **电子记录** 指电子形式文本、图表、数据、声音、图像或其他信息的总和，电子记录的创建、修改、维护、归档、检索或分发是由计算机系统完成的。

(7) **电子签名** 指对个人创建、采用或认可的某一符号或一系列符号汇编的计算机数据，使它与个人手写签名具有相同的法律效力。

(8) **手写签名** 指个人创建或采用的手写签名或合法标识，表达当前的意愿并永久保留。签署行为用手写签名或使用标识设备（如钢笔或触控笔）保存下来。手写签名或合法标识一般适用于纸质，但也适用于其他采集签名或标识设备。

(9) **开放系统** 指一种环境，在此环境中，系统的登录不受电子记录系统负责人控制。

## 子部分 B 电子记录

### 11.10 封闭系统的控制

使用封闭系统来创建、修改、维护或发送电子记录的人们应该采用能够保证记录真实性、完整性和保密性的操作程序和控制系统，以保证签名者不能轻易否认签名的真实性而否认已经签署的记录。这些程序和控制系统应包含如下内容：

(a) 验证系统，以保证达到准确、可靠、稳定的预期性能，以及具有识别无效记录或记录已被更改的能力。

(b) 能产生准确、完整的记录副本，既有可供人阅读的形式，也有适合供 FDA 视察、审核和拷贝的电子版形式。如果对 FDA 进行电子记录审核和对电子记录进行拷贝的资格有任何疑问，应该联络 FDA。

(c) 对记录进行保护以使记录能够在整个文件保存期内准确且易于得到。

(d) 对系统的登录设限，只开放给经授权的人。

(e) 使用可靠的、计算机产生的、带时间印迹的稽查轨迹，以便独立地记录操作者登录及产生、修改或删除电子记录的行为，以及行为发生的日期和时间。更改记录不能覆盖以前的记录信息。带稽查轨迹的记录将被保留一段时间，至少与受试者的电子记录一样长久，以保证在FDA审核和拷贝时可以得到。

(f) 必要时，进行操作系统检查，以实施系统允许的对操作步骤和事件的排序。

(g) 审查权限以确保仅经授权者能使用系统、电子化签署文件、登录操作系统或计算机的输入或输出装置、更改记录或进行手动操作。

(h) 必要时检查设备（如终端）以确定原始数据输入或操作指令的正确性。

(i) 确定开发、维护或使用电子记录/电子签名系统的人员具备与其执行指派任务相应的教育背景、培训和经验。

(j) 为震慑伪造记录和签名，制定个人对其签署的电子签名行为负责任的书面政策，并要求依从。

(k) 在系统记录方面采取适当管控，包括：

(1) 对于分发、登录和使用系统操作和维护记录有足够的管控。

(2) 有修订和更改控制操作规程，以保留按时间顺序记录系统文件产生和修改的稽查轨迹。

## 11.30 开放系统的控制

使用开放系统来创建、修改、维护或发送电子记录的人们应该采用能够保证电子记录从其创建开始直至被接收为止均真实、完整和机密的操作程序和控制系统。必要时，操作程序和控制系统应包含11.10列出的措施，并增加额外的方法，如文档加密术及使用适当的数字签名标准以确保记录的真实性、完整性和保密性。

## 11.50 签名显示

(a) 签署的电子记录应能清晰显示如下所有签名相关信息：

(1) 签署者名字的印刷体。

(2) 签名生效的日期和时间。

(3) 与此签署相关的含意（如审核、批准、职责或作者身份）。

(b) 已在此节（a）(1)、(a)(2)和（a）(3)段提出的条款，应同样服从于对电子记录的管控，并且应成为可读形式电子记录的一部分（例如电子显示或打印输出）。

### 11.70 签名/记录链接

电子签名及将手写签名转化成的电子记录应该关联到其各自的电子记录上，以保证电子签名不被删除、拷贝或转移，防止使用一般手段伪造电子记录。

## 子部分 C 电子签名

### 11.100 一般要求

(a) 每一电子签名应唯一对应特定个人，且不能被再使用或再分配给其他任何人。

(b) 在创建、分配、证明或批准个人的电子签名或电子签名要素前，所在组织应核实此人的身份。

(c) 使用电子签名者应该在使用前或使用时向 FDA 证明：在其系统上的电子签名（从 1997 年 8 月 20 日之后开始使用的系统）与传统的手写签名具有同等的法律效力。

(1) 证明应以书面形式并采用传统的手写签名提交到地方运营办公室（HFC-100）（地址：5600 Fishers Lane, Rockville, MD 20857）。

(2) 应 FDA 要求，使用电子签名者应提供附加证明或证书，明确电子签名与手写签名具有同等的法律效力。

### 11.200 电子签名构成要素及管控

(a) 不依据生物测定的电子签名应：

(1) 使用至少两种不同的身份证明要素，例如识别码和密码。

(i) 如个人在一次登录控制系统持续期间签署了一系列签名，签署的第一个签名将使用电子签名所有的要素，后续签名应至少使用一种电子签名要素。该要素只能由本人签署，并且设计成只供本人使用。

(ii) 如个人在间断性登录控制系统期间签署一个或多个签名，每一个签名均应含所有的电子签名要素。

(2) 仅由签名的真正所有者使用。

(3) 进行管理和执行，以确保除真正所有者外，其他人使用该电子签名时需要有两人或更多人协作。

(b) 设计依据生物测定的电子签名时应确保其不能被真正所有者之外的其他人使用。

## 11.300 识别码/密码的管控

使用基于识别码和密码混合的电子签名时应采用控制系统以保证安全性和完整性，这些控制措施应包括：

(a) 保持每一识别码和密码结合的唯一性，即不会有两个人拥有相同的识别码和密码。

(b) 确保生成识别码和密码的装置定期接受检查、收回或修订（例如，解决类似密码老化问题）。

(c) 依据丢失管理的操作程序，对丢失、被盗、找不到或其他潜在受损的令牌、卡片及其他携带或创建识别码或口令信息的装置进行电子失效，并用适当的严格管控手段生成临时或永久的替代品。

(d) 采用交易安全装置以防止未经授权使用密码和/或识别码，发现并立即以紧急方式将任何未经授权使用系统的企图报告至安全部门，必要时报告至组织管理层。

(e) 在初始时进行设备测试并定期进行设备测试，以保证设备正常工作且所有的更改均经授权，这些设备带有或生成识别代码或密码信息，如令牌或卡片。

[2016 年 4 月 1 日修改]

# 21CFR 第 50 部分 保护人类受试者

## 子部分 A 总则

### 50.1 范围

(a) 本部分法规适用于根据《联邦食品、药品和化妆品法案》第 505(i) 和 520(g) 节，受美国食品药品管理局（FDA）监管下进行的所有临床研究，以及用来支持目的是申请获得 FDA 监管下产品上市许可的临床研究，包括食品、含营养成分声明或健康声明的膳食补充剂、婴儿配方奶粉、食品和色素添加剂、人用药品、人用医疗器械、人用生物制品及电子产品。涉及特定检查条款而对申办者或监查临床试验人员制定额外具体义务、承诺以及行为准则，可在 21CFR 其他部分法规（如第 312 和 812 部分法规）中找到。遵守这些部分法规的目的是保护受试者的权利和安全，这些受试者参与 FDA 根据《联邦食品、药品和化妆品法案》第 403，406，409，412，413，502，503，505，510，513-516，518-520，721 和 801 节以及《公共卫生服务法》第 351 和 354-360F 节列出的研究。

(b) 本部分法规参考的法案是指《美国联邦法案》第 21 篇的第Ⅰ章，另有说明除外。

### 50.3 定义

本部分法规定义如下：

(a) **法案** 指经修正的《联邦食品、药品和化妆品法案》。

(b) **研究或上市许可申请** 包括：

(1) 色素添加剂申请，第 71 部分描述。

(2) 食品添加剂申请，第 171 和 571 部分描述。

(3) 申报过程中，为确立某物质可安全使用，使其成为食品的成分或直接或间接地对食物特性造成影响，所需要递交相关的数据和信息，在 170.30 和 570.30 中描述。

(4) 申报过程中，当食品添加剂用于内服申请的获批需要依靠补充的研究结果时，需递交的相关数据和信息，在 180.1 中描述。

(5) 申报过程中，为说明某一物质可耐受食品和食品包装材料的污染，需递交相关的数据和信息，在本法第 406 节中描述。

(6) 研究新药申请在本章第 312 部分描述。

(7) 新药申请在本章第 314 部分描述。

(8) 申请颁发、修改或废除生物等效性要求的过程中，需提交关于人用药物生物利用度或生物等效性的数据和信息，在第 320 部分描述。

(9) 申请将药品归为公认安全有效且不易被误服类别的过程中，需提交关于人用非处方药（OTC）的数据和信息，在第 330 部分描述。

(10) 申请将药品归为公认安全有效且不易被误服类别的过程中，需提交关于人用处方药物的数据和信息，在本章描述。

(11) [保留]

(12) 生物制品上市许可申请，在本章第 601 部分描述。

(13) 申报过程中，为判断有专利的生物制品安全有效且正确标记，需提交有关生物制品的数据和信息，在第 601 部分描述。

(14) 为某些体外诊断产品申请建立、修改或废除体外诊断产品标准的过程中，需提交的有关体外诊断产品的数据和信息，在第 809 部分法规描述。

(15) 研究器械豁免申请，在第 812 部分描述。

(16) 申报医疗器械分类过程中，需提交有关医疗器械的数据和信息，在第 513 节描述。

(17) 为某些医疗器械申请建立、修改或废除医疗器械标准的过程中，需提交的有关医疗器械的数据和信息，在第 514 节描述。

(18) 医疗器械上市前批准申请，在第 515 节描述。

(19) 用于医疗器械的产品开发方案，在第 515 节描述。

(20) 为电子产品申请建立、修改或废除电子产品标准的过程中，需提交有关电子产品的数据和信息，在《公共卫生服务法》第 358 节描述。

(21) 为电子产品申请认可其与任何现有电子产品性能标准有差异时的过程中，需提交相关电子产品的数据和信息，在 1010.4 描述。

(22) 为电子产品申请授予、修改或延长对其免除辐射安全性能标准要求的过程中，需提交有关电子产品的数据和信息，在 1010.5 描述。

(23) 申报婴儿配方奶粉通告的过程中，需提交婴儿配方奶粉临床研究的数据和信息，按《联邦食品、药品和化妆品法案》第 412(c) 节的要求提交。

(24) 递交含营养成分声明申请所需提交的数据和资料，在本章 101.69 描述，或递交其有益健康声明申请所需提交的数据和资料，在本章 101.70 描述。

(25) 申请获得涉及儿童的新膳食成分通告的批准，需包含的研究数据和信息，在本章 190.6 描述。

(c) **临床研究** 指任何涉及试验物品及一位或多位人类受试者的试验，或者符合根据本法案第 505 (i) 或 520 (g) 节规定需事先提交给 FDA 的要求，或者虽不需要事先按照本法案要求提交 FDA 审批，但其结果用于获得上市许可的申请，将稍后提交给 FDA 或由 FDA 进行视察。临床研究不包括符合本章 58 部分法规关于非临床实验室研究的实验。

(d) **研究者** 指实际执行临床研究的个人，即，在其直接指导下，将试验物品施用或分发，或给受试者使用。若临床研究由团队执行，研究者是该团队的责任领导。

(e) **申办者** 指发起临床研究但不实际执行研究的人员，即试验物品是在其他人的直接指导下被施用或分发，或给受试者使用。由一名或多名雇员开展其发起的临床研究的非个体（如公司或机构），被认为是申办者（非申办研究者），其雇员被认为是研究者。

(f) **申办-研究者** 指既发起研究也单独或与其他人一起实际执行临床研究的个人。在申办-研究者的直接指导下，试验物品被施用或分发，或给受试者使用。该术语不包括个人以外的实体，如公司或机构。

(g) **人类受试者** 指作为试验物品或对照品接受者参与研究的个体。受试者可以是健康人或患者。

(h) **机构** 指任何公立或私立实体或管理当局（包括联邦、州和其他管理局）。本法案第 520（g）节的所用的服务机构（*Facility*）与本部分法规使用的“机构”为同义词。

(i) **机构审查委员会**（*Institutional review board*，简称 IRB） 指任何由机构正式指派，审核涉及人类作为受试者的生物医学研究的管理会、委员会或其他组织，以批准启动研究以及定期审核研究。此术语与法案第 520（g）节中使用的 *institutional review committee* 一词含义相同。

(j) **试验物品** 指在本法案或《公共卫生服务法》（42U. S. C 262 及 263b-263n）第 351 和第 354—360F 节下的任何药品（包括人用生物制品）、人用医疗器械、人用食品添加剂、色素添加剂、电子产品或任何其他物品。

(k) **最低风险** 指研究中预期对受试者造成的伤害或不适发生概率和程度不比受试者在日常生活中或在常规体检或心理检查中所遇到的更高。

(l) **法定授权代表** 指适用法律授权的个人或司法机构或其他代表，替潜在受试者同意参与临床研究。

(m) **家庭成员** 指以下任一有合法资格的个人：配偶；父母；子女（包括领养子女）；兄弟，姐妹，兄弟姐妹配偶；任何有血缘关系或与受试者关系亲密、相当于家庭关系的亲属。

(n) **同意** 指儿童对参与临床研究的正面肯定。儿童仅仅未反对参与，未肯定地同意参与试验，不应该被解释为同意。

(o) **儿童** 指根据临床研究所在地适用法律，尚未达到可以同意参与临床研究相关治疗或操作的法定年龄者。

(p) **父母** 指儿童的生物父母或收养父母。

(q) **受监护人** 指根据适用联邦、州或当地法规，被安置在国家或其他机关、机构或实体的合法监护下的儿童。

(r) **许可** 指父母或监护人同意其子女或受监护人参与临床研究。

(s) **监护人** 指根据适用州或当地法律，有权为了儿童的利益而同意进行常规医学治疗的个人。

## 子部分 B 人类受试者知情同意

### 50.20 对知情同意的一般要求

除非研究人员已经获得受试者或受试者法定授权代表有法律效力的知情同意书，否则研究者不得将潜在受试者作为研究对象，50.23 和 50.24 中另有规定除外。研究者只有在提供潜在受试者或其代表足够的机会考虑是否参与试验，并尽量减少胁迫或不当影响的情况下，才能寻求受试者的知情同意书。告知受试者或其代表的信息应使用受试者或其代表可理解的语言。无论是口头知情还是书面知情同意书均不得包含任何使受试者或其授权代表放弃或似乎放弃该受试者的任何合法权利的内容，或使研究者、申办者、机构或其代理人对疏忽免除或似乎免除责任的免责声明。

### 50.23 一般要求之外的例外情形

(a) 在使用试验物品之前，应事先获取知情同意书［本节 (b) 段规定情况除外］。除非研究者和未参与临床研究的医师均书面证明出现了如下所有情形，可在未获取知情同意书的情况下使用试验物品：

(1) 受试者正面临生命危险，需要使用试验物品。

(2) 由于无法与受试者沟通或进行知情同意，导致无法从受试者处获得有法律效力的知情同意书。

(3) 没有充足的时间，不能从该受试者的法定代表处获得知情同意书。

(4) 没有其他经批准的或普遍认可的替代治疗方法能提供同等或更大的机会以挽救受试者的生命。

(b) 如果研究者认为需要立即使用试验物品以保护受试者生命，并且没有足够时间在使用试验物品之前获得本节（a）段要求的独立判定（其他非研究医生的判定），临床研究者应该做出决定使用试验物品，并在使用试验物品后5个工作日内由未参与临床研究的医师进行审查和评估，并作书面记录。

(c) 本节（a）或（b）段要求的书面记录文件应在使用试验物品后5个工作日内提交给机构审查委员会（IRB）。

(d) (1) 在10U. S. C. 1107（f）条款下，总统可以决定对参与特定军事行动的武装部队成员使用研究新药，免除参加临床试验前需要获得知情同意的要求。法规明确规定总统只有在判断出现以下情形，且总统需要以书面形式确定获得知情同意：不可行；违反了军事成员的最佳利益；或不符合国家安全利益的情况下方可免除对知情同意的要求。法规进一步规定，以获得知情同意书不可行或者以违背相关军事成员最佳利益的理由而做出免除知情同意要求的决定时，总统应采用FDA设立的美国《联邦食品、药品及化妆品法案》[21U. S. C. 355(i)(4)] 第505(i)(4) 节中规定的，对免除开展研究之前获得知情同意要求相关的标准和准则。对于国防部（DOD）赞助的仅限于特定军事行动军事人员的特殊方案的研究新药申请（IND），在做出军事人员在使用研究用药（包括抗生素或生物制品）之前获得知情同意不可行，或违反相关军事人员最大利益的决定前，国防部长必须先请求总统做出免除知情同意的决定，并向总统提供证明和记录，表明本段（d)(1) 至（d)(4) 所列的标准和要求已得到满足。

(i) 与在军事行动中可能遇到的医疗风险相比，研究新药的安全性和有效性证据支持使用研究用药。

(ii) 军事行动存在很大风险，军事人员可能暴露于化学制品、生物制品、核能或其他物质，可能导致死亡、严重或危及生命的伤害或疾病。

(iii) 与拟使用的研究新药相比，没有满意的替代治疗或预防方法。

(iv) 对自愿参与研究的成员有条件使用研究新药可能会严重危及个体成员的安全和健康，这些成员可能会拒绝使用，因此可能危及其他军事人员的安全以及军事任务的完成。

(v) 为符合本节 (d)(2) 和 (d)(3) 段的要求，正式组建运作的负责审核此研究的 IRB 已经审查和批准新药研究方案以及未获得知情同意也可以使用研究新药。国防部的申请需包含本章56.115(a)(2) 所要求的文件。

(vi) 国防部已解释：

(A) 研究药物的具体用法，如：设定是否是自行注射，或由卫生专业人员给药；

(B) 所预防或治疗的疾病或症状的性质；

(C) 根据现有数据或可用信息，以及在某些条件下研究用药疗效可能发生变化的信息。

(vii) 国防部的记录保存系统能够进行追踪，并将用于跟踪从供应者到每位药品接受者的治疗情况。

(viii) 每位参与军事行动成员在使用研究用药前，会给予特定的书面信息页［包含 10U. S. C. 1107 (d) 所要求的信息］，介绍研究用新药的风险和益处、潜在不良反应以及正确使用药物的其他相关信息。

(ix) 参与军事行动成员的医疗档案将准确记录成员收到本节 (d)(1)(viii) 段所要求告知的信息。

(x) 根据 FDA 法案（包括本章第 312 部分法规），将在医疗记录上准确记录参与军事行动成员收到的任何研究新药。

(xi) 国防部将进行适当随访，以评估使用研究用药是否对健康造成有益或不利的后果。

(xii) 国防部正在进行药物开发，包括提供开发时间表，和积极进行上市批准申请。

(xiii) FDA 已经确定，如总统提出免除知情同意请求，可以开始执行新药研究方案。

(xiv) 国防部将在用药前对适当的医务人员和潜在受试者提供如何使用研究用药的培训。

(xv) 国防部已经说明所需免除知情同意的期限不超过一年，如需延长，则需根据这些标准和指标另行更新。

(xvi) 如相关情况发生变化，可能影响到上述标准和指标［包括本节 (d)(1)(xv) 中提到的时间段］，或可能会影响到是否做出在无知情同意的情况下使用研究新药的决定，国防部有责任继续向 FDA 和总统报告。

(xvii) 国防部需尽快通过联邦公报公告，依据信息分类级别的要求，描述每个免除知情同意书的决定，提供对研究用药最新科学信息摘要以及其他相关信息。

(xviii) 其他符合适用法律的未经知情同意使用研究药物的情况。

(2) 本节 (d)(1)(v) 段所述的适时组建的机构审查委员会成员必须包括至少 3 名非隶属人员，他们不能是联邦政府雇员或官员（担任本研究的 IRB 成员除外），并且需要通过必要的安全调查。此 IRB 应在召开的会议上审核提交的 IND 方案，需有机构审查委员会多数成员出席会议，其中至少包含 1 名主要关注点不在科学领域的成员。如果可行，还应包括非隶属人员中的大多数成员。本章 56.115(a)(2) 所要求的信息需提交给国防部长以进行进一步的审核。

(3) 本节 (d)(1)(v) 段描述的适时组建的机构审查委员会必须审查和批准：

(i) 必需的信息页；

(ii) 发布信息的计划是否充分，包括对潜在药品接受者发布研究用药信息的形式（例如，以非书面形式）；

(iii) 给医务人员传递的信息和计划是否充分，包括潜在不良反应、禁忌证、潜在的药物间相互作用以及其他相关考虑；

(iv) 本章第 50 部分法规要求的，以及国防部在某种情况下决定的可从部分或全部相关受试者处获得的知情同意书。

(4) 机构审查委员会完成审核提交的方案后，国防部需将会议摘要提交给 FDA。

(5) 这些标准或指标中的内容均不得取代或限制 FDA 和国防部在适用法律法规下的权力或义务。

(e) (1) 对于确定化学物品、生物、放射性或核物质的体外诊断器械的试验，需在使用试验物品之前获得知情同意书。如要免除知情同意，需要研究者（如临床实验室主任或其他负责人）和不参加临床研究的医生共同做出决定，且需要他们在其后书面证实符合如下所有条件：

(i) 受试者正面临危及生命的情形，需要使用研究性体外诊断器械来识别可能成为恐怖事件或其他危及公共健康紧急情况的化学、生物、放射性或核物质。

(ii) 无法从受试者处获得知情同意书，因为：

(A) 在收集样本时，下令收集样本的人员无合理方法预知可能需要使用研究性体外诊断器械来测试受试者的标本；

(B) 受试者冒着生命危险，没有足够时间从受试者处获得知情同意。

(iii) 没有足够时间从受试者法定授权代表处获得知情

同意。

(iv) 无明确的或经批准的其他诊断方法可识别化学、生物、放射性或核物质，或提供相同或更大的可能性挽救受试者的生命。

(2) 如研究者（如临床实验室主任或其他负责人员）认为为保全受试者的生命需要使用研究性器械，且无足够的时间事先获得本节 (e)(1) 段要求的使用研究器械的独立判定（其他非研究医生的判断），研究者应该做出决定，且需在使用器械后 5 个工作日内由不参与临床研究的医生进行书面审核和评估。

(3) 研究者必须在使用研究器械 5 个工作日内向 IRB 和 FDA 提交本节 (e)(1) 或 (e)(2) 段所要求的由研究者和非研究医生做出的书面判断证明。

(4) 研究人员必须在向受试者的医生以及公共健康部门提交的报告中披露体外诊断器械的研究状况以及已知的该研究器械性能特征。研究者须向 IRB 提供 50.25 中所要求的信息 [50.25(a)(8) 描述的信息除外]，以及当试验结果已经提供给受试者的医生和公共健康部门时，如何向每位受试者或其法定代表提供研究信息的流程。

(5) IRB 负责确认 50.25 节 [50.25 (a)(8) 所描述情况除外] 所需信息已经充足，并确认已采取措施将此信息提供给每位受试者或其法定授权代表。

(6) 任何国家或国家的政治分支机构均不得制定或继续实施与本条例要求不一致的法律、法规、条例或其他要求，要求在使用研究性体外诊断器械来识别涉嫌恐怖事件及其他潜在危及公共健康突发事件的化学、生物、放射性或核物质前需获得知情同意，或在此法规上增加额外要求。

## 50.24 为急救研究豁免知情同意的要求

(a) 负责审查、批准和持续审查本节描述临床研究的 IRB 可以在不要求获得所有受试者知情同意书的情况下批准临床研究，条件是 IRB（经 IRB 成员/顾问中未参与该临床研究的执业医生同意）发现并记录以下每一项：

（1）受试者正处于危及生命的状况，目前可用的治疗方法疗效未经证实或结果不令人满意，需要收集有效的科学证据（包括通过随机安慰剂对照性研究获得的证据）以确定某种干预措施的安全性和有效性。

（2）不能获得知情同意书，因为：

（i）受试者由于身体疾病状况而无法给予知情同意书。

（ii）临床研究的干预措施须在受试者法定代表可以进行知情同意之前进行。

（iii）没有合理的方法前瞻性地识别可能有资格参与此临床研究的受试者。

（3）参与研究可能对受试者直接受益，因为：

（i）受试者正面临危及生命的情形，需要进行干预。

（ii）已进行了适当的动物和其他临床前研究，来自这些研究的信息及相关证据支持采取干预措施可能使受试者直接受益。

（iii）已知潜在受试者的疾病状况及标准治疗的风险与受益（如有）和已知拟进行的研究性干预措施或行动带来的风险与受益相比，进行研究性干预措施带来的风险是合理的。

（4）如不豁免知情同意要求，临床研究不能实际执行。

（5）基于科学证据，拟进行的研究计划确定了潜在治疗窗的范围，研究者已尽力在此治疗窗范围内努力尝试联系每位受试者的法定授权代表，要求联系到的法定授权代表在治疗窗内进行知情同意（如可行），而非未签署知情同意书就进行研究。研究者将记录总结尝试联系法定授权代表的努力，并在持续审核时向 IRB 提供此信息。

（6）IRB 已经审核并批准知情同意过程及符合 50.25 要求的知情同意书。在可进行知情同意的情况下，对受试者或其法定授权代表进行知情同意过程，且将经批准的知情同意书交给受试者或其法定授权代表。IRB 已经审查并批准了知情同意过程和信息，采用这种过程和提供这些信息为家庭成员提供了反对受试者参与本节（a)(7)(v)段所述临床研究的机会。

(7) 对受试者权利和福祉提供额外保护，至少包括：

(i) 向实施临床试验地区的社区代表及受试者来源社区的代表进行咨询（包括，如可行，由IRB举行咨询）。

(ii) 在临床研究开始前，对实施临床研究的社区以及受试者来源社区进行信息公开披露，披露研究计划、研究的风险和预期受益。

(iii) 完成临床研究后向社区和研究者公开披露足够的信息，包括研究人群的人口学特征及研究结果。

(iv) 成立独立数据监查委员会，对临床研究进行监督。

(v) 以及如果不能获得知情同意书，且未找到法定授权代表，研究者在可行的情况下已在治疗窗范围内尝试联系非法定授权代表的受试者家属，询问他/她是否反对该受试者参加临床研究。研究者将记录总结尝试与受试者家庭成员联系的努力，并在持续审核时向IRB提供此信息。

(b) IRB有责任确保已有操作规程将患者已经参加临床研究的事实、研究细节以及在知情同意书中描述的其他信息尽可能早地告知每位受试者，如该受试者仍无行为能力，告知受试者的法定授权代表，如法定授权代表不在，告知受试者的家庭成员。IRB还应确认有告知受试者的操作流程，或如该受试者仍无行为能力，告知受试者的法定授权代表，或如果法定授权代表不在，告知受试者的家庭成员，受试者可以在任何时候停止参加试验，停止试验将不会受到处罚或丧失原有利益。如果已将受试者参加临床试验的情况告知了受试者法定授权代表或家庭成员，在受试者健康状况有所改善的情况下，也应在可行的情况下尽快告知受试者。如果受试者没签署知情同意书入组临床研究，且在联系到受试者法定授权代表或家庭成员前受试者死亡，如可行，应向受试者的法定授权代表或家庭成员提供有关该受试者参与临床研究的信息。

(c) 根据本章 56.115 (b)，本节 (a) 段要求 IRB 做出的决定以及本节 (e) 段要求的记录应由 IRB 在该临床研究完成后保留至少 3 年，记录应供 FDA 视察和复印。

(d) 涉及本节描述的豁免知情同意要求例外情况的方案需在特殊的研究新药申请 (IND) 或研究器械豁免 (IDE) 中分开递交，需明确标注此方案为可能需要入组无法事先进行知情同意的受试者。即使同一药品已有 IND 或同一器械已有 IDE，仍需分开以 IND/IDE 递交这种类型的方案。根据本节提交的研究申请不能根据本章 312.30 或 812.35 按方案增补进行提交。

(e) 如因为研究不符合本节 (a) 段规定的例外标准或基于其他相关伦理考虑，IRB 决定不能批准此临床研究，IRB 必须记录其发现的问题并将这些问题及时以书面形式提供给临床研究者和申办者。申办者必须及时向 FDA 和相关研究者以及相关 IRB 披露这些信息。相关研究者指正参加或被邀参加此研究或此申办者开展的其他实质上相同的临床研究；相关 IRB 指已经审核或被邀审核此研究或其他实质上相同的临床研究。

## 50.25 知情同意要素

(a) 知情同意的基本要素。在寻求知情同意书时，应向每位受试者提供以下信息：

  (1) 试验涉及研究的陈述，解释研究目的以及预期受试者参与的期限，描述所需遵循的试验步骤，并指出哪些步骤是试验性的。

  (2) 对受试者可能遇到的风险或不适的描述。

  (3) 对受试者或其他人可能从研究中获得益处的描述。

  (4) 公布可能对该受试者有利的替代治疗手段或治疗方案（如有）。

(5) 描述对受试者身份记录保密及保密程度的声明（如有），且注明 FDA 可能视察受试者的记录。

(6) 对于涉及高于最低风险的研究，解释是否有任何补偿，以及解释如发生伤害是否有医疗措施可用，如有，包括什么，或从哪里能获得进一步信息。

(7) 解释如有与研究和受试者权利相关的疑问时联系谁，如发生与研究相关的对受试者造成的伤害时联系谁。

(8) 声明参与试验是自愿的，拒绝参与不会使受试者受到处罚或有任何利益损失，并且受试者可随时停止参与试验，不会受到处罚或有任何利益损失。

(b) 知情同意的附加要素。如可行，还应向每位受试者提供以下信息：

(1) 声明某特定治疗或措施可能对受试者（或在受试者怀孕或可能怀孕情况下对其胚胎或胎儿）造成的风险，这些风险在当前不可预知。

(2) 可能出现的研究者可在不需要考虑受试者同意的情形下终止受试者参与试验的情况。

(3) 受试者由于参与研究而可能产生的任何额外费用。

(4) 受试者决定退出研究的后果及有序终止受试者参与试验的步骤。

(5) 声明在研究过程中发生可能影响到受试者是否愿意继续参与试验意愿的重大新发现时，将向受试者提供相关信息。

(6) 参与研究的大概受试者人数。

(c) 在为临床试验寻求相关的知情同意书时，如 42U. S. C. 282 (j) (1) (A) 所定义，在寻求知情同意书和知情同意过程中，应向每位受试者做如下声明，告知受试者的临床试验信息已经或将要提交至根据《公共卫生服务法》第 402 节第 (j) 段建立的临床试验注册数据库。该声明是：“根据美国法律的规定，对本临床试验的介绍可从 http://www.ClinicalTrials.gov 查到。该网页不会包含您的可识别信息。至多，网站将包括试验结果的总结，您可以随时搜索本网页。”

(d) 本条例所规定的对知情同意的要求并不意图高过任何联邦、州或当地适用法律，那些法律可能要求披露额外的信息以使知情同意书具有法律效力。
(e) 本条例无意限制医生根据适用联邦、州或当地法律在权限范围内提供紧急医疗救护的权利。

### 50.27 记录知情同意过程

(a) 除第 56.109（c）条另有规定外，知情同意应使用 IRB 批准的知情同意书进行记录，并在同意时由受试者或受试者法定授权代表签署姓名和日期。应提供给签字人签署后的知情同意书副本。
(b) 除 56.109(c) 条另有规定外，知情同意书可能是以下之一：
  (1) 含 50.25 要求的知情同意要素的书面同意文件。知情同意书可以宣读给受试者或受试者法定授权代表。无论采用何种方式，研究者应在受试者或受试者法定授权代表签署前给他们提供足够的时间进行阅读。
  (2) 简要版书面知情同意书说明 50.25 所要求的知情同意要素已向受试者或受试者法定授权代表口头表述。当使用此方法时，应该有口头表述的见证人。此外，IRB 还应批准向该受试者或其法定代表所表达内容的书面摘要。受试者或其法定代表只需签署简要版知情同意书。见证人应当签署简要版知情同意书和摘要副本，实际获得知情同意书的人应当签署摘要副本。除了简要版知情同意书副本之外，还应给予受试者或其法定代表摘要副本。

## 子部分 C [保留]

## 子部分 D 在临床研究中对儿童的额外保护

### 50.50 IRB 责任

除了本章本部分法规和第 56 部分法规分配给 IRB 的其他职责外，

IRB 必须审核本子部分 D 所监管的涉及儿童作为受试者的临床研究，仅批准满足 50.51、50.52 或 50.53 及本子部分 D 所有其他适用条款中所述标准的临床研究。

**50.51 不高于最低风险的临床研究**

本章第 50.1 和 56.101 所述范围内的临床研究，对儿童的风险不高于最低风险，只有在 IRB 发现下列情况时才能将儿童作为受试者：

(a) 未表现出对儿童有高于最低风险的风险。

(b) 按照第 50.55 的规定，对征求儿童的知情同意及得到其父母或监护人的许可有足够的规定。

**50.52 涉及高于最低风险，但呈现出对受试者直接受益前景的临床研究**

本章 50.1 和 56.101 描述通过干预措施或治疗手段可能对儿童造成高于最低风险的损害，但同时也呈现对儿童直接受益的前景，或通过监测手段，可能有助于受试者福祉的临床研究，只有在 IRB 确定下列情况下，才可能同意将儿童作为受试者：

(a) 相对于受试者的预期受益，风险是值得的。

(b) 对受试者预期的利益与风险至少优于现有替代方法。

(c) 按照第 50.55 的规定，对征求儿童的知情同意及得到其父母或监护人的许可有足够的规定。

**50.53 临床研究涉及高于最低风险，且对受试者没有直接有益的前景，但可能获得对受试者的机能失调或健康状况的一般性知识**

本章 50.1 和 56.101 所述范围内的临床研究，通过干预或治疗手段可能带给儿童的风险超过最低风险，且这种干预或治疗手段不能让受试者直接受益，或通过监测手段不大可能改善受试者的福祉，在这种情况下，只有在 IRB 发现下列情形时才有可能将儿童作为受试者：

(a) 风险只稍高于最低风险。

(b) 干预措施或治疗手段带给受试者的体验与他们原有的或预期的医疗、牙科、心理、社会或教育情形基本类似。

（c）通过干预措施或治疗手段可能获得对受试者的机能失调或健康状况的一般性知识，这些知识对于了解或改善受试者的机能失调或健康状况至关重要。

（d）按照 50.55 的规定，对征求儿童的知情同意及得到其父母或监护人的许可有足够的规定。

**50.54 只有通过进行临床研究才有机会了解、预防或减轻影响儿童健康或福祉的严重问题的临床研究**

如果 IRB 不认为本章第 50.1 和 56.101 所描述的涉及儿童作为受试者的临床研究符合 50.51、50.52 或 50.53 的要求，临床研究仅可在以下情形下进行：

（a）IRB 发现临床研究提供进一步了解、预防或减轻影响儿童健康或福祉的严重问题的合理机会。

（b）FDA 专员通过咨询相关专业专家小组（如科学、医学、教育、伦理、法律），并有机会进行公众审核和评论后，判定：

（1）临床研究事实上符合 50.51、50.52 或 50.53 的适用条件。

（2）或满足以下条件：

（i）临床研究提供了进一步了解、预防或减轻影响儿童健康或福祉的严重问题的合理机会。

（ii）临床研究将根据良好的道德准则进行。

（iii）按照 50.55 的规定，对征求儿童的知情同意及得到其父母或监护人的许可有足够的规定。

**50.55 由家长或监护人代替儿童同意参加试验的要求**

（a）除其他适用部分法规及本子部分 D 的规定外，在 IRB 判断儿童能够提供知情同意的情况下，IRB 还必须确定在寻求儿童知情同意时制定了足够的规定。

（b）在判断儿童是否有能力提供知情同意书时，IRB 必须考虑到所涉儿童的年龄、成熟程度和心理状态。此决定可根据特定方案，为全部临床试验所涉儿童做出，或 IRB 认为合适时，为每一位儿童单独做出。

（c）如果 IRB 认为存在下列情况，儿童的知情同意不是实施临床研究的必要条件：

(1) 部分或全部儿童的能力太受限，询问其意见不合理。

(2) 或临床研究涉及的干预措施或治疗手段有直接受益的前景，这对于儿童的健康或福祉非常重要，而这个前景仅能通过临床研究才能得以实现。

(d) 即使IRB认为受试者有能力进行知情同意，如发现并记录以下情形，IRB仍然可以放弃对知情同意的要求：

(1) 临床研究涉及的对受试者的风险不高于最低风险。

(2) 免除知情同意不会对受试者的权利和福祉产生不利影响。

(3) 若不免除对知情同意的要求，临床研究无法实际执行。

(4) 受试者参加临床研究后，适当时，将获得额外的相关信息。

(e) 除本子部分D的其他适用部分所需的判断外，IRB还必须根据第50部分法规对知情同意的要求，确保获得每位儿童的父母或监护人的同意。

(1) 如果需要获得家长许可，IRB发现根据50.51或50.52，获得一方家长的知情同意就足够进行临床研究。

(2) 如临床研究涉及50.53或50.54，对临床研究的许可应来自父母双方，除非父母有一方死亡、未知、不称职或不在，或父母只有一方有照顾和监护子女的法律责任。

(f) 父母或监护人的准许必须按照50.27规定进行记录。

(g) 当IRB判定需要知情同意时，必须确定是否以及如何记录知情同意过程。

## 50.56 受监护的儿童

(a) 受国家或其他机关、机构或实体监护的儿童，只有在以下情况下，才能被纳入根据50.53或50.54批准的临床研究：

(1) 与他们作为受监护儿童的身份相关。

(2) 或在学校、营地、医院、机构或类似地方进行，大多数以受试者身份参与的儿童都不是受监护的儿童。

(b) 如是根据本节（a）段批准的临床研究，IRB必须要求为每位受监护儿童任命一名代言人。

(1) 作为监护人或代理家长之外的补充，代言人将为儿童工作。

(2) 一个人可以担任多位子女的代言人。

(3) 代言人必须有相应背景和经验来行使职责，并同意在儿童参与临床研究期间行使职责，保证儿童的最大利益。

(4) 代言人不得以任何方式与临床研究、研究者或监护人组织相关联（担任本研究儿童代言人或IRB成员除外）。

[2016 年 4 月 1 日修改]

# 21CFR 第 54 部分 临床研究者财务公开

## 54.1 目的

(a) 根据法律要求，美国食品药品管理局（FDA）评估目的在于获得新的人用药品和生物制品上市许可和医疗器械上市许可及重新分类申请的临床研究。

(b) FDA 审核从临床研究中产生的数据，以判定按法规要求是否可以批准申请。如未在设计、实施、报告和研究分析中采取适当措施以尽量减少偏倚带来的误差，FDA 会认为临床研究不够充分，数据不够充足。临床研究中发生偏倚的潜在来源之一是研究者可以如获得所安排的报酬（如版税），基于得出的研究结果而获取经济利益，或研究者对在研产品拥有资本权益（如专利）或申办者股权。此节以及相应法规要求：申报结果部分依赖于临床数据的申请人需披露申办者与研究者之间的财务安排以及研究者从所研产品或从申办者处获得某些利益的情况。FDA 将使用这些信息，连同研究的设计方法和研究目的以及通过现场视察获得的信息来评估数据的可靠性。

## 54.2 定义

本部分法规的定义：

(a) **受临床研究结果影响的补偿** 指有利的试验结果比不利的结果研究者获得的补偿高，如好的结果得到的补偿明显高于不好的结果，或以申办者权益的形式，或以捆绑产品销售的形式，如以特许专属权益的形式补偿研究者。

(b) **数量相当大的股权利益** 指接受申办者的股东权益、股票期权，或指价值不易通过参考公开价格确定（通常指非上市公司的利益）的其他财务利益，或指从临床研究开始起直至研究完成后 1 年内，从上市公司获得的任何超过 50000 美元的权益。

(c) **测试产品的资本权益** 指产品的资产或其他经济利益，包括但不限于，专利、商标、版权或许可协议。

(d) **临床研究者** 仅指被列出或被指定的研究者或协助研究者，他们直接参与治疗或评估研究受试者。该术语也包括研究者的配偶和每位受其赡养的子女。

(e) **受覆盖的临床研究** 指在本部分法规下提交人用药品或医疗器械上市申请或重新分类申请的研究，申请人或 FDA 根据此研究确立产品的有效性（包括表明其与某有效产品等效的研究）或某一研究者对显示药品的安全性方面有重大贡献的研究。一般来说，此术语不包含Ⅰ期耐受性研究或药代动力学研究、大多数临床药理学研究（除非其对评定疗效至关重要）、大型多中心开放性安全性研究、治疗方案和平行非交叉方案。申请人可向 FDA 就哪类临床研究属于“受覆盖的临床研究”进行咨询，其目的是依从 FDA 对财务公开的要求。

(f) **其他类别的大额支付** 指进行受覆盖研究的申办者除支付开展此临床研究或其他临床研究的费用（例如，对正在进行的研究提供资金，以仪器设备的形式补偿或预付咨询费用或酬金）外，在研究者开展研究期间和研究完成后 1 年内，为支持研究者的活动支付给研究者或研究机构货币价值超过 25000 美元的费用。

(g) **申请人** 指提交药品、医疗器械或生物制品上市申请至 FDA 的当事人。申请人负责提交本部分法规所要求的适当证明和财务公开声明。

(h) **受覆盖临床研究申办者** 指在研究实施时资助特定研究的一方。

## 54.3 范围

本部分法规的要求适用于任何提交人用药品、生物制品或医疗设备上市申请以及提交受覆盖临床研究的申请人。对于与申请人签署研究合同以进行试验的研究者，以及未签署合同的其他研究者，申请人负责为他们提供适当的财务证明或财务公开声明。

## 54.4 财务证明和财务公开声明要求

为符合本部分法规要求，申请人必须提交所有进行受覆盖研究的研究者名单，以判断申请人的产品是否符合 FDA 的上市要求，指出那些在受覆盖研究中是申办者全职或兼职雇员的研究者。申请人还必须完整准确地披露或认证每位在受覆盖临床研究中非申办者专职或者兼职雇员的研究者的经济利益信息。受新药研究或研究器械豁免规定监管的研究者必须向申办者提供足够准确的信息以供后续披露或认证要求。申请人需要为每位参加受覆盖研究的研究者向 FDA 提交财务证明，说明不存在 54.2 中描述的财务安排，或向 FDA 公开已有财务安排的性质。当申请人已努力寻求但未得到本节所要求的信息时，申请人应当证明尽管申请人已尽力寻求此类信息，但仍无法获得，且应包含无法获得的原因。

(a) 全部或部分依赖临床研究结果的申请人［根据美国《联邦食品、药品和化妆品法案》第 505，506，510（k），513，或 515 节，或根据《公共卫生服务法》第 351 节提交申请］应为每位参加受覆盖研究的研究者提交本节（a)(1) 段描述的财务证明或本节（a)(3) 段描述的财务公开声明。

(1) 财务证明：本节适用申请人应替所有适用研究者［54.2（d）中定义］提交填好的 FDA3454 表格，证明无经济利益及无本节（a)(3) 段中描述的财务安排。表格须由申办者财务总监或公司其他负责人或代表签署并签注日期。

(2) 如果财务证明未覆盖申请中所有受覆盖的临床数据，申请人应在财务证明中包含受覆盖研究的列表。

(3) 财务公开声明：对 54.2（d）中定义的任何研究者，如申请人未提交本节（a)(1) 段描述的财务证明，申请人应当提交已填妥的 FDA 3455 表，完整准确地披露以下内容：

(i) 任何受覆盖研究申办者和实施研究的研究者之间的财务安排，给研究者进行研究补偿的金额可能因研究结果的好坏而受到影响。

(ii) 受覆盖研究申办者支出的其他类别的大额支付，

如给正在进行研究的资助基金、以仪器设备形式进行的补偿、提供预付咨询费或酬金。

(iii) 研究者持有的在研产品的任何资本权益。

(iv) 涉及临床研究的研究者持有大量的受覆盖临床研究申办者的股权。

(v) 为尽量减少因披露的财务安排、利益或付款而产生的偏倚而采取的行动措施。

(b) 研究者应向受覆盖研究申办者提供足够准确的财务信息，使申办者能够按照本节（a）段要求提交完整准确的财务证明或财务公开声明。如在研究过程中或研究完成后1年内财务信息发生变化，研究者应及时更新相关财务信息。

(c) 拒绝申请文件。如果申请不包含此节所需财务公开信息，或无申办者已尽力寻求获取信息但仍未得到并陈述其理由的声明，FDA可能会拒绝此节（a）段描述的上市申请。

## 54.5 FDA对财务利益的评估

(a) 评估财务公开声明。FDA将根据54.4（a)(2）评估每个递交申请的受覆盖临床研究的信息披露，以确定公开的财务利益对研究可靠性的影响。FDA可能会考虑披露财务利益的大小和性质（包括如果产品被批准后潜在利益的增加）以及已采取的减少潜在偏倚的措施。

(b) 研究设计的影响。在评估研究者经济利益可能对研究造成的偏差时，FDA将考虑研究设计和研究目的。研究设计如果采用某些措施如使用多位研究者（其中大多数人没有可支配的股份)、设盲、客观终点，或由其他人而非研究者测量试验终点，可对试验进行充分保护，不受由于披露的经济利益而造成偏倚的影响。

(c) FDA采取措施以确保数据可靠性。如果FDA认定研究者经济利益对试验数据的公正产生严重问题，FDA将采取任何其认为必要的措施来保证数据的可靠性，包括：

(1) FDA启动对问题数据来源的研究者进行稽查。

(2) 要求申请人提交对数据进一步的分析，例如，评估问题研究者的数据对整体试验结果的影响。

(3) 要求申请人进行额外的独立研究，以确认被质疑的研究结果。

(4) 拒绝将此受覆盖临床研究视为已提交资料供 FDA 审批的研究。

## 54.6 保存记录及记录保留

(a) 保留临床研究者的财务记录。提交受覆盖临床研究上市许可申请的申请人应将研究者的相关财务信息保留归档，申请人依靠研究者进行试验，且研究者不是申办者专职或兼职雇员。

(1) 如 54.4 (a)(3)(i) 所述，显示由受覆盖研究的申办者支付给研究者任何财务利益或安排的完整记录。

(2) 如 54.4 (a)(3)(ii) 所述，显示由受覆盖研究的申办者支付给研究者大额付款的完整记录。

(3) 如 54.4 (a)(3)(iii) 和 (a)(3)(iv) 所述，显示任何研究者的经济利益的完整记录。

(b) 保存研究者财务记录的要求。

(1) 对受覆盖产品提交的任何申请，申请人应保留此节 (a) 段描述的记录，直至申请批准后 2 年。

(2) 维护财务记录者应该根据相应授权官员或 FDA 职员要求，在适当时间，准许 FDA 官员或职员查阅、复制及核实财务记录。

[2016 年 4 月 1 日修订]

# 21CFR 第 56 部分 机构审查委员会

## 子部分 A 总则

### 56.101 范围

(a) 本部分法规包含机构审查委员会(IRB)的组成、操作规程和责任的一般标准。IRB 负责审核法案第 505(i)和 520(g)节 FDA 监管下的研究以及用来支持 FDA 上市许可申请的临床研究。上述研究涉及食品、含有营养成分声明或健康声明的膳食补充剂、婴儿奶粉、食品和色素添加剂、人用药品、人用医疗器械、人用生物制品和电子产品。依从此部分法规要求是为了保护参与研究的人类受试者的权利和福祉。

(b) 本部分法规参考的法案是指《美国联邦法案》第 21 篇的第Ⅰ章,另有说明除外。

### 56.102 定义

在本部分法规中:

(a) **法案** 指《联邦食品、药品和化妆品法案》及修订版本。

(b) **研究或上市许可申请** 包括:

(1) 色素添加剂申请,第 71 部分描述。

(2) 申报过程中,为确认某物质被普遍认为可安全使用,导致或可合理预期将导致其直接或间接成为食物成分或对食物特性造成影响,所需要递交的数据和信息,在 170.35 描述。

(3) 食品添加剂申请,第 171 部分描述。

(4) 在申报过程中,当食品添加剂用于内服的获批依赖于补充研究结果时,需递交的相关数据和信息,在 180.1 中描述。

(5) 申报过程中，为说明某一物质可耐受食品和食品包装材料的污染，需递交的相关数据和信息，在本法案第406节中描述。

(6) 研究新药申请在本章第312部分描述。

(7) 新药申请在第314部分描述。

(8) 申请颁发、修改或废除生物等效性要求的过程中，需提交关于人用药物生物利用度或生物等效性的数据和信息，在第320部分描述。

(9) 申请将药品归为公认安全有效且不被误服类别的过程中，需提交关于人用非处方药（OTC）的数据和信息，在第330部分描述。

(10) 生物制品上市许可申请，在本章第601部分描述。

(11) 申报过程中，为判断有专利的生物制品安全有效且正确标记，需提交有关生物制品的数据和信息，在第601部分描述。

(12) 研究器械豁免（IDE）的申请，在第812部分描述。

(13) 申请将器械列为人用医疗器械分类的申报过程中，需提交的有关人用医疗器械的数据和信息，在第860部分描述。

(14) 为某些医疗器械申请建立、修改或废除人用医疗器械标准的申报过程中，需提交的有关人用医疗器械的数据和信息，在第861部分描述。

(15) 人用医疗器械上市前批准申请，在本法案第515节描述。

(16) 人用医疗器械的产品开发方案，在本法案第515节描述。

(17) 为某些电子产品申请建立、修改或废除电子设备标准过程中，需提交的有关电子产品的数据和信息，在《公共卫生服务法》第358节描述。

(18) 为电子产品申请获得该电子产品的性能标准不同于任何其他电子产品证明过程中，需提交的电子产品的数据和信息，在1010.4描述。

(19) 为电子产品申请授予、修改或延长豁免辐射安全性能标准要求过程中，需提交的有关电子产品的数据和信息，在1010.5描述。

(20) 为电子产品申请获得豁免辐射安全缺陷或不符合辐射安全性能标准通告过程中，需提交的有关电子产品的数据和信息，在第1003部分的子部分D中描述。

(21) 申报婴儿配方奶粉通知过程中，需提交婴儿配方奶粉临床研究的数据和信息，按《联邦食品、药品和化妆品法案》第412 (c) 节要求提交。

(22) 为递交营养成分声明的申请，所需提交的数据和资料，见本章101.69描述；营养成分有益健康声明的申请，所需提交的数据和资料，见本章101.70描述。

(23) 为获得涉及儿童新膳食成分通知申请的批准，需包含的研究数据和信息，在本章190.6描述。

(c) **临床研究** 指任何涉及试验物品及一位或多位人类受试者的试验，或者符合根据本法第505 (i) 或520 (g) 节需事先提交给FDA的规定，或者虽不需要事先按法规要求提交给FDA审批，但其结果将作为获得研究或上市许可申请的部分资料，稍后将提交给FDA审核或受FDA视察。该术语不包括符合本章58部分法规关于非临床实验室的研究。本部分术语“research”，“clinical research”，“clinical study”，“study”，“clinical investigation”被认为是同义词。

(d) **急救使用** 指在没有可被接受的标准治疗方法且无足够时间获得IRB批准的危及生命的情形下，对人类受试者使用研究物品。

(e) **人类受试者** 指作为研究物品或对照品的接受者参与研究的个体。受试者可以是健康人或患者。

(f) **机构** 指任何公立或私立实体或管理当局（包括联邦、州和其他管理局）。本法第520 (g) 节中使用的服务机构（Facility）一词与本部分使用的“机构”为同义词。

(g) **机构审查委员会（IRB）** 指任何由研究机构正式指派，来审核涉及人类作为受试者的生物医学研究管理会、委员会或其他组织，用来批准启动研究以及定期审核研究。审核的主要目的是为了保护受试者的权利和福祉。

(h) **研究者** 指实际进行临床研究的个人，如，在其直接指导下，将试验物品施用或分发，或给受试者使用。若临床研究由团队执行，研究者是该团队的责任领导。

(i) **最低风险** 指研究中预期对受试者造成伤害或不适的概率和程度不比受试者在日常生活中或在常规体检或心理检查中所遇到的更高。

(j) **申办者** 指发起临床研究的人或其他实体，但不实际执行研究，即研究物品是在其他人的直接指导下被施用或分发，或供受试者使用。使用所属一名或多名雇员开展其发起的临床研究的公司或机构，被认为是申办者（非申办-研究者），其雇员被认为是研究者。

(k) **申办-研究者** 指既发起研究也实际执行临床研究的个人，在其直接指导下，试验物品被施用或被分发，或给受试者使用。该术语不包括个人以外的实体，如公司或机构。本部分所指的申办-研究者的义务包含申办者的义务和研究者的义务。

(l) **试验物品** 指在本法案或《公共卫生服务法》第 351 和第 354—360F 节监管下的任何药品（包括人用生物制品）、人用医疗器械、人用食品添加剂、色素添加剂、电子产品或任何其他物品。

(m) **IRB 批准** 指 IRB 确认临床研究已经通过其审核，可以在 IRB 和联邦要求范围内的研究机构进行。

## 56.103 需要 IRB 审核的情形

(a) 除 56.104 和 56.105 另有规定外，任何有要求需事先向 FDA 递交申请的临床试验（第 312、812 和 813 部分法规要求），在未得到符合本部分法规要求的 IRB 审核及批准前，不得启动，且临床试验将持续受到该 IRB 的审核。

(b) 除 56.104 和 56.105 另有规定外，如果临床研究尚未获得符合本部分法规要求的 IRB 批准，不符合 IRB 初次和持续审核要求，FDA可决定不使用其得到的研究数据或资料来支持其研究或上市许可申请。FDA对临床研究不支持上市许可申请的裁定，不能免除申请人根据其他适用法规需向FDA提交研究结果的义务。

(c) 遵守本规定不会违背适用的联邦、州或当地法律或法规。

**56.104 豁免IRB要求**

以下类别临床研究可豁免本部分法规对IRB审核的要求：

(a) 1981年7月27日前开始的任何研究，前提是研究仍需接受符合FDA在1981年7月27日前要求的IRB审核。

(b) 1981年7月27日前开始的任何研究，且研究不需接受符合FDA在该日期前要求的IRB审核。

(c) 紧急使用试验物品，前提是在5个工作日内向IRB报告此类紧急使用试验物品的情况。随后在该研究机构使用研究物品仍需经过IRB审核。

(d) 评估口味和食品质量以及消费者接受度的研究，如果摄入的是无添加剂的健康食品，或摄入的食物所含食品成分在安全范围内，或农业、化学或环境污染物等于或低于FDA认定的安全水平，或被环境保护局或美国农业部食品安全检验局批准使用。

**56.105 免除IRB要求**

根据申办者或申办-研究者的申请，FDA可以对特定研究活动或特定研究活动类别免除本条例中的要求，其中包括需接受IRB审核的要求。

## 子部分B 组织和人员

**56.106 登记**

(a) **谁必须注册？** 审核法案第505 (i) 或520 (g) 节条例下FDA监管的临床研究的IRB，以及审核目的在于获得FDA上市许可申请的临床研究的IRB，都必须在美国卫生与公众服务部维护中心注册。[在本法案第505（i）节下的研究申请通常称为研究新药申请（IND），在本法案第520（g）节下的研究申请通常称为研究器械豁免（IDE）。] IRB的授权代表必须提交注册信息。所有其他的IRB可以自愿注册。

(b) IRB **必须注册什么信息？** 每个IRB必须提供以下信息：

(1) 使用IRB的研究机构名称、邮寄地址和街道地址（如不同于邮寄地址）以及该研究机构负责监督IRB执行活动的高级管理人员姓名、邮寄地址、电话号码、传真号码和电子邮件地址。

(2) IRB的名称、邮寄地址、街道地址（如果与邮寄地址不同）、电话号码、传真号码和电子邮件地址；IRB主席的姓名、电话号码和电子邮件地址；以及注册信息联系人的姓名、邮寄地址、电话号码、传真号码和电子邮件地址。

(3) 已审核的涉及FDA监管产品的在研方案的大概数量。本规则中，“在研方案”是指IRB在近12个月内，经召集会议或经快速审核程序进行的初步审核或持续审核的方案。

(4) 对IRB审核方案中涉及的FDA监管产品（如生物制品、色素添加剂、食品添加剂、人用药品或医疗器械）的描述。

(c) **什么时候需要进行IRB注册？** 所有IRB必须提交初始注册登记。初次登记必须在IRB开始审核本节（a）段所述临床研究之前进行。所有IRB必须每3年更新注册登记。IRB注册登记在美国卫生与公众服务部审核和验收后生效。

(d) **在哪里进行IRB注册？** IRB可以通过http：//ohrp. cit. nih. gov/efile进行电子注册。如果IRB不能以电子方式注册，则必须以书面形式将注册信息寄给FDA特殊医学项目办公室，GCP办公室（地址：10903 New Hampshire Ave.，Bldg. 32，Rm. 5129，Silver Spring，MD 20993）。

(e) IRB **如何修改其注册信息？** 如果IRB联系人或伦理委员会主席的联系信息发生变化，IRB必须在变化发生后90天内提交更新的信息以修改注册信息。IRB 对 FDA 监管产品做出新的类别审核的更改（例如，IRB 以前审核与药品有关的研究，现决定审核与食品添加剂有关的研究），或决定停止审核 FDA 监管的临床研究，必须在变更后的 30 天内报告。涉及 IRB 解散决定的变更，必须在 IRB 做出永久停止审核研究决定后的 30 天内报告。所有其他信息更改可在 IRB 更新注册时报告。修改后的信息必须按照本节（d）段的要求以电子方式或以书面形式发送给 FDA。

## 56.107 IRB 组成成员

(a) 每个 IRB 应至少有 5 名成员，具有不同的背景，以促进对该研究机构通常进行的研究活动进行完整而充分的审核。IRB 应足够称职，通过其组成成员的经验和专长以及成员的多样性，考虑到不同种族、性别、文化背景以及对社区态度等问题的敏感性等因素，促进对其维护人类受试者权利和福祉的咨询意见和建议的尊重。除了拥有审核具体研究活动所需的专业能力外，IRB 还应能够根据研究机构的承诺和相关法规、适用法律和专业行为及实践标准，判断拟进行研究的可接受性。因此，IRB 应包括在这些领域有丰富知识的专业人员。如果 IRB 定期审核涉及弱势群体的研究，如儿童、囚犯、孕妇或残障人士，则应考虑纳入 1 名或多名对这些受试者有了解和有与他们有一起工作经验的人员。

(b) 尽力防止歧视，确保 IRB 不完全由男性或女性组成，考虑 IRB 内有两种性别的合格成员，使 IRB 会不根据性别做出抉择。IRB 不能完全由一个职业的成员组成。

(c) IRB 应至少包括 1 名主要关注点在科学领域的成员，一名主要关注点在非科学领域的成员。

(d) IRB 应至少包括 1 名不隶属于该研究机构且不是该研究机构雇员直系亲属的成员。

(e) IRB 的初始或后续审核不得让有经济利益冲突的成员参与，IRB 要求提供研究信息的情况除外。

(f) IRB 可以酌情邀请在特定领域有能力的专家，协助审核超出该 IRB 成员专业知识范围的复杂问题或对 IRB 的知识进行补充。这些专家不得参与投票。

## 子部分 C　IRB 的功能及运营

### 56.108　IRB 的功能及运营

为符合规则要求，每个 IRB 应：

(a) 遵循书面操作规程：(1) 对研究进行初步和持续审核，并向研究者和研究机构报告其发现和采取的行动；(2) 确定哪些项目需要进行比年度审核更为频繁的审核，哪些项目需要对非来源于研究者的其他信息进行审核，证明自 IRB 上次审核以来没有发生实质性变化；(3) 确保及时向 IRB 报告研究活动的变化；(4) 对于已批准的研究，确保在 IRB 批准期间，如果未经过 IRB 审核和批准，不得对已批准的研究进行任何变更，需立即消除对人类受试者明显直接危害的情形除外。

(b) 遵循书面操作规程，以确保及时向 IRB、相应机构官员和 FDA 报告：(1) 给人类受试者或其他人带来风险的非预期性问题；(2) 严重或重复违反本条例或 IRB 要求或决定的情况；(3) 暂停或终止 IRB 的批准。

(c) 除了使用快速审核程序外（见 56.110)，在大多数 IRB 成员列席的审评会议上审核拟议研究，应至少包含 1 名主要关注点在非科学领域的成员。为使研究获得批准，应当获得出席会议的大多数成员的批准。

### 56.109　IRB 审核研究

(a) 对本法规监管的研究活动，IRB 应进行审核并有权批准、要求修改（以获得批准）或不予批准。

(b) 知情同意过程中，IRB 应要求提供给受试者的信息符合 50.25 要求。除 50.25 中具体列出的信息外，当 IRB 判断某些其他信息有助于保护受试者的权利和福祉时，IRB 可以要求提供给受试者。

(c) 为符合本章第 50.27 要求，IRB 应要求提供知情同意书，下列情况除外：

(1) 对于某些或所有受试者，如果发现研究对受试者造成伤害不高于最低风险，且不涉及通常需要签署书面同意的研究操作，IRB可以不要求受试者或其法定授权代表签署书面知情同意书。

(2) 对于某些或所有受试者，IRB发现研究满足本章50.24因急救研究而免于知情同意的要求。

(d) 如果根据本节(c)(1)段规定免除知情同意书的要求，IRB可要求研究者向受试者提供有关研究的书面陈述。

(e) IRB应以书面形式通知研究者和研究机构IRB做出的批准或不批准的决定，或为了获得IRB批准而应做出的修改。如果IRB决定不批准研究活动，应在书面通知中陈述其做出不批准决定的理由，并向研究者提供研究者亲自或以书面形式做出回应的机会。对于涉及本章50.24规定的知情同意例外情形的研究，当IRB因判断研究并不符合本章50.24规定的情形或由于其他相关道德考虑而不批准研究时，IRB应立即以书面形式通知研究者和申办者。书面通知应包含IRB做出不批准决定的理由。

(f) IRB应根据风险程度以适当的时间间隔对研究进行持续审核，但间隔不得少于每年一次，并有权观察或让第三方观察知情同意过程和研究。

(g) 对涉及本章50.24知情同意特殊情形的研究，IRB应以书面形式给予申办者根据本章50.24(a)(7)(ii)和(a)(7)(iii)要求公开披露信息的副本。IRB应及时向申办者提供此类信息，以便申办者知晓已经发生此类披露。收到后，申办者应向FDA提供披露信息的副本。

(h) 当研究中的部分或所有受试者是儿童时，IRB必须在初步审核研究时判断研究是否符合本章第50部分子部分D的要求。对2001年4月30日在进行的部分或所有受试者是儿童的研究，IRB必须对其进行审核，以确定研究是否符合本章第50部分子部分D的要求，审核可在规定的持续审核期间进行，如IRB认为有必要，可在更早的日期内进行。

## 56.110 快速审核程序：涉及不高于最低风险及对已批准的研究进行微小变更

(a) 美国食品药品管理局已经建立且在联邦公报上公布了IRB可以通过快速审核程序进行审核的研究类别清单。该清单将在适当情况下通过联邦公报定期公布所进行的修订。

(b) IRB可以使用快速审核程序审核以下任一类或两类研究：(1) 列表中出现的部分或全部研究，审评者发现其风险不高于最低风险，(2) 对之前已批准的研究，在授权批准期间(1年或以内)发生的微小变更。根据快速审核程序，审核可由IRB主席或由IRB主席从IRB成员中指定的一名或多名有经验的审评员执行。在审核此类研究时，审评人员可以行使IRB除“不批准”以外的所有权力。只有采用非快速审核程序，按56.108 (c) 规定进行审核后才能否决研究活动。

(c) 所有使用快速审核程序的IRB均应采取措施，使得所有成员知晓采用快速审核程序已经获得批准的研究。

(d) 必要时，为保护受试者的权利或福祉，FDA可以限制、暂停或终止研究机构或IRB使用快速审核程序。

## 56.111 IRB审核研究的标准

(a) 为批准本法规监管下的研究，IRB应确定以下所有要求均得到满足：

(1) 对受试者的风险减到最小：(i) 通过良好的研究设计，且不会不必要地将受试者暴露于风险中，(ii) 为诊断或治疗的目的，适当时维持使用以往受试者使用过的治疗措施。

(2) 考虑到受试者的预期福祉，以及预期从试验获得疾病知识的重要性，受试者所冒风险是合理的。在评估风险和受益时，IRB应仅考虑研究可能带来的风险和受益(这些风险和受益有别于受试者即使不参与研究而接受治疗的医学风险和受益)。IRB不应考虑应用研究所得知识可能带来的长期效果(例如，研究对公共政策的可能影响）。

（3）受试者的选择是公平的。在做出此类评估时，IRB应考虑到研究的目的及研究进行的环境，并应该特别认识到涉及弱势人群研究的特殊问题，如儿童、囚犯、孕妇、残疾人，或精神障碍人士，或经济或受教育弱势人群。

（4）按照第50部分规定的要求，向每个潜在受试者或受试者法定授权代表征求知情同意。

（5）知情同意过程将按照50.27规定的要求进行适当记录。

（6）在适当情况下，研究计划内制定了对收集数据进行适当监查的规定，以确保受试者安全。

（7）在适当情况下，有足够条款保护受试者隐私，并保持数据的保密性。

（b）当部分或全部受试者为弱势人群，如儿童、囚犯、孕妇、残疾人，或精神障碍人士，或经济或受教育弱势人群等，容易受到强制或不当伤害影响时，附加额外的保障措施以保护这些受试者的权利和福祉。

（c）为了批准部分或所有受试者是儿童的研究，IRB必须确定所有研究均依从本章第50部分子部分D的要求。

### 56.112 机构审查委员会审核

本法规监管下的研究经IRB批准后可能会被FDA官员进一步审核，以决定批准或不批准进行该研究。如果未得到IRB的批准，FDA官员不能批准该研究。

### 56.113 暂停或终止IRB对研究的批准

IRB有权暂停或终止未按照IRB要求进行的研究，或对受试者造成意外严重伤害的研究。任何暂停或终止批准均应包含IRB采取此行动理由的陈述，并应及时向研究者、相应研究机构官员和FDA报告。

### 56.114 合作研究

按照规定，涉及多中心研究的机构可采用联合审核，依靠另一合格的IRB进行审核，或做类似安排，以避免重复工作。

# 子部分 D 记录和报告

## 56.115 IRB 记录

(a) 研究机构，或在适当情况下 IRB，应对 IRB 的活动充分记录和维护，记录应包括以下内容：

(1) 经审核的所有研究提案副本，与提案相关的科学评估(如有)，经批准的知情同意书样本，研究者提交的进度报告以及对受试者造成伤害的报告。

(2) IRB 会议记录要足够详细地记录出席会议人员；IRB 采取的行动措施；对这些行动进行的表决，包括投票赞成、反对和弃权的人数；要求进行修改或不批准研究的理由；以及对有争议问题及其解决方案进行讨论的书面摘要。

(3) 持续审核活动的记录。

(4) IRB 与研究者之间所有通信副本。

(5) IRB 成员名单：包含姓名；获得的学位；代表资格；经验证明（如专业委员会认证、执照等)；说明每位成员对 IRB 审核工作的主要预期贡献；以及每位成员与研究机构之间的工作或其他关系，例如，全职雇员、兼职雇员、理事会成员或董事会成员、股东、有酬或无酬顾问等。

(6) 56.108 (a) 和 (b) 要求的 IRB 书面操作规程。

(7) 按照 50.25 要求，向受试者提供重要新发现的声明。

(b) 本条例要求的记录应保留至研究完成后至少 3 年，记录应在合理时间内和以合适的方式供 FDA 授权代表视察和复印。

(c) 如果研究机构或审核研究的 IRB 不允许 FDA 根据本节对此研究进行视察，FDA 可以拒绝考虑以此临床研究来支持研究或上市许可的申请。

## 子部分 E　对不依从的行政处罚

### 56.120　行政措施

(a) 如果 FDA 的视察员在视察期间观察到 IRB 的操作明显不符合本法规规定，视察员将向 IRB 相应代表提供口头或书面视察摘要。FDA 随后会向 IRB 及其母机构发信函描述该违规事件。FDA 将要求 IRB 或其母机构在 FDA 指定时间内对发出信函做出回应，描述 IRB、研究机构或两者都将采取的纠正措施，以达到依从法规的要求。

(b) 根据 IRB 或研究机构的回应，FDA 可以安排再次视察以确认纠正措施是否适当。此外，在 IRB 或母机构采取适当纠正措施之前，FDA 可能要求 IRB：

(1) 暂停批准受本部分法规条例监管、在此研究机构进行或受此 IRB 审核的新研究。

(2) 指示不得对正在进行的受本部分法规监管的研究增加新受试者。

(3) 或终止正在进行的受本部分法规监管的研究，以免受试者受到危害。

(c) 当明显的违规行为对人类受试者的权利和福祉造成重大威胁时，FDA 将通知相关国家和联邦监管机构以及因 FDA 对 IRB 操作不当而采取行动有直接利益关系的其他方。

(d) 母机构应对 IRB 的运作负责，FDA 通常会根据本子部分法规针对该研究机构采取行政措施。然而，根据视察期间确认的研究缺陷责任证据，FDA 可以只对 IRB 或其母机构指派的 IRB 负责部门采取行政措施。

### 56.121　取消 IRB 或研究机构的资格

(a) 当 IRB 或研究机构未能采取足够措施以纠正 FDA 根据 56.120 (a) 发送信件中所描述的违规情形，FDA 专员确定，有理由根据这种违规行为取消 IRB 或母机构的资格时，专员将按照第 16 部分法规规定的监管听证要求提起行政程序。

(b) 如确定以下情况，FDA 专员可以取消 IRB 或母机构的资格：

(1) IRB 拒绝或多次未遵守本部分法规下的任何规定，并且

(2) 违规行为对临床研究中受试者的权利或福祉产生了不利影响。

(c) 如判定取消资格是正确的，FDA 专员会发出指令，解释做出该决定的依据，并说明将对接受此 IRB 审核的正在进行的临床研究采取的行动。FDA 将向 IRB 和母机构发送取消资格的通知。其他直接利益方，如申办者和临床研究者，也可能会收到取消资格的通知。此外，FDA 可以选择在联邦公报上公布其采取的行动通知。

(d) FDA 不会批准由不合格 IRB 审核或由不合格研究机构进行的临床研究许可申请。在审核上市申请时，FDA 不会考虑由不合格 IRB 审核或由不合格研究机构产生的临床数据，除非该 IRB 或母机构按照 56.123 规定被恢复职能。

### 56.122 公开披露撤销信息

FDA 取消机构资格的决定，以及关于该项决定的行政记录可根据第 20 部分法规向公众公开。

### 56.123 恢复 IRB 或机构

IRB 或研究机构向 FDA 递交该机构或 IRB 计划采取纠正措施的书面说明，FDA 专员对此解释进行评估后确定：IRB 或研究机构已经提供足够保证将依从本部分法规的标准运行，则可恢复 IRB 或研究机构的资格。恢复资格的信息应下达至 56.121 (c) 中列出的曾收到过撤销资格通知的所有相关人员。

### 56.124 取消资格的替代措施或补充措施

取消 IRB 或研究机构资格的行动是独立的，不是授权行为的替代或先决条件。在取消资格之前、之时或之后，作为取消资格的补充或替代处罚，FDA 可随时通过司法部门提起适当的司法程序（民事或刑事）和采取任何适当的监管措施。FDA 还可以将相关事宜提交给另一联邦、州或地方政府机构，以便机构确定采取适当的行动。

[2017 年 4 月 1 日更新版本]

# 21CFR 第 312 部分 研究新药申请

## 子部分 A 一般条款

### 312.1 范围

(a) 本部分法规包含管理使用研究新药的程序和要求，包括向美国食品药品管理局（FDA）提交研究新药申请（IND）及受 FDA 审核的程序与要求。依从本部分法规得到有效 IND 即可免除原本适用的上市前批准要求，可合法运输药品以进行临床研究。

(b) 本部分法规参考的法案指《美国联邦法案》第 21 篇的第Ⅰ章，另有说明除外。

### 312.2 适用性

(a) 适用性。除本节另有规定外，本部分法规适用于《联邦食品、药品和化妆品法案》第 505 节或《公共卫生服务法》(58 Stat. 632）监管的所有临床研究。

(b) 豁免。

(1) 如满足以下条件，在美国合法上市销售的药品制剂的临床研究可免除本部分法规要求：

(i) 研究目的既不是为向 FDA 申请新适应证而进行的严格对照研究，也不是为了对药品标签进行重大变更的临床研究。

(ii) 在研药品如果是合法上市销售的处方药品，研究目的不是用于支持对其产品广告进行重大变更。

(iii) 研究不涉及明显增加药品使用风险（或降低风险接受度）的有关因素，如给药途径、剂量水平、患者群体或其他因素。

(iv) 研究依从第56部分法规规定的对机构审核的要求和第50部分法规规定的对知情同意的要求进行。

(v) 研究按照312.7要求实施。

(2) (i) 涉及本节(b)(2)(ii)段列出的体外诊断生物制品的临床研究可豁免此部分法规要求，如果符合以下条件：该体外诊断制品是用于在诊断过程中证实由另一诊断制品或诊断步骤得出的医学诊断，并且按照312.160的要求进行运输。

(ii) 根据本节(b)(2)(i)段，以下产品可免除本部分法规要求：分型血清；红细胞试剂；和抗人球蛋白。

(3) 如按照312.160要求运输，仅用于体外试验或实验室动物研究的药品，可免除本部分法规要求。

(4) FDA不接受根据本节(b)(1)段条款得到豁免的研究申请。

(5) 如无提交IND的要求，涉及使用安慰剂的临床研究可免除本部分法规要求。

(6) 涉及本章50.24规定的因急救研究而豁免事先获得知情同意要求的例外情形的临床研究，不得免除本部分法规要求。

(c) 生物利用度研究。本部分法规对于人体体内生物利用度研究的适用性条款是320.31。

(d) 未标签的适应证。本部分法规不适用于根据第314部分法规获批的新药或生物制品用于未经批准适应证的临床研究。

(e) 指导原则。FDA可自行就本部分法规对特定研究用药的适用性发布指导原则。根据要求，FDA将就本部分法规对计划临床研究的适用性提供建议。

### 312.3 定义和释义

(a) 本法案第201节术语的定义和解释适用于本部分法规使用的术语。

(b) 对以下术语的定义也适用于本部分法规：

**法案** 指美国《联邦食品、药品和化妆品法案》。

**临床研究** 指任何涉及试验物品及一名或多名人类受试者的试验。本部分法规中，研究是指在医疗实践过程中使用除市售药物之外的任何药物。

**合同研究组织** 指作为申办者的独立承包商，承担申办者一项或多项义务的实体，例如：方案设计、选择或监查研究者、评估报告，以及准备提交给美国食品药品管理局的材料。

**FDA** 指美国食品药品管理局。

**IND** 指研究新药申请。本部分，"IND"与"研究新药豁免申请"同义。

**独立伦理委员会（IEC）** 指审查小组，负责确保参与临床研究人类受试者的权利、安全和福祉得到保护，且其组成能充分提供此种保护。本章 56.102（g）中定义的机构审查委员会（IRB）是 IEC 的一种类型，需要符合本章第 56 部分法规的要求。

**研究新药** 指用于临床研究的新药或生物制品。该术语还包括用于诊断目的体外生物制品。"研究性药品"和"研究新药"在本部分法规中被认为是同义词。

**研究者** 指实际实施临床研究的个人（即在他/她直接指导下将药物施用或分发给受试者）。如果研究由一研究小组实施，研究者是小组的责任领导。"协作研究者"包括该团队的任何其他成员。

**上市申请** 是指根据此法案第 505（b）条提交的新药申请或根据《公共卫生服务法》提交的生物制品许可申请。

**申办者** 指负责发起临床研究的人员。申办者可以是个人或制药公司、政府机构、学术机构、私人组织或其他组织。除非申办者是申办-研究者，实际上申办者并不实施研究。由自己的一名或多名雇员开展其发起的临床研究的非个体（如公司或机构），被认为是申办者（非申办-研究者），其雇员被认为是研究者。

**申办-研究者** 指既发起也执行研究的个人，在其直接指导下，试验物品被施用或被分发。该术语不包括个人以外的实体，如公司或机构。本部分法规下，申办-研究者的义务既包括研究者的义务也包括申办者的义务。

**受试者** 是指参与研究的人，既可以是研究新药的接受者，也可以是作为对照者。受试者可以是健康人或患者。

## 312.6 研究新药标签

(a) 拟用于人体的研究新药的直接包装上应贴有标签，标明“注意：新药——根据联邦（或美国）法律，仅限用于研究用途”。

(b) 研究新药的标签不得有任何虚假或误导性的陈述，不得表述研究新药对研究的疾病安全或有效。

(c) 根据本章 201.26 或 610.68 规定的程序，相应 FDA 中心主管可以豁免对此节的要求或对本条款（a）的规定采取替代措施，前提是对于列入或将被列入在战略性国家储备中的人用药品的指定批次或单位，法令并未对本条款有明确要求。

## 312.7 研究用药的推广

(a) 研究新药的推广。申办者、研究者或申办者/研究者代表，均不得在研究过程中对其研究新药的安全性或有效性进行任何宣传或对研究药物进行推广。这项规定并不是为了限制对相关药物进行全面的科学信息交流（包括在科学或大众媒体上传播科学发现），而是为了限制在研究中对研究用药安全性或有效性的推广诉求，以及禁止研究用药在获得批准上市之前的商业行为。

(b) 研究新药的商业分销。申办者或研究者不得在市场上销售或试销研究新药。

(c) 研究期限的延长。发现可能获得了足够的数据支持其上市许可申请的结果后，申办者不得过度延长研究期限。

## 312.8 对 IND 下研究用药的收费

(a) 收费的一般标准。

(1) 申办者必须满足本节（b）段对临床研究收费或本节（c）段对将研究用药扩大至治疗范围而收费的适用要求。申办者对从非隶属关系实体单位购得的已上市药品用于临床研究评估而进行收费时（例如，对已批准上市药品进行新用法的临床研究、使用已批准药品作为阳性对照药的研究），无需满足本节要求。

(2) 申办者必须依照本节（d）段规定合理收费。

(3) 申办者必须在获得 FDA 书面授权后才能对研究用药进行收费。

(4) 如果 FDA 认定对试验药物的收费干扰了药品上市许可的开发进程或不再符合授权标准，FDA 将撤销收费授权。

(b) 临床试验中收费。

(1) 对申办者的药物收取费用。申办者拟对研究用药（包括已上市药品的研究性使用）进行收费，必须满足以下条件：

(i) 提供证据表明：如临床试验已显示出试验药物具有潜在临床益处，相比现有产品将在疾病或病症的诊断、治疗、缓解或预防方面具有明显优势。

(ii) 证据表明：从临床试验中得到的数据有望确立药品的有效性或安全性，获得药品的初步批准，或将支持对已上市药品的标签进行重大变更申请的批准（例如，新适应证、加入比较性安全信息）。

(iii) 证据表明：考虑到申办者要承担巨大的药品成本，在未收费情况下，临床试验将不能实施。巨大成本可能源于生产工艺的复杂性、自然资源的稀缺性、对研究用药的大量需求（例如，由于试验规模大或持续时间长）或以上因素的组合或其他特殊情况的组合（例如，申办者可用的资源少等）。

(2) 临床试验收费期限。除非 FDA 规定了更短的期限，否则可在临床试验期间持续收费。

(c) 对研究用药扩大至治疗用途的收费。

(1) 在本部分子部分 I，拟将研究用药扩大至治疗用途并进行收费的申办者，必需提供合理证据，证实对试验用药的收费不会影响药品上市许可的开发进程。

(2) 对于 312.320 监管下的扩展性研究（治疗用 IND 或治疗方案），必须包含以下保证：

(i) 对于在研临床试验，已有药品上市批准所要求的足够受试者入组试验的证据，向 FDA 保证试验将按计划成功完成。

(ii) 证据显示申请上市许可的药物开发进程进展顺利。

(iii) 总体研究计划［312.23 (a)(3)(iv)］提交的信息明确了申办者计划在下一年度达成的药物开发里程碑事件。

(3) 如有限制，授权收费仅限于获准接受药物治疗的患者人群。

(4) 除非FDA规定了更短期限，否则根据本部分子部分I对扩大研究用药至治疗用途的收费可持续至FDA授权后1年。申办者可向FDA申请追加收费期限。

(d) 对研究用药收费时可收回的费用。

(1) 申办者只能收回生产研究用药的直接成本。

(i) 直接成本是指由申办者发生的，可具体地、专属地归于为FDA批准的研究提供研究用药而发生的费用。直接成本包括生产药物的单位成本（例如，原材料、劳动力、生产所需数量的授权收费研究用药而花费的一次性物料和设备成本），或从其他生产来源获得药物的成本，以及运送和处理（如储存）药物的直接费用。

(ii) 间接成本包括主要用于生产商业销售规模的药物而发生的费用（例如，生产研究用药的设施和设备成本，但这些设备设施主要用于最终为商业化大规模销售而生产药物），以及研究与开发、行政、劳动力，或其他即使临床研究或治疗未授权收费也会发生的费用。

(2) 对于312.315（中等规模患者人群）和312.320（治疗用IND或治疗方案）监管下的将研究用药扩展至治疗用药，除本节(d)(1)(i)段所描述的直接成本外，申办者还可以收回因监查扩展性使用IND或方案、遵守IND报告要求而发生的成本，以及因扩展使用IND而发生的其他行政管理成本。

(3) 为支持其对成本收回的计算，申办者必须提供支持文件以显示申办者的计算与本节(Ld)(1)和(d)(2)段的要求一致（如适用）。证明文件必须附有独立注册会计师已审核和认可计算的声明。

### 312.10 免除要求

(a) 申办者可以要求 FDA 免除本部分法规的适用要求。免除要求的申请可以在 IND 或 IND 信息增补中提交。紧急情况下，可以通过电话或其他快速沟通方式提出申请。免除申请至少包含以下内容之一：
  (1) 解释为什么申办者不必或无法依从本部分法规要求。
  (2) 描述满足本部分法规要求的备选方案或行动措施。
  (3) 其他信息说明免除要求是合理的。

(b) 如果 FDA 认为申办者的不依从行为不会对受试者造成重大不合理风险，并符合以下条件之一，FDA 可准许免除对本部分法规的要求：
  (1) FDA 审核申请时不需要评估申办者对该要求的依从情况，或申办者无法依从规定要求。
  (2) 申办者提出的替代方案满足此项要求。
  (3) 申办者提交的免除申请有道理。

## 子部分 B 研究新药申请（IND）

### 312.20 对 IND 的要求

(a) 如果申办者想要进行 312.2 (a) 监管的新药临床研究，申办者应向 FDA 提交研究新药申请（IND)。

(b) 根据 312.40，对 312.2 (a) 监管的研究，在 IND 生效前，申办者不得开展临床研究。

(c) 申办者应根据 50.24 的规定，对任何涉及无需事先获得知情同意的急救临床研究提交单独的 IND。未经 FDA 事先书面授权，不得进行此类临床研究。FDA 应在收到 IND 之后 30 天内以书面形式提供其做出的决定。

### 312.21 研究阶段

一个或多个阶段的临床研究可以提交一份 IND。新药临床研究通常分为三个阶段。一般来说，各阶段应依次进行，但也可以重叠进行。临床研究三个阶段如下所示：

(a) Ⅰ期临床研究

(1) Ⅰ期临床研究为研究新药首次应用于人体。Ⅰ期临床研究通常需要进行密切监测，可在患者或正常志愿者中进行。此阶段研究目的是确定药物在人体中的代谢和药理作用、因剂量增加引起的不良反应，以及获得早期有效性证据（如果可能）。Ⅰ期临床研究应获得有关药代动力学和药理作用的充分信息，以便设计出严格对照、科学有效的Ⅱ期临床研究。Ⅰ期临床研究中受试者和患者总数随药物的不同而有所差异，通常人数为20～80例。

(2) Ⅰ期临床研究还包括药物代谢研究、构效关系研究、对人体作用机制研究，以及以研究用药作为研究手段进行生物学现象或疾病过程的探索性研究。

(b) Ⅱ期临床研究。Ⅱ期临床研究包括对照性临床研究，用来评估药物对特定适应证的有效性，并确定常见的短期不良反应以及与研究用药相关的风险。Ⅱ期临床研究通常为严格对照试验，需要密切监测，并在相对较少数量的患者中进行，通常涉及的受试者不超过几百例。

(c) Ⅲ期临床研究。Ⅲ期临床研究是扩大的对照和非对照性试验。在获得初步证据表明药物具有疗效后进行，目的在于收集有关有效性和安全性的更多信息，评估药物整体利益-风险关系，同时为处方说明提供充分依据。Ⅲ期临床研究通常包括数百到数千名受试者。

## 312.22 提交IND的一般原则

(a) FDA审核IND的主要目的是在所有研究阶段都确保受试者的安全和权利，且Ⅱ期、Ⅲ期试验对药物的科学评估质量良好，可以评估药物的有效性和安全性。因此，尽管FDA对提交的Ⅰ期试验申请审核侧重于安全性评估，FDA对提交的Ⅱ、Ⅲ期试验申请审核还包括评估临床研究的科学质量以及该研究产生的数据能否符合上市许可法定标准。

(b) 对于特定的药物，在提交IND申请时必须提交足够的信息以确保能够达到本节（a）段的目标，所需提供的信息量取决于多种因素：如药物的创新性、既往对药物研究的程度、已知或怀疑的风险、药物的开发阶段等。

（c）IND首次提交报告的中心要点应放在总体研究计划和为特定研究人群制定的研究方案上。随后包含新方案或修订方案的IND增补应以先前提交的资料为逻辑依据，并应有额外的信息加以支持，包括相应的动物毒理学研究或其他对人类研究的结果。IND年度报告将重点报告研究现状，并应为来年更新总体研究计划。

（d）申办者应常规采用312.23规定的IND申请格式，以使FDA对申请的审核更有效率。但是，根据所研药物的种类及已有信息，申办者对每部分提交的信息有相当大的酌处权。312.23节列出了新分子实体上市申请IND所需的信息。将生产商已获得IND或上市许可申请的研究新药作为研究工具的申办-研究者应使用统一格式，但一般情况下，如果有生产商授权，可以参考生产商的IND或上市许可申请来提供技术信息，支持拟进行的临床研究。除非可从科学文献中引用技术信息，申办-研究者使用非生产商IND或上市申请监管的研究用药时，通常需要提交支持其IND的所有技术信息。

## 312.23 IND内容和格式

（a）拟在本部分法规规定下进行临床研究的申办者，应当按照以下顺序提交“研究新药申请”（IND）：

（1）**封面（FDA-1571表）**。申请封面应包含以下内容：

（i）申办者姓名、地址和电话号码，申请日期以及研究新药名称。

（ii）确定拟进行临床研究的阶段。

（iii）承诺该IND生效前不启动临床研究。

（iv）承诺符合第56部分法规要求的IRB将负责对每项拟议临床研究进行首次及持续的审核和批准，且研究者将根据第56部分法规要求将研究活动变更计划报告给IRB。

(v) 承诺按所有其他适用监管要求实施研究。

(vi) 负责监查临床研究执行和进展人员的姓名和职务。

(vii) 按312.32规定，负责审核和评估药物安全相关信息人员的姓名和职务。

(viii) 如果申办者将临床研究任何一项义务转交给合同研究组织（CRO），需提供书面声明。此声明需包含CRO的名称和地址、临床研究编号及所转交义务的清单。如果将所有临床研究执行义务都转交给CRO，则可以提交一份关于转交义务的一般性声明，来代替所转交的具体义务清单。

(ix) 申办者或申办者授权代表签名。如果申请签署人在美国境内无居住地或营业地，则IND中还必须包含律师、代理人，或在美国居住或有营业场所的其他授权人员的姓名和地址，并由其联合签署。

(2) **目录。**

(3) **介绍性声明和研究计划。**

(i) 简要介绍药物名称、所有活性成分、药物药理学类别、药物结构式（如已知）、所用剂型配方、给药途径、拟进行临床研究的目标和计划期限。

(ii) 简要总结既往该药在人体的应用经验，如相关，可参考其他IND申请，以及在其他国家可能与拟进行临床研究安全性相关的临床研究或上市后经验。

(iii) 如果药物曾因安全性或有效性原因而在任何国家被撤回研究或撤市，确定药物被撤回的国家和撤回原因。

(iv) 简要说明来年该药研究的总体规划。计划应包括以下内容：药物或研究的基本原理；研究的适应证；药物评估所采用的一般方法；在提交申请后的第一年要进行临床研究类别（如果不是全年计划，申办者应加以说明）；对研究中接受药物患者人数的预估；根据动物毒理学数据或既往人体研究中此药物或相关药物数据而预期的任何特定的严重或重大风险。

(4) ［保留］

(5) **研究者手册。**按 312.55 规定，研究者手册副本应包含以下信息：

(i) 原料药和制剂的简要说明，包括结构式（如已知）。

(ii) 药物在动物和人体内（如已知）药理学和毒理作用的总结。

(iii) 药物在动物和人体内（如已知）药代动力学和生物处置的总结。

(iv) 既往临床研究中获得的对人体安全性和有效性信息总结（如有用，可附上此类研究发表文章的复印件）。

(v) 根据研究用药或相关药物既往经验，对可能风险及预期不良反应进行描述，以及作为药物研究性应用的一部分，对注意事项或特别监查措施的描述。

(6) **方案。**

(i) 计划研究的方案［起初未在 IND 中提交的研究方案应按照 312.30 (a) 要求提交］。一般来说，与Ⅱ、Ⅲ期临床研究方案相比，Ⅰ期临床研究方案不太详细，更为灵活。Ⅰ期研究方案应着重提供研究大纲（包括：对受试者人数的预估，安全性排除标准的描述，包括在确定给药剂量时对给药持续时间、剂量或给药方式等的描述），仅对研究中影响安全性的重要因素加以详细说明，如对生命体征和血液生化的必要监测。对不影响关键安全性评估的Ⅰ期试验设计修改仅需要在年度报告中向 FDA 报告。

(ii) 对于Ⅱ、Ⅲ期临床研究，应提交详尽描述试验各部分的研究方案。对于Ⅱ、Ⅲ期临床研究方案，如果申办者预期随着研究进展会出现方案偏离，那么在一开始制定时就应在方案中加入避免发生偏离的替代方法或应急措施。例如，短期对照性研究方案可能包含对无应答受试者早期交叉至替代治疗的计划。

(iii) 临床试验方案需要包含以下内容，具有反映各研究阶段差异的具体要素和细节：

(A) 研究目标和目的陈述。

(B) 每位研究者姓名、地址和资格声明（简历或其他资格证明），主要研究者监管下每位协助研究者（如进修医生、住院医生）姓名，研究场所名称和地址，以及相应IRB的名称和地址。

(C) 患者入选标准和排除标准以及对参加研究患者人数的预估。

(D) 对研究设计的描述，包括要使用的对照组类型（如有对照组），以及为减少受试者、研究者和分析人员发生偏离而采用方法的说明。

(E) 确定给药剂量、计划最大剂量以及患者个体暴露于药物持续时间的方法。

(F) 对为达到研究目标需进行的观察和测量的描述。

(G) 对临床措施、实验室检测或其他为监测药物对人类受试者的影响并尽量减少受试者风险而采取的措施的描述。

(7) **化学、生产和质量控制信息。**

(i) 适用于IND监管的特定研究，需要有一章节描述原料药和药物制剂的组成、生产和质量控制内容。虽然在每一研究阶段都需要提供足够信息来确保研究用药的鉴别、质量、纯度和活性强度，但所需信息量仍将随研究阶段、研究持续时间、药物剂型和其他已有信息而变化。FDA 承认随着研究进行，很可能需要修改新药原料药和剂型的制备方法，或者改变剂型。因此，首次提交Ⅰ期临床研究的重点一般应放在原材料和新药原料药的鉴别和质量控制上。药物原料和药物制剂的最终说明在研究结束时才确定。

(ii) 应当强调的是，提交的信息量取决于拟进行临床研究的范围。例如，尽管在 IND 所有阶段都需要稳定性数据，来表明在拟进行临床研究计划实施期间，新原料药和药物制剂在可接受的化学和物理限度范围内；如果只需做非常短期的测试，支持稳定性的数据可相应地减少。

(iii) 随着药物开发进行和随着规模或产量的进展（从最初限制性临床研究的中试规模到扩大临床研究所需的大规模生产），申办者应提交修正信息以补充初期提交的化学、生产和质量控制过程信息，以适应扩大的临床研究。

(iv) 为反映本段（a)(7) 所述的差异，根据研究阶段，提交材料需包含以下内容：

(A) **原料药。** 对原料药进行描述，包括物理、化学或生物学特性，生产商名称和地址，原料药一般制备方法，确保原料药的鉴别、活性强度、质量和纯度的可接受限度以及分析方法，足够支持原料药在毒理学研究和预期临床研究期间保持稳定的信息。参考现行版《美国药典-国家处方集》可以满足本段的有关要求。

(B) **药物制剂。** 用于生产研究药物制剂的所有成分列表（其中可包括非活性化合物的合理替代物），包括预期出现在药物制剂中的成分和在生产过程中使用但并未添加到药物制剂中的成分，以及临床研究药物制剂的定量组成成分（如适用），包括在研究阶段可能发生的任何对成分的合理改动；药物制剂生产商的名称和地址；药物制剂生产和包装程序的简要概述；确保药物制剂的鉴别、活性强度、质量和纯度的可接受限度和分析方法；以及能够确保药物制剂在预期临床研究期间维持稳定的充足信息。参考现行版《美国药典-国家处方集》可以满足本段的有关要求。

(C) 对用于对照性临床研究中安慰剂的组成、生产和质量控制的简要总体描述。

(D) **标签。**提供给每位研究者的所有标签副本。

(E) **环境分析要求。**根据 25.30 或 25.31 规定作出的分类排放声明或根据 25.40 规定作出的环境评估。

(8) **药理学和毒理学信息。**根据已有实验动物或体外药理学和毒理学研究的足够信息，申办者得出进行拟议临床研究较为安全的结论。随拟进行临床研究的持续时间和性质不同，实验动物的种类、持续时间和范围以及其他测试有所差异。可从 FDA 处获得满足这些要求方法的指导文件。这些信息还包括评价这些研究结果的个人身份和资质。审批者评估试验结果后得出开展拟进行临床研究相当安全的结论，以及研究开展的地点和何处可查阅研究记录以供视察的说明。随着药物开发进展，申办者须酌情提供安全性补充信息。

(i) 药理学和药物处置。此节描述药物在动物体内的药理作用和作用机制，以及药物的吸收、分布、代谢和排泄信息（如已知）。

(ii) 毒理学。

(A) 药物动物试验和体外试验的毒理作用综合总结。根据药物性质和不同研究阶段，包含急性、亚急性和慢性毒性试验结果；药物对生殖和胎儿发育的影响；与特定给药方式或使用条件（例如，吸入、透皮、眼毒理学）相关的任何特殊毒性试验以及任何旨在评估药物毒性的体外研究结果。

(B) 对于为支持临床研究安全性而进行的所有毒理学研究，列出全面研究数据表格，供详细审核。

(iii) 对于需遵守第 58 部分法规药物非临床研究质量管理规范（GLP）的非临床实验室研究，声明该研究将依从第 58 部分法规规定的 GLP，如果该研究未依从 GLP，需简要说明未依从 GLP 的原因。

(9) **既往研究用药人体使用经验。**申请人已知的既往人体使用研究用药经验（如有）的总结。所需信息包括如下内容：

(i) 如果研究用药已经在美国或其他国家进行过研究或已上市，需提供这些研究安全性或合理性的相关经验详细信息。如果该药已成为对照性试验的研究用药，还应提供与评估药物有效性相关试验的详细信息。任何与研究安全性相关的或关于药物对拟进行研究用途有效性的出版资料应全部提供。非直接相关的出版材料可通过参考书目提供。

(ii) 如果药物在既往研究或上市后以联合用药方式使用，应为每个药物活性成分提供本节 (a)(9)(i) 所需信息。然而，如果组合用药中的任何组分已获得上市许可申请批准或已在美国合法销售，申办者不需要提交该药物活性成分的已发表资料，除非这些资料与拟进行的研究用途直接相关（包括各成分之间相互作用有关的出版物）。

(iii) 如果该药物在美国境外上市，则列出该药物已上市国家名单以及该药物因潜在安全性或有效性问题而撤市的国家名单。

(10) **附加信息。**如下所述，在某些申请中，可能需要特殊信息。应在本节中提交以下信息：

(i) 药物依赖和滥用的可能性。如果是精神类药物或有滥用可能的其他药物，需要有描述相关临床研究和用药经验以及在实验动物研究的章节。

(ii) 放射性药物。如果是放射性药物，则需要有足够的动物或人类研究数据来对人类受试者全身和重要器官进行辐射吸收剂量的合理计算。放射性药物Ⅰ期临床研究必须包括能获取足够数据以满足剂量计算要求的研究。

(iii) 儿科研究。评估儿童用药安全性和有效性计划。

(iv) 其他资料。简要说明能够有助于评估拟进行临床研究的安全性或设计规划的其他信息，以及作为对照性临床试验支持药物上市的可能性。

(11) **相关信息。**如果FDA要求，审核申请所需的任何其他相关信息。

(b) 已提交的信息。申办者通常不需要重新提交已提交的信息，但可以包含参考资料。引用提交过的信息时须注明文件名称、参考号、卷和页码以方便查找。由申办者以外的代理人提交引用信息时须附加已获授权引用信息的书面声明，并由提交信息者签署。

(c) 外国语材料。对于非英文材料，申办者应提交IND各部分准确完整的英文翻译件。申办者还应提交各部分原始文献出版物的副本。

(d) 副本数量。对所有IND文件，包括最初提交文件、所有修订文件和报告，申办者均应提交一份原件和两份副本。

(e) IND提交文件编号。提交的所有IND文件都需要使用唯一的三位数序列号进行连续编号。IND文件初始编号为000，每个后续文件（如修订版、报告、信函）都需要按时间顺序进行编号。

(f) 不需要事先知情同意的例外情况。如果研究涉及本章50.24部分规定的紧急情况下不需要事先知情同意的例外情形，则申办者应在封面突出标明：该研究符合本章 50.24 部分法规要求。

### 312.30 方案增补

一旦 IND 生效，申办者应根据需要修改方案，以确保临床研究依照方案进行。本节阐述了提交新方案以及更改已提交方案的规定。如果申办者拟进行 50.24 所述的知情同意例外的急救研究，申办者应单独提交这类研究的 IND。

(a) 新方案。如果 IND 未包含申办者拟进行的研究方案，申办者应向 FDA 提交含此研究方案的增补文件。在满足以下两条件时，可以开展此类研究：申办者向 FDA 提交了研究方案供 FDA 审核；方案已根据第 56 部分法规要求获得相关 IRB 批准。申办者可以按照任一顺序遵守这两个条件。

(b) 方案变更。

(1) 申办者应在提交的方案增补文件中描述所做更改，如，在Ⅰ期研究方案中描述对受试者安全造成显著影响之处的更改，在Ⅱ、Ⅲ期研究方案中描述对受试者安全、研究范围或研究的科学质量造成显著影响之处的更改。需要改动的例子包括：

(i) 受试者药物暴露的剂量或持续时间超过现行方案中的剂量或时间，或显著增加受试者人数。

(ii) 在方案设计方面的任何重大改变（如添加或删除对照组）。

(iii) 增加新的检测或实验程序，目的是改善对不良反应或不良事件的监测，或降低不良反应或不良事件的风险；或减少针对安全性监测的检测。

(2) (i) 根据本节 (b)(1) 段规定，方案变更需要满足以下两条件：

(A) 申办者已向 FDA 提交变更申请，供 FDA 审核。

(B) 变更已获相关 IRB 批准。申办者可以按任何顺序遵守这两个条件。

(ii) 尽管有本节 (b)(2)(i) 的规定，如果是为了消除对受试者明显直接危害，可以立即执行方案变更，随后向 FDA 通知方案增补，并按照 56.104（c）的规定通知 IRB 进行审核。

(c) 新研究者。一般来说，增加新研究者实施已提交的方案时，申办者应提交方案增补（根据 312.315 或 312.320 的规定，在实施治疗性研究方案时，增加执业医师不需要进行方案增补的情况除外）。一旦允许新研究者加入临床研究，该研究者即可接收研究用药并开始参与临床研究。申办者应在增加新研究者后 30 天内通知 FDA。

(d) 内容和格式。方案增补需醒目地标识相应内容（例如，“方案增补：新方案”，“方案增补：方案变更”，或“方案增补：新研究者”），并包含如下内容：

(1) (i) 对于新方案，提供新方案副本以及与先前方案具有临床上显著差异的简要说明。

(ii) 对于方案变更，简要说明方案变更的内容和参考资料（含日期和编号）。

(iii) 对于新研究者，提供研究者姓名、实施临床研究资质、已提交的相关方案，以及 312.23（a)(6)(iii)(B) 要求的所有研究者的其他额外信息。

(2) 如有必要，申办者在 IND 或其后 IND 增补中加入具体技术信息的参考文献，以此来支持新方案或方案增补中的重大临床变更。如用参考文献来支持 IND 中已提交的信息，申办者应标明其名称、参考文献编号、信息所在的卷和页码。

(3) 如果申办者希望 FDA 对提交内容提出意见，应说明希望 FDA 给予评论的请求以及希望得到 FDA 回答的具体问题。

(e) 提交时间。申办者应在实施增补前提交方案增补或方案变更。添加新研究者或提供研究者补充信息的方案增补可间隔 30 天一并提交。如预估在短时间内需多次提交新方案或方案变更时，鼓励申办者在情况许可时将这些内容全部汇总，统一提交。

## 312.31 信息增补

(a) 信息增补要求。申办者应在 IND 信息增补中报告不属于方案增补、IND 安全性报告或年度报告范围内的 IND 核心信息。需要进行信息增补的例子包括：

(1) 新的毒理学、化学或其他技术信息；或

(2) 有关停止临床研究的报告。

(b) 信息增补的内容和格式。信息增补需显著标明相应内容（例如，“信息增补：化学、生产和质量控制”，“信息增补：药理学-毒理学”，“信息增补：临床”），并包含以下内容：

(1) 陈述增补的性质和目的。

(2) 以有利于科学审核的格式系统性地提交数据。

(3) 如果申办者希望 FDA 对信息增补给予评论时，提出对此评论的申请。

(c) 提交时间。对 IND 的信息增补应在必要时提交，在可行情况下，不得比每 30 天的间隔更密集。

## 312.32 IND 安全性报告

(a) 定义。以下术语定义适用于本节：

**不良事件** 指任何与人类用药相关或无关的不良医学事件。

**危及生命的不良事件或危及生命的疑似不良反应** 如果研究者或申办者认为事件的发生将患者或受试者置于死亡的紧迫风险中，则此不良事件或疑似不良反应被认为是“危及生命的”。它不包括如果病情进一步发展可能导致死亡的不良事件或可疑不良反应。

**严重不良事件或严重疑似不良反应** 如果研究者或申办者认为不良事件或疑似不良反应导致以下任一结果，则该事件被认为是“严重的”：死亡、危及生命的不良事件、住院或延长现有住院时间、持续或重大的功能丧失或实质性破坏正常生活功能、先天性异常/出生缺陷。重要医学事件是指未必导致死亡、危及生命或严重到需要住院治疗的事件，基于医学判断，患者或受试者可能受到危害，需要医疗或外科手术干预以防止出现上述定义中列出的任一结果。这类医疗事件

的例子包括：需要在急救室或家中进行强化治疗的过敏性支气管痉挛、不会导致住院治疗的血液恶液质或惊厥、或导致药物依赖或药物滥用的情形。

**疑似不良反应** 指有合理的可能性是由试验药物引起的不良事件。IND安全性报告时，"合理可能性"意味着有证据表明药物与不良事件之间有因果关系。疑似不良反应意味着对因果关系的确定程度较不良反应低，不良反应意味着不良事件是由药物引起的。

**非预期不良事件或非预期疑似不良反应** 以下情况的不良事件或疑似不良反应将被认为是"非预期"的：未列入研究者手册或未列出所观察到的特异性或严重程度；当不需要或无研究者手册时，事件的发生与申请材料中的总体研究计划和别处描述的风险信息不一致。例如，如果研究者手册中仅提及转氨酶升高或肝炎，则发生肝坏死将是非预期的（由于更严重）。同样，如果研究者手册仅列出脑血管意外，则脑血栓和脑血管炎将是非预期的（由于更大的特异性）。本定义中使用的"非预期"也指研究者手册中提到的在同一类药物中发生过或可从该药药理学特性中预期、但未具体提到在特定研究用药中出现的不良事件或疑似不良反应。

(b) 审核安全性信息。申办者必须及时审核现有的或其他国内外收集到的所有药物安全性相关信息，包括从临床或流行病学研究而获得的资料、动物或体外研究资料以及国外监管机构报告和在美国未上市但在美国以外的国家上市的药物经验报告。

(c) (1) IND安全性报告。申办者必须尽快将从临床研究或任何其他来源得到的潜在严重风险信息，通过IND安全性报告，通知FDA和所有参与研究者（即接受申办者提供研究用药的所有研究者）。申办者一旦判断出此信息是根据本节(c)(1)(i)、(c)(1)(ii)、(c)(1)(iii)、(c)(1)(iv)规定要上报的信息，需在15天内上报。在IND安全性报告中，申办者必须鉴别既往提交给FDA的所有类似的疑似不良反应的IND安全性报告，必须根据既往类似报告或其他相关信息来分析该疑似不良反应的意义。

(i) 严重非预期疑似不良反应。申办者必须报告所有严重非预期疑似不良反应。仅当有证据表明药物与不良事件之间存在因果关系时，申办者必须将不良事件报告为疑似不良反应，例如：

(A) 单一发生且已知与药物暴露密切相关的罕见事件（如血管性水肿、肝损伤、Stevens-Johnson 综合征）。

(B) 单次或多次发生的事件与药物暴露很少相关，但在药物暴露的人群中也不常见（如肌腱断裂）。

(C) 综合分析临床研究中观察到的特定事件（例如，正在研究的潜在疾病或症状的已知后果或在受试人群中经常发生的独立于药物治疗的其他事件），发现与同期或历史对照组相比，这些事件更频繁地发生在药物治疗组。

(ii) 其他研究结果。无论研究是否受 IND 监管或是否由申办者实施，申办者都必须报告所有因药物暴露而带来重大风险的流行病学研究、多项研究的荟萃分析或临床研究结果［根据本节（c)(1)(i)段报告的结果除外］。通常情况下，这些研究发现将导致方案、知情同意书、研究者手册中的安全性信息改变（文件日常更新除外）或对临床研究整体运行其他方面的变更。

(iii) 动物或体外检测结果。无论试验是否由申办者实施，申办者必须报告所有提示药物暴露可引起对人体重大风险的动物或体外检测结果，如致突变性、致畸性、致癌性或在接近预期人体药物暴露剂量时对重要器官的毒性。通常情况下，这些研究发现将导致对方案、知情同意书、研究者手册中的安全性信息更改（文件日常更新除外）或对临床研究整体运行其他方面的变更。

(iv) 严重疑似不良反应发生率增加。如果严重疑似不良反应发生率较方案或研究者手册中列出的发生率有明显增加，申办者必须报告。

(v) 提交IND安全性报告。申办者必须以叙述格式或使用FDA3500A表格或以FDA能够处理、审核和归档的电子格式提交IND安全性报告。FDA将定期就如何进行电子提交发布指导原则（如传输方式、媒体、文件格式、文件的准备和组织等）。对在美国以外发生的疑似不良反应，申办者可以向国际医学科学组织（CIOMS）提交（CIOMS）Ⅰ表，而不使用FDA3500A表格。已出版的和未发表的体外、动物、流行病学或临床研究的所有结果或汇总分析报告必须以叙述格式提交。提交给FDA的报告必须对其内容进行显著标识（如"IND安全性报告"），并将其发送给负责审查IND的药物评价和研究中心、生物制品评估和研究中心审核部门。根据FDA要求，申办者必须尽快向FDA提交FDA认为有必要的附加数据或信息，并在收到要求后15日内提交。

(2) 非预期的致命性或危及生命的疑似不良反应报告。申办者必须尽快通知FDA非预期的致命性或危及生命的疑似不良反应，不得迟于申办者初次收到此信息后7日内提交。

(3) 报告格式或报告频率。FDA可要求申办者以不同于本段要求的报告格式或报告频率递交IND安全性报告。如果FDA负责审核该IND的负责人事先同意对其进行改变，则申办者也可以提议并采用不同的报告格式或报告频率。

(4) 对已上市药物的研究。对在美国已上市或已经批准的药物进行IND临床研究，申办者须为美国国内或国外的研究中心在临床研究中观察到的疑似不良反应提交IND安全性报告。申办者还须按照上市后安全性报告要求（如310.305、341.80、600.80要求）提交临床研究中的安全信息。

(5) 报告研究终点。申办者必须将研究终点（如死亡率或主要并发症）按方案所述报告给 FDA，通常不在本节（c）段下报告。但如果发生严重非预期不良事件，有证据表明药物与该事件之间存在因果联系的情况（如由过敏反应引起死亡），即使它属于研究终点的组成部分（如全因死亡率），此类事件也必须按照 312.32（c）(1)(i) 规定将其作为严重非预期疑似不良反应报告。

(d) 跟进。

(1) 申办者必须及时研究收到的全部安全信息。

(2) IND 安全性报告的相关后续信息必须在得到相关信息后立即提交，且必须明确标记为“跟进 IND 安全性报告”。

(3) 如果申办者的研究结果表明当初根据本节（c）段判定为不需要上报的不良事件其实需要上报，则申办者必须尽快（在确定之后 15 日内）在 IND 安全性报告中报告此疑似不良反应。

(e) 免责声明。由申办者根据本部分法规提交的安全性报告或其他资料（以及 FDA 对该报告发布的任何信息）不一定反映申办者或 FDA 根据此报告或信息得出药物引起或导致不良事件发生的结论。申办者不需要承认根据申办者提交的报告或信息而得出药物引起或导致不良事件的结论，也可以否认此结论。

## 312.33 年度报告

申办者应当在 IND 生效满一周年前 60 日内，提交研究进展的简要报告，内容包括：

(a) 单个研究信息。简要总结正在进行的以及上一年度完成的每项研究。总结应包括每项研究的以下信息：

(1) 研究题目（有相应研究编号，如方案号）、研究目的、适用患者人群简短陈述以及研究是否已完成的陈述。

(2) 计划纳入研究的受试者总人数，按年龄、性别和种族列出已进入研究的受试者人数，已按计划完成研究的人数以及因任何原因退出研究的人数。

(3) 如果已完成研究或已知中期研究结果，则简要说明已知研究结果。

(b) 总结。上一年度获得的临床和非临床研究信息，包括：

(1) 采用叙述或图表格式，按人体系统总结最常见和最严重的不良经历。

(2) 过去一年提交的所有 IND 安全性报告总结。

(3) 参加研究期间死亡的受试者名单以及每位受试者的死亡原因。

(4) 无论是否与用药相关，因任何不良经历而中途退出试验的受试者名单。

(5) 简要说明获得的有关药物作用的认识（如有），包括，如：量效关系、对照性试验得到的信息以及生物利用度。

(6) 列出过去一年完成的或正在进行的临床前研究（包括动物研究）的清单以及主要临床前研究发现的总结。

(7) 总结过去一年药物生产的重要变化或微生物学的重大变化。

(c) 说明关于下一年的总研究计划，以取代一年前提交的旧计划。总研究计划应包含 312.23 (a)(3)(iv) 所规定的信息。

(d) 如果研究者手册经过修订，则需对修订和新手册副本进行说明。

(e) 如上一年对Ⅰ期临床试验方案有重大修改，但并未在 IND 方案增补中报告，则需对此加以说明。

(f) 简要总结过去一年内药物在美国以外市场的新进展，如在任何国家批准上市、撤销或暂停上市。

(g) 如果申办者要求或期望对 IND 相关某些未决事宜能得到回复、评论或开会讨论，则申办者需要提供这些未决事宜列表。

## 312.38 撤销 IND

(a) 申办者可在任何时候撤回生效的 IND，而不受到偏见。

(b) 如果申办者撤销 IND 应通知 FDA，应终止进行与 IND 相关的所有临床研究，应通知所有研究者，且应根据申办者的要求，依据 312.59 规定将所有库存药物均退回至申办者或按申办者要求以其他方式进行处置。

(c) 如果因安全原因撤销 IND，申办者应立即通知 FDA、所有参与研究者和所有审核研究的机构审查委员会，并给出撤销原因。

## 子部分 C 行政措施

### 312.40 在临床研究中对使用研究新药的一般要求

(a) 如果满足以下条件，则可以在临床研究中使用研究新药：

(1) 申办者向 FDA 提交 IND 申请；根据本节 (b) 段该 IND 已生效；申办者遵从本部分、第 50 和 56 部分法规中关于临床研究的所有适用要求；和

(2) 参与临床研究的研究者均遵从本部分、第 50 和 56 部分法规要求进行临床研究。

(b) IND 生效：

(1) 除 FDA 通知申办者因 312.42 规定暂不批准 IND 的情况外，FDA 收到 IND 申请后 30 天，IND 自动生效。

(2) 或在更早的时候 FDA 通知可以开始进行 IND 临床研究。FDA 将书面通知申办者 FDA 收到 IND 申请的日期。

(c) 申办者可以向 IND 中指定的研究者运送研究新药：

(1) FDA 收到 IND 申请后 30 天。

(2) 或 FDA 更早时授权运送此药。

(d) 在根据本节 (b) 段 IND 生效前，研究者不得在人类受试者身上使用研究新药。

### 312.41 对 IND 的意见和建议

(a) 研究过程中的任何时候，FDA 可以就 IND 不足之处或需要更多的数据或信息时口头或书面与申办者沟通。

(b) 应申办者要求，FDA 将就 IND 相关具体事宜提供建议，例如，是否有充足技术数据支持研究计划、临床试验设计以及拟议研究能否产生满足上市许可申请所需的数据和信息。

(c) 除非 FDA 依据 312.42 规定下达暂停临床研究命令，否则 FDA 根据本节内容与申办者的沟通仅为建议。申办者不需要对计划或正进行的临床研究作任何修改，不需对 FDA 的建议进行回复。

## 312.42 临床研究暂停和修改要求

(a) 总则。临床研究暂停是指 FDA 向申办者发布命令，以延迟拟进行临床研究或中止在研临床研究。临床研究暂停命令可适用于 IND 监管的一项或多项研究。当暂停拟进行临床研究时，不能给予受试者研究用药。暂停在研临床研究时，不能再招募新受试者进入研究及使用研究用药；已参与临床研究患者应停止使用研究用药，FDA 从患者安全利益角度考虑而特别允许的情况除外。

(b) 临床研究暂停理由

(1) 暂停 IND Ⅰ期临床研究。如发现以下情况，FDA 将暂停申请或已在研Ⅰ期临床研究：

(i) 受试者正暴露于或将暴露于不合理及重大的疾病或伤害风险。

(ii) IND 指定的临床研究者不具备科学培训和经验来进行 IND 申请中描述的临床研究。

(iii) 研究者手册存在误导、错误、较严重信息不全；或

(iv) IND 未包含 312.23 要求的足够信息，不能评估拟进行研究对受试者的风险。

(v) IND 是对用来治疗危及生命的疾病或病症（男女均患有）研究用药的研究。考虑使用研究用药可能的生殖毒性（影响生殖器官）或对生长发育毒性（影响潜在后代）的风险或潜在风险，具有生殖潜力的男性或女性患者被排除在研究范围。“具有生殖潜力的女性”一词不包括孕妇。就本条款而言，“危及生命的疾病或病症”被定义为“除非中断疾病发展，否则死亡可能性很高的疾病或病症”。临床研究暂停不适用于以下临床研究：

(A) 在特殊情况下，如仅与一种性别相关的研究

（例如，评估精液中的药物浓度或药物对月经的影响）。

(B) 仅针对男性或女性的研究，只要有不排除具有生殖潜力的其他性别患者的研究在同时进行、已经进行或将在FDA同意的合理时间内进行。

(C) 或只选择未患有待研究疾病或病症受试者的研究。

(2) 暂停Ⅱ、Ⅲ期IND临床研究。如发现以下情况，FDA将暂停正在申请或正在进行的Ⅱ、Ⅲ期临床研究：

(i) 适用于本节 (b)(1)(i) 至 (b)(1)(v) 段的任何条件。

(ii) 或研究计划、方案有明显设计缺陷，不能达到既定目标。

(3) 对扩展IND或扩展方案的临床研究暂停。FDA可在以下情况下暂停扩展IND或扩展方案：

(i) 最终用途。如确认以下情况，FDA将暂停拟进行扩展IND或治疗使用研究用药方案：

(A) 不符合本部分子部分Ⅰ规定的允许扩大研究适用范围的有关标准。

(B) 或扩展使用IND或扩展使用研究方案不符合本部分子部分Ⅰ规定的提交扩展性研究申请的要求。

(ii) 持续使用。如果确定本部分子部分I中关于允许药物研究的相关标准不再适用，则FDA可以暂停正在进行的扩展IND或扩展方案。

(4) 暂停设计不恰当、未严格对照的研究。如果发现以下任意情况，FDA将暂停拟进行或正在进行的设计不当、未严格对照的临床研究：

(i) 适用于本节 (b)(1) 或 (b)(2) 段的任何条件。

(ii) 合理证据表明，设计不当、未严格对照的研究正妨碍受试者入组，或以其他方式干扰设计良好和严格对照的同一个或其他研究用药研究的执行或完成。

(iii) 研究用药数量不够，不足以进行设计不当、未严格对照的研究以及设计良好、严格对照的研究。

(iv) 该药已进行一项或多项设计良好且严格对照的临床试验，结果有力表明该药物缺乏疗效。

(v) 另一种正在研究或已获批准的用于同一患者群体、相同适应证的药物已显示出更好的潜在利益/风险平衡。

(vi) 已有针对同一患者人群、相同适应证的药物获准上市。

(vii) 进行设计良好且严格对照研究的申办者并未积极推进研究用药的上市批准。

(viii) FDA专员认为开展拟议研究或继续进行研究不符合公众利益，FDA会根据本节（b)(4)(ii)，（b)(4)(iii) 和（b)(4)(v) 段要求暂停临床研究。该情况一般仅适用于限制对照性试验受试者的继续入组，而并非对已接受研究用药的受试者停止继续用药。

(5) 暂停符合本章50.24规定的涉及知情同意例外情形的临床研究。如果确认以下情况，FDA可以暂停拟进行或正在进行的符合本章50.24规定涉及知情同意例外情形的临床研究：

(i) 适用于本节（b)(1) 或（b)(2) 段的任何条件；或

(ii) 未提交或不符合本章50.24规定开展或继续研究的相关标准。

(6) 暂停本章50.23(d) 规定的涉及知情同意例外情形的临床研究。如果确定以下情况，FDA可暂停拟进行或正在进行的涉及本章50.23(d) 规定知情同意例外情形的临床研究：

(i) 适用于本节（b)(1) 或（b)(2) 段的任何条件；或

(ii) 总统尚未做出免除使用研究新药前需事先获得知情同意书要求的决定。

(c) 对存在缺陷的讨论。当FDA得出因临床研究中存在缺陷可能需要暂停临床研究的结论时，除非患者面临直接且严重的风险，FDA 会在发布暂停临床研究命令前，尝试与申办者讨论并妥善解决问题。

(d) 下达暂停临床研究命令。暂停临床研究命令可以通过电话或其他快速沟通方式或以书面形式下达。暂停临床研究命令将标明适用于暂停命令的 IND 临床研究，并简要说明采取该项措施的依据。暂停临床研究命令将由负责审核 IND 的部门主管或其指定代表发出。部门主管将尽快（发出命令 30 天内）向申办者提供书面说明，解释暂停研究的理由。

(e) 恢复暂停临床研究。只有在 FDA（通常是负责审核 IND 的部门主管或主管指定人员）通知申办者研究可以继续进行后，临床研究才可恢复进行。当申办者纠正先前指出的缺陷或达到 FDA 所提出的进行临床研究的其他要求，FDA 才可以授权恢复已暂停的临床研究。FDA 可以通过电话或其他快速沟通方式通知申办者暂停临床研究的决定。如果被暂停临床研究的 IND 申办者要求 FDA 以书面形式证明临床研究暂停命令已被撤销，同时申办者对暂停命令中指出问题给出完整答复，则 FDA 应在收到申请 30 日内以书面形式对申办者做出完整回复。FDA 的回复有可能是撤销暂停命令或维持暂停状态，并会对此决定做出解释。在 30 天的回复时间内，申办者在接到 FDA 取消暂停通知前，不得重新启动已下令暂停的临床试验。

(f) 上诉。如果申办者不认可暂停临床研究的理由，申办者可根据 312.48 规定，请求 FDA 重新考虑该决定。

(g) 将暂停状态 IND 转为非活动状态。如果 IND 监管的所有研究持续保持暂停状态达 1 年以上，则 FDA 将根据 312.45 规定将其置于非活动状态。

### 312.44 终止

(a) 总论。本节介绍 FDA 终止 IND 的程序。如果 IND 要被终止，申办者将终止该 IND 下进行的所有临床研究，并召回或以其他方式处置所有未使用药物。终止行动可能基于 IND 本身或进行 IND 研究过程中存在的缺陷。除本节（d）段外，终止前应先由 FDA 提议终止，并给予申办者答复的机会。通常，FDA 启动本节终止试验行动前会先尝试非正式地解决分歧，或在适当的时候按照 312.42 规定启动临床研究暂停程序。

(b) 终止的理由

(1) Ⅰ期临床研究。如果发现以下情况，FDA 可提出终止Ⅰ期临床研究的研究新药申请（IND）：

(i) 人类受试者将面临不合理和重大疾病或伤害的风险。

(ii) IND 未包含 312.23 要求的足够信息，不能评估对临床研究受试者的安全性。

(iii) 生产、加工和包装研究用药的方法、设备和管控措施未达到和维持对药物的鉴别、活性强度、质量和纯度的适当标准，不能保护受试者的安全。

(iv) 正在进行的临床研究方式与在 IND 中提交的方案实质上不一致。

(v) 用于商业目的对药物进行宣传或分销，不符合研究的要求或不被 312.7 允许。

(vi) IND（或 IND 增补或报告）中含对重要事实的虚假陈述或遗漏本部分要求的重要信息。

(vii) 申办者未按照 312.32 的规定及时将严重非预期不良反应通报给 FDA 和所有研究者，或未提供本部分要求的其他报告。

(viii) 申办者未按照 312.33 要求提交准确的研究年度报告。

(ix) 申办者未能遵守本部分、第 50 或第 56 部分法规的其他适用要求。

(x) IND 已经处于非活动状态 5 年或 5 年以上。

(xi) 申办者未依照 312.42(b)(4) 规定延迟拟议 IND 研究或暂停正在进行的研究。

(2) Ⅱ期或Ⅲ期临床研究。如发现以下任意情况，FDA 可提出终止Ⅱ期或Ⅲ期新药临床研究。

(i) 符合本节 (b)(1)(i) 至 (b)(1)(xi) 段的任何条件。

(ii) 研究计划或方案不合理，科学性不强，无法确定药物的安全性、有效性。

(iii) 已有可靠证据表明该药物对正进行临床研究的目的无效。

(3) 如果发现如下情况，FDA可提出终止治疗性IND：

(i) 符合本节 (b)(1)(i) 至 (x) 段的任何条件；或

(ii) 符合312.42(b)(3) 规定中的任何条件。

(c) 申办者回应机会。

(1) 如果建议终止IND，FDA将以书面形式通知申办者，且要求申办者在30天内做出纠正或进行解释。

(2) 申办者接到通知后可提供书面解释或纠正措施，也可要求与FDA开会讨论，做出解释或纠正措施。如果申办者未在规定的时间内对通知做出回应，IND将被终止。

(3) 如果申办者做出回应，但FDA不接受其提交的解释或纠正措施，FDA将以书面形式通知申办者FDA不接受的原因，并根据第16部分法规向申办者提供监管听证的机会，以讨论该IND是否应被终止。申办者召开监管听证会的请求须在收到FDA不予接受通知的10天内提出。

(d) 立即终止IND。尽管有本节 (a) 至 (c) 段规定，但是一旦FDA得出继续进行临床研究会对个人健康造成直接和重大危害的结论时，FDA药物研究中心主管或生物制品评估和研究中心主管应立即以书面形式通知申办者终止IND。如果要恢复以这种方式终止的IND，需要递交额外材料说明危险已排除，由FDA主管予以恢复。如果依据此段法规终止IND，则FDA将根据第16部分法规规定，提供给申办者监管听证会机会，讨论是否恢复IND事宜。

## 312.45 非活动状态

(a) 如果IND临床研究2年或2年以上无受试者入组，或IND

下所有研究已长达 1 年或 1 年以上处于暂停状态，则 FDA 会将此 IND 置于非活动状态。FDA 可根据申办者的要求发起此行动，FDA 也可自行决定发起此行动。如果 FDA 根据本节主动采取行动，则应首先以书面形式通知申办者。收到此类通知后，申办者应该在 30 天内回应为什么此 IND 应继续保持活动状态。

(b) 如果 IND 被置于非活动状态，则应通知所有研究者，并按照 312.59 规定退回或以其他方式处置所有库存药物。

(c) 对于被置于非活动状态的 IND，申办者无须提交年度报告。然而，非活动状态的 IND 仍然需要公开披露 312.130 规定的数据和信息。

(d) 申办者如果想将非活动状态 IND 恢复为活动状态，应根据 312.30 要求提交方案增补，其中包含拟进行的下一年度总体研究计划和相应方案。如果根据已提交信息进行方案增补，则研究计划应参考此类信息。用于支持拟进行研究的额外信息（如有），应以信息增补的形式提交。尽管有 312.30 的规定，非活动状态 IND 只能在以下情形下恢复：(1) FDA 接收方案增补 30 天后，除非 FDA 通知申办者：方案增补中所描述研究符合 312.42 规定的临床研究暂停条款；(2) FDA 在早于收到方案增补 30 天的日期内通知申办者可以开始方案增补中描述的临床研究。

(e) 根据 312.44 规定，应终止处于非活动状态 5 年或 5 年以上的 IND。

### 312.47 会议

(a) 总论。通常申办者和 FDA 间的会议有助于解决临床研究过程中提出的疑问和出现的问题。在资源允许情况下，FDA 鼓励类似会议，以帮助评估药物及解决有关科学问题。举行会议的一般原则是：应就临床研究中可能出现的任何科学或医学问题进行自由、全面和公开的沟通。根据第 10 部分法规，应该开展这类会议并进行记录。

(b) “Ⅱ期末”会议及提交上市许可申请前举行的会议。在药物研究过程中的特定阶段，FDA 和申办者之间的会议特别有助于尽量减少时间和金钱的浪费，从而加速药物开发和评估进程。尤其是，FDA 发现Ⅱ期研究结束时会议（“Ⅱ期末”会议）对规划后续研究特别有帮助；Ⅲ期快完成时提交上市许可申请前的会议（“NDA 前”会议）有助于找到在上市许可申请中呈现和提交数据的方法，便于 FDA 审核并及时进行回复。

(1)“Ⅱ期末”会议。

(i) 目的。“Ⅱ期末”会议目的是明确Ⅲ期临床研究的安全性、评估Ⅲ期研究计划和方案，以及目前的研究和计划是否足以对儿童的安全性和有效性进行评估，并明确是否需要任何补充信息来支持上市许可申请。

(ii) 会议资格。虽然“Ⅱ期末”会议主要针对涉及新分子实体或上市药物新用途的 IND，但所有 IND 申办者都可以申请并召开“Ⅱ期末”会议。

(iii) 时间。为对申办者最为有利，在申办者对Ⅲ期临床研究做出努力和重大资源投入前，应举行“Ⅱ期末”会议。然而，“Ⅱ期末”会议的安排不应延误研究从Ⅱ期临床试验过渡到Ⅲ期临床试验的进程。

(iv) 事先准备的信息。“Ⅱ期末”会议前至少一个月，申办者应提交有关Ⅲ期研究计划的背景资料，包括Ⅰ期和Ⅱ期临床研究总结、Ⅲ期临床研究具体方案、额外的非临床实验计划、儿科研究计划（包括方案定稿、入组、完成研究和数据分析时间表，或任何对免除或推迟儿科研究申请计划的支持信息）和暂定的药物标签（如有）。《FDA 工作人员手册指南》4850.7 中更全面地介绍了建议提交的内容，该手册指南可在第 20 部分法规 FDA 的公开信息条例中找到。

(v) 召开会议。“Ⅱ期末”会议将由负责审核该 IND 的 FDA 药物审评与研究中心或生物制品审评与研究中心安排。FDA将把会议安排在对FDA和申办者都方便的时间。申办者和FDA都可以带顾问参加会议。会议主要是为了FDA与申办者对Ⅲ期临床研究的总体规划以及具体研究的目标和设计达成共识。此会议还可讨论支持Ⅲ期临床研究和/或上市许可申请的技术信息是否充足的问题。FDA还将提供当时对于药物用于儿科所需的儿科研究，以及提交儿科研究申请是否会推迟到批准之后的最佳判断。在会议上对这些问题达成的共识将以会议纪要的形式记录，由FDA根据10.65规定记录并提交给申办者。会议纪要以及向申办者提供的任何其他书面材料将作为达成共识的永久记录。除非出现重大科学进展而另有要求，否则根据共识所做的研究应被认定为按照足以获得药物上市许可申请的设计进行。

(2)“NDA前”和“BLA前”会议（“新药申请前会议”和“生物制品许可申请前会议”）。FDA发现，交流上市申请信息可减少上市许可申请初步审核的延迟。这种沟通的主要目的是发现任何重大未解决问题，明确申办者依靠充分及严格对照研究来判断药物有效性的研究；明确正进行研究的状况或拟进行研究能否评估药物对儿童的安全性和有效性；使FDA审核人员了解在上市许可申请中需提交的综合信息（包括技术信息）；讨论数据统计分析的适当方法，并讨论上市许可申请时最佳的数据呈现方式和格式。应由申办者与FDA负责审核该IND的部门安排会议。为了便于FDA向申办者提供准备上市许可申请的最有用建议，申办者应至少在会前1个月向FDA审核部门提交以下信息：

(i) 需提交申请的临床研究简要总结。

(ii) 拟定的提交格式及组织形式，包括数据呈现方法。

(iii) 需要进行或正在进行的儿科研究现状。

(iv) 会议需讨论的其他信息。

## 312.48 解决争议

(a) 总论。FDA致力于通过合作交流信息和意见，尽可能迅速友好地解决申办者和FDA审核部门之间关于IND要求的分歧。

(b) 行政和程序问题。当出现行政或程序上的争议时，申办者应首先与制定该申请的消费者安全官员联系，尝试和负责审核IND的药物审评与研究中心或生物制品审评与研究中心解决争议。如果争议未解决，申办者可向指定调查官员申述，调查官员的职能是调查发生的问题并帮助及时公平地解决问题。向调查官员提出的问题可包括解决会议安排的困难，以及及时获得对质疑的答复等。《FDA工作人员手册指南》4820.7中详细地介绍了具体操作步骤，该手册指南可在FDA的公开信息条例第20部分中找到。

(c) 科学和医学争议。

(1) 药物研究过程中出现科学或医学争议时，申办者应直接与负责审核官员商讨。如需要，申办者可以要求与审核官员和管理层代表召开会议以寻求解决方案。此类会议应直接向FDA负责审核IND的药物评估和研究中心或生物制品评估和研究中心的部门主管申请。FDA将尽力满足涉及重大问题的会议请求，并安排在双方便利的时间。

(2) 312.47(b)中描述的“Ⅱ期末”和“NDA前”会议也将及时提供讨论和解决申办者和FDA在科学和医学问题分歧的机会。

(3) 申请举办会议以解决科学或医学争议时，申请人可以建议FDA咨询外部专家。在这种情况下，FDA也可以酌情自行指定邀请一名或多名咨询委员会成员或其他顾问参加会议。申请人可以依靠自己的顾问，带顾问参会。对于非正式会议中未解决的重大科学和医学政策问题，FDA可提交给其常设咨询委员会，供其考虑和提出建议。

# 子部分 D　申办者和研究者的责任

## 312.50　申办者的一般责任

申办者有以下职责：选择合格的研究者，向他们提供规范进行临床研究所需信息，确保对研究进行适当监查，确保研究按照 IND 的总体研究计划和方案进行，保持 IND 有效，并确保 FDA 及所有参与研究者及时了解有关该药物重大的新的不良事件或风险。申办者的额外具体责任将在本部分法规其他地方进行描述。

## 312.52　向合同研究组织（CRO）转让义务

（a）申办者可将本部分法规中列出的任一或全部义务转让给合同研究组织（CRO）。转让义务均应以书面形式描述。如果并非转让所有义务，则需书面描述 CRO 应该承担的每项义务。如果转让所有义务，则须提供转让所有义务的一般性声明。未在书面说明中提及的任何义务，均视为未被转让。

（b）承担申办者任何义务的 CRO 应依从本章法规中适用于该义务的具体规定，如果任何义务有未依从本条例的情况，则需接受与申办者相同的行政处罚。因此，只要合同研究组织（CRO）承担申办者的一项或多项义务，本部分中“申办者”的相应责任都适用于 CRO。

## 312.53　选择研究者和监查员

（a）选择研究者。申办者只能选择接受过培训和有临床经验的合格研究者作为合适的专家来研究研究用药。

（b）管控药物。申办者仅向参与临床研究的研究者运送研究新药。

（c）从研究者处获取信息。在允许研究者开始参与临床研究之前，申办者应获得以下文件：

（1）签署的研究者声明（FDA-1572 表），其中包含：

（i）研究者姓名和地址。

（ii）IND 中确定研究者将要实施的研究方案名称和编

码（如有）。

(iii) 将进行临床研究的医学院校、医院或其他研究机构名称和地址。

(iv) 研究中将使用的临床实验室名称和地址。

(v) 负责审核和批准该临床研究的 IRB 名称和地址。

(vi) 研究者承诺：

(A) 将按照相关的现行方案进行研究，只有在通知申办者之后才会修改方案，为保护受试者安全、权利、福祉而需立即修改方案的特殊情形除外。

(B) 将依从本部分法规关于研究者义务的要求和所有其他相关要求。

(C) 将亲自实施或直接指导所述研究。

(D) 将告知潜在受试者该药物用于临床研究的目的，并确保满足获得知情同意（21CFR 第 50 部分）的相关要求和机构审查委员会审核和批准（21CFR 第 56 部分）的要求。

(E) 将按照 312.64 规定，向申办者报告研究过程中发生的不良体验。

(F) 已阅读并理解研究者手册中信息，包括药物潜在风险和不良反应的信息。

(G) 将确保已经告知所有帮助进行临床试验的助手、同事和雇员他们各自的义务，履行以上承诺。

(vii) 研究者承诺，对于第 56 部分监管的需经机构审核的研究，符合本部分法规要求的 IRB 负责对临床研究进行初步和持续审核和批准。研究者将及时向 IRB 报告研究活动中所有变化，以及涉及对人类受试者或其他人带来风险的所有非预期问题。没有 IRB 的批准，研究者不得对研究进行任何修改，有必要消除对人类受试者明显直接伤害的情况除外。

(viii) 列出所有帮助研究者进行临床研究的协助研究者名单（如进修医生、住院医生）。

(2) 简历。提供研究者简历或其他资格证明，需要显示教育背景、培训情况和经验，以显示研究者有资格作为专家进行临床研究。

(3) 临床方案。

(i) 对于Ⅰ期临床研究，需提供研究计划大纲，其中包括研究预期期限和预期参与受试者人数。

(ii) 对于Ⅱ期或Ⅲ期临床研究，需要提供研究方案大纲，其中包括：预计接受研究用药的受试者人数以及试验对照组人数（如有）；研究的临床用途；受试者特点，包括年龄、性别和身体状况；需进行的临床观察和实验室检查；预估研究期限；以及所使用的病例报告表（CRF）说明或副本。

(4) 披露财务信息。有了足够准确的财务信息，申办者就能够提交本章第54部分法规要求的完整准确的财务证明或财务披露声明。研究者应向申办者承诺，如果在研究中和完成研究后1年内财务状况发生变化，研究者将及时更新信息。

(d) 选择监查员。申办者应选择经过培训和有经验的合格监查员来监督研究进程。

## 312.54 符合本章50.24规定的急救研究

(a) 申办者应监查符合本章50.24涉及因急救研究而不要求事先获得知情同意例外情形的研究的进展情况。当申办者从IRB处收到依照本章50.24(a)(7)(ii) 和 (a)(7)(iii) 要求需公开的信息时，申办者应及时将用IND号识别的公开信息副本提交到IND档案（档案号95S-0158），并储存在文档管理部（HFA-305）。地址：FDA，5630 Fishers Lane，rm.1061，Rockville，MD20852。

(b) 申办者应监查此类研究以发现IRB判定研究不符合本章50.24(a) 的知情同意例外标准或因其他相关伦理问题的考虑而决定不予批准研究的情况。申办者应及时以书面形式向

FDA、向被要求参加此项或类似临床研究的研究者、以及向被要求对此项研究或其他类似研究进行审核的 IRB 提供相关信息。

## 312.55 告知研究者

(a) 在研究开始之前，申办者（非申办-研究者）应向每位临床研究参与者提供含 312.23(a)(5) 要求信息的研究者手册。

(b) 随着整个研究的开展，申办者应告知参与试验的研究者研究用药的新发现，特别是涉及不良反应和安全使用方面的信息。可以通过定期修订研究者手册、转载或出版研究结果、向研究者提供报告或信件或以其他适当方式将这些信息发布给研究者。根据 312.32 要求，重要安全信息需递交给研究者。

## 312.56 审核正在进行的研究

(a) 申办者应监查在 IND 下进行的所有临床研究的进展情况。

(b) 当申办者发现研究者不依从签署的研究者声明（FDA-1572 表），不依从研究总体计划、不依从本部分法规或其他适用部分法规要求时，应立即采取行动，保证合规或停止向该研究者提供研究用药，并终止该研究者参与研究。如果终止研究者参与研究，申办者应要求研究者按照 312.59 要求处置或退回研究用药，并通知 FDA。

(c) 申办者应审核和评估从研究者处获得的有关研究用药安全性和有效性证据。申办者应按 312.32 要求，向 FDA 提交有关药物安全性信息。申办者应当按照 312.33 要求，对研究进展情况进行年度报告。

(d) 如果申办者确定研究用药对受试者有不合理和重大风险，则应停止研究，并通知 FDA、所有机构审查委员会以及所有参与研究的研究者。确保按 312.59 要求处理所有研究用药的库存，并向 FDA 提供申办者所采取行动的完整报告。申办者应尽快停止研究，不得迟于决定停止研究后 5 个工作日。如有要求，FDA 将向申办者发送有关停止研究的要求。

## 312.57 记录保存和记录保留

(a) 申办者应保存适当记录，展示对研究用药的接收、运输或其他处置。记录须包括接收药物的研究者姓名、每次运送日期、数量和批次或代码标记。

(b) 申办者应保存完整准确的记录，显示本章中 54.4(a)(3)(i)，(a)(3)(ii)，(a)(3)(iii) 和 (a)(3)(iv) 描述的由申办者支付给研究者的所有经济利益。对本章第 54 部分法规有要求的研究者，申办者还应保存该研究者所有其他财务利益的完整准确记录。

(c) 申办者应当在药物上市申请批准后 2 年，保留本部分法规要求的记录和报告。如果申请未被批准，则保留直到研究用药的运输和交付都被停止后 2 年，且已经通知了 FDA。

(d) 申办者应保留本章 320.38 或 320.63 所述的在生物等效性或生物利用度研究中用作试验用药和参照标准品的储备样品，并按照 320.38 规定的期限将储备样品交给 FDA（如 FDA 要求）。

## 312.58 对申办者记录和报告的视察

(a) FDA 视察。在 FDA 授权官员或雇员的要求下，申办者应在合理的时间内允许 FDA 官员或雇员访问并复制和核实按本部分法规进行临床研究的相关记录和报告。根据 FDA 书面要求，申办者应将记录或报告（或其副本）递交给 FDA。申办者应当停止向未按本部分要求维护或提供研究记录或研究报告的研究者运送药物。

(b) 受管制物质。如果研究新药是在受管制物质法中（21USC801；21CFR 第 1308 部分）列出的物质，则应按照本部分法规或其他适用部分法规要求保存该药物的运输、运送、接收和处置记录，应在美国司法部执法管理部门正式授权雇员的要求下，由研究者或者申办者提供，以供视察和复制。此外，申办者应确保采取充分的预防措施，包括将研究用药储存在牢固锁定的柜体或其他牢固锁定的场所内，仅授权人员可以进入，以防止盗窃或转移药物至非法渠道。

### 312.59 处置未使用的研究用药

申办者应确保每位研究者在停止或终止研究后，归还所有未使用的研究用药。申办者可以授权研究者对未使用研究用药采用替代处置方法，前提是此替代处置方法不会将人暴露于药物的风险之下。申办者应按 312.57 要求保存药物处置的书面记录。

### 312.60 研究者的一般责任

研究者负责确保该研究按签署的研究者声明、研究计划和适用法规进行；保护研究者照护受试者权利、安全和福祉；并管控研究用药。除 50.23 或 50.24 规定外，研究者应按照本章第 50 部分法规规定获得每位受试者的知情同意。临床研究者的其他具体职责在本章本部分和第 50 和 56 部分法规列出。

### 312.61 对研究用药的管控

在研究者或协助研究者监督下研究用药仅可用于受试者。根据本部分法规规定，研究者不得向任何未授权的个人提供研究用药。

### 312.62 研究者记录和记录保留

（a）发药。研究者须有详细的发药记录，包括日期、数量和受试者使用情况。如果研究被终止、暂停、停止或已完成，研究者应将未使用药物归还给申办者，或根据 312.59 规定另行处置未使用药物。

（b）受试者记录。研究者须准备与维护适当、准确的受试者记录，记录对接受研究用药或作为对照组参与研究的每个受试者的所有观察结果和其他研究相关数据。受试者记录包括病例报告表（CRF）和支持数据，包括签署和注明日期的知情同意书及医疗记录（如医师记录的病程进展记录、医院病历和护士记录）。在每个受试者病历上应记录："在参与研究之前获得了知情同意书"。

（c）记录保留。研究者应根据本部分法规要求保留研究记录，至少为进行该适应证研究上市许可申请批准之日起 2 年；或如果未提交申请或此适应证申请未被批准，则需要保留记录直到临床研究停止后 2 年内，并通知 FDA。

## 312.64 研究者报告

(a) 进度报告。研究者应向申办者提供所有报告，申办者负责收集和评估所得结果。根据 312.33 要求，申办者须向 FDA 提交有关临床研究进展情况的年度报告。

(b) 安全性报告。研究者必须立即向申办者报告所有严重不良事件，不论其是否被视为与研究用药相关，包括那些在研究方案或研究者手册中列出的事件，并必须评估是否由于药物引起该事件发生的可能性。研究终点为严重不良事件的（如全因死亡率），除非有证据表明药物与该事件之间存在因果关系（如由过敏反应引起死亡），否则必须按照方案要求报告。在这种情况下，研究者必须立即将此事件报告给申办者。研究者必须记录非严重不良事件并在方案规定的时间内报告给申办者。

(c) 最终报告。当完成临床研究后，研究者应尽快向申办者提供适当的研究报告。

(d) 财务公开报告。按照本章第 54 部分法规规定，临床研究者应向申办者提供足够准确的财务信息，以便申办者提交完整准确的财务证明或财务公开声明。如果在研究过程中及研究完成后 1 年内发生相关变化，研究者应及时更新此信息。

## 312.66 IRB 审核的保证

研究者应该保证依从第 56 部分法规要求由 IRB 负责初步及持续审核和批准拟议临床研究。研究者还应保证他/她能及时向 IRB 报告研究活动中的所有变化，以及涉及人类受试者或其他人风险的所有非预期问题。此外，除有必要消除对人类受试者明显直接危害外，研究者应保证他/她不会在无 IRB 批准的情况下对研究作任何改动。

## 312.68 对研究者记录和报告的视察

根据 312.62 要求，应 FDA 授权官员或雇员的要求，研究者应在合理时间内，允许 FDA 官员或雇员访问、复制及核实研究者的记录或报告。研究者不需要泄露受试者姓名，除非需要对个别病例的记录进行更详细的研究，或除非有理由相信记录不代表实际研究病例或不代表所获得的实际结果。

### 312.69 处理受管制物质

如果研究用药是受管制药品，被受管制物质法规约束，则研究者应采取充分的预防措施，包括将研究用药储存在牢固锁定的柜体中或在其他能够满足牢固锁定要求的场所内，仅授权人员可以进入，以防止盗窃或将药物转移用于非法渠道。

### 312.70 取消临床研究者的资格

(a) 如果有信息表明，研究者（包括申办-研究者）已屡次或故意不遵守本章第50部分或第56部分法规的要求，或已屡次或故意在要求的报告中提交虚假信息给FDA或申办者，则FDA药品审评与研究中心或生物制品审评与研究中心将向研究者递交书面投诉通知，并向研究者提供书面解释的机会，研究者也可选择在非正式会议上进行解释。如果FDA适用中心接受研究者的解释，则适用中心将停止取消资格程序。如果FDA适用中心未接受研究者提供的解释，根据第16部分法规要求，研究者将有机会就研究者是否有资格接受本部分法规要求的试验物品以及是否有资格进行FDA监管下的支持产品上市许可申请的临床研究举行监管听证会。

(b) 在评估所有现有资料（包括研究者提供的解释）后，如果FDA专员确定研究者已屡次或故意不遵守本章第50部分或第56部分法规的要求，或已屡次或故意在要求的报告中提交虚假信息给FDA或申办者，FDA专员将通知研究者、指定研究者参加研究的申办者以及审核研究的IRB，表明在本部分法规要求下，该研究者无资格接收试验物品。提供给研究者、申办者和IRB的通知中将包含做出此决定的依据声明。该声明还将解释：根据本部分法规确定无资格接受试验药物的研究者将无资格进行任何FDA监管下的用来支持产品研究和上市许可申请的临床研究，包括药物、生物制剂、医疗设备、动物用新药、食品（包括含营养成分声明或健康声明的膳食补充剂、婴儿配方奶粉、食品和色素添加剂以及烟草制品）。

(c) 本章规定下向FDA提交的任何申请，如含有已确定无资格接收 FDA 监管试验物品研究者报告的数据，均须接受审核，以确定该研究者是否提交了对继续进行研究或批准上市许可特别重要的数据，或是否提交了对 FDA 监管产品的持续销售特别重要的不可靠数据。

(d) 如果 FDA 专员确定：清除研究者提交的不可靠数据后，剩余的数据不足以支持继续进行研究合理安全的结论，则 FDA 专员将会通知申办者，申办者有机会按本章第 16 部分法规要求举行监管听证。然而，如果对公共健康有危害，FDA 专员应立即终止 IND，并通知申办者和 IRB 其终止研究的决定。此种情况下，申办者有机会按本章第 16 部分法规举行监管听证，以确定是否可以恢复新药研究。不支持研究或上市许可申请或听证申请的决定并不能免除申办者按照其他适用法规向 FDA 提交研究结果的义务。

(e) 如果 FDA 专员确定，剔除研究者提交的不可靠数据后，继续批准产品不合理，专员将按照相关适用法规条款撤回对该产品的批准。

(f) 对于根据本节 (b) 段确定为不合格的研究者，如果 FDA 专员确定，该研究者已经充分保证将依照本章适用法规使用试验物品进行临床研究，以支持 FDA 监管产品的研究或上市许可申请（仅支持符合本章适用条款），可恢复该研究者资格。

## 子部分 E　用于治疗危及生命和严重衰弱疾病的药物

### 312.80　目的

本节目的是为治疗危及生命和严重衰弱疾病的新治疗方法的开发、评估和上市进程设立规则，加快开发进程，特别是在目前尚无有效治疗手段的情况下。如本章 314.105(c) 所述，虽然法定安全和有效性标准适用于所有药物，但药品种类的多样性及药品的广泛应用，需要在使用操作标准时更为灵活。美国食品药品管理局（FDA）已经确定，可以在保证安全性和有效性的同时，在适用法定标准方面行使最广泛的灵活性。这些措施反映医生和患者通常在治疗危及生命和严重衰弱疾患时较治疗不太严重疾病时更愿意接受风险高或有不良反应的制剂。这些措施也反映了认识到需要根据所治疗疾病的严重程度评估药物的益处。本节中列出的措施应被认为与这一目的保持一致。

### 312.81 范围

本节适用于评估用来治疗危及生命或严重衰弱疾患的新药和生物制品的安全性和有效性。

(a) 本节，“危及生命”一词指：

(1) 除非疾病进展中断，否则死亡可能性很高。

(2) 疾病或病症可能致命，临床研究分析的终点为生存。

(b) 本节，“严重衰弱”指导致严重不可逆转病情发作的疾病或病症。

(c) 鼓励申办者就这些特殊措施对特定制剂的适用性向 FDA 咨询。

### 312.82 提早咨询

对于用来治疗危及生命或严重衰弱疾患的制剂，申办者可在药物开发早期申请与 FDA 审核官员会面，进行审核并就所需的临床前和临床研究设计要求达成一致。FDA 可邀请一名或多名外部专家、科学顾问或咨询委员会成员参加此类会议。在 FDA 资源许可范围内，FDA 审核官员将同意开会讨论的申请。

(a) 研究新药申请（IND）前会议。提交 IND 前，申办者可以申请与 FDA 审核官员举行会议。会议主要目的是审核为启动人体研究而进行的动物研究设计，且对设计达成一致意见。会议还可提供机会讨论相关问题，如：Ⅰ期临床研究的范围和设计、研究新药在儿童中的研究计划，以及研究新药申请中数据呈现的最佳方法和格式等。

(b) “Ⅰ期末”会议。当得到Ⅰ期临床试验数据时，申办者可再次申请与 FDA 审核官员会面。主要目的是审核并对Ⅱ期对照性临床研究设计方案达成共识，并讨论对儿科患者药物研究的必要性以及研究设计和时间安排。Ⅱ期临床研究目的是提供足够药物安全性和有效性相关数据，以支持其上市许可申请的批准。对于治疗危及生命疾患的药物，FDA 将做出对是否需要进行儿科研究以及研究是否会推迟到批准之后再提交的最佳判断。312.47(b)(1) 中列出的关于“Ⅱ期末”会议的程序，包括达成共识的文件记录，也适用于“Ⅰ期末”会议。

### 312.83　治疗方案

如果Ⅱ期临床试验试验结果的初步分析结果很有希望，FDA 可能会要求申办者根据 312.305 和 312.320 中列出的程序和标准提交待审核的治疗方案。这种治疗方案申请如果得到批准，通常会在申办者收集上市许可申请所需要的完整数据时以及在 FDA 审核期间保持有效［除非出现 312.42(b)(3)(ii) 描述的研究暂停情况］。

### 312.84　审核用于治疗危及生命和严重衰弱疾患药物上市许可申请的风险利益分析

(a) FDA 依照上市许可申请批准的法定标准做出最终是否批准的决定时，需进行医疗风险利益判断。为依从 312.80 声明，在评估时，FDA 将考虑到药物的益处是否超过已知和潜在的风险，以及对评价药物的风险和益处尚未解决的问题，考虑到疾病严重程度和缺乏满意替代疗法的现况。

(b) 对于根据 312.82 规定符合召开“Ⅰ期末”会议的药物做出是否批准上市许可申请决定前，FDA 通常会征求外部专家科学顾问或咨询委员会意见。根据本章 314.101 或第 601 部分提交上市许可申请时，FDA 将通知有关常设咨询委员会成员申请已备案，可供审核。

(c) 如果 FDA 认定提供的数据不足以批准上市，FDA 将根据本章 314.110 或生物制品许可程序发出完整答复信。答复信在描述申请不足之处时，将提到为什么在根据 312.82 召开或之后的会议中达成一致意见的研究设计未能提供足够的上市许可批准证据。这封信还将描述咨询委员会对申请提出的建议。

(d) 根据本节所述程序提交的上市许可申请将受本章第 314 部分或第 600 部分以及本部分法规要求和程序的约束。

### 312.85 Ⅳ期临床研究

上市批准时，FDA可与申办者达成共识，进行上市后（Ⅳ期）研究，以描述药物风险、受益和最佳使用的额外信息。这些研究可能包括但不限于使用不同于Ⅱ期临床研究中的剂量或用药时间间隔、在不同患者群体或疾病不同阶段使用或更长时间使用该药物的研究。

### 312.86 FDA重点监管的研究

FDA可以根据实际情况对药物开发和评估过程中的临床前、化学/生产和临床研究阶段的关键限速步骤进行重点监管。一旦启动，FDA将进行此项工作，作为满足公共卫生需求的手段，促进开发对危及生命或严重衰弱疾患的治疗方法。

### 312.87 主动监查临床研究的实施和评估

受本节监管的药物，FDA专员和其他机构官员将监查临床研究的进展，评估临床研究，并参与促进其适当进展。

### 312.88 受试者安全保护

本章第50、56、312、314和600部分法规包含的所有保障措施是为了确保临床试验的安全性以及受本节监管申请获得上市许可批准药物的安全性。其中包含对知情同意（本章第50部分法规）和机构审查委员会（本章第56部分法规）的要求。这些保障措施还包括在初次人体试验前审核对动物的研究（312.23），以及通过审核IND安全性报告（312.32）、上市许可申请安全性报告更新（314.50）和上市后不良反应报告（314.80）的要求监查药物不良事件。

## 子部分F 其他

### 312.110 进出口要求

(a) 进口。如果312.40监管的IND有效，进口到美国的研究新药需依从本部分法规要求，且（1）在美国的收货人是IND的申办者；（2）收货人是IND指定的合格研究者；（3）或者收货人是申办者在美国的代理人，负责研究用药的管控和分发，且在IND中指明收货人并描述收货人对于研究用药将采取的行动（如有）。

(b) 出口。在以下条件下研究新药可从美国出口：

(1) 312.40监管的IND，药物符合出口所在国家的法律，药物接收者均为在IND中被提名并获准进行IND研究的研究者。

(2) 该药物在澳大利亚、加拿大、以色列、日本、新西兰、瑞士、南非或欧盟或欧洲经济区的任何国家有有效营销授权，并符合所出口国家的法律，符合本法案802(b)(1)(A)，(f) 和 (g) 以及本章1.101要求。

(3) 该药物出口到澳大利亚、加拿大、以色列、日本、新西兰、瑞士、南非或欧盟或欧洲经济区的任何国家，并符合所出口国家的法律，符合本法案802(c)，(f) 和 (g) 适用条款和本章1.101要求。根据本段法规出口的药物如不属于IND，则免除312.6(a) 标签要求。

(4) 除本节 (b)(5) 段另有规定外，药物首次出口时，出口人向FDA国际计划办公室（HFG-1）（地址：5600 Fishers Lane，Rockville，MD20857）发书面证明书并保存依从本段要求的记录。该证明书应描述出口药物［如商品名（如有）、通用名和剂］，确定出口药物国家或地区，并确认：

(i) 该药物用于出口。

(ii) 该药物用于在美国以外的研究。

(iii) 该药物符合美国以外买方或收货人要求。

(iv) 该药物不与进口国法律相抵触。

(v) 外部运输包装贴上标签表明该包裹是从美国出口。

(vi) 该药物不在美国上市或出售。

(vii) 临床研究将按照312.120的要求进行。

(viii) 该药物的生产、加工、包装符合现行GMP标准。

(ix) 该药物不得有此法案501(a)(1)，501(a)(2)(A)，

501(a)(3)，501(c)，或 501(d) 节定义的掺假。

(x) 不论是在美国内（如果药物要重新进口），或在美国以外，药物不会对公共健康构成危险。

(xi) 药物按照美国以外国家的法律要求贴标签。

(5) 如果在美国以外国家出现国际紧急情况，须出口研究新药，则适用本节 (b)(4) 段的规定：

(i) 预期在国家紧急情况下需要储存研究新药的情形。有可能需要出口研究新药，以便在出现国家紧急情况时，有储存的药物供进口国使用。在这种情况下：

(A) 出口人可以通过本节 (b)(4) 段出口研究新药，而无需对本节 (b)(4)(i)，(b)(4)(iv)，(b)(4)(vi)，(b)(4)(vii)，(b)(4)(viii) 和/或 (b)(4)(ix) 中的任何一项或多项做出肯定，只要他/她：

① 提供书面声明，解释为什么遵守那些规定不可行或违背了研究新药可能接受者的最佳利益；

② 提供进口国政府授权官员书面声明。声明必须证明该官员同意出口商根据本节 (b)(5)(i)(A)①做出的声明；解释只能在所进口国国家紧急情况下储存该药物；并描述在哪些可能出现的国家紧急情况下按此条例规定出口该药物；

③ 提供书面声明，表明美国卫生与公众服务部部长或其指定官员同意进口国政府授权官员的发现。希望获得部长书面声明者应向 Secretary′s Operations Center，Office of Emergency Operations and Security Programs，Office of Public Health Emergency Preparedness，Office of the Secretary，Department of Health and Human Services

官员提出申请，地址为 200 Independence Ave. SW. ,Washington，DC 20201。

(B) 在获得 FDA 出口批准前，研究新药不得出口。如果根据本节 (b)(5)(i)(A) ①或(b)(5)(i)(A) ②段提供的声明不充分或出口违反公共健康，FDA 会拒绝授权。

(ii) 研究新药用于突发和国家紧急状态的情形。可能需要出口研究新药，以便该药物可在已发生或正发生的突发和紧急的国家紧急情况下使用。在此情况下：

(A) 出口人可以通过本节 (b)(4) 段出口研究新药，而不需对本节 (b)(4)(i)，(b)(4)(iv)，(b)(4)(vi)，(b)(4)(vii)，(b)(4)(viii) 和/或 (b)(4)(ix) 中的任何一项或多项做出肯定，只要他/她：

① 提供书面陈述，解释为什么遵守此段规定不可行或违背研究新药接受人最佳利益；

② 进口国政府授权官员提供足够资料，使部长或其指定人员能够判断国家紧急情况是否在进口国进行或正在发展，是否将进口的研究新药仅针对该国家紧急情况，以及是否需要立即出口研究新药。如希望得到部长答复，应将其要求提交至 Secretary′s Operations Center，Office of Emergency Operations and Security Programs，Office of Public Health Emergency Preparedness，Office of the Secretary，Department of Health and Human Services，200 Independence Ave. SW.，Washington，DC 20201。

(B) 未得到 FDA 事先授权可以出口的情形。

(c) 限制。如果出现以下情况，则不能按照本节 (b) 段规定出口：

(1) 根据本节 (b)(1) 出口药物的IND不再有效；

(2) 根据本节 (b)(2) 出口的药物，不再符合本法规 802 (b)(1)，(f)，或 (g) 规定；

(3) 根据本节 (b)(3) 出口的药物，不再符合 802(c)，(f)，或 (g) 的规定；

(4) 根据本节 (b)(4) 出口的药物，不再符合本节 (b)(5) 段所述的认证或提交声明的条件；

(5) 本节监管的研究新药，不再符合进口国法律规定的要求。

(d) 胰岛素和抗生素。研究用新胰岛素和抗生素药物可以根据此法案 801(e)(1) 出口用于研究，不需要符合本节要求。

**312.120　不受IND监管的美国以外的临床研究**

(a) 对研究的接受。

(1) 对于不受 IND 监管的临床研究，如果满足以下条件，对于良好设计和良好执行的、美国以外不受 IND 管辖的临床试验，FDA 支持其 IND 或上市许可申请［根据此法案 505 节或《公共卫生服务法》(PHS 法案) 第 351 节］：

(i) 该研究是按照临床试验质量管理规范 (GCP) 进行的。本节中，GCP 被定义为临床研究的设计、实施、操作、监查、稽查、记录、分析和报告的标准，保证数据和报告结果可靠准确以及受试者的权利、安全和福祉受到保护。GCP 包括试验前由独立伦理委员会 (IEC) 审核和批准 (或提供有利意见)，以及随着研究的开展，IEC 持续审核该研究，并且在开始研究之前获得和记录受试者自愿给予的知情同意 (或如受试者无法提供知情同意，由受试者法定授权代表签署)。在危及生命情况下，当 IEC 在研究开始前审核研究时发现事先获得知情同意不可行，或出现本章 50.23 或 50.24(a) 中描述的情形，或研究方案中或其他方面描述的措施将保护受试者的权利、安全和福祉的情况下，GCP不要求事先获得知情同意。

(ii) 如果FDA认为有必要，FDA可以通过现场视察验证研究数据。

(2) 虽然FDA不会接受不符合本节(a)(1)条件的IND研究或上市许可申请，但FDA将检查从此类研究中得到的数据。

(3) 仅基于美国以外临床数据的新药上市批准受本章314.106节管制。

(b) 支持信息。对于提交的数据是来自美国以外未在IND监管下的临床研究，申办者或申请人除须向FDA提交本章第312、314或601部分法规要求信息外，还需描述本节(a)(1)(i)中指出的申办者或申请人为确保研究符合GCP而采取的行动。描述中不需要重复已经在IND或上市批准申请中提交过的信息。但是，描述中必须提供以下信息或引用提交中其他部分的信息：

(1) 研究者资格。

(2) 研究设施描述。

(3) 研究方案和结果的详细总结，如FDA要求，研究者保存的病例记录或其他背景数据，如医院或其他机构记录。

(4) 研究中使用的药物和药物成分的描述，包括对临床研究中使用的具体药物成分、分子式、规格以及生物利用度(如有)的描述。

(5) 如果研究用来支持药物有效性，则信息显示在本章314.126监管下，研究为充分及严格对照的研究。

(6) 审核研究的IEC名称和地址以及IEC符合本章312.3定义的声明。申办者或申请人必须保存此类声明记录，包括IEC成员的名单和资格记录，并根据要求将这些记录提供给FDA审核。

(7) IEC关于批准或修改后批准或提供正面意见决定的总结。

(8) 如何获得知情同意书的描述。

(9) 对受试者参与研究的激励措施（如有）。

(10) 关于申办者如何监查研究并确保研究按研究方案开展的说明。

(11) 对研究者如何接受培训以依从 GCP［如本节（a)(1)(i) 所述］，并按照研究方案进行研究的说明，以及是否获得研究者遵守 GCP 和方案的承诺。研究者的书面承诺书必须由申办者或申请人保留，并可按要求供 FDA 审核。

（c）免除。

(1) 申办者或申请人可以要求 FDA 免除本节（a)(1) 和（b）段适用要求。免除申请可在 IND 中或 IND 信息增补中提交，也可按本章第 314 或 601 部分法规在申请或申请增补中提交。要求免除的申请至少包含以下内容：

(i) 解释为什么申办者或申请人无需或无法符合此项要求。

(ii) 描述满足此要求的备选方案或行动措施。

(iii) 或其他信息证明免除要求合理。

(2) 如果发现该行为符合公共健康利益，FDA 可以免除要求。

（d）记录。申办者或申请人必须保留本节所要求的不受 IND 监管的在美国以外进行的临床研究记录：

(1) 如果提交支持上市批准申请，在 FDA 对该申请做出决定后保留 2 年。

(2) 如果提交研究报告支持 IND，但不支持上市批准申请，则在提交 IND 后保留 2 年。

## 312.130 公开披露 IND 数据和信息

（a）除非先前已经公开披露或承认，否则 FDA 不会披露研究新药申请的存在。

（b）在研究新药申请中，公开披露数据和信息将按照 314.430 规定进行处理，以保护 314 部分法规规定的提交申请中数据和信息的保密性。公开披露生物制品研究新药申请中所有数据和资料的使用将受到 601.50 和 601.51 规定约束。

(c) 尽管有 314.430 的规定，根据申请，FDA 应向服用研究新药的个人披露该受试者个人使用药物发生的相关 IND 安全性报告副本。

(d) 公开披露涉及本章 50.24 规定的因急救研究无需事先获得知情同意例外情形的研究信息处理措施如下：要求在 IND 中公开披露信息的人员应根据信息自由法规定向地址为 5630 Fishers Lane，rm. 1061，Rockville，MD 20852 的 FDA 案卷管理部门（HFA-305）提交文件，案卷号：95S-0158。

## 312.140 通信地址

(a) 申办者必须向药品审评与研究中心（CDER）或生物制品审评与研究中心（CBER）发送初始的 IND 提交文件，具体向哪个中心提交取决于负责管理产品的中心，如下所示。

(1) 由 CDER 管制的药物。IND 提交文件至：Central Document Room，Center for Drug Evaluation and Research，Food and Drug Administration，5901-B Ammendale Rd.，Beltsville，MD 20705-1266。简约版新药申请人体体内生物利用度或生物等效性研究的 IND 提交文件发送至：Office of Generic Drugs（HFD-600），Center for Drug Evaluation and Research，Food and Drug Administration，Metro Park North Ⅶ，7620 Standish Pl.，Rockville，MD 20855。

(2) 由 CDER 管制的生物制品。IND 提交文件的地址为 Central Document Room，Center for Drug Evaluation and Research，Food and Drug Administration，5901-B Ammendale Rd.，Beltsville，MD 20705-1266。

(3) 由 CBER 管制的生物制品。IND 提交文件需发送至：Food and Drug Administration，Center for Biologics Evaluation and Research，Document Control Center，10903 New Hampshire Ave.，Bldg. 71，Rm. G112，

Silver Spring，MD 20993-0002。

(b) 负责中心收到 IND 后，告知申办者 CDER 或 CBER 中哪个部门负责申办者的 IND。应将 IND 相关事项的增补、报告和其他信函按本节所述地址发送到责任中心，并加以标明以引起责任部门注意。提交文件外部包装应说明其中所含内容，如“IND 申请”、“方案增补”等。

(c) 根据 312.110(b)(2) 规定，所有与研究用药出口相关的信件都应提交至：International Affairs Staff (HFY-50)，Office of Health Affairs，Food and Drug Administration，5600 Fishers Lane，Rockville，MD 20857。

### 312.145 指南文件

(a) FDA 在本章 10.115 下提供指南文件，以帮助依从本部分的某些要求。

(b) 药品审评与研究中心 (CDER) 和生物制品审评与研究中心 (CBER) 有适用于中心条例的文件指南清单。这些清单在互联网上保存，并每年在联邦公报上刊登。希望得到 CDER 清单副本应将申请提交至：Office of Training and Communications，Division of Drug Information，Center for Drug Evaluation and Research，Food and Drug Administration，10903 New Hampshire Ave.，Silver Spring，MD 20993-0002。希望得到 CBER 清单副本应将申请提交至：Food and Drug Administration，Center for Biologics Evaluation and Research，Office of Communication，Outreach and Development，10903 New Hampshire Ave.，Bldg. 71，Rm. 3103，Silver Spring，MD 20993-0002。

## 子部分 G 用于实验室动物研究和体外试验的研究用药

### 312.160 用于实验室动物研究和体外试验的研究用药

(a) 授权运输。

(1) (i) 如果使用如下标签，则可运送仅为实验室研究目的供体外试验或动物实验的药物：

注意事项：所含研究新药仅用于实验室动物研究或体外测试研究，不供人类使用。

(ii) 如果使用如下标签，则可以运送 312.2(b)(2)(ii) 所列供体外诊断的生物制品：

注意事项：研究用生物制品仅用于体外诊断测试。

(2) 按照本节 (a) 段规定运送药物的人员应当尽职，确保收货人定期进行检测，保证运输新药确实只用于体外或动物实验室研究。

(3) 按本节 (a) 段规定运送药物的人员应维护正确运输药物的记录，记录接受药物专家姓名和邮局地址，以及药物的每次装运和交货日期、数量、批次或代码标记。按本节 (a)(1)(i) 段规定运输记录应在装运之日起保存 2 年。按本节 (a)(1)(ii) 段规定对相关数据和运输的记录和报告应按照 312.57(b) 要求进行维护。运送药物人员应满足 FDA 授权官员或雇员的要求，在合理时间内，允许 FDA 官员或雇员获得并复制、核实本节所需记录。

(b) 终止授权运输。如发现以下任意情况，FDA 可根据本节终止运送药物的授权：

(1) 申办者未能遵守本节规定的装运条件。

(2) 继续开展研究不安全、或违背公共利益、或研究用于科学研究以外的用途。FDA 将通知运输药物人员 FDA 发现的问题，要求立即采取纠正措施。如未立即采取纠正措施，在 FDA 执行第 16 部分法规处理措施前，运输药物人员将有机会进行监管听证。

(c) 处置未使用的药物。根据本节 (a) 段运送药物人员应在研究停止或研究终止时，确保研究者返还所有未使用药物。运送药物人员可以书面授权采用替代方法来处置未使用药物，条件是替代处置方法不会直接或间接地（如通过食用动物）有使人类暴露于药物的风险。运输人员应保存采用替代处置方法的所有记录。

## 子部分H [保留]

## 子部分I 扩展研究用药的治疗用途

### 312.300 总论

(a) 范围。本子部分包含对研究性新药和限制性批准药物的使用要求。当临床研究主要目的是诊断、监测或治疗患者的疾病或病症时，因评估风险和降低风险策略（REMS），研究性药物的适用范围受到限制。本子部分目的是当患者患严重疾病或病症，且没有类似或满意的其他方法诊断、监测或治疗时，促进这些患者得到这些药物。

(b) 定义。以下定义适用于本子部分：

**危及生命的疾病或病症** 指患者或受试者很有可能在数月内死亡或如未进行早期治疗，将会过早死亡的疾病阶段。

**严重疾病或病症** 指对日常生活产生重大影响的疾病或病症。短暂的和自限性疾病通常不视为严重疾病。如果疾病是持久性的或复发性的，即使不是不可逆转的，也可以判断为严重疾病或病症。对疾病或病症是否严重的临床判断基于疾病对生存、日常功能等因素的影响，或基于如果不及时治疗，疾病从不太严重发展到严重疾病的可能性而进行判断。

### 312.305 对扩展研究用药治疗范围的要求

本节规定的标准、提交要求、保障措施和初始治疗信息适用于本子部分中描述的扩展研究用药的治疗用途。在312.310至312.320中描述了适用于特定类型的扩展研究用药治疗用途的附加标准、提交要求和安全措施。

(a) 标准。FDA必须明确：

(1) 有严重或立即危及生命的疾病或病症，并且目前尚无有效替代治疗方法诊断、监测或治疗疾病或病症的患者。

(2) 患者潜在受益与使用研究用药治疗的潜在风险相比合理，且考虑到需治疗疾病或病症的严重性，治疗使用的潜在风险并非不合理。

(3) 提供按要求使用的研究用药，不会干扰支持拓展性使用的上市批准的临床研究启动、执行或完成，也不会损害扩展性使用的开发进程。

(b) 提交。

(1) 本部分中描述的每种类型的扩大药物治疗范围研究都需要提交扩展研究申请。可用新 IND 或用现有 IND 方案增补的形式提交。如果现 IND 申办者同意授权，所需递交信息可参考现有 IND 中包含的相关信息。

(2) 扩大药物治疗范围研究必须提交：

(i) 封面（FDA1571）满足 312.23(a) 要求。

(ii) 药物预期用途的合理性，包括在使用研究用药之前，通常会尝试的现有治疗选择清单；或解释为什么优先使用研究用药而非现有治疗方法的原因。

(iii) 选择患者标准，描述患者疾病或病症，包括现病史和既往疾病或病症治疗史。

(iv) 药物给药途径、剂量和治疗时间。

(v) 对药物生产设施的描述。

(vi) 足够的化学、生产和质量控制信息以确保研究用药的鉴别、质量、纯度和活性强度。

(vii) 药理学和毒理学信息足以得出以下结论：该药物在扩展研究中的剂量和持续时间应是安全的（通常这些信息足以允许在预计需治疗人群中进行药物临床试验）。

(viii) 对临床操作步骤、实验室检查或其他为评估药物有效性和降低风险所进行监查活动的描述。

(3) 扩展性研究的申请和邮寄封面必须明确标记**"扩展性研究申请"**。如果扩展性研究申请用于治疗性 IND 或治疗性方案，则 FDA1571 表格上的适用框必须勾选。

(c) 保障。本部分子部分 D 规定的申办者和研究者责任适用于本段描述的本子部分下的扩展性研究。

(1) 本部分规定，直接指导管理或分配研究用药用于扩展性研究的执业医师被视为研究者，如适合于扩展性研究，他/她必须遵守本部分子部分 D 中规定的研究者职责。

(2) 在本子部分中，提交扩展性研究 IND 或方案的个人或机构被视为申办者。当适合于扩展性研究时，他们必须遵守本部分子部分 D 规定的申办者职责。

(3) 在本部分规定下，直接指导执业医师管理或分配研究用药用于扩展性研究，并提交扩展性研究 IND 申请的个人是申办-研究者。当适合于扩展性研究时，他/她必须遵守本部分子部分 D 中规定的申办者和研究者责任。

(4) 研究者。对于扩展性研究，研究者负责向申办者报告药物不良事件，确保满足本章第 50 部分对知情同意的要求，确保 IRB 对扩展性研究的审核与本章第 56 部分要求一致，并按照 312.62 要求的方式保存准确的病史、药物处置记录。根据扩展性研究类型，子部分 D 其他研究者的职责也可能适用。

(5) 申办者。对扩展性研究，申办者负责根据 312.32 和 312.33 的要求向 FDA 提交 IND 安全性报告和年度报告（当 IND 或方案持续 1 年或更久），确保执业医师有资格管理用于扩展性研究的研究用药，提供执业医师所需的研究用药信息使风险最小化和益处最大化（如果有，则必须提供研究者手册），维护用于扩展性研究的有效 IND，并按 312.57 要求的方式保留详细的药物处置记录。根据扩展性研究类型，子部分 D 其他申办者责任也可能适用。

(d) 初始治疗

(1) IND。扩展性研究 IND 在 FDA 收到 IND 申请后 30 天生效，或在 FDA 在 30 天内通知扩展性研究可以开始时生效。

(2) 方案。在现有 IND 下提交的扩展性研究方案可按 312.30(a) 所述开始进行，以下例外情况除外。

(i) 312.310(d) 中描述的急救情况下的扩展性研究可

在 FDA 审核官员授权时开始。

(ii) 312.320 下的扩展性研究可在 FDA 收到方案 30 天后开始，或在 FDA 于 30 天内通知时开始。

(3) 临床研究暂停。FDA 可以按 312.42 所述方式将扩展性研究 IND 或方案置于临床暂停状态。

## 312.310 个别患者，包括急救使用药物者

根据本节规定，FDA 可以允许执业医师使用研究用药救治个别患者。

(a) 标准。必须符合 312.305(a) 中的标准，并做出以下决定：

(1) 医生必须明确，使用研究用药可能引起的风险不会大于疾病或病症本身所造成的风险。

(2) FDA 必须明确，患者不能通过另一种 IND 或方案而获得该药物。

(b) 提交。申请扩大药物治疗范围必须提交充足信息，满足 312.305(a) 和本节 (a) 段要求。申请扩大药物治疗范围必须符合 312.305(b) 要求。

(1) 如果药物是现有 IND 的研究对象，可以由申办者或执业医师提交扩大药物治疗范围研究的申请。

(2) 申办者可以通过修改现有 IND，包含修改对个体患者扩大用药范围的方案，以满足提交申请的要求。

(3) 执业医师可以从申办者处获得 FDA 许可参照 IND 中的任何信息，这些信息能用于支持扩大药物适用范围研究的需要，以及其他未包含在 IND 中的信息（通常只针对个体患者的特定信息）。

(c) 保障。

(1) 除非 FDA 明确授权进行多次治疗或长期治疗，否则治疗通常仅限于在指定时间内的单次治疗。

(2) 在治疗结束时，执业医师或申办者必须向 FDA 提供扩大药物适用范围研究结果的书面总结，包括不良反应。

(3) 如果药物使用期限延长，FDA 可以要求申办者监查参与扩大用药范围研究的个体患者。

(4) 当 FDA 收到大量类似个体患者要求扩大研究用药治疗

范围的申请时，FDA 可以要求申办者根据 312.315 或 312.320 要求提交 IND 或方案。

(d) 紧急程序。如果在提交书面申请材料之前，出现患者需要接受治疗的紧急情况，FDA 可以在未提交书面申请的情况下，授权进行扩大药物适用范围的研究。FDA 审核官员可以通过电话授权急救使用研究用药。

(1) 可以通过电话、传真或其他电子通信方式急救使用扩展性研究用药。对于受生物制品审评与研究中心监管的试验性生物制品，提交申请至：Office of Communication, Outreach and Development，Center for Biologics Evaluation and Research，电话：240-402-8010 或 1-800-835-4709，电子邮件：ocod@fda.hhs.gov。对于所有其他研究用药，申请应提交至 Division of Drug Information, Center for Drug Evaluation and Research，电话：301-796-3400，电子邮件：druginfo@fda.hhs.gov。正常工作时间是上午 8 时至下午 4 时 30 分，非工作时间的申请应提交至 FDA 紧急呼叫中心，电话：866-300-4374，电子邮件：emergency.operations@fda.hhs.gov。

(2) 执业医生或申办者必须解释扩大药物适用范围的研究如何满足 312.305 和 312.310 的要求，并须同意在 FDA 授权的 15 个工作日内提交扩大药物适用范围研究申请。

## 312.315 中等规模患者人群

本节规定，FDA 可以允许研究用药用于治疗相比典型的治疗性 IND 或治疗方案人群更小的患者群体。当 FDA 收到大量个体患者因为相同原因要求扩大研究用药治疗范围的申请时，FDA 可能会要求申办者在本节规定下扩大药物治疗范围。

(a) 扩大药物治疗范围的需求。在以下情况下，可能需要根据本部分规定扩大药物治疗范围：

(1) 尚未开发的药物。药物尚未被开发，例如，由于疾病或病症非常罕见，申办者无法招募患者进行临床研究。

(2) 正在开发的药物。正在进行该药物临床研究，但要求获得药物的患者不能参与扩展性研究。例如，患者可能因以下各种原因无法参加试验：因所患疾病不同于正在研究的疾病或疾病阶段而不符合入选标准；试验入组已关闭；受试者因为试验中心的地理位置问题而不能参加。

(3) 已批准的或相关的药物。

(i) 该药物已被批准，但因安全原因不再销售，或由于未达到批准条件而无法通过商业渠道获得。

(ii) 或该药物含有与已批准药物制剂相同的活性成分，由于不符合批准条件或由于药物短缺而无法通过销售渠道获得。

(b) 标准。必须符合 312.305(a) 标准；FDA 必须确定：

(1) 有足够证据表明在扩大治疗范围时使用的药物剂量和持续时间是安全的，证明在预期人数的患者中进行扩大使用范围的临床研究是合理的。

(2) 至少有初步的临床证据表明该药物有效或有合理的药理作用，在预期患者人群中扩大使用是合理的治疗选择。

(c) 提交。申请扩大药物治疗范围必须提交充足信息，以符合 FDA 在 312.305(a) 和本节（b）中的标准。申请扩大药物治疗范围也必须符合 312.305(b) 要求。此外：

(1) 扩大药物治疗范围必须提交药物是否正在开发或尚未开发的说明，以及对需要治疗患者群体的描述。

(2) 如果未积极开发药物，申办者必须解释目前未能将药物用于扩大使用范围的原因以及表明在何种情况下可以开发药物。

(3) 如果正在进行临床研究，申办者必须解释需要治疗患者未能入组的原因，以及表明何种情况下申办者将对这些患者进行临床试验。

(d) 保障。

(1) 经过对 IND 年度报告审核，FDA 将判断在本节监管下继续进行扩大药物使用范围的研究是否合宜。

(i) 如果申办者未积极开发药物或尚未开发扩大药物使用范围（但正在开发另一种用途），FDA 将考虑是否有可能进行扩大药物使用范围的临床研究。

(ii) 如果正在积极开发药物，FDA 将考虑研究用药用于扩大治疗范围的研究是否干扰了正在进行的临床研究。

(iii) 随着入组患者人数的增加，FDA 可能会要求申办者根据 312.320 规定提交 IND 或方案。

(2) 申办者负责监查扩大药物使用范围的研究方案，以确保执业医生依从方案以及对研究者的适用法规。

**312.320 治疗性 IND 或治疗性方案**

在本节规定下，FDA 可允许使用研究用药进行广泛的治疗应用。

(a) 标准。必须满足 312.305(a) 标准，FDA 必须确定：

(1) 试验状况。

(i) 该药物在 IND 规定下正在进行对照性临床研究，以获得对扩大研究用药治疗范围的上市许可申请。

(ii) 或已经完成了药物的所有临床研究。

(2) 上市状况。申办者正在积极努力并尽力寻求扩大研究用药治疗范围的上市许可批准。

(3) 证据。

(i) 当扩大药物治疗范围是为了治疗严重的疾病或病症时，需要有足够的安全性和有效性临床证据支持。这些证据通常来自Ⅲ期临床研究数据，但也可包含已完成的Ⅱ期试验数据；或

(ii) 当扩大药物治疗范围是为了治疗紧急危及生命的疾病或病症时，从已有的科学证据可合理推论：研究用药在扩大药物治疗范围的应用是有效的，且不会将患者置于不合理的重大疾病或受伤害的风险中。证据通常来自Ⅲ期或Ⅱ期临床研究数据，也可来自更早期临床证据。

(b) 提交。申请扩大药物治疗范围必须提交足够信息，符合 FDA 在 312.305(a) 和本节 (a) 段中的标准。申请扩大药物治疗范围也必须符合 312.305(b) 的要求。

(c) 保障。申办者负责监查治疗方案，以确保执业医生依从方案以及研究者适用法规。

[2017 年 6 月 30 日电子版更新版本]

# 21CFR　第 812 部分　研究器械豁免

## 子部分 A　一般规定

### 812.1　范围

(a) 本部分法规的目的是在符合公共健康安全及道德标准的范围内，鼓励发现和开发有用的人用医疗器械，为科学研究者实现此目标维持最适宜的自由度。本部分法规提供医疗器械临床研究操作规程。如获得研究器械豁免（IDE）的批准，则允许合法运送研究器械进行临床研究；如未获得 IDE 批准，则运送研究性器械需要器械达到性能标准要求或获得上市前批准。根据 812.30 批准的 IDE 或根据 812.2(b) 被视为经批准的 IDE 可以对器械豁免《联邦食品、药品和化妆品法案》以下章节相关管理措施的要求：本法案（21 CFR）下 502 节监管的错误标签，510 节监管下的注册、列表和上市前通知，514 节监管下的执行标准，515 节监管下的上市前批准，516 节监管下的取缔器械的规章制度，519 节监管下的记录和报告，520(e) 监管下的限制器械要求，520(f) 监管下生产质量管理规范（GMP）要求 [但适用于 820.30 要求除外，除非申办者声明将依从 812.20(b)(3) 或 812.140(b)(4)(v) 的要求]，以及 721 节监管下对色素添加剂的要求。

(b) 本部分法规参考的法案是指《美国联邦法案》第 21 篇的第Ⅰ章，另有说明除外。

### 812.2　适用性

(a) 总则。本部分法规适用于所有为确定医疗器械的安全性和有效性而进行的临床研究，本节（c）段除外。

(b) 简化要求。下列研究被认为已经获得 IDE 申请批准，除非 FDA 根据 812.20(a) 通知申办者其申请仍需要得到批准：

(1) 对无重大风险的医疗器械进行研究，如非禁用器械，且申办者：

(i) 按照 812.5 的要求对器械进行标签。

(ii) 向审核 IRB 简要说明该器械不是具有重大风险器械的原因后，获得 IRB 对研究的批准，并保留此批准。

(iii) 确保参与器械研究的研究者根据第 50 部分法规要求从每位受试者处获得知情同意书，并将过程记录在案，除非 IRB 根据 56.109(c) 免除对记录的要求。

(iv) 依从 812.46 关于对研究进行监查的要求。

(v) 根据 812.140(b)(4) 和 (5) 的要求维护记录，并根据 812.150(b)(1) 至 (3) 和 (5) 至 (10) 的规定进行报告。

(vi) 确保参与试验的研究者依从 812.140(a)(3)(i) 要求，保留试验记录，并按照 812.150(a)(1)、(2)、(5) 和 (7) 规定进行报告。

(vii) 依从 812.7 禁止宣传和其他行为的禁令。

(2) 于 1980 年 7 月 16 日前开始，并于 1981 年 1 月 19 日前完成的医疗器械研究，被认为已经获得 IDE 申请批准[符合本节 (e) 段的研究除外]。

(c) 豁免研究。除了 812.119 外，本部分法规不适用于以下类别器械的研究：

(1) 1976 年 5 月 28 日前按有效标签中的适应证使用或进行研究的医疗器械，这里指的不是过渡性器械。这些器械当时在商业流通中。

(2) 1976 年 5 月 28 日后进入商业流通的器械（非过渡性器械），FDA 确认其与在 1976 年 5 月 28 日前商业流通中的器械实质上一致，且根据标签的适应证使用或进行研究。FDA根据第807部分法规子部分E在确定器械的实质等同性时审核过器械的标签。

(3) 诊断器械，如果申办者依从809.10(c) 的适用要求，并且测试表明：

(i) 无创。

(ii) 不需要采取高风险的侵入性抽样措施。

(iii) 设计的意图不是向受试者引入能量。

(iv) 且在无另外的医学诊断物品或程序确认的情况下，不用于诊断。

(4) 对器械进行消费者偏好测试、进行修改测试或测试商业流通中的两个或多个器械的组合。这种测试不是为了确定器械的安全性或有效性，且不会将受试者置于风险之中。

(5) 仅用于兽医用途的器械。

(6) 仅用于实验动物的器械，并按照812.5(c) 的要求标签。

(7) 812.3(b) 定义的定制器械（对用于商业流通的器械确定其安全性或有效性的除外）。

(d) 限制某些豁免。对于本节（c)(1）或（2）段所述Ⅱ类或Ⅲ类器械，自FDA要求未经批准的Ⅲ类器械提交上市前批准申请或为Ⅱ类器械建立性能标准的法令生效之日起，此部分法规开始适用。

(e)（略）

## 812.3 定义

(a) **法案** 指美国《联邦食品、药品和化妆品法案》。

(b) **定制器械** 指《联邦食品、药品和化妆品法案》第520(b)节所指的器械。

(c) **FDA** 指美国食品药品管理局。

(d) **植入物** 指该器械被置入外科手术形成的或天然形成的人体空腔内，且其目的是在体内保留30天或更长时间。为了保护公共健康，FDA可能会判断放置在受试者体内较短时间的器械在本部分法规内也被称为“植入物”。

(e) **机构** 指从事临床研究或以向人们提供医学服务为主要活动或作为为人们提供居住或照护的辅助活动的团体，不指特定个人。该术语包括医院、退休所、分娩设施、学术机构和器械制造商。该术语与本法案 520(g) 节中的“设施”一词具有相同的含义。

(f) **机构审查委员会（Institutional Review Board，IRB）** 指研究机构正式指定的任何董事会、委员会或其他组织，负责审核涉及受试者的生物医学研究，并按照第 56 部分法规的要求而建立、运作和正常工作。该术语与本法案 520(g) 节中的“Institutional Review Committee”意思相同。

(g) **研究器械** 指作为研究对象的器械，包括过渡器械。

(h) **研究** 指涉及一位或多位受试者的临床研究，以确定器械的安全性或有效性。

(i) **研究者** 指实际实施临床研究的个人，例如，将试验物品施用或分发，或给受试者使用。在研究团队进行研究的情况下，研究者是该团队的负责领导。

(j) **Monitor（监查员）** 用作名词时，指由申办者或合同研究组织（CRO）指定的监督研究过程的个人。监查员可以是申办者的雇员或是申办者的顾问，或 CRO 的雇员或顾问。Monitor 用作动词时，意思是监查研究。

(k) **非侵入性** 当此词用于诊断器械或操作过程时，指其设计意图不是：(1) 穿透或刺穿身体、眼眶或尿道的皮肤或黏膜；(2) 进入耳道超越外耳道，进入鼻超越鼻腔、进入口腔部位超越咽部、进入肛管超越直肠、进入阴道超越宫颈口。对本部分法规而言，涉及简单静脉穿刺的血液采样被认为是非侵入性的，因非研究目的采集体液或组织的剩余样本也被认为是非侵入性的。

(l) **人员** 包括任何个人、合伙人、公司法人、协会、科学或学术机构、政府机构的组织单位以及任何其他法人实体。

(m) **重大风险器械** 指研究器械：

(1) 目的是作为植入物使用，且对受试者的健康、安全或福祉造成潜在高风险。

(2) 为了支持或维持生命，显示出对受试者的健康、安全或福祉有潜在的严重风险。

(3) 在诊断、治愈、缓解或治疗疾病或以其他方式预防对人体健康的损害方面有重要意义，但对受试者的健康、安全或福祉具有潜在的严重高风险。

(4) 或可能对受试者的健康、安全或福祉造成严重风险。

(n) **申办者** 指启动研究但不实际执行研究的人员，即研究器械是在其他人的直接指导下被施用、分发或使用。组织一名或多名自己的雇员进行研究的人员（非个体）是申办者，而不是申办-研究者，雇员是研究者。

(o) **申办-研究者** 指既启动也实际执行临床试验的个人，单独或与他人一起进行研究。在申办-研究者直接指导下施用、分发或使用研究器械。该术语不包括个人以外的任何实体。申办-研究者的义务既包括研究者的义务也包括申办者的义务。

(p) **受试者** 指参与研究的个人，在其身体上或身体样本上使用研究器械或使用对照器械。受试者可能是正常健康人，也可能是有医学症状或患有疾病的个人。

(q) **终止** 意味着在研究完成之前被申办者或IRB或FDA停止研究。

(r) **过渡器械** 指符合本法案第520(Ⅰ)节规定的器械，1976年5月28日前这些器械被FDA认作新药或抗生素。

(s) **器械的非预期不良反应** 指对健康或安全性造成严重不良影响或危及生命、或由使用器械造成死亡，且此种影响、问题或死亡的本质、严重程度或发生频度以前未在研究计划或申请（包括补充计划或申请）中标明，或其他任何与器械相关的影响受试者权利、安全或福祉的非预期的严重问题。

## 812.5 研究器械标签

(a) 内容。研究器械或其直接包装标签应包含以下信息：制造商、包装商或经销商的名称和营业地址（根据801.1）、所含内容及数量（如适用），和以下声明：“小心——研究器械。根据联邦（或美国）法律，仅限用于研究。”此标签或其他标签应描述所有相关禁忌证、危害、不良反应、干扰物质或器械、警告和注意事项。

(b) 禁止　研究器械标签不得有任何虚假或误导性的陈述，不得表示该器械对研究的目的安全或有效。

(c) 动物研究　仅用于实验动物研究的器械，应在标签上标明以下声明：“小心——研究器械，供实验室动物研究或不涉及人类受试者的其他测试”。

(d) 根据本章 801.128 或 809.11 规定的程序，FDA 相应的中心主任可以对本节（a）和（c）段规定授予例外或提供替代，前提是这些条例没有被法规明确要求，且特定的器械批次或器械部件已经或将被纳入国家战略库存。

## 812.7　禁止宣传和其他行为

申办者、研究者、申办者或研究者代表均不得：

(a) 在 FDA 批准器械可进行商业流通之前，推广或试销研究器械。

(b) 通过向受试者或研究者收取高于研究器械的制造、研究、开发和处置成本的费用而牟利。

(c) 不适当地延长研究期限。如果研究数据显示，Ⅲ类器械无法获得上市前批准，或者Ⅱ类器械不符合适用操作标准或修正标准，申办者应及时终止研究。

(d) 表示研究器械对于正在进行的研究安全或有效。

## 812.10　免除要求

(a) 申请。申办者可以请求 FDA 免除对本部分法规的要求。免除要求的申请与支持文件可以单独提交，也可以作为申请的一部分提交到 812.19 所列出的地址。

(b) FDA 行动。如 FDA 发现此法规并未提出要求，且没有必要对于保护受试者权利、安全或福祉方面提出对本部分法规的要求，FDA 可以通过信件免除这些要求。

(c) 申请的效力。所有免除要求的申请将持续有效，除非和直到 FDA 终止。

### 812.18 进出口要求

(a) 进口。除依从本部分法规的其他要求外，进口或提供受本法规监管的进口器械人员，应为外国出口研究器械的代理人，并担任临床研究的申办者，或确保其他人担任外国出口器械代理人和研究申办者。

(b) 出口。根据本部分法规 801(e) 要求，出口本法规监管的研究器械人员应事先获得 FDA 批准，或依从本法案第 802 节规定。

### 812.19 IDE 通信地址

(a) 如果发送申请、补充申请、报告、免除要求的申请、进口或出口许可申请，或与本部分法规所涉事宜相关的其他通信，须将这些申请发送到以下相应地址：

(1) 对于由放射健康中心监管的器械，请发送给 FDA 器械和放射健康中心的文档邮件中心（地址：10903 New Hampshire Ave.，Bldg. 66，rm. G609，Silver Spring，MD 20993-0002）。

(2) 对于由生物制品评估和研究中心监管的器械，请发送给 FDA 生物制品评估和研究中心的文档管理中心（地址：10903 New Hampshire Ave.，Bldg. 71，Rm. G112，Silver Spring，MD 20993-0002）。

(3) 对于由药品评估和研究中心监管的器械，请发送给 FDA 药品评估和研究中心的中心文档管理室（地址：5901-B Ammendale Rd.，Beltsville，MD 20705-1266）。

(b) 必须在每个提交文档的外包装上标明提交的内容，例如 “IDE 申请”，“补充 IDE 申请” 或 “关于 IDE（或 IDE 申请）的信件”。

## 子部分 B　申请和行政措施

### 812.20 申请

(a) 提交。

(1) 如果申办者打算在研究中使用有重大风险的器械，计划进行本章 50.24 规定的因急救不能事先获得知情同意的例外情形的临床研究，或如果 FDA 通知申办者需要递交研究申请，申办者应向 FDA 提交申请。

(2) 对于需要得到 FDA 对申请批准的研究，申办者不得自行开始，需要在 FDA 批准申请后才能开始研究。

(3) 申办者应当通过挂号邮件或亲手递交 3 份签署的“研究器械豁免申请书”（IDE 申请书）副本和附带材料到 812.19 所述地址。有关申请或补充申请的后续信件应通过挂号邮件或亲手提交。

(4) (i) 申办者应为本章 50.24 监管下的涉及知情同意例外情形的临床研究单独提交 IDE。未经 FDA 事先书面授权，不得进行此类临床研究。FDA 将在收到申请后的 30 天内提供书面确认。

(ii) 如果涉及本章 50.24 的知情同意例外情形的临床研究，申办者应在封面显著标识，显示研究受本章 50.24 要求的监管。

(b) 内容。IDE 申请应按以下顺序，包括：

(1) 申办者的姓名和地址。

(2) 对器械先前进行研究的完整报告，以及 812. 25 (a) 至 (e) 中描述的研究计划部分的准确总结，或用完整的研究计划代替总结。如果研究未经 IRB 审核，或如果 FDA 已经发现 IRB 的审核不够充分，或如果 FDA 要求提供，申办者应向 FDA 提交完整的研究计划和对器械之前研究的完整报告。

(3) 对器械制造、加工、包装、储存、安装（合适时）采用的方法、设施和质量管控的描述，足够详细，以便熟悉生产质量管理规范（GMP）的人可以对器械制造中使用的质量管控做出专业判断。

(4) 本部分法规下所有研究者需签署的遵守研究者义务的协议样本，以及所有已签署协议的研究者姓名和地址清单。

(5) 所有参与研究的研究者签署协议的证明书，研究者名单包括参与研究的所有研究者，并且在签署协议之前研究者不得参与研究。

(6) 已经或将要审核研究的 IRB 名称、地址和主席清单，以及 IRB 对研究所采取行动的证明。

(7) 尚未根据本节 (b)(6) 段确认但可能进行部分研究的机构名称和地址。

(8) 如果要出售器械，要收取的费用以及解释为什么这种销售不被视为器械的商品化。

(9) 受 25. 30 或 25. 34 监管的分类排除申请或受 25. 40 监管对环境评估的申请。

(10) 所有器械标签副本。

(11) 获得知情同意书，提供给受试者的所有表格和信息副本。

(12) FDA 审核申请所需的其他相关信息。

(c) 补充信息。FDA 可要求在研究计划中提供关于研究或修正的额外信息。申办者可以将此类要求视为对申请的不批准，要求根据第 16 部分法规，申请举行听证会。

(d) 以前提交的信息。以前提交给 FDA 器械和放射健康中心、生物制品审评与研究中心或药品审评与研究中心的信息，根据本章节法规，通常不需要重新提交，但可以以参考资料的形式嵌入。

## 812.25 研究计划

研究计划应按以下顺序，包括：

(a) 目的。器械的名称和预期用途，以及研究目的和持续时间。

(b) 方案。书面描述研究将采用的方法，对方案进行的分析表明研究科学可靠。

(c) 风险分析。描述和分析暴露于研究的受试者所有增加的风险；使这些风险最小化的方法；研究的合理性；以及对患者人群的描述，包括人数、年龄、性别和身体状况。

(d) 器械描述。在研究过程中描述器械的每个重要组成部件、组成部分、成分、特性和器械操作原理以及预期器械在研究中的变化。

(e) 监查程序。申办者监查研究的书面程序以及每名监查员的姓名和地址。

(f) 标签。器械所有标签的副本。

(g) 知情同意书材料。获得知情同意书时，提供给受试者的所有表格和信息材料副本。

(h) IRB 信息。所有已经或将要对研究进行审核的 IRB 名称、地点和伦理委员会主席名单列表，以及 IRB 对研究采取行动的证明。

(i) 其他机构。本节（h）段尚未确定的可能进行部分研究的机构名称和地址。

(j) 附加记录和报告。除子部分 G 所述规定外，对研究中需要维护的记录和报告进行说明。

## 812.27 研究前报告

(a) 总则。研究前报告应包括所有对器械的临床前动物和实验室测试报告，并应全面充分证明拟进行研究的合理性。

(b) 具体内容。报告还应包括：

(1) 所有与评估器械安全性或有效性相关的出版物参考书目(无论是支持的或不支持的)，所有发表的和未发表的负面信息副本，以及如果 IRB 或 FDA 要求的其他重要出版物副本。

(2) 申办者拥有或可合理获得的，与评估器械的安全性或有效性相关的，所有其他未发表信息的汇总（无论其是支持或反对研究的信息)。

(3) 如提供有关非临床实验室研究的信息，则声明所有此类研究均符合第 58 部分法规药物非临床研究质量管理规范（GLP）中的适用要求，或者如果此类研究未按照 GLP 执行，则简要说明未遵守的原因。未遵守或不能遵守 GLP 要求并不能成为未提供有关非临床实验研究信息的借口。

## 812.30 FDA 对申请的行动措施

(a) 批准或不批准。FDA 将书面通知申办者收到申请的日期。

FDA可以根据申请批准研究、经修改后批准或不批准。研究不能开始直至：

(1) FDA在812.19所列地址收到非禁用器械研究申请后30天，除非FDA通知申办者研究不可进行。

(2) 或FDA正式批准，发放研究IDE。

(b) 不同意或撤销申请的理由。如果发现以下情况，FDA可能会不批准申请或撤销已批准的申请：

(1) 未能遵守本部分法规或本法案，以及任何其他适用法规或条例，或由IRB或FDA施加的任何批准条件。

(2) 申请书或报告中含对客观事实严重虚假的陈述，或者遗漏本部分法规要求的重要信息。

(3) 申办者未能在FDA规定的时间内回复FDA提出的需提供进一步信息的要求。

(4) 有理由认为对受试者预期利益以及将获得知识的重要性未高过预期风险，或知情同意不够充分，或研究的科学性不够充足，或有理由让人相信所使用的器械无效。

(5) 由于该器械的使用方式或在下列方面存在不足，因此启动或持续进行研究不合理：

(i) 以前的研究报告或研究计划。

(ii) 用来制造、加工、包装、储存和安装（适当时）器械的方法、设施和管控。

(iii) 或对研究的监查和审核。

(c) 不同意或撤回通知。如果FDA不批准申请或提议撤销已批准的申请，FDA将以书面形式通知申办者。

(1) 不批准的命令将包含关于不批准理由的完整陈述，以及申办者有机会根据第16部分法规，要求举行听证会的声明。

(2) 建议撤销已批准申请的通知将包含完整的撤回理由声明，以及申办者有机会根据第16部分法规，要求举行听证会的声明。FDA将在撤销批准前提供听证会的机会，除非FDA在通知中确认继续测试将导致对公众健康造成不合理风险，并命令在听证会前撤销批准。

## 812.35 补充申请

（a）研究计划的变更

（1）需经事先批准的变更。除本节（a）（2）至（a）（4）段所述外，在实施变更的研究计划前，申办者必须根据812.30（a）获得补充申请批准，适当时，还需获得IRB批准（见本章56.110和56.111）。如果申办者打算进行涉及本章50.24规定的因急救研究而无需事先获得知情同意的例外情形的研究时，则申办者应根据812.20（a），提交单独的研究器械豁免（IDE）申请。

（2）因急救使用而导致的变更。本节（a）（1）段关于FDA对补充申请批准的要求，不适用于在急救情况下偏离研究计划以保护受试者生命或身体健康的情况。这种偏离应在申办者了解情况后5个工作日内向FDA报告［见812.150（a）（4）］。

（3）在5天内需通知FDA的变更。如果申办者认定变更符合此节（a）（3）（i）和（a）（3）（ii）段所述的标准，且根据本节（a）（3）（iii）段中定义的信息可靠，申办者可以在未事先根据本条（a）（1）获得补充申请的批准情况下对研究计划进行某些更改。申办者应在实施这些更改后5个工作日内向FDA通告。

（i）开发过程的变更。本节（a）（1）段关于FDA批准补充申请的要求不适用于器械开发过程中做出的不会对设计或基本操作原则造成重大变化的变更（包括制造变更），也不适用于根据研究过程中收集到信息产生反馈，对器械开发过程进行的变更。

（ii）临床方案变更。本节（a）（1）段关于FDA对补充申请批准的要求不适用于所作修改不影响如下方面的临床方案修改：

（A）完成批准方案而产生的数据或信息的有效性，或依据批准方案得出可能的受试者风险与受益关系。

(B) 研究计划的科学性；或

(C) 参与研究的人类受试者的权利、安全或福祉。

(iii) 对可靠信息的定义。

(A) 支持器械研发变更（包括制造变更）的可靠信息包含按照820.30设计管控流程而生成的数据、临床前/动物实验、同行审评出版文献或其他可靠信息，如在临床试验或上市许可试验中收集到的数据。

(B) 支持临床方案变更的可靠信息被定义为变更不会对研究设计或计划的统计学分析造成重大影响，且不会影响受试者权利、安全或福祉。文件应包括诸如同行审评出版文献的信息，临床研究者的建议和/或在临床试验或上市许可期间或上市后收集的信息。

(iv) IDE 变更的通知。符合本节（a）(3)（i）和（a）(3)（ii）段条件且本节（a）(3)（iii）定义为可靠信息支持的变更，可以在未经 FDA 批准的情况下进行变更，条件是申办者需在进行变更后不迟于5个工作日内提交 IDE 变更通知。将设计或制造变更后生产出来的器械发给研究者的日期，即为器械变更的发生日期。当申办者通知临床研究者执行修正的方案，或者在研究中申办-研究者在方案中加入变更时，即临床方案发生变更。这种通知应被标记为“IDE 变更通知”。

(A) 对于器械的研发或生产变更，通知应包括在研究过程中收集到的相关信息，以此作为变更依据；描述器械或生产过程的变更（参考器械或制造过程相应部分的原始描述）；如果使用设计控制来评估变更，则声明通过适当风险分析未发现新的风险，并且核实和验证测试（如适当）结果证明设计成果符合设计要求。如果使用另一种评估方法，通知应对支持变更的可靠信息进行总结。

(B) 对于方案变更，通知应包含对方案变更的描述（参考原方案相应章节）；支持该变更对研究设计或计划的统计分析无重大影响的评估；以及用来支持申办者认定变更不影响受试者权利、安全或福祉的可靠信息摘要。

(4) 年度报告中提交的变更。本节 (a) (1) 段的要求不适用于对研究目的、风险分析、监查程序、标签、知情同意材料和 IRB 信息做出微小变更，这种变更不会影响如下方面：

(i) 方案批准后产生的数据或信息的有效性，或依据批准方案带给患者可能的风险与受益。

(ii) 研究计划的科学可靠性。

(iii) 或参与研究受试者的权利、安全或福祉。这些变更应按 812.150 (b) (5) 在 IDE 年度进度报告中报告。

(b) IRB 对新机构的批准。申办者应向 FDA 提交未包括在 IDE 申请中的 IRB 对研究或部分研究批准的证明。如果研究没有其他变化，补充申请应包含 812.20 (b) 和 (c) 所要求的更新信息，以及作为批准条件，IRB 要求的对研究计划修改的描述。IRB 批准证明不需要包含在补充申请的初次提交中，且该证明不是 FDA 考虑申请的前提条件。但直至 IRB 批准了此研究，FDA 已收到 IRB 批准证明，且根据 812.30 (a)，FDA 批准了与部分研究相关的补充申请后[见 56.103 (a)]，申办者才能在新机构开始部分研究。

## 812.36 研究器械的治疗使用

(a) 综合。对于患有严重且即刻危及生命疾病或症状的患者，如果找不到可与研究器械相比的或满意的替代器械或其他治疗方法，可以使用未获上市批准的器械进行临床研究。在临床试验期间或在对上市申请作最终判定之前，根据治疗性研究器械豁免（IDE）规定，将该器械用于治疗非试验中的患者是适当的。本节的目的是在器械上市之前，尽早在器械开发过程中使用有前景的新器械，用于治疗极度严重的患者，并获得有关器械安全性和有效性的其他数据。在严重疾病的情况下，在所有临床试验完成后，通常可以将该器械用于本节法规监管下的治疗用途。对于即刻危及生命的疾病，可以在完成所有临床试验前，将本器械用于本部分法规监管下的治疗用途。本节，“即刻危及生命”的疾病是指在几个月内有可能死亡，或若无早期治疗，可能发生过早死亡的疾病阶段。本节，器械的“治疗使用”包括用于诊断目的的器械。

(b) 标准。如 FDA 发现下列情况，应考虑在治疗 IDE 规定下使用研究器械：

(1) 该器械用于治疗或诊断严重或即刻危及生命的疾病或症状。

(2) 没有可与之相比的或满意的替代设备或治疗方法来治疗或诊断特定患者群体的疾病或症状。

(3) 该器械正在进行已批准的用于相同用途的对照性 IDE 临床试验，或该器械已经完成了此类临床试验。

(4) 研究申办者正在积极推动上市审批/许可。

(c) 治疗用途的申请。

(1) 治疗性 IDE 的申请应按以下顺序，包括：

(i) 治疗性 IDE 申办者的名称、地址和电话号码。

(ii) 器械的预期用途、患者选择标准以及描述治疗用途的书面方案。

(iii) 解释使用该器械的理由，包括列出使用研究器械之前现有常备治疗方案清单，或说明使用研究器械较已上市常规治疗更优的原因。

(iv) 对临床措施、实验室检查或其他用于评估器械疗效并尽量减少风险的描述。

(v) 监查治疗性用途的书面操作程序以及监查员的姓名和地址。

(vi) 根据 812.5（a）和（b）的要求，器械使用说明和所有其他标签。

(vii) 与治疗用器械相关的安全性和有效性信息。可合并参考来自其他IDE的信息，支持器械用于治疗用途。

(viii) 申办者承诺履行本章本部分和第56部分法规所有适用职责的声明，并确保所有参与研究者依从第50部分法规对知情同意的要求。

(ix) 参与治疗性IDE的所有研究者需签署的协议样本，且声明在签署协议之前，研究者未参与治疗IDE。

(x) 如果要出售器械，收取的费用仅限于制造和管理成本。

(2) 接收治疗用研究器械的执业医师是IDE下的“研究者”，承担本章本部分法规及第50和56部分法规中所有研究者适用职责。

(d) FDA对治疗性IDE申请的行动。

(1) 批准治疗性IDE。FDA在812.19所述地址收到IDE申请30天后可开始治疗性使用试验器械，除非FDA在30天内以书面形式通知申办者可以或不可以开始治疗使用。FDA可根据申请批准治疗性使用或建议进行修改后予以批准。

(2) 不批准或撤销治疗性IDE批准。如果出现以下情况，FDA将不批准或撤销治疗性IDE的批准：

(i) 不符合812.36 (b) 规定或治疗性IDE未提供812.36 (c) 中要求的信息。

(ii) FDA判定符合812.30 (b) (1) 至 (5) 所列的不予批准或取消批准的情况。

(iii) 该器械的目的是用于治疗严重疾病或症状，但没有足够的安全性和有效性证据来支持这种使用。

(iv) 该器械的目的是用于治疗即刻危及生命的疾病或症状，但总的说来，已有的科学证据未能提供合理依据表明该器械：

(A) 可能对选定人群有预期的疗效。

(B) 或不会将该器械使用者暴露于不合理的额外的重大疾病或伤害的风险。

(v) 合理证据表明，器械的治疗性使用妨碍了同一或另一研究器械对照性研究的受试者入组，或已干扰研究的进行或完成。

(vi) 该器械已经获得上市批准/许可，或针对使用研究器械的同一患者人群，已经有了类似的器械或治疗方法来治疗或诊断相同的适应证。

(vii) 对照性临床试验的申办者不积极寻求上市批准/许可。

(viii) 该器械对照性临床研究 IDE 的批准已被撤销。

(ix) 或治疗性 IDE 中任命的临床研究者在科学训练和/或使用研究器械进行预期治疗性使用试验器械的经验等方面不合格。

(3) 不批准或撤销批准的通知。如果 FDA 不赞成或提议撤销对治疗性 IDE 的批准，FDA 将遵循 812.30（c）中规定的程序。

(e) 保障措施。治疗性使用研究器械的条件是申办者和研究者依从 IDE 过程的保障措施以及知情同意（本章第 50 部分法规）和机构审查委员会（本章第 56 部分法规）的规定。

(f) 报告要求。治疗性 IDE 的申办者应每半年向 IRB 和 FDA 提交研究进度报告，直至提交上市申请。这些报告应从治疗性 IDE 初始批准时起，应包括治疗性 IDE 下使用器械治疗的患者人数、参与治疗性使用研究器械的研究者姓名以及申办者努力寻求批准研究器械上市的简单描述。提交上市申请后，应按照 812.150（b）（5）的要求每年提交进度报告。治疗性 IDE 的申办者负责提交 812.150 所要求的所有其他报告。

## 812.38 数据和信息的保密

(a) IDE 的存在。除非之前已公开披露或承认 IDE 的存在，在 FDA 批准受 IDE 监管的器械上市前申请之前，或在公布该器械的产品开发方案已经完成的声明生效之前，FDA 不得透露 IDE 的存在。

(b) 总结或数据的可获得性。

(1) FDA将根据申请，公开有关器械安全性和有效性信息的详细总结，此总结是做出批准、不批准或撤销禁用器械IDE申请批准的基础。总结应包含该器械对健康造成不良影响的信息。

(2) 如果是禁用器械，或者已有的IDE已被公开披露或承认，则在获得器械的上市前申请批准或已完成产品开发方案的通知生效之前，不得向公众公开文件中包含的数据或信息，除非按本节的要求提供。FDA可以酌情选定器械安全性和有效性数据部分的总结进行披露，即披露器械临床、动物或实验室研究和测试的信息，供公众思考某些尚无定论的问题。

(3) 如果尚未公开披露或承认IDE档案的存在，除此节(b)(1)和(c)段另有规定外，档案中的数据或信息均不得公开披露。

(4) 尽管有本节(b)(2)段的规定，FDA将根据申请向公众提供涉及本章50.24监管下知情同意例外情形的IDE研究的某些信息，这些信息需要在FDA档案管理部门(HFA－305)卷宗编号95S-0158处归档(地址：5630 Fishers Lane，rm. 1061，Rockville，MD 20852)。希望得到此类信息的人应根据“信息自由法案”提交申请。

(c) 不良反应报告。在收到披露信息的申请后或出于主动，FDA应向研究器械使用者披露与该用途有关的器械不良反应报告副本。

(d) 其他规则。不符合本节规定时，获得公开披露的IDE档案文件中的数据和信息应根据814.9进行处理。

## 子部分C 申办者责任

### 812.40 申办者的一般责任

申办者负责选择合格的研究者，并向他们提供进行研究所需的正确信息，确保对研究进行适当监查，确保研究获得IRB审核和批准，向FDA提交IDE申请，并确保向审核研究的IRB和FDA及时告知有关研究的新的重要信息。申办者的其他责任在子部分B和G中描述。

**812.42 FDA和IRB批准**

在IRB和FDA均批准与研究或部分研究有关的申请或补充申请之前，申办者不得开展研究或部分研究。

**812.43 选择研究者和监查员**

(a) 选择研究者。申办者应选择接受过培训和有经验的合格研究者来进行器械研究。

(b) 器械的管控。申办者只能向参加研究的合格研究者运送研究器械。

(c) 获得同意。申办者应从每位参与研究者处获得一份签署的同意书，其中包括：

(1) 研究者的履历。

(2) 适用时，研究者相关经验的陈述，包括进行研究的日期、地点、范围和经验类型。

(3) 研究者参与过的研究，或如果研究被终止，对导致出现终止情形的解释。

(4) 研究者的承诺声明。

(i) 按协议、研究计划、本部分法规和其他适用FDA法规，以及IRB或FDA审核的批准条件进行研究。

(ii) 监督所有涉及人类受试者的器械测试。

(iii) 确保满足获得受试者知情同意书的要求。

(5) 足够且准确的财务披露信息，使申办者能够按照本书第54部分法规要求提交完整及准确的财务证明或财务披露声明。申办者应获得临床研究者的承诺：在研究过程中以及研究完成后1年内，研究者将及时更新其发生的任何相应的财务变化信息。该信息不得在研究器械豁免(IDE)申请中提交，应在涉及该器械的上市申请中提交。

(d) 选择监查员。根据本部分法规和其他适用 FDA 法规，申办者应选择接受过培训和有经验的合格监查员监查临床研究。

## 812.45 告知研究者

申办者应向参与研究的所有研究者提供研究计划副本和之前的器械研究报告。

## 812.46 监查研究

(a) 确保合规。一旦申办者发现研究者未依从签署的方案、研究计划、本部分法规或其他适用 FDA 法规的要求或 IRB 或 FDA 所规定的任何批准条件，应及时确保合规或停止向研究者运送器械，并终止该研究者参与研究。申办者还应要求该研究者处理或退回研究器械，除非这样做会危害受试者的权利、安全或福祉。

(b) 器械的非预期不良反应。

(1) 申办者应立即对任何器械的非预期不良反应进行评估。

(2) 一旦申办者确定器械的非预期不良反应对受试者造成不合理的风险，申办者应尽快终止所有或部分造成风险的研究。终止时间不得迟于申办者做出此项决定后的 5 个工作日内，且不得迟于申办者首次收到此不良反应通知后 15 个工作日内。

(c) 恢复被终止的研究。如果是有重大风险的器械，申办者不能在无 IRB 和 FDA 批准的情况下恢复被终止的研究。如果不是有重大风险的器械，申办者不能在无 IRB 批准的情况下恢复被终止的研究；如果研究是根据本节 (b)(2) 段的要求被终止，则需要 FDA 的批准。

## 812.47 本章 50.24 监管下的急救研究

(a) 申办者应监查所有涉及本章 50.24 监管下的因急救而无需事先知情同意的例外情形的研究进展情况。当申办者从 IRB 收到根据本章 50.24 (a) (7) (ii) 和 (a) (7) (iii) 公开披露的信息时，申办者应及时将标识 IDE 号码的披露信息副本提交到 IDE 文件档案夹和 FDA 档案管理部门（HFA-305），卷宗号 95S-0158，地址：5630 Fishers Lane，rm. 1061，Rockville，MD 20852。

(b) 申办者还应监查这类研究，以确定当研究不符合本章 50.24 (a) 的知情同意例外情形标准或其他相关道德标准时，IRB 不得批准此类研究。申办者应及时向 FDA 和受邀参加此研究或类似临床研究的研究者，以及其他受邀审核此项目或类似项目的 IRB 书面提供此信息。

## 子部分 D　IRB 审核和批准

### 812.60　IRB 的组成，职责和职能

根据本部分法规进行审核和批准临床研究的 IRB 应在各方面依从第 56 部分法规的所有要求，包括 IRB 的组成、职责和职能。

### 812.62　IRB 批准

(a) IRB 应审核并有权批准、要求修改（以获得批准）或不批准本部分法规所涉及的所有研究。

(b) 如果没有 IRB，或者如果 FDA 发现 IRB 的评估不够充分，则申办者可以向 FDA 提交申请。

### 812.64　IRB 持续审核

IRB 应根据第 56 部分法规对研究进行持续审核。

### 812.65　[保留]

### 812.66　重大风险器械确定

如果 IRB 根据 812.2 (b) (1) (ii) 确定提交批准申请的研究涉及有重大风险的器械，则应通知研究者，并在适当情况下通知申办者。除 812.30 (a) 规定的情况外，申办者不得开始研究。

# 子部分 E　研究者的责任

## 812.100　研究者的一般责任

研究者负责确保按照签署的方案、研究计划和适用 FDA 法规进行研究，保护受研究者照护的受试者的权利、安全和福祉，以及对研究器械的管控。研究者还负责确保根据本章第 50 部分法规获得知情同意书。研究者的额外责任在子部分 G 中描述。

## 812.110　研究者的具体责任

(a) 等待批准。研究者可判断潜在受试者是否有兴趣参与研究，但不得要求参加的受试者签署书面知情同意书，并且在获得 IRB 和 FDA 批准之前不得允许任何受试者参与试验。

(b) 依从。研究者应根据与申办者签署的方案、研究计划、本部分法规和其他适用 FDA 法规，以及 IRB 或 FDA 强制要求的限定条件进行研究。

(c) 器械使用管控。研究者管控研究器械，仅在研究者监管的情况下供受试者使用研究器械。根据本部分法规，研究者不得向任何未经授权的人提供研究器械。

(d) 财务披露。临床研究者应向申办者披露充分且准确的财务信息，以供申请人提交本章第 54 部分法规要求的完整准确的财务证明或财务披露声明。研究者如在研究过程中及研究完成后 1 年内财务信息发生了变化，应及时更新财务信息。

(e) 处置器械。在完成或终止临床研究或研究者完成其所负责临床研究部分后，或根据申办者的要求终止试验时，研究者应向申办者退还试验器械的全部剩余供应品，或按申办者的指示以其他方式处置试验器械。

## 812.119　取消临床研究者的资格

(a) 如果 FDA 有信息表明研究者（包括申办-研究者）屡次或故意不遵守本章本部分、第 50 部分或第 56 部分法规的要求，或屡次或故意在任何要求的报告中向 FDA 或申办者提交虚假信息，FDA器械和放射健康中心、生物制品审评与研究中心或药品审评与研究中心将向研究者提交书面投诉通知，并向研究者提供以书面形式进行解释的机会，或由研究者选择通过以非正式会议的形式解释。如果研究者提供解释而且解释被FDA相应中心所接受，相应中心将中断取消资格的程序。如果研究者提供解释未被FDA相应中心接受，根据本章第16部分法规，研究者将有机会举行监管听证，判断研究者是否有资格接受本部分法规监管的研究物品，以及是否有资格进行由FDA监管的、支持研究或设备上市许可申请的临床研究。

(b) 在评估所有现有信息（包括研究者提供的解释）后，如果FDA专员确定研究者屡次或故意不遵守本章本部分、第50部分或第56部分法规的要求，或在要求的报告中屡次或故意提交给FDA或申办者虚假信息，FDA专员将通知研究者、指定研究者参与试验的申办者，以及正在审核该研究的IRB，该研究者不符合本部分法规监管下接收试验器械的要求。给研究者、申办者和IRB的通知将提供做出此判断的依据声明。该通知还将解释根据本部分法规而确认不适合接收研究器械的研究者将无资格进行任何FDA监管的研究或上市许可申请的临床研究，包括药品、生物制品、器械、新的动物药物、食品（包括标有营养成分说明或健康说明的膳食补充剂）、婴儿配方奶粉、食品和色素添加剂，以及烟草制品。

(c) 根据本章条款的规定，对于每一项提交给FDA的申请或文件，如其中包含已确认为不符合接收FDA监管研究物品资格的研究者提交的数据，需要接受检查，以确定该研究者是否提交了不可靠的数据，此数据对于研究的继续进行、对于上市许可批准、对于FDA管制产品的持续销售至关重要。

(d) 如FDA专员判定：在清除该研究者提交的不可靠数据后，根据剩余数据不能得出继续进行研究安全合理的结论，则FDA专员会通知申办者，申办者将有机会按本章

第 16 部分法规进行监管听证。但如果一旦发现存在对公共健康带来危险的情形，专员应立即终止研究器械豁免（IDE），并通知申办者和审核 IRB 其做出的终止研究决定。在这种情况下，申办者应有机会根据本章第 16 部分法规进行 FDA 监管听证会，以判断是否可以恢复 IDE。即使裁定不考虑用某项研究支持其研究上市许可的申请、通告或申诉申请，也不能免除申办者依据其他适用法规向 FDA 提交研究结果的义务。

(e) 在清除该研究者提交的不可靠数据后，仍无法证明持续许可或批准已提交数据的产品合理，则 FDA 专员将按照相关法规的适用规定废除批准或撤回批准。

(f) 根据本节（b）段确定的不合格研究者，如果 FDA 专员确定该研究者已经提供了充分的保证，比如研究者将仅依照本章的适用法规使用所有试验物品、进行支持 FDA 监管产品的研究或上市许可申请的临床研究，该研究者可以被重新恢复原职。

## 子部分 F [保留]

## 子部分 G 记录和报告

### 812.140 记录

(a) 研究者记录。参与研究者应保留下列在研究过程中产生的，与研究者参与研究相关的记录，保证其准确、完整和及时：

(1) 所有与其他研究者、IRB、申办者、监查员或 FDA 的通信，包括报告。

(2) 有关器械的接收、使用或处理记录：

(i) 器械类型和数量、收货日期以及批号或代码。

(ii) 所有接收、使用或处置器械人员的姓名。

(iii) 退回申办者、维修或以其他方式处置器械的原因及数量。

(3) 受试者病历和使用器械的记录。病历包括病例报告表和辅助资料，包括签署和注明日期的知情同意书；医疗记录，包括医师对病情进展的说明、受试者医院病历和护士记录。此类记录应包括：

(i) 证实进行知情同意的文件；以及研究者在无知情同意情况下，使用器械的执业医师书面同意，及对未能获得知情同意情况的简要说明。每个受试者的病历上应记录在参与研究之前已获得知情同意书。

(ii) 所有相关观察，包括关于器械的不良反应记录(无论预期或非预期)，每位受试者参加试验时，以及在研究过程中，病情的信息和数据，包括既往相关病史和所有诊断测试的结果。

(iii) 每个受试者使用研究器械的记录，包括每次使用的日期和时间以及任何其他治疗。

(4) 方案，以及记录每次方案偏离的日期和原因的文件。

(5) 根据法规、研究类别或某项特定研究的要求，FDA要求保留的其他记录。

(b) 申办者记录。申办者应保存以下研究有关的记录，保证其准确、完整和及时：

(1) 所有与其他申办者、监查员、研究者、IRB或FDA的通信及所要求的报告。

(2) 运输和处置研究器械的记录。运输记录应包含收货人名称和地址、器械类型和数量、运输日期、批号或代码。处理记录应描述任何由研究者或其他人退回给申办者，进行修理或以其他方式处置的器械批号或代码，以及所采用对器械处置方法的理由。

(3) 根据本章第54部分法规签署的研究者协议，包括根据812.43(c)(5)要求收集的财务披露信息。

(4) 对每个812.2(b)(1)监管下不造成重大风险的器械研

究，本节（b）（5）段描述的记录和下列记录，合并放在同一位置，供FDA视察和复制：

(i) 器械名称和计划用途以及研究目的。

(ii) 解释器械不是有重大风险器械的简要说明。

(iii) 每位研究者的姓名和地址。

(iv) 审核研究的IRB名称和地址。

(v) 关于在生产器械时将遵循第820部分法规GMP要求的声明。

(vi) FDA要求的任何其他信息。

(5) 关于器械不良反应（无论预期或非预期）和投诉的记录。

(6) 根据法规、研究类别或某项特定研究要求，FDA要求保留的其他记录。

(c) IRB记录。IRB应根据本章第56部分法规要求保存记录。

(d) 保留期限。研究者或申办者应在研究期间及以下两个日期（以两者中后一日期为准）之后2年，保留本子部分法规所要求的记录：研究终止或完成日期，或不再要求为支持上市前批准申请或获得产品开发方案已完成的通知而保留记录的日期。

(e) 记录保管。研究者或申办者可以不再负责维护本节（d）所要求的记录，并将保管记录的责任转移给其他依照本部分法规（包括812.145）要求对其承担责任的人。移交通知应在转移发生后不迟于10个工作日内提交FDA。

## 812.145 视察

(a) 进入和视察。具有审阅权限的申办者或研究者应允许被授权的FDA雇员在合理时间以合理的方式进入和视察器械所在的场所（包括器械制造、加工、包装、安装、使用，或被植入的场所，或者保存使用器械结果记录的场所）。

(b) 视察记录。申办者、IRB或研究者、或其代表，应在合理的时间、以合理的方式允许经授权的FDA雇员视察和复制与研究相关的所有记录。

(c) 可确认受试者身份的记录。如果FDA有理由怀疑知情同意不够充分，或需要由研究者提交给申办者或IRB的报告未提交、不完整、不准确、虚假或误导，研究者应允许授权的FDA雇员视察和复制可确认受试者身份的记录。

## 812.150 报告

(a) 研究者报告。研究者应准备并提交以下完整、准确和及时的报告：

(1) 器械的非预期不良反应。研究者应尽快向申办者和审核IRB提交研究期间发生的任何非预期不良反应报告，不得迟于研究者首次知道不良反应发生后的10个工作日内。

(2) 撤销IRB批准。审核IRB撤销研究者参与研究的批准后，研究者应在5个工作日内向申办者报告。

(3) 进展。研究者应定期向申办者、监查员和审核IRB提交研究进度报告，不得少于每年一次。

(4) 研究计划偏离。研究者应通知申办者和审核IRB在紧急情况下，为保护受试者的生命或身体健康而对研究计划的偏离[见56.108 (a) (3)和 (4)]。该通知应尽快发出，不得迟于紧急情况发生后的5个工作日。除此种紧急情况外，改变或偏离计划需获得申办者事先批准，如果这些变化或偏离会影响到研究计划的科学合理性或人类受试者的权利、安全或福祉，为依从812.35 (a)，还需要事先得到FDA和IRB的批准。

(5) 知情同意。如果研究者在没有获得知情同意的情况下使用器械，研究者应在该事件发生后的5个工作日内向申办者和审核IRB报告。

(6) 最终报告。研究者应在研究终止或研究完成后，或在研究者完成其研究部分后，3个月内向申办者和审核IRB提交最终报告。

(7) 其他。研究者应根据审核IRB或FDA的要求，提供全部关于研究的准确、完整和最新信息。

(b) 申办者报告。申办者应准备并提交以下完整、准确和及时的报告：

(1) 器械的非预期不良反应。根据 812.46 (b)，对器械非预期不良反应进行评估的申办者应在首次收到不良反应通知后 10 个工作日内向 FDA 及所有审核 IRB 和所有参与研究者报告评估结果。此后，申办者应按 FDA 要求提交关于此不良反应的附加报告。

(2) 撤销 IRB 批准。对于任何已批准的研究或已批准的部分研究被 IRB 撤销批准的情况，申办者应当在收到该撤销批准通知后的 5 个工作日内向 FDA 和所有审核 IRB 以及参与研究者通告。

(3) 撤销 FDA 批准。申办者应在收到撤销批准通知后 5 个工作日内向所有审核 IRB 和参与研究者通告所有 FDA 撤销批准研究的情况。

(4) 当前研究者名单。申办者应每 6 个月向 FDA 提交目前所有参与研究的研究者姓名和地址清单。申办者应在 FDA 批准 6 个月内提交首个研究者名单。

(5) 进度报告。申办者应至少每年向所有审核 IRB 提交一次进度报告。对有重大风险的器械，申办者还应向 FDA 提交进度报告。按 812.36 (f) 要求，治疗 IDE 的申办者应向所有审核 IRB 和 FDA 提交半年度进度报告，以及按本节法规要求，提供年度报告。

(6) 召回和器械处置。申办者应通知 FDA 及所有审核 IRB 任何要研究者退还、修理或以其他方式处理器械部件的要求。该通知应在提出要求后 30 个工作日内发布，并说明提出此要求的原因。

(7) 最终报告。如是重大风险的器械，申办者应在研究完成或终止后的 30 个工作日内通知 FDA，并在试验完成或终止后 6 个月内向 FDA 和审核 IRB 以及所有参与研究者提交最终报告。如果不是重大风险器械，申办者应在研究终止或完成后 6 个月内向所有审核 IRB 提交最终报告。

(8) 知情同意。研究者根据本节 (a) (5) 段报告未得到知情同意而使用本器械，申办者应在收到报告后5个工作日内，向FDA提交报告副本。

(9) 重大风险器械的确定。如果IRB判定器械是有重大风险的器械，但申办者已声明器械不是有重大风险的器械，则申办者应在首次知道IRB的判定后5个工作日内向FDA提交IRB的判定。

(10) 其他。申办者应根据审核IRB或FDA要求，提供全部关于研究的准确、完整和最新信息。

[2009年7月14日生效]

# 45CFR 第46部分 保护人类受试者

## 子部分A 保护人类受试者的基本卫生和公共服务（HHS）政策

### 46.101 政策适用范围（略）

### 46.102 定义

（a）**部门或政府机构负责人** 指美国联邦部门或政府机构负责人，以及被部门或政府机构授权的其他政府官员或雇员。

（b）**机构** 指公立或私立实体或管理局（包括美国联邦、州和其他管理局）。

（c）**法定授权代表** 指在适用法律下获得授权的个人或司法机构或其他代表，代表可能的受试者同意参与研究。

（d）**研究** 指设计用来开发或为获得一般性知识作出贡献的系统性学术研究，包括研究开发、测试和评估。在本部分政策下，符合此定义的活动即为研究，无论它是否属于其他的研究项目，是否因其他目的进行研究。例如，某些示范和服务项目可能包括研究活动。

（e）**受法规监管的研究** 类似的术语包括由联邦部门或政府机构具体负责管理的研究活动（例如，FDA管理的新药研究要求）。此术语不包括偶尔由联邦部门或政府机构监管的研究活动，也不包括仅作为部门或政府机构广泛职责的一部分所管理的活动，无论其为研究性质或非研究性质（例如，由劳工部监管的对薪水和工作时间的要求不属于受法规监管的研究）。

（f）**人类受试者** 指研究者（无论是专业人员还是学生）对其进

行研究，并获得以下信息的个体：

(1) 通过对受试者进行干预或互动而得到的数据。

(2) 或可识别的私人信息。

**干预**包括为研究目的采取措施（如静脉穿刺）而收集数据的过程以及对受试者或受试者的环境进行操控。**互动**包括研究者和受试者之间的沟通或人与人之间的接触。**私人信息**包括在某种环境下发生，行为者本人有理由期望不被观察或不被记录的行为信息，以及因某种目的而提供但行为者本人有理由期望不被公示的信息（如医疗记录）。私人信息必须可辨识相应个体（即根据信息、研究者或其同事可以轻易识别受试者的身份），以获得可成为涉及人类受试者的研究信息。

(g) **IRB** 指为本政策所表达的目标而设立、符合本政策的机构审查委员会。

(h) **IRB 批准** 指 IRB 确定研究已被审核，可在 IRB 规定的以及在其他机构或联邦要求限制下的机构进行研究。

(i) **最小风险** 指研究中预期的伤害或不适发生概率和程度不高于受试者本身在日常生活中或在常规体检或心理检查中所遇到的。

(j) **证书** 指机构根据本政策要求向支持部门或政府机构正式通知涉及人类受试者的研究项目或活动已经得到 IRB 审核和批准。

## 46.103 确保遵守本政策——由联邦部门或政府机构进行或支持的研究

(a) 从事本政策覆盖研究、由联邦部门或政府机构执行或支持的研究机构，应提供符合本政策规定要求的书面保证，获得联邦部门或政府机构负责人肯定。特定部门或政府机构负责人应接受人类研究保护办公室、美国卫生与公众服务部或任何后续办公室已存档的适用于有关研究的保证书，并批准其可在联邦范围内使用，以替代对提交符合本政策规定的书面保证的要求。当接受经美国卫生与公众服务部批准的已有的保证书而替代了提交书面保证的要求时，根据本政策，对部门和机构负责人要求的报告（除证书）也应提交给人类研究保护办公室、美国卫生与公众服务部或任何后续办公室。

(b) 政府部门和机构只有在机构有本节规定的批准保证，且只有该机构已向政府部门或政府机构负责人确认IRB已经审核和批准此项研究，并将接受IRB的持续审核后，才能进行或支持本政策所涉及的研究。适用于联邦支持或进行研究的保证至少需包含如下内容：

(1) 在该机构实施或该机构资助的研究活动中履行保护人类受试者权利和福祉原则的声明，不论该研究是否受美国联邦法案监管。可包括适用现行法规、声明或道德原则声明，或机构本身提出的声明。此要求不会取代本政策对受政府部门或政府机构支持或监管研究的相关条款，不适用于根据46.101 (b) 或 (i) 豁免或免除的任何研究。

(2) 指定根据本政策要求设立的一个或多个IRB，并制作条款保证有足够会议空间和足够工作人员来支持IRB执行其审核和记录职责。

(3) IRB成员名单包括：姓名；获得的学位；成员的能力；经验证明，如医学认证、执照等，描述每位成员对IRB审核工作的主要预期贡献；以及每个成员与机构之间的工作或其他关系，例如，全职雇员、兼职雇员、理事会成员或董事会成员、股东、有酬或无酬顾问。IRB成员的变更应报告至部门或政府机构负责人，除非符合本政策46.103 (a) 规定，已接受现存美国卫生与公众服务部批准的保证书。在这种情况下，IRB成员的变更应向人类研究保护办公室、美国卫生与公众服务部或后续办公室报告。

(4) IRB进行下列活动时将遵循的书面操作规程：

(i) 进行研究的初步和持续审核，并向研究者和研究机构报告审核发现和采取的行动。

(ii) 确定哪些项目需要较年审更为频繁的审核，哪些项目需要对从研究者以外的其他来源的信息进行核查，指出自从上次 IRB 审核以来未发生重大变化。

(iii) 确保及时向 IRB 报告研究活动的拟议变更，并确保在审批期间，在未得到 IRB 审核和批准的情况下，不得启动对已批准研究的变更，为消除对受试者明显直接危害的紧急情况除外。

(5) 确保及时向 IRB、适当机构官员以及政府部门或政府机构负责人书面报告下列情况：

(i) 对受试者或其他人非预期风险，或对严重或持续不依从本政策或 IRB 的要求或决定。

(ii) IRB 批准的研究暂停或终止。

(c) 保证应由经机构授权的人执行，代表机构承担本政策规定的义务，并以政府部门或政府机构负责人规定的格式和方式归档。

(d) 政府部门或政府机构负责人将通过政府部门或机构官员和职员以及负责人和当时为此聘用的专家或顾问，评估依照本政策而制定和提交的所有保证。政府部门或政府机构负责人评估 IRB 是否考虑到机构研究活动的预期范围和可能涉及的受试人群类型，依据可能的风险、机构的规模和复杂性，进行初始和持续审核程序是否适当。

(e) 在此评估的基础上，政府部门或政府机构负责人可以批准或者不批准此保证，或者进行谈判，制定可以批准的保证。政府部门或政府机构负责人可以限制期限，在此期限内，任何特定批准保证或保证类别将保持有效，或以其他方式限制批准期限。

(f) 当研究得到联邦部门或政府机构支持，且根据 46.101 (b) 或 (i) 不得豁免或免除证书时，则需要证书。获得批准证书的机构应证明：保证本政策 46.103 监管下的每项研究申请或提案均已获得 IRB 的审核和批准。此类证明必须在提交申请或提案时提交，或在政府部门或政府机构规定的申请或提案提交日之后提交。未收到研究已获 IRB 审核和批准认证报告前，本政策46.103所覆盖的研究在任何情况下均不能得到支持。未得到覆盖研究批准保证的机构应在收到政府部门或政府机构对证书的要求后30天内，证明申请或提案已经得到IRB批准。如果未在此时限内提交证书，申请或提案可能会被退回至机构。

**46.104—46.106 ［保留］**

**46.107 IRB会员资格**

(a) 每个IRB应至少有5名成员，具有不同的背景，以促进对该机构通常进行的研究活动进行完整和充分的审核。IRB成员的经验和专业知识应足够合格，在成员的多样性方面应考虑到各种因素，包括种族、性别、文化背景，以及社区态度问题的敏感性，以促进维护受试者权利和福祉，尊重其咨询意见和建议。除拥有审核具体研究活动所需的专业能力外，IRB还可以依照机构承诺和法规、适用法律以及专业行为和实践标准确定拟议研究的可接受性。因此IRB应包含在这些领域有专业知识的人员。如果IRB定期审核涉及弱势群体的研究，如儿童、囚犯、孕妇、残障人士，则应考虑纳入一名或多名对这类受试者有专业知识和工作经验的成员。

(b) 需尽力避免歧视，保证IRB不完全由男性或完全由女性组成，包括该机构对两种性别人员胜任能力的考虑，保证IRB的决策不基于性别作出。IRB不能完全由同一职业的成员组成。

(c) 每个IRB应至少包括一名其主要关注点在科学领域的成员，至少有一名其主要关注点在非科学领域的成员。

(d) 每个IRB应至少包括一名不附属于该机构的成员，且该成员无附属于该机构的直系亲属。

(e) 除提供IRB要求的信息外，IRB不得有与项目有利益冲突的成员参与项目的初始或持续审核。

(f) IRB可以自行决定邀请在特殊领域有专业能力的专家协助审核超出IRB专业知识范围的问题，或作为已有IRB的补充。这些人不得参与IRB投票。

## 46.108 IRB 的功能和操作

为了满足本政策的要求，IRB 应：

(a) 遵循 46.103 (b) (4) 及 46.103 (b) (5) 里详细描述的书面程序。

(b) 除使用快速审核程序外（见 46.110），在大多数成员参加的会议上审核拟议研究，其中至少有一名主要关注点在非科学领域的成员。为使研究获得批准，应当获得出席会议的大多数成员批准。

## 46.109 IRB 审核研究

(a) IRB 应审核并有权批准、要求修改（以获得批准）或不批准本政策覆盖的研究活动。

(b) IRB 应要求作为知情同意的一部分提供给受试者的信息符合 46.116 的要求。除了 46.116 中特别提到的信息外，如 IRB 认为额外的信息有助于保护受试者的权利和福祉，IRB 可要求向受试者提供额外的信息。

(c) IRB 应要求提供知情同意书，或根据 46.117 的规定放弃对知情同意书的要求。

(d) IRB 应以书面形式通知研究者和机构 IRB 批准或不批准、或通过修改才能批准研究活动的决定。如果 IRB 决定不批准研究活动，应书面给出 IRB 做出不批准决定的理由，并提供研究者亲自或以书面形式做出回应的机会。

(e) IRB 应对本政策覆盖的研究按研究的风险程度每隔一段时间适当地进行持续审核，不得少于一年一次，并有权观察或让第三方观察知情同意过程。

## 46.110 快速审核程序，涉及不高于最低风险的某些研究，以及批准研究的微小变更

(a) 美国卫生与公众服务部部长已建立并公布了联邦登记通知，列表说明可由 IRB 通过快速审核程序的研究种类。在咨询其他部门和机构后，将酌情对清单进行增补，通过部长在联邦登记处定期公布。该清单副本可从人类研究保护办公室、美国卫生与公众服务部或任何后续办公室获得。

(b) IRB 可采用快速审核程序审核以下任一种或两种试验：

（1）列表中出现的部分或全部研究，审评员发现其涉及的风险不高于最低风险。

（2）以前批准的研究在授权期内（一年或更短）有微小改变。

快速审核程序下，审核可由 IRB 主席或主席指定的一名或多名有经验的审评员执行。在审核研究时，审评员可以行使 IRB 的所有权利，但不能做出否决研究的决定。研究活动只能按 46.108（b）的规定进行非快速程序审核之后才能被否决。

（c）使用快速审核程序的 IRB 应采用某种方法使所有成员均了解根据快速审核程序批准的研究提案。

（d）政府部门或政府机构负责人可以限制、暂停、终止或选择不授权给机构或 IRB 使用快速审核程序。

## 46.111 IRB 批准研究的标准

（a）为了批准本政策所涉及的研究，IRB 应确定满足以下所有要求：

（1）对受试者的风险最小化：（i）通过使用良好研究设计程序，避免不必要地将受试者暴露于风险中，以及（ii）在适当的时候，使用受试者曾接受过的治疗措施为受试者进行诊断和治疗。

（2）受试者的风险与预期利益（如有）以及可合理预期获得知识的重要性相比是合理的。在评估风险和受益时，IRB 应仅考虑研究可能带来的风险和受益（这些风险和受益有别于受试者即使不参与研究而接受治疗的医学风险和受益）。IRB 不应考虑应用研究所得知识可能带来的长期效果（例如，研究对公共政策的可能影响），因为评估研究风险属于其职责范围。

（3）受试者的选择公平。在进行评估时，IRB 应考虑研究的目的和研究的背景，特别关注涉及弱势群体，如儿童、囚犯、孕妇、精神障碍人士、经济或教育弱势群体的特殊问题。

（4）根据 46.116，将要求对每个潜在受试者或其法定授权代表进行知情同意。

(5) 根据46.117要求，将适当记录知情同意过程。

(6) 适当时，研究计划中对监查收集的数据有充分规定，以确保受试者安全。

(7) 适当时，有充分规定来保护受试者的隐私，并维护数据的保密性。

(b) 当部分或全部受试者为易受到胁迫或不当影响的弱势人群，如儿童、囚犯、孕妇、精神障碍人士、经济或教育弱势群体，研究还应有额外保障措施来保护这些受试者的权利和福祉。

## 46.112 机构审核

由IRB批准的本政策覆盖的研究可能会受到FDA官员进一步审核，FDA官员可批准或不批准研究。如未获得IRB的批准，FDA官员不能批准研究。

## 46.113 暂停或终止IRB批准的研究

研究未按照IRB要求进行或出现与研究相关的受试者意外严重伤害时，IRB有权暂停或终止已批准的研究。IRB应提供暂停或终止批准行动的理由，并及时向研究者、相关机构官员以及政府部门或FDA负责人报告。

## 46.114 合作研究

合作研究项目是指本政策监管的涉及多个研究机构的项目。在开展合作研究项目时，各研究机构负责保护人类受试者的权利和福祉，并遵守此政策。在政府部门或政府机构负责人的批准下，对参与合作项目的研究机构可以安排联合审核，依靠另一合格IRB进行审核，或做类似安排，避免重复工作。

## 46.115 IRB记录

(a) 机构或IRB应充分准备和维护对IRB活动的记录，记录包含以下内容：

(1) 所有研究项目的审核副本，配合提案的科学评估（如有），批准的知情同意书样本，研究者提交的进度报告以及对受试者造成伤害的报告。

(2) IRB会议纪要应详细列出出席会议人员；IRB采取的行

动；对所述行动进行的表决，包括赞成、反对和弃权的成员人数；要求进行更改或不批准研究的原因；以及就有争议问题及其解决方案进行讨论的书面摘要。

(3) 持续审核活动记录。

(4) IRB与研究者之间的所有通信副本。

(5) 如46.103 (b) (3) 所描述的具体IRB成员名单。

(6) 如46.103 (b) (4) 和46.103 (b) (5) 所描述的具体IRB书面操作规程。

(7) 根据46.116 (b) (5) 要求，将向受试者提供重要新发现的声明。

(b) 本政策要求记录应保留至少3年，进行研究的记录在研究完成后至少保留3年。所有记录应在合理时间以合理方式供政府部门或FDA授权代表视察和复印。

**46.116 知情同意的一般要求**

除非已经获得受试者或其法定授权代表具有法律效力的知情同意书，研究者不得将人作为研究的受试者，本政策其他地方另有规定除外。研究者只有在提供潜在受试者或法定授权代表足够多的时间考虑是否参与，并在尽可能减少强制或不当影响的情况下才能寻求知情同意。受试者或其授权代表提供信息时，应使用该受试者或授权代表可以理解的语言。无论是口头还是书面知情同意书均不得包含任何免责声明，以及不得通过免责声明，让受试者或其授权代表放弃或看似放弃合法权利，或免除或看似免除研究者、申办者、研究机构或其代理机构的疏忽责任。

(a) 知情同意的基本要素。本节 (c) 或 (d) 段规定除外，在寻求知情同意时应向每个受试者提供以下信息：

(1) 试验涉及研究的陈述，解释研究目的以及预期受试者参与期限，对需遵循试验步骤的描述以及指出哪些步骤是试验性的。

(2) 对受试者合理可预见风险或不适的描述。

(3) 对受试者或他人可合理预期益处的描述。

(4) 对受试者可能有利的适当的替代操作或治疗方案的披露（如有）。

(5) 对维护受试者身份记录的保密性及保密程度的陈述（如有）。

(6) 对涉及高于最低风险的研究，解释是否有任何补偿，以及如果发生伤害，是否有任何可采取的医疗措施，如有，包含什么，或从何处可以获得更多信息。

(7) 解释与谁联系来解答关于研究和受试者权利的相关问题，以及在出现与研究相关的对受试者造成损害的情况下与谁联系的说明。

(8) 声明参与研究是自愿的，拒绝参与研究不会给受试者带来惩罚或失去任何原本享有的利益，且受试者可以随时停止参与研究，而不会给受试者带来惩罚或失去原本享有的利益。

(b) 知情同意的附加要素。在适当的情况下，应向每位受试者提供以下一个或多个信息：

(1) 特定的治疗方法或手术可能对受试者（或若受试者已经或可能怀孕，对胚胎或胎儿）造成目前不可预见风险的声明。

(2) 研究者可在不考虑受试者同意的情况下终止受试者参与试验的情形。

(3) 可能因参与研究而对受试者产生的任何额外费用。

(4) 受试者决定退出研究的后果，以及有序终止受试者参与研究的程序。

(5) 当研究过程中出现重大新问题，可能影响到受试者继续参与试验的意愿时，将向受试者提供该新信息的声明。

(6) 参与研究受试者的大概数量。

(c) IRB可以批准不包含或改变上述知情同意部分或全部要素的知情同意书，或者放弃对获得知情同意书的要求，前提是IRB发现和记录如下情形：

(1) 研究或示范项目是由国家或地方政府官员执行或经其批准，目的是研究、评估或检查：(i) 公益或服务项目；(ii) 在这些项目下获得利益或服务的程序；(iii) 这些项目或程序的可能变化或替代方案；(iv) 这些项目利益或服务的付款方法或数额的可能变化。

(2) 如果不豁免或变更要求，研究无法实际进行。

(d) IRB 可以批准未包含或改变本节所列部分或全部知情同意要素的知情同意书，或者放弃获得知情同意书的规定，前提是 IRB 发现且记录如下情形：

(1) 研究涉及受试者的风险不高于最低风险。

(2) 豁免或变更不会对受试者权利和福祉产生不利影响。

(3) 如果不豁免或变更要求，研究无法实际进行。

(4) 适当时，受试者在参加试验后将获得额外相关信息。

(e) 本政策中对知情同意的要求并不是为了取代适用的联邦、州或当地法规，这些法规可要求披露额外信息以使知情同意具有法律效力。

(f) 根据适用的联邦、州或当地法规，本政策中的任何内容均不得限制医生在其许可范围内提供紧急医疗服务的权力。

### 46.117 知情同意记录

(a) 除本节（c）段另有规定外，知情同意记录应使用 IRB 批准的书面知情同意书，由受试者或受试者法定授权代表签署。应向签署人发放所签署的知情同意书副本。

(b) 除本节（c）段另有规定外，知情同意书可能是以下之一：

(1) 书面知情同意文件包含 46.116 要求的知情同意要素。知情同意书可宣读给受试者或受试者法定授权代表，但无论采用哪种方式，研究者应在签署之前给予该受试者或授权代表足够的机会阅读。

(2) 简短版书面知情同意文件，声明 46.116 要求的知情同意要素已向受试者或受试者法定授权代表口头表述。当采用这种方法时，应该有口头表达的见证人。此外，IRB 还应批准对该受试者或授权代表所说内容的书面摘要。受试者或其授权代表只需签署简短知情同意文件。见证人应当签署简短知情同意文件和摘要副本，实际获得知情同意的人应当签署摘要副本。除简短知情同意文件副本外，还应给予受试者或其授权代表摘要副本。

(c) IRB 可以放弃对研究者获得某些或所有受试者签署知情同意

书的要求，如果IRB发现如下情形：

(1) 联系受试者和研究的唯一记录是知情同意书，主要风险来自于违反保密性而造成的潜在危害。将向每个受试者询问受试者是否想要有与研究关联的记录，且满足受试者的意愿。

(2) 研究表明对受试者造成伤害的风险不高于最低风险，在研究背景外通常也不涉及需要进行书面同意的操作程序。

在免除知情同意要求的情形下，IRB可能要求研究者向受试者提供书面声明。

### 46.118　申请和提案缺乏明确的人类受试者参与计划

提交给政府部门或政府机构的某些类型基金申请、合作协议或合同，在提交时已知在支持期内研究可能涉及人类受试者，但通常不会在申请或提案中说明明确的计划。其中包括机构负责选择特定项目的基金；需选择人类受试者的研究培训基金；也包括人类受试者对项目的参与程度决取决于仪器的完备、先前动物研究的实验结果或化合物的纯化程度的项目。在给出资金之前，不需要IRB对这些申请进行审核。但是，除非根据46.101(b)或(i)，对研究进行豁免，根据本政策规定，在项目被IRB审核批准并由机构提交给政府部门或政府机构认证前，任何人类受试者不得参与由这些基金支持的项目。

### 46.119　无意涉及人类受试者的研究

对事先无意涉及人类受试者进行研究，但之后提议将人类受试者纳入研究，本政策规定：该研究应首先由IRB进行审核批准，由研究机构向政府部门或政府机构提交认证，由政府部门或政府机构对拟议的变更进行最终批准。

### 46.120　评估和处理由联邦部门或政府机构执行或支持的研究申请与提案

(a) 政府部门或政府机构负责人将通过政府官员和雇员以及政府部门或政府机构负责人指定的专家和顾问，评估提交给政府部门或政府机构涉及人类受试者的所有申请和提案。该评估将考虑到对受试者的风险，对这些风险的保护是否足够，研究对受试者和其他人的潜在利益，以及已获得或将获得知识的重要性。

(b) 在此评估基础上，政府部门或政府机构负责人可以批准或不批准申请或提案，或者经过谈判制定可批准的申请。

**46.121 ［保留］**

**46.122 使用联邦资金**

除非符合本政策要求，否则由政府部门或政府机构管理的联邦基金不得用于涉及人类受试者的研究。

**46.123 提前终止研究支持：评估申请和提案**

(a) 当政府部门或政府机构负责人发现研究机构实质上未能遵守本政策时，可要求支持项目的政府部门或政府机构以规定的方式，终止或暂停项目。

(b) 在做出支持或批准本政策监管的申请或建议时，除了所有资格要求和项目标准之外，政府部门或政府机构负责人还应考虑一些其他因素，诸如申请是否符合本条 (a) 段监管的终止或暂停条款，以及政府部门或政府机构负责人判断申请人或科学和技术方面的指导者是否履行了保护人类受试者权利和福祉的责任（无论研究是否受美国联邦法案监管）。

**46.124 条件**

对于所有研究项目，当政府部门或政府机构负责人判断需要附加条件来保护受试者时，可以在批准前或批准时施加附加条件。

## 子部分 B 涉及孕妇、胎儿和新生儿研究的额外保护

**46.201 规定适用范围？(略)**

**46.202 定义**

46.102 中的定义也适用于该子部分。另外，在该子部分中：

(a) **死胎** 指不显示心跳、自发呼吸活动、自发性肌肉运动、也无脐带脉动的胎儿。

(b) **分娩** 指通过排出或取出或以其他方式将胎儿与母亲完全分离。

(c) **胎儿** 指从着床到分娩的受精产物。

(d) **新生儿** 指刚出生的婴儿。

(e) **无法存活的新生儿** 指分娩后的新生儿，虽然存活，但不可能生存。

(f) **怀孕** 包括从着床到分娩的过程。如果妇女出现任何相关的妊娠迹象，例如不来月经，直至妊娠测试结果转为阴性或直至分娩，均视为孕妇。

(g) **部长** 指美国卫生与公众服务部部长，以及获授权的美国卫生与公众服务部其他政府官员或雇员。

(h) **存活的** 当此词与新生儿相关联时是指在分娩后能够生存（靠已有药物治疗）到独立维持心跳和呼吸。考虑到医疗的进步，部长将不定时在“联邦登记册”中公布用以帮助确定按本部分定义新生儿是否判断为存活的指南。如果新生儿是存活的，那么只有在允许的范围内才能将其纳入研究，并且需符合本部分子部分 A 和子部分 D 的要求。

### 46.203 IRB 在涉及孕妇、胎儿和新生儿相关研究的职责

除了根据本部分法规分配给 IRB 的其他职责外，IRB 还应审核本子部分法规监管的研究，IRB 仅能批准满足本子部分法规所有适用部分要求和本部分法规其他子部分要求的研究。

### 46.204 涉及孕妇或胎儿的研究

如果满足以下所有条件，孕妇或胎儿可以参与研究：

(a) 科学上可行，已经进行了包括对怀孕动物的临床前研究，以及对非妊娠妇女的临床研究，并提供对孕妇和胎儿潜在风险的评估数据。

(b) 对胎儿的风险仅由干预措施或干预过程造成，这些措施或过程对妇女或胎儿具有直接受益的前景；或者，如没有受益前景，但对胎儿的风险不高于最低风险，且研究目的是获得不能以其他方式获得的重要生物医学知识。

(c) 实现研究目标的风险已最小化。

(d) 如果研究对孕妇有直接受益的前景，直接受益的前景是针对

孕妇和胎儿，或虽然对孕妇和胎儿没有受益，但对他们的风险不高于最低风险，且研究目的是获得不能以其他方式获得的重要生物医学知识，孕妇的知情同意是根据本部分子部分A的知情同意规定获得的。

(e) 如果研究只对胎儿有直接受益的前景，则根据本部分法规子部分A的知情同意规定，需获得孕妇和胎儿父亲的知情同意，除非胎儿父亲由于不在、不胜任、暂时丧失行为能力，或怀孕是因强奸或乱伦而造成无法知情同意，则不要求胎儿父亲知情同意。

(f) 根据本节（d）或（e）段提供知情同意的每个人完全了解研究对胎儿或新生儿合理可预见的影响。

(g) 对46.402 (a) 所定义的儿童，按本部分子部分D的条款，获得知情同意和许可。

(h) 不提供任何货币或其他形式的诱惑，来终止妊娠。

(i) 从事研究的个人不会就终止妊娠的时间、方法或程序做出任何决定。

(j) 从事研究的个人不会参与判断新生儿的存活能力。

## 46.205 涉及新生儿的研究

(a) 如果满足以下所有条件，难以判断是否可以存活的新生儿和无法存活的新生儿可参与研究：

(1) 在科学可行情况下，已经进行了临床前研究和临床研究，并提供了对新生儿潜在风险的评估数据。

(2) 根据本节（b）(2）或（c）(5）段提供知情同意的每个人完全了解研究对新生儿的合理可预见的影响。

(3) 从事这项研究的个人不会参与判断新生儿的生存能力。

(4) 满足本节（b）或（c）段的适用要求。

(b) 生存能力不确定的新生儿。在确定新生儿是否可存活之前，除非符合以下附加条件，否则新生儿不能参与本子部分法规所涉及的研究：

(1) IRB确定：

(i) 研究有提高新生儿存活率的前景，并且为实现该目标，已将风险降至最低；或

(ii) 研究目的是得到不能以其他方式获得的重要生物医学知识，且不会对新生儿造成额外的风险。

(2) 获得新生儿父母中一方的法定有效知情同意书，或父母双方均因不在、不胜任、暂时丧失行为能力无法知情同意时，根据本部分子部分 A，需获得父母法定授权代表具有法律效力的知情同意。因强奸或乱伦造成怀孕，不需要获得父亲或其法定授权代表的知情同意。

(c) 无法存活的新生儿。分娩后，无法存活的新生儿不能参与本子部门监管的研究，除非满足以下所有附加条件：

(1) 新生儿生命功能不会靠人为维持。

(2) 研究不会终止新生儿心跳或呼吸。

(3) 研究不会对新生儿造成额外的风险。

(4) 研究目的是得到不能以其他方式获得的重要生物医学知识。

(5) 根据本部分子部分 A，需获得新生儿双亲法定有效知情同意书，授予豁免和不适用于 46.116 (c) 和 (d) 的规定除外。但是，如果一方父母由于不在、不胜任或临时丧失行为能力而无法知情同意，则获得不能存活新生儿的父母中另一方的知情同意就足以满足 (c)(5) 段要求。如果因强奸或乱伦造成的怀孕，不需要获得父亲的知情同意。无法存活新生儿父母一方或两方的法定授权代表的知情同意不足以满足 (c)(5) 的要求。

(d) 存活的新生儿。分娩后被确定为存活的新生儿仅在符合本部分子部分 A 和 D 的要求下才能被纳入研究。

## 46.206 研究涉及分娩后胎盘、死胎或胎儿物质

(a) 涉及分娩后胎盘、死胎、胎儿物质，或者从死胎得到的细胞、组织或器官的研究，只能根据适用的联邦、州或当地有关此类活动的法律和法规进行。

(b) 如果出于研究目的，记录与本节 (a) 段所述物质有关的信息，可以直接或通过与受试者个体相关联的标识符号识别参与研究的个体，这些个体为研究受试者，本部分法规所有相关的子部分条款均对其适用。

### 46.207 不批准研究就没有机会进行了解、预防或减轻影响孕妇、胎儿或新生儿健康或福祉的严重问题

仅在满足以下条件下，美国卫生和公众服务部部长可以同意执行或资助 IRB 认为未满足 46.204 或 46.205 要求的研究：

(a) IRB 发现研究提供了合理机会来进一步理解、预防或减轻影响孕妇、胎儿或新生儿健康或福祉的严重问题；

(b) 部长经咨询相关专业的专家小组（如科学、医药、伦理、法律），并提供机会进行公众意见审核，包括在联邦登记机构公布的公开会议上讨论，并已确定：

(1) 研究事实上符合 46.204 的适用条件。

(2) 或以下内容：

(i) 研究提供了合理机会来进一步了解、预防或减轻影响孕妇、胎儿或新生儿健康或福祉的严重问题。

(ii) 研究将按照良好道德原则进行。

(iii) 按照子部分 A 和本部分法规其他适用子部分的知情同意规定，将获得知情同意书。

## 子部分 C　涉及将囚犯作为受试者的生物医学和行为研究的附加保护

### 46.301 适用范围（略）

### 46.302 目的

囚犯因监禁而受到限制，可能会影响到他/她做出真正自愿和非强迫的、是否作为受试者参与研究的决定。本子部分的目的是为参与该子部分适用活动的囚犯提供更多的保障措施。

### 46.303 定义

在本子部分中：

(a) **部长**　指美国卫生与公众服务部部长，以及获美国卫生与公众服务部授权的其他政府官员或雇员。

(b) **DHHS**　指美国卫生与公众服务部。

(c) **囚犯** 指在刑事机构内非自愿受限制或被拘留的个人。该术语包括根据刑事或民事法规判刑的个人；依照法令，或作为刑事起诉或在刑罚机关监禁的替代，被扣留在其他设施的个人；以及在审讯期间被羁押等候审判或判刑的个人。

(d) **最低风险** 指研究中预期对受试者造成的伤害或不适发生概率和程度不比受试者在日常生活中或在常规体检或心理检查中所遇到的更高。

## 46.304 囚犯参与研究时机构审查委员会的组成

除符合本部分46.107的要求外，机构审查委员会对本部分法规涉及的研究工作承担责任，也应符合下列具体要求：

(a) 除委员会成员外，委员会的多数（不包括囚犯成员）与参与研究的监狱无关。

(b) 至少有一名委员会成员是具有适当背景和经验、具有审核能力的囚犯或囚犯代表。除非特定研究项目需由一个以上的机构审查委员会审核，其他研究仅一个机构审查委员会可以满足这一要求。

## 46.305 机构审查委员会对囚犯参与研究的附加职责

(a) 除本部分法规规定的机构审查委员会所有其他责任外，机构审查委员会应审核本子部分所涉及的研究，只有在满足下列条件时才能批准研究：

(1) 研究是受46.306 (a) (2) 监管允许的研究类别之一。

(2) 与一般生活条件、医疗保健、食物质量、设施和在监狱的收入机会相比，囚犯通过参与研究而得到的可能优势不特别巨大，不会影响他/她在监狱有限的选择环境中衡量研究风险与优势的判断。

(3) 囚犯所接受的因研究所涉及的风险与不受监禁的志愿者接受的风险相等。

(4) 在监狱内选择受试者的程序对所有囚犯都是公平的，不受监狱当局或囚犯的任意干预。除非主要研究者向机构审查委员会提供书面说明要求遵循其他程序及其理由，否则对照性研究必须从满足特定研究项目所需特征的囚犯中随机选择对照受试者。

(5) 以受试者人群可以理解的语言表达相关信息。

(6) 有充分的保证说明假释委员会不会在做出是否同意假释决定时考虑到囚犯参与研究的事实，并且向每个囚犯事先明确告知：参与研究对他/她的假释没有影响。

(7) 审查委员会认为，在参与研究结束后可能需要对参与者进行后续检查或照料，已经对这种检查或照料做了适当的规定，将考虑到个别囚犯判刑时间的长短，并向参与者告知这一事实。

(b) 审查委员会须履行部长指派的其他职责。

(c) 研究机构须以部长规定的格式及方式，向部长证明该审查委员会已履行本节所述职责。

## 46.306 允许涉及囚犯的研究

(a) 仅在以下情况下，美国卫生与公众服务部进行或支持的生物医学或行为研究可能会涉及将囚犯作为受试者：

(1) 负责执行研究的机构已向部长证明，机构审查委员会已批准本子部分 46.305 监管的研究。

(2) 部长判断拟议研究仅涉及以下内容：

(i) 研究监禁可能的原因、影响、程序，以及犯罪行为，条件是该研究造成的风险不高于最低风险，仅仅对受试者造成不方便。

(ii) 对监狱体制结构或被监禁囚犯的研究，条件是该研究造成的风险不高于最低风险，仅仅对受试者造成不方便。

(iii) 将囚犯作为特别受影响的一类人的研究（例如，疫苗试验和肝炎的研究，肝炎在监狱中比其他地方更普遍发生；以及关于社会和心理问题如酗酒、吸毒成瘾和性侵的研究），只有在部长与包括刑事、医学和伦理学方面的相关专家咨询，并在联邦登记册上公布其批准这种研究的意向后，研究才能进行。

(iv) 在实践方面的研究，既创新又可被接受，有改善受试者健康或福祉的意图且有合理的可能性。如果这些研究需要以符合IRB批准方案的方式将囚犯分配到对照组，囚犯可能无法从研究中获益，则只有在部长咨询相关刑罚学、医药和道德专家，并在联邦注册局公布了批准此类研究的意向后才能进行研究。

(b) 除本节（a）段另有规定外，美国卫生与公众服务部进行或支持的生物医学或行为研究不得将囚犯作为受试者。

## 子部分D　研究中涉及儿童作为受试者的其他保护

### 46.401　本规定适用范围（略）

### 46.402　定义

子部分A 46.102中的定义也适用于本子部分。另外，在本子部分中：

(a) **儿童**　指按照研究实施地的适用法律，尚未达到法定年龄，不能知情同意接受研究治疗或试验程序的人。

(b) **同意**　指儿童对参与研究的肯定协议。仅未反对，没有提供肯定的同意，不应被解释为同意。

(c) **许可**　指家长或监护人同意其子女或受监护人参与研究。

(d) **父母**　指儿童的生物或收养父母。

(e) **监护人**　指根据适用国家或地方法规授权的个人，代表儿童同意进行常规医疗。

### 46.403　IRB的职责

除了根据本部分法规IRB的其他责任外，每个IRB都应审核本子部分所监管的研究，仅批准满足本子部分所有适用条件的研究。

### 46.404　不涉及高于最低风险的研究

在IRB发现研究的风险不高于最低风险，且在寻求儿童父母或监护人的知情同意方面已遵守46.408规定的情况下，美国卫生与公众服务部将进行或资助研究。

### 46.405 研究涉及的风险高于最低风险，但对受试者有直接受益的前景

IRB 发现干预或治疗措施的风险高于最低风险，但这些干预或治疗措施可以对受试者有直接受益的前景，或通过监控手段可能对受试者的福祉有帮助，只有在 IRB 发现下列情况时，美国卫生与公众服务部将进行或资助研究：

(a) 相对于受试者预期利益，所冒的风险是合理的。

(b) 对受试者预期利益与风险的关系至少与现有替代方法相比有利。

(c) 根据 46.408 规定，已对寻求儿童父母或监护人知情同意做了足够的规定。

### 46.406 研究涉及的风险大于最低风险，对个体受试者无直接受益前景，但可能获得关于受试者的疾病或病症的一般性知识

IRB 发现干预或治疗措施的风险高于最低风险，这些干预或治疗措施并未为受试者提供直接受益的前景，或通过监控手段不能对受试者的福祉有帮助，只有在 IRB 发现下列情况时，美国卫生与公众服务部将进行或资助研究：

(a) 增加的风险仅稍高于最低风险。

(b) 干预或治疗措施给受试者的体验与实际或预期的医疗、牙科、心理、社会或教育情形中原有的内容基本相同。

(c) 干预或治疗措施可能获得关于受试者功能失调或病症的一般性知识，这对于了解或改善受试者的功能失调或病症至关重要。

(d) 根据 46.408 规定，已对寻求儿童父母或监护人知情同意做了足够的规定。

### 46.407 不批准研究就没有机会了解、预防或减轻影响儿童健康或福祉的严重问题

IRB 认为研究未符合 46.404、46.405 或 46.406 要求时，只有在以下情况下，美国卫生与公众服务部将进行或资助研究：

(a) IRB 认为研究提供了合理机会进一步了解、预防或减轻影响

儿童健康或福祉的严重问题。

(b) 部长经咨询有关专业的专家小组（如科学、医学、教育、道德、法律），并提供机会进行公众审核和评论后，并已确定。

(1) 该研究事实上符合 46.404，46.405 或 46.406 的条件。

(2) 或以下条件：

(i) 研究提供了合理机会进一步了解、预防或减轻影响儿童健康或福祉的严重问题。

(ii) 研究将按照良好道德原则进行。

(iii) 根据 46.408 规定，已对寻求儿童父母或监护人知情同意做了足够的规定。

## 46.408 父母或监护人许可儿童参与研究的要求

(a) 在本子分部其他适用规定的基础上，IRB 在判断儿童有能力提供知情同意时，还应明确已经为征求儿童知情同意做出足够的规定。在判断儿童是否有能力进行知情同意时，IRB 应考虑到相关儿童的年龄、成熟度和心理状态等因素。此判断可根据特定方案，为所有参与研究的儿童做出；或 IRB 认为适当时，为每一个儿童单独做出。如果 IRB 判断某些或全部儿童的能力都非常受限，以致无法合理地进行咨询，或者该研究所涉及的干预或治疗措施有对儿童直接受益的前景，可能对儿童的健康或福祉至关重要，且只有通过研究才能得到，在此情况下，儿童的知情同意不是进行研究的必要条件。即使 IRB 确定受试者能够进行知情同意，IRB 仍可以在符合子部分 A 46.116 的情况下放弃对知情同意的要求。

(b) 在本子部分其他适用规定的基础上，根据子部分 A 46.116 要求，IRB 还应明确已经为寻求每个儿童父母或监护人的知情同意做出足够的规定。在需获得父母同意的情况下，IRB 可能会发现根据 46.404 或 46.405 进行的研究，只需要父母中一方许可。如果研究受 46.406 和 46.407 监管，并需得到父母双方的许可，则必须父母双方均给出他们的知情同意，除非父母中一方死亡、未知、没有能力或不在或只有一方在照顾和监护儿童。

(c) 在子部分 A46.116 规定的豁免条款的基础上，如果 IRB

确定研究方案是为特殊的情况或特殊的受试者群体设计，从保护受试者的角度考虑，获得这部分人群父母或监护人知情同意并不合理（如被忽视或被虐待的儿童），可以放弃本部分子部分 A 和本节（b）段对知情同意的要求，而采用适当替代机制来保护作为受试者参与研究的儿童，并进一步规定：豁免知情同意并不违背联邦、州或当地法律。适当替代机制的选择将取决于方案中描述的活动性质和目的、受试者风险和预期利益，以及受试者年龄、成熟度、状态和健康状况。

（d）父母或监护人的知情同意应按照子部分 A 46.117 的要求进行记录。

（e）当 IRB 确定需要知情同意时，还应明确是否以及如何记录知情同意过程。

### 46.409 受监护的儿童

（a）根据 46.406 或 46.407，只有下列情况下才能将在国家或其他机关、机构或实体受监护的未成年人纳入研究：

（1）研究与儿童受监护的状况相关；

（2）或在学校、营地、医院、机构或类似场所进行，其中参与研究的大多数儿童不是受监护的儿童。

（b）如果研究是根据本节（a）段批准的，IRB 除了要求为每位受监护的儿童有监护人或以父母身份代表其利益外，还应要求为每位受监护的儿童指定代言人。一个人可以担任多个儿童的代言人。代言人应是具有保护儿童背景和经验的个人，在儿童参与研究期间介入且同意介入，帮助儿童获得最大利益。他们与此研究、与研究者或监护组织都无关联（作为代言人或 IRB 的成员除外）。

## 子部分 E 机构审查委员会的登记（略）

# ICH

## GUIDELINE FOR GOOD CLINICAL PRACTICE (GCP)
## (E6_R2)

Current Step 4 version
dated 9 November 2016

## E6 (R1)
## Document History

| First Codification | History | Date | New Codification November 2005 |
|---|---|---|---|
| E6 | Approval by the Steering Committee under Step 2 and release for public consultation. | 27 April 1995 | E6 |
| E6 | Approval by the Steering Committee under Step 4 and recommended for adoption to the three ICH regulatory bodies. | 1 May 1996 | E6 |

## E6 (R1) Step 4 version

| | | | |
|---|---|---|---|
| E6 | Approval by the Steering Committee of Post-Step 4 editorial corrections. | 10 June 1996 | E6 (R1) |

### Current E6 (R2) Addendum Step 4 version

| Code | History | Date |
|---|---|---|
| E6 (R2) | Adoption by the Regulatory Members of the ICH Assembly under Step 4.<br>Integrated Addendum to ICH E6 (R1) document. Changes are integrated directly into the following sections of the parental Guideline: Introduction, 1.63, 1.64, 1.65, 2.10, 2.13, 4.2.5, 4.2.6, 4.9.0, 5.0, 5.0.1, 5.0.2, 5.0.3, 5.0.4, 5.0.5, 5.0.6, 5.0.7, 5.2.2, 5.5.3 (a), 5.5.3 (b), 5.5.3 (h), 5.18.3, 5.18.6 (e), 5.18.7, 5.20.1, 8.1 | 9 November 2016 |

***Legal notice**: This document is protected by copyright and may be used, reproduced, incorporated into other works, adapted, modified, translated or distributed under a public license provided that ICH's copyright in the document is acknowledged at all times. In case of any adaption, modification or translation of the document, reasonable steps must be*

*taken to clearly label, demarcate or otherwise identify that changes were made to or based on the original document. Any impression that the adaption, modification or translation of the original document is endorsed or sponsored by the ICH must be avoided.*
*The document is provided "as is" without warranty of any kind. In no event shall the ICH or the authors of the original document be liable for any claim, damages or other liability arising from the use of the document.*
*The above-mentioned permissions do not apply to content supplied by third parties. Therefore, for documents where the copyright vests in a third party, permission for reproduction must be obtained from this copyright holder.*

# Introduction

Good Clinical Practice (GCP) is an international ethical and scientific quality standard for designing, conducting, recording and reporting trials that involve the participation of human subjects. Compliance with this standard provides public assurance that the rights, safety and well-being of trial subjects are protected, consistent with the principles that have their origin in the Declaration of Helsinki, and that the clinical trial data are credible.
The objective of this ICH GCP Guideline is to provide a unified standard for the European Union (EU), Japan and the United States to facilitate the mutual acceptance of clinical data by the regulatory authorities in these jurisdictions.
The guideline was developed with consideration of the current good clinical practices of the European Union, Japan, and the United States, as well as those of Australia, Canada, the Nordic countries and the World Health Organization (WHO).
This guideline should be followed when generating clinical trial data that are intended to be submitted to regulatory authorities.
The principles established in this guideline may also be applied to other clinical investigations that may have an impact on the safety and well-being of human subjects.

**Addendum**

Since the development of the ICH GCP Guideline, the scale, complexity, and cost of clinical trials have increased. Evolutions in technology and risk management processes offer new opportunities to increase efficiency and focus on relevant activities. When the original ICH E6 (R1) text was prepared, clinical trials were performed in a largely paper-based process. Advances in use of electronic data recording and reporting facilitate implementation of other approaches. For example, centralized monitoring can now offer a greater advantage, to a broader range of trials than is suggested in the original text. Therefore, this guideline has been amended to encourage implementation of improved and more efficient approaches to clinical trial design, conduct, oversight, recording and reporting while continuing to ensure human subject protection and reliability of trial results. Standards regarding electronic records and essential documents intended to increase clinical trial quality and efficiency have also been updated.

This guideline should be read in conjunction with other ICH guidelines relevant to the conduct of clinical trials (e. g. , E2A (clinical safety data management) , E3 (clinical study reporting) , E7 (geriatric populations) , E8 (general considerations for clinical trials) , E9 (statistical principles) , and E11 (pediatric populations) ) .

This ICH GCP Guideline Integrated Addendum provides a unified standard for the European Union, Japan, the United States, Canada, and Switzerland to facilitate the mutual acceptance of data from clinical trials by the regulatory authorities in these jurisdictions. In the event of any conflict between the E6 (R1) text and the E6 (R2) addendum text, the E6 (R2) addendum text should take priority.

# 1. Glossary

## 1. 1 Adverse Drug Reaction (ADR)

In the pre-approval clinical experience with a new medicinal product or its new usages, particularly as the therapeutic dose (s) may not be established: all noxious and unintended responses to a medicinal product related to any dose should be considered adverse drug reactions. The phrase responses to a medicinal product means that a causal relationship between a medicinal product and an adverse event is at least a reasonable possibility, i. e., the relationship cannot be ruled out.

Regarding marketed medicinal products: a response to a drug which is noxious and unintended and which occurs at doses normally used in man for prophylaxis, diagnosis, or therapy of diseases or for modification of physiological function (see the ICH Guideline for Clinical Safety Data Management: Definitions and Standards for Expedited Reporting).

### 1.2 Adverse Event (AE)

Any untoward medical occurrence in a patient or clinical investigation subject administered a pharmaceutical product and which does not necessarily have a causal relationship with this treatment. An adverse event (AE) can therefore be any unfavourable and unintended sign (including an abnormal laboratory finding), symptom, or disease temporally associated with the use of a medicinal (investigational) product, whether or not related to the medicinal (investigational) product (see the ICH Guideline for Clinical Safety Data Management: Definitions and Standards for Expedited Reporting).

### 1.3 Amendment (to the protocol)

See Protocol Amendment.

### 1.4 Applicable Regulatory Requirement(s)

Any law(s) and regulation(s) addressing the conduct of clinical trials of investigational products.

### 1.5 Approval (in relation to Institutional Review Boards)

The affirmative decision of the IRB that the clinical trial has been reviewed and may be conducted at the institution site within the constraints set forth by the IRB, the institution, Good Clinical Practice (GCP), and the applicable regulatory requirements.

### 1.6 Audit

A systematic and independent examination of trial related activities and documents to determine whether the evaluated trial related activities were conducted, and the data were recorded, analyzed and accurately reported according to the protocol, sponsor's standard operating procedures (SOPs), Good Clinical Practice (GCP), and the applicable regulatory requirement(s).

### 1.7 Audit Certificate

A declaration of confirmation by the auditor that an audit has taken place.

### 1.8 Audit Report

A written evaluation by the sponsor's auditor of the results of the audit.

### 1.9 Audit Trail

Documentation that allows reconstruction of the course of events.

### 1.10 Blinding/Masking

A procedure in which one or more parties to the trial are kept unaware of the treatment assignment(s). Single-blinding usually refers to the subject(s) being unaware, and double-blinding usually refers to the subject(s), investigator(s), monitor, and, in some cases, data analyst(s) being unaware of the treatment assignment(s).

### 1.11 Case Report Form (CRF)

A printed, optical, or electronic document designed to record all of the protocol required information to be reported to the sponsor on each trial subject.

### 1.12 Clinical Trial/Study

Any investigation in human subjects intended to discover or verify the clinical, pharmacological and/or other pharmacodynamic effects of an investigational product(s), and/or to identify any adverse reactions to an investigational product(s), and/or to study absorption, distribution, metabolism, and excretion of an investigational product(s) with the object of ascertaining its safety and/or efficacy. The terms clinical trial and clinical study are synonymous.

### 1.13 Clinical Trial/Study Report

A written description of a trial/study of any therapeutic, prophylactic, or diagnostic agent conducted in human subjects, in which the clinical and statistical description, presentations, and analyses are fully integrated into a single report (see the ICH Guideline for Structure and Content of Clinical Study Reports).

### 1.14 Comparator (Product)

An investigational or marketed product (i.e., active control), or placebo, used as a reference in a clinical trial.

### 1.15 Compliance (in relation to trials)

Adherence to all the trial-related requirements, Good Clinical Practice (GCP) requirements, and the applicable regulatory requirements.

### 1.16 Confidentiality

Prevention of disclosure, to other than authorized individuals, of a sponsor's proprietary information or of a subject's identity.

### 1.17 Contract

A written, dated, and signed agreement between two or more involved parties that sets out any arrangements on delegation and distribution of tasks and obligations and, if appropriate, on financial matters. The protocol may serve as the basis of a contract.

### 1.18 Coordinating Committee

A committee that a sponsor may organize to coordinate the conduct of a multicentre trial.

### 1.19 Coordinating Investigator

An investigator assigned the responsibility for the coordination of investigators at different centres participating in a multicentre trial.

### 1.20 Contract Research Organization (CRO)

A person or an organization (commercial, academic, or other) contracted by the sponsor to perform one or more of a sponsor's trial-related duties and functions.

### 1.21 Direct Access

Permission to examine, analyze, verify, and reproduce any records and reports that are important to evaluation of a clinical trial. Any party (e. g., domestic and foreign regulatory authorities, sponsor's monitors and auditors) with direct access should take all reasonable precautions within the constraints of the applicable regulatory requirement (s) to maintain the confidentiality of subjects' identities and sponsor's proprietary information.

### 1.22 Documentation

All records, in any form (including, but not limited to, written, electronic, magnetic, and optical records, and scans, x-rays, and electrocardiograms) that describe or record the methods, conduct, and/or results of a trial, the factors affecting a trial, and the actions taken.

### 1. 23 Essential Documents

Documents which individually and collectively permit evaluation of the conduct of a study and the quality of the data produced (see 8. Essential Documents for the Conduct of a Clinical Trial).

### 1. 24 Good Clinical Practice (GCP)

A standard for the design, conduct, performance, monitoring, auditing, recording, analyses, and reporting of clinical trials that provides assurance that the data and reported results are credible and accurate, and that the rights, integrity, and confidentiality of trial subjects are protected.

### 1. 25 Independent Data-Monitoring Committee (IDMC) (Data and Safety Monitoring Board, Monitoring Committee, Data Monitoring Committee)

An independent data-monitoring committee that may be established by the sponsor to assess at intervals the progress of a clinical trial, the safety data, and the critical efficacy endpoints, and to recommend to the sponsor whether to continue, modify, or stop a trial.

### 1. 26 Impartial Witness

A person, who is independent of the trial, who cannot be unfairly influenced by people involved with the trial, who attends the informed consent process if the subject or the subject's legally acceptable representative cannot read, and who reads the informed consent form and any other written information supplied to the subject.

### 1. 27 Independent Ethics Committee (IEC)

An independent body (a review board or a committee, institutional, regional, national, or supranational), constituted of medical professionals and non-medical members, whose responsibility it is to ensure the protection of the rights, safety and well-being of human subjects involved in a trial and to provide public assurance of that protection, by, among other things, reviewing and approving/providing favourable opinion on, the trial protocol, the suitability of the investigator(s), facilities, and the methods and material to be used in obtaining and documenting informed consent of the trial subjects.

The legal status, composition, function, operations and regulatory requirements pertaining to Independent Ethics Committees may differ among countries, but should allow the Independent Ethics Committee to act in agreement with GCP as described in this guideline.

### 1. 28 Informed Consent

A process by which a subject voluntarily confirms his or her willingness to participate in a particular trial, after having been informed of all aspects of the trial that are relevant to the subject's decision to participate. Informed consent is documented by means of a written, signed and dated informed consent form.

### 1. 29 Inspection

The act by a regulatory authority (ies) of conducting an official review of documents, facilities, records, and any other resources that are deemed by the authority (ies) to be related to the clinical trial and that may be located at the site of the trial, at the sponsor's and/or contract research organization's (CRO's) facilities, or at other establishments deemed appropriate by the regulatory authority (ies).

### 1. 30 Institution (medical)

Any public or private entity or agency or medical or dental facility where clinical trials are conducted.

### 1. 31 Institutional Review Board (IRB)

An independent body constituted of medical, scientific, and non-scientific members, whose responsibility is to ensure the protection of the rights, safety and well-being of human subjects involved in a trial by, among other things, reviewing, approving, and providing continuing review of trial protocol and amendments and of the methods and material to be used in obtaining and documenting informed consent of the trial subjects.

### 1. 32 Interim Clinical Trial/Study Report

A report of intermediate results and their evaluation based on analyses performed during the course of a trial.

### 1. 33 Investigational Product

A pharmaceutical form of an active ingredient or placebo being tested or used as a reference in a clinical trial, including a product with a marketing authorization when used or assembled (formulated or packaged) in a way different from the approved form, or when used for an unapproved indication, or when used to gain further information about an approved use.

## 1. 34 Investigator

A person responsible for the conduct of the clinical trial at a trial site. If a trial is conducted by a team of individuals at a trial site, the investigator is the responsible leader of the team and may be called the principal investigator. See also Subinvestigator.

## 1. 35 Investigator/Institution

An expression meaning "the investigator and/or institution, where required by the applicable regulatory requirements" .

## 1. 36 Investigator's Brochure

A compilation of the clinical and nonclinical data on the investigational product(s) which is relevant to the study of the investigational product (s) in human subjects (see 7. Investigator's Brochure) .

## 1. 37 Legally Acceptable Representative

An individual or juridical or other body authorized under applicable law to consent, on behalf of a prospective subject, to the subject's participation in the clinical trial.

## 1. 38 Monitoring

The act of overseeing the progress of a clinical trial, and of ensuring that it is conducted, recorded, and reported in accordance with the protocol, Standard Operating Procedures (SOPs), Good Clinical Practice (GCP), and the applicable regulatory requirement(s) .

## 1. 39 Monitoring Report

A written report from the monitor to the sponsor after each site visit and/or other trial-related communication according to the sponsor's SOPs.

## 1. 40 Multicentre Trial

A clinical trial conducted according to a single protocol but at more than one site, and therefore, carried out by more than one investigator.

## 1. 41 Nonclinical Study

Biomedical studies not performed on human subjects.

## 1. 42 Opinion (in relation to Independent Ethics Committee)

The judgement and/or the advice provided by an Independent Ethics Committee (IEC) .

### 1. 43 Original Medical Record

See Source Documents.

### 1. 44 Protocol

A document that describes the objective (s), design, methodology, statistical considerations, and organization of a trial. The protocol usually also gives the background and rationale for the trial, but these could be provided in other protocol referenced documents. Throughout the ICH GCP Guideline the term protocol refers to protocol and protocol amendments.

### 1. 45 Protocol Amendment

A written description of a change(s) to or formal clarification of a protocol.

### 1. 46 Quality Assurance (QA)

All those planned and systematic actions that are established to ensure that the trial is performed and the data are generated, documented (recorded), and reported in compliance with Good Clinical Practice (GCP) and the applicable regulatory requirement(s).

### 1. 47 Quality Control (QC)

The operational techniques and activities undertaken within the quality assurance system to verify that the requirements for quality of the trial-related activities have been fulfilled.

### 1. 48 Randomization

The process of assigning trial subjects to treatment or control groups using an element of chance to determine the assignments in order to reduce bias.

### 1. 49 Regulatory Authorities

Bodies having the power to regulate. In the ICH GCP Guideline the expression Regulatory Authorities includes the authorities that review submitted clinical data and those that conduct inspections (see 1. 29). These bodies are sometimes referred to as competent authorities.

### 1. 50 Serious Adverse Event (SAE) or Serious Adverse Drug Reaction (Serious ADR)

Any untoward medical occurrence that at any dose:

- results in death,
- is life-threatening,
- requires inpatient hospitalization or prolongation of existing hospitalization,

- results in persistent or significant disability/incapacity,

or

- is a congenital anomaly/birth defect

(see the ICH Guideline for Clinical Safety Data Management: Definitions and Standards for Expedited Reporting).

### 1.51 Source Data

All information in original records and certified copies of original records of clinical findings, observations, or other activities in a clinical trial necessary for the reconstruction and evaluation of the trial. Source data are contained in source documents (original records or certified copies).

### 1.52 Source Documents

Original documents, data, and records (e.g., hospital records, clinical and office charts, laboratory notes, memoranda, subjects' diaries or evaluation checklists, pharmacy dispensing records, recorded data from automated instruments, copies or transcriptions certified after verification as being accurate copies, microfiches, photographic negatives, microfilm or magnetic media, x-rays, subject files, and records kept at the pharmacy, at the laboratories and at medico-technical departments involved in the clinical trial).

### 1.53 Sponsor

An individual, company, institution, or organization which takes responsibility for the initiation, management, and/or financing of a clinical trial.

### 1.54 Sponsor-Investigator

An individual who both initiates and conducts, alone or with others, a clinical trial, and under whose immediate direction the investigational product is administered to, dispensed to, or used by a subject. The term does not include any person other than an individual (e.g., it does not include a corporation or an agency). The obligations of a sponsor-investigator include both those of a sponsor and those of an investigator.

### 1.55 Standard Operating Procedures (SOPs)

Detailed, written instructions to achieve uniformity of the performance of a specific function.

### 1.56 Subinvestigator

Any individual member of the clinical trial team designated and supervised by the investigator at a trial site to perform critical trial-related procedures and/or to make important trial-related decisions (e. g. , associates, residents, research fellows) . See also Investigator.

### 1. 57 Subject/Trial Subject

An individual who participates in a clinical trial, either as a recipient of the investigational product(s) or as a control.

### 1. 58 Subject Identification Code

A unique identifier assigned by the investigator to each trial subject to protect the subject's identity and used in lieu of the subject's name when the investigator reports adverse events and/or other trial related data.

### 1. 59 Trial Site

The location(s) where trial-related activities are actually conducted.

### 1. 60 Unexpected Adverse Drug Reaction

An adverse reaction, the nature or severity of which is not consistent with the applicable product information (e. g. , Investigator's Brochure for an unapproved investigational product or package insert/summary of product characteristics for an approved product) (see the ICH Guideline for Clinical Safety Data Management: Definitions and Standards for Expedited Reporting) .

### 1. 61 Vulnerable Subjects

Individuals whose willingness to volunteer in a clinical trial may be unduly influenced by the expectation, whether justified or not, of benefits associated with participation, or of a retaliatory response from senior members of a hierarchy in case of refusal to participate. Examples are members of a group with a hierarchical structure, such as medical, pharmacy, dental, and nursing students, subordinate hospital and laboratory personnel, employees of the pharmaceutical industry, members of the armed forces, and persons kept in detention. Other vulnerable subjects include patients with incurable diseases, persons in nursing homes, unemployed or impoverished persons, patients in emergency situations, ethnic minority groups, homeless persons, nomads, refugees, minors, and those incapable of giving consent.

### 1. 62 Well-being (of the trial subjects)

The physical and mental integrity of the subjects participating in a clinical trial.

**Addendum**

### 1. 63 Certified Copy

A copy (irrespective of the type of media used) of the original record that has been verified (i. e., by a dated signature or by generation through a validated process) to have the same information, including data that describe the context, content, and structure, as the original.

### 1. 64 Monitoring Plan

A document that describes the strategy, methods, responsibilities, and requirements for monitoring the trial.

### 1. 65 Validation of Computerized Systems

A process of establishing and documenting that the specified requirements of a computerized system can be consistently fulfilled from design until decommissioning of the system or transition to a new system. The approach to validation should be based on a risk assessment that takes into consideration the intended use of the system and the potential of the system to affect human subject protection and reliability of trial results.

# 2. The Principles of ICH GCP

**2. 1** Clinical trials should be conducted in accordance with the ethical principles that have their origin in the Declaration of Helsinki, and that are consistent with GCP and the applicable regulatory requirement(s).

**2. 2** Before a trial is initiated, foreseeable risks and inconveniences should be weighed against the anticipated benefit for the individual trial subject and society. A trial should be initiated and continued only if the anticipated benefits justify the risks.

**2. 3** The rights, safety, and well-being of the trial subjects are the most important considerations and should prevail over interests of science and society.

**2. 4** The available nonclinical and clinical information on an investigational product should be adequate to support the proposed clinical trial.

**2. 5** Clinical trials should be scientifically sound, and described in a clear, detailed protocol.

**2. 6** A trial should be conducted in compliance with the protocol that has received prior institutional review board (IRB) /independent ethics committee (IEC) approval/favourable opinion.

**2. 7** The medical care given to, and medical decisions made on behalf of, subjects should always be the responsibility of a qualified physician or, when appropriate, of a qualified dentist.

**2. 8** Each individual involved in conducting a trial should be qualified by education, training, and experience to perform his or her respective task(s) .

**2. 9** Freely given informed consent should be obtained from every subject prior to clinical trial participation.

**2. 10** All clinical trial information should be recorded, handled, and stored in a way that allows its accurate reporting, interpretation and verification.

**Addendum**

This principle applies to all records referenced in this guideline, irrespective of the type of media used.

**2. 11** The confidentiality of records that could identify subjects should be protected, respecting the privacy and confidentiality rules in accordance with the applicable regulatory requirement(s) .

**2. 12** Investigational products should be manufactured, handled, and stored in accordance with applicable good manufacturing practice (GMP) . They should be used in accordance with the approved protocol.

**2. 13** Systems with procedures that assure the quality of every aspect of the trial should be implemented.

**Addendum**

Aspects of the trial that are essential to ensure human subject protection and reliability of trial results should be the focus of such systems.

# 3. Institutional Review Board/Independent Ethics Committee (IRB/IEC)

## 3. 1 Responsibilities

3. 1. 1 An IRB/IEC should safeguard the rights, safety, and well-being of all trial subjects. Special attention should be paid to trials that may include vulnerable subjects.

3. 1. 2 The IRB/IEC should obtain the following documents:
trial protocol(s)/amendment(s), written informed consent form(s) and consent form updates that the investigator proposes for use in the trial, subject recruitment procedures (e. g., advertisements), written information to be provided to subjects, Investigator's Brochure (IB), available safety information, information about payments and compensation available to subjects, the investigator's current curriculum vitae and/or other documentation evidencing qualifications, and any other documents that the IRB/IEC may need to fulfil its responsibilities.
The IRB/IEC should review a proposed clinical trial within a reasonable time and document its views in writing, clearly identifying the trial, the documents reviewed and the dates for the following:
- approval/favourable opinion;
- modifications required prior to its approval/favourable opinion;
- disapproval/negative opinion; and
- termination/suspension of any prior approval/favourable opinion.

3. 1. 3 The IRB/IEC should consider the qualifications of the investigator for the proposed trial, as documented by a current curriculum vitae and/or by any other relevant documentation the IRB/IEC requests.

3. 1. 4 The IRB/IEC should conduct continuing review of each ongoing trial at intervals appropriate to the degree of risk to human subjects, but at least once per year.

3. 1. 5 The IRB/IEC may request more information than is outlined in paragraph 4. 8. 10 be given to subjects when, in the judgement of the IRB/IEC, the additional information would add meaningfully to the

protection of the rights, safety and/or well-being of the subjects.

3. 1. 6 When a non-therapeutic trial is to be carried out with the consent of the subject's legally acceptable representative (see 4. 8. 12, 4. 8. 14), the IRB/IEC should determine that the proposed protocol and/or other document (s) adequately addresses relevant ethical concerns and meets applicable regulatory requirements for such trials.

3. 1. 7 Where the protocol indicates that prior consent of the trial subject or the subject's legally acceptable representative is not possible (see 4. 8. 15), the IRB/IEC should determine that the proposed protocol and/or other document(s) adequately addresses relevant ethical concerns and meets applicable regulatory requirements for such trials (i. e., in emergency situations).

3. 1. 8 The IRB/IEC should review both the amount and method of payment to subjects to assure that neither presents problems of coercion or undue influence on the trial subjects. Payments to a subject should be prorated and not wholly contingent on completion of the trial by the subject.

3. 1. 9 The IRB/IEC should ensure that information regarding payment to subjects, including the methods, amounts, and schedule of payment to trial subjects, is set forth in the written informed consent form and any other written information to be provided to subjects. The way payment will be prorated should be specified.

## 3. 2 Composition, Functions and Operations

3. 2. 1 The IRB/IEC should consist of a reasonable number of members, who collectively have the qualifications and experience to review and evaluate the science, medical aspects, and ethics of the proposed trial. It is recommended that the IRB/IEC should include:

(a) At least five members.

(b) At least one member whose primary area of interest is in a non-scientific area.

(c) At least one member who is independent of the institution/trial site.

Only those IRB/IEC members who are independent of the investigator and the sponsor of the trial should vote/provide opinion on a trial-related matter.

A list of IRB/IEC members and their qualifications should be maintained.

3. 2. 2 The IRB/IEC should perform its functions according to written operating procedures, should maintain written records of its activities and minutes of its meetings, and should comply with GCP and with the applicable regulatory requirement(s) .

3. 2. 3 An IRB/IEC should make its decisions at announced meetings at which at least a quorum, as stipulated in its written operating procedures, is present.

3. 2. 4 Only members who participate in the IRB/IEC review and discussion should vote/provide their opinion and/or advise.

3. 2. 5 The investigator may provide information on any aspect of the trial, but should not participate in the deliberations of the IRB/IEC or in the vote/opinion of the IRB/IEC.

3. 2. 6 An IRB/IEC may invite nonmembers with expertise in special areas for assistance.

## 3. 3 Procedures

The IRB/IEC should establish, document in writing, and follow its procedures, which should include:

3. 3. 1 Determining its composition (names and qualifications of the members) and the authority under which it is established.

3. 3. 2 Scheduling, notifying its members of, and conducting its meetings.

3. 3. 3 Conducting initial and continuing review of trials.

3. 3. 4 Determining the frequency of continuing review, as appropriate.

3. 3. 5 Providing, according to the applicable regulatory requirements, expedited review and approval/favourable opinion of minor change (s) in ongoing trials that have the approval/favourable opinion of the IRB/IEC.

3. 3. 6 Specifying that no subject should be admitted to a trial before the IRB/IEC issues its written approval/favourable opinion of the trial.

3. 3. 7 Specifying that no deviations from, or changes of, the protocol should be initiated without prior written IRB/IEC approval/favourable opinion of an appropriate amendment, except when necessary to eliminate immediate hazards to the subjects or when the change (s) involves only logistical or administrative aspects of the trial (e. g. ,

change of monitor(s), telephone number(s)) (see 4. 5. 2).

3. 3. 8 Specifying that the investigator should promptly report to the IRB/IEC:

(a) Deviations from, or changes of, the protocol to eliminate immediate hazards to the trial subjects (see 3. 3. 7, 4. 5. 2, 4. 5. 4).

(b) Changes increasing the risk to subjects and/or affecting significantly the conduct of the trial (see 4. 10. 2).

(c) All adverse drug reactions (ADRs) that are both serious and unexpected.

(d) New information that may affect adversely the safety of the subjects or the conduct of the trial.

3. 3. 9 Ensuring that the IRB/IEC promptly notify in writing the investigator/institution concerning:

(a) Its trial-related decisions/opinions.

(b) The reasons for its decisions/opinions.

(c) Procedures for appeal of its decisions/opinions.

### 3. 4 Records

The IRB/IEC should retain all relevant records (e. g., written procedures, membership lists, lists of occupations/affiliations of members, submitted documents, minutes of meetings, and correspondence) for a period of at least 3-years after completion of the trial and make them available upon request from the regulatory authority(ies).

The IRB/IEC may be asked by investigators, sponsors or regulatory authorities to provide its written procedures and membership lists.

## 4. Investigator

### 4. 1 Investigator's Qualifications and Agreements

4. 1. 1 The investigator(s) should be qualified by education, training, and experience to assume responsibility for the proper conduct of the trial, should meet all the qualifications specified by the applicable regulatory requirement(s), and should provide evidence of such qualifications through up-to-date curriculum vitae and/or other relevant documentation requested by the sponsor, the IRB/IEC, and/or

the regulatory authority (ies) .

4. 1. 2 The investigator should be thoroughly familiar with the appropriate use of the investigational product (s) , as described in the protocol, in the current Investigator's Brochure, in the product information and in other information sources provided by the sponsor.

4. 1. 3 The investigator should be aware of, and should comply with, GCP and the applicable regulatory requirements.

4. 1. 4 The investigator/institution should permit monitoring and auditing by the sponsor, and inspection by the appropriate regulatory authority (ies) .

4. 1. 5 The investigator should maintain a list of appropriately qualified persons to whom the investigator has delegated significant trial-related duties.

## 4. 2 Adequate Resources

4. 2. 1 The investigator should be able to demonstrate (e. g. , based on retrospective data) a potential for recruiting the required number of suitable subjects within the agreed recruitment period.

4. 2. 2 The investigator should have sufficient time to properly conduct and complete the trial within the agreed trial period.

4. 2. 3 The investigator should have available an adequate number of qualified staff and adequate facilities for the foreseen duration of the trial to conduct the trial properly and safely.

4. 2. 4 The investigator should ensure that all persons assisting with the trial are adequately informed about the protocol, the investigational product (s) , and their trial-related duties and functions.

### Addendum

4. 2. 5 The investigator is responsible for supervising any individual or party to whom the investigator delegates trial-related duties and functions conducted at the trial site.

4. 2. 6 If the investigator/institution retains the services of any individual or party to perform trial-related duties and functions, the investigator/institution should ensure this individual or party is qualified to perform those trial-related duties and functions and should implement procedures to ensure the integrity of the trial-related duties and functions performed and any data generated.

## 4. 3 Medical Care of Trial Subjects

4. 3. 1 A qualified physician (or dentist, when appropriate), who is an investigator or a sub-investigator for the trial, should be responsible for all trial-related medical (or dental) decisions.

4. 3. 2 During and following a subject's participation in a trial, the investigator/institution should ensure that adequate medical care is provided to a subject for any adverse events, including clinically significant laboratory values, related to the trial. The investigator/institution should inform a subject when medical care is needed for intercurrent illness(es) of which the investigator becomes aware.

4. 3. 3 It is recommended that the investigator inform the subject's primary physician about the subject's participation in the trial if the subject has a primary physician and if the subject agrees to the primary physician being informed.

4. 3. 4 Although a subject is not obliged to give his/her reason(s) for withdrawing prematurely from a trial, the investigator should make a reasonable effort to ascertain the reason(s), while fully respecting the subject's rights.

## 4. 4 Communication with IRB/IEC

4. 4. 1 Before initiating a trial, the investigator/institution should have written and dated approval/favourable opinion from the IRB/IEC for the trial protocol, written informed consent form, consent form updates, subject recruitment procedures (e. g., advertisements), and any other written information to be provided to subjects.

4. 4. 2 As part of the investigator's/institution's written application to the IRB/IEC, the investigator/institution should provide the IRB/IEC with a current copy of the Investigator's Brochure. If the Investigator's Brochure is updated during the trial, the investigator/institution should supply a copy of the updated Investigator's Brochure to the IRB/IEC.

4. 4. 3 During the trial the investigator/institution should provide to the IRB/IEC all documents subject to review.

## 4. 5 Compliance with Protocol

4. 5. 1 The investigator/institution should conduct the trial in compliance with the protocol agreed to by the sponsor and, if required, by the

regulatory authority(ies) and which was given approval/favourable opinion by the IRB/IEC. The investigator/institution and the sponsor should sign the protocol, or an alternative contract, to confirm agreement.

4.5.2 The investigator should not implement any deviation from, or changes of the protocol without agreement by the sponsor and prior review and documented approval/favourable opinion from the IRB/IEC of an amendment, except where necessary to eliminate an immediate hazard(s) to trial subjects, or when the change(s) involves only logistical or administrative aspects of the trial (e.g., change in monitor(s), change of telephone number(s)).

4.5.3 The investigator, or person designated by the investigator, should document and explain any deviation from the approved protocol.

4.5.4 The investigator may implement a deviation from, or a change of, the protocol to eliminate an immediate hazard(s) to trial subjects without prior IRB/IEC approval/favourable opinion. As soon as possible, the implemented deviation or change, the reasons for it, and, if appropriate, the proposed protocol amendment(s) should be submitted:

(a) to the IRB/IEC for review and approval/favourable opinion,

(b) to the sponsor for agreement and, if required,

(c) to the regulatory authority(ies).

## 4.6 Investigational Product(s)

4.6.1 Responsibility for investigational product(s) accountability at the trial site(s) rests with the investigator/institution.

4.6.2 Where allowed/required, the investigator/institution may/should assign some or all of the investigator's/institution's duties for investigational product(s) accountability at the trial site(s) to an appropriate pharmacist or another appropriate individual who is under the supervision of the investigator/institution.

4.6.3 The investigator/institution and/or a pharmacist or other appropriate individual, who is designated by the investigator/institution, should maintain records of the product's delivery to the trial site, the inventory at the site, the use by each subject, and the return to the sponsor or alternative disposition of unused product(s). These records should include dates, quantities, batch/serial numbers, expiration dates (if applicable), and the unique code numbers assigned to the investigational product(s) and trial subjects. Investigators should maintain records that document adequately that the subjects were provided the doses specified by the protocol and reconcile all investigational product(s) received from the sponsor.

4.6.4 The investigational product(s) should be stored as specified by the sponsor (see 5.13.2 and 5.14.3) and in accordance with applicable regulatory requirement(s).

4.6.5 The investigator should ensure that the investigational product(s) are used only in accordance with the approved protocol.

4.6.6 The investigator, or a person designated by the investigator/institution, should explain the correct use of the investigational product(s) to each subject and should check, at intervals appropriate for the trial, that each subject is following the instructions properly.

## 4.7 Randomization Procedures and Unblinding

The investigator should follow the trial's randomization procedures, if any, and should ensure that the code is broken only in accordance with the protocol. If the trial is blinded, the investigator should promptly document and explain to the sponsor any premature unblinding (e.g., accidental unblinding, unblinding due to a serious adverse event) of the investigational product(s).

## 4.8 Informed Consent of Trial Subjects

4.8.1 In obtaining and documenting informed consent, the investigator should comply with the applicable regulatory requirement(s), and should adhere to GCP and to the ethical principles that have their origin in the Declaration of Helsinki. Prior to the beginning of the trial, the investigator should have the IRB/IEC's written approval/favourable opinion of the written informed consent form and any other written information to be provided to subjects.

4.8.2 The written informed consent form and any other written information to be provided to subjects should be revised whenever important new information becomes available that may be relevant to the subject's consent. Any revised written informed consent form, and written information should receive the IRB/IEC's approval/favourable opinion in advance of use. The subject or the subject's legally acceptable representative should be informed in a timely manner if new information becomes available that may be relevant to the subject's willingness to continue participation in the trial. The communication of this information should be documented.

4. 8. 3 Neither the investigator, nor the trial staff, should coerce or unduly influence a subject to participate or to continue to participate in a trial.

4. 8. 4 None of the oral and written information concerning the trial, including the written informed consent form, should contain any language that causes the subject or the subject's legally acceptable representative to waive or to appear to waive any legal rights, or that releases or appears to release the investigator, the institution, the sponsor, or their agents from liability for negligence.

4. 8. 5 The investigator, or a person designated by the investigator, should fully inform the subject or, if the subject is unable to provide informed consent, the subject's legally acceptable representative, of all pertinent aspects of the trial including the written information and the approval/ favourable opinion by the IRB/IEC.

4. 8. 6 The language used in the oral and written information about the trial, including the written informed consent form, should be as non-technical as practical and should be understandable to the subject or the subject's legally acceptable representative and the impartial witness, where applicable.

4. 8. 7 Before informed consent may be obtained, the investigator, or a person designated by the investigator, should provide the subject or the subject's legally acceptable representative ample time and opportunity to inquire about details of the trial and to decide whether or not to participate in the trial. All questions about the trial should be answered to the satisfaction of the subject or the subject's legally acceptable representative.

4. 8. 8 Prior to a subject's participation in the trial, the written informed consent form should be signed and personally dated by the subject or by the subject's legally acceptable representative, and by the person who conducted the informed consent discussion.

4. 8. 9 If a subject is unable to read or if a legally acceptable representative is unable to read, an impartial witness should be present during the

entire informed consent discussion. After the written informed consent form and any other written information to be provided to subjects, is read and explained to the subject or the subject's legally acceptable representative, and after the subject or the subject's legally acceptable representative has orally consented to the subject's participation in the trial and, if capable of doing so, has signed and personally dated the informed consent form, the witness should sign and personally date the consent form. By signing the consent form, the witness attests that the information in the consent form and any other written information was accurately explained to, and apparently understood by, the subject or the subject's legally acceptable representative, and that informed consent was freely given by the subject or the subject's legally acceptable representative.

4. 8. 10 Both the informed consent discussion and the written informed consent form and any other written information to be provided to subjects should include explanations of the following:

(a) That the trial involves research.

(b) The purpose of the trial.

(c) The trial treatment(s) and the probability for random assignment to each treatment.

(d) The trial procedures to be followed, including all invasive procedures.

(e) The subject's responsibilities.

(f) Those aspects of the trial that are experimental.

(g) The reasonably foreseeable risks or inconveniences to the subject and, when applicable, to an embryo, fetus, or nursing infant.

(h) The reasonably expected benefits. When there is no intended clinical benefit to the subject, the subject should be made aware of this.

(i) The alternative procedure(s) or course(s) of treatment that may be available to the subject, and their important potential benefits and risks.

(j) The compensation and/or treatment available to the subject in the event of trial-related injury.

(k) The anticipated prorated payment, if any, to the subject for participating in the trial.

(l) The anticipated expenses, if any, to the subject for participating in the trial.

(m) That the subject's participation in the trial is voluntary and that the subject may refuse to participate or withdraw from the trial, at any time, without penalty or loss of benefits to which the subject is otherwise entitled.

(n) That the monitor (s), the auditor (s), the IRB/IEC, and the regulatory authority (ies) will be granted direct access to the subject's original medical records for verification of clinical trial procedures and/or data, without violating the confidentiality of the subject, to the extent permitted by the applicable laws and regulations and that, by signing a written informed consent form, the subject or the subject's legally acceptable representative is authorizing such access.

(o) That records identifying the subject will be kept confidential and, to the extent permitted by the applicable laws and/or regulations, will not be made publicly available. If the results of the trial are published, the subject's identity will remain confidential.

(p) That the subject or the subject's legally acceptable representative will be informed in a timely manner if information becomes available that may be relevant to the subject's willingness to continue participation in the trial.

(q) The person(s) to contact for further information regarding the trial and the rights of trial subjects, and whom to contact in the event of trial-related injury.

(r) The foreseeable circumstances and/or reasons under which the subject's participation in the trial may be terminated.

(s) The expected duration of the subject's participation in the trial.

(t) The approximate number of subjects involved in the trial.

4.8.11 Prior to participation in the trial, the subject or the subject's legally acceptable representative should receive a copy of the signed and dated written informed consent form and any other written information provided to the subjects. During a subject's participation in the trial, the subject or the subject's legally acceptable representative should receive a copy of the signed and dated consent form updates and a copy of any amendments to the written information provided to subjects.

4. 8. 12 When a clinical trial (therapeutic or non-therapeutic) includes subjects who can only be enrolled in the trial with the consent of the subject's legally acceptable representative (e. g. , minors, or patients with severe dementia), the subject should be informed about the trial to the extent compatible with the subject's understanding and, if capable, the subject should sign and personally date the written informed consent.

4. 8. 13 Except as described in 4. 8. 14, a non-therapeutic trial (i. e. , a trial in which there is no anticipated direct clinical benefit to the subject), should be conducted in subjects who personally give consent and who sign and date the written informed consent form.

4. 8. 14 Non-therapeutic trials may be conducted in subjects with consent of a legally acceptable representative provided the following conditions are fulfilled:

(a) The objectives of the trial can not be met by means of a trial in subjects who can give informed consent personally.

(b) The foreseeable risks to the subjects are low.

(c) The negative impact on the subject's well-being is minimized and low.

(d) The trial is not prohibited by law.

(e) The approval/favourable opinion of the IRB/IEC is expressly sought on the inclusion of such subjects, and the written approval/ favourable opinion covers this aspect.

Such trials, unless an exception is justified, should be conducted in patients having a disease or condition for which the investigational product is intended. Subjects in these trials should be particularly closely monitored and should be withdrawn if they appear to be unduly distressed.

4. 8. 15 In emergency situations, when prior consent of the subject is not possible, the consent of the subject's legally acceptable representative, if present, should be requested. When prior consent of the subject is not possible, and the subject's legally acceptable representative is not available, enrolment of the subject should require measures described in the protocol and/or elsewhere, with docu-

mented approval/favourable opinion by the IRB/IEC, to protect the rights, safety and well-being of the subject and to ensure compliance with applicable regulatory requirements. The subject or the subject's legally acceptable representative should be informed about the trial as soon as possible and consent to continue and other consent as appropriate (see 4. 8. 10) should be requested.

## 4. 9 Records and Reports

**Addendum**

4. 9. 0 The investigator/institution should maintain adequate and accurate source documents and trial records that include all pertinent observations on each of the site's trial subjects. Source data should be attributable, legible, contemporaneous, original, accurate, and complete. Changes to source data should be traceable, should not obscure the original entry, and should be explained if necessary (e. g. , via an audit trail) .

4. 9. 1 The investigator should ensure the accuracy, completeness, legibility, and timeliness of the data reported to the sponsor in the CRFs and in all required reports.

4. 9. 2 Data reported on the CRF, that are derived from source documents, should be consistent with the source documents or the discrepancies should be explained.

4. 9. 3 Any change or correction to a CRF should be dated, initialed, and explained (if necessary) and should not obscure the original entry (i. e. , an audit trail should be maintained) ; this applies to both written and electronic changes or corrections (see 5. 18. 4 (n)) . Sponsors should provide guidance to investigators and/or the investigators' designated representatives on making such corrections. Sponsors should have written procedures to assure that changes or corrections in CRFs made by sponsor's designated representatives are documented, are necessary, and are endorsed by the investigator. The investigator should retain records of the changes and corrections.

4. 9. 4 The investigator/institution should maintain the trial documents as specified in Essential Documents for the Conduct of a Clinical Trial (see 8. ) and as required by the applicable regulatory requirement (s) .

The investigator/institution should take measures to prevent accidental or premature destruction of these documents.

4. 9. 5 Essential documents should be retained until at least 2-years after the last approval of a marketing application in an ICH region and until there are no pending or contemplated marketing applications in an ICH region or at least 2-years have elapsed since the formal discontinuation of clinical development of the investigational product. These documents should be retained for a longer period however if required by the applicable regulatory requirements or by an agreement with the sponsor. It is the responsibility of the sponsor to inform the investigator/institution as to when these documents no longer need to be retained (see 5. 5. 12) .

4. 9. 6 The financial aspects of the trial should be documented in an agreement between the sponsor and the investigator/institution.

4. 9. 7 Upon request of the monitor, auditor, IRB/IEC, or regulatory authority, the investigator/institution should make available for direct access all requested trial-related records.

## 4. 10 Progress Reports

4. 10. 1 The investigator should submit written summaries of the trial status to the IRB/IEC annually, or more frequently, if requested by the IRB/IEC.

4. 10. 2 The investigator should promptly provide written reports to the sponsor, the IRB/IEC (see 3. 3. 8) and, where applicable, the institution on any changes significantly affecting the conduct of the trial, and/or increasing the risk to subjects.

## 4. 11 Safety Reporting

4. 11. 1 All serious adverse events (SAEs) should be reported immediately to the sponsor except for those SAEs that the protocol or other document (e. g. , Investigator's Brochure) identifies as not needing immediate reporting. The immediate reports should be followed promptly by detailed, written reports. The immediate and follow-up reports should identify subjects by unique code numbers assigned to the trial subjects rather than by the subjects' names, personal identification numbers, and/or addresses. The investigator should also comply with the applicable regulatory requirement (s)

related to the reporting of unexpected serious adverse drug reactions to the regulatory authority(ies) and the IRB/IEC.

4. 11. 2 Adverse events and/or laboratory abnormalities identified in the protocol as critical to safety evaluations should be reported to the sponsor according to the reporting requirements and within the time periods specified by the sponsor in the protocol.

4. 11. 3 For reported deaths, the investigator should supply the sponsor and the IRB/IEC with any additional requested information (e. g., autopsy reports and terminal medical reports).

## 4. 12 Premature Termination or Suspension of a Trial

If the trial is prematurely terminated or suspended for any reason, the investigator/institution should promptly inform the trial subjects, should assure appropriate therapy and follow-up for the subjects, and, where required by the applicable regulatory requirement(s), should inform the regulatory authority (ies). In addition:

4. 12. 1 If the investigator terminates or suspends a trial without prior agreement of the sponsor, the investigator should inform the institution where applicable, and the investigator/institution should promptly inform the sponsor and the IRB/IEC, and should provide the sponsor and the IRB/IEC a detailed written explanation of the termination or suspension.

4. 12. 2 If the sponsor terminates or suspends a trial (see 5. 21), the investigator should promptly inform the institution where applicable and the investigator/institution should promptly inform the IRB/IEC and provide the IRB/IEC a detailed written explanation of the termination or suspension.

4. 12. 3 If the IRB/IEC terminates or suspends its approval/favourable opinion of a trial (see 3. 1. 2 and 3. 3. 9), the investigator should inform the institution where applicable and the investigator/institution should promptly notify the sponsor and provide the sponsor with a detailed written explanation of the termination or suspension.

## 4. 13 Final Report(s) by Investigator

Upon completion of the trial, the investigator, where applicable, should inform the institution; the investigator/institution should provide the IRB/IEC with a summary of the trial's outcome, and the regulatory authority(ies) with any reports required.

# 5. Sponsor

## Addendum

### 5. 0 Quality Management

The sponsor should implement a system to manage quality throughout all stages of the trial process.

Sponsors should focus on trial activities essential to ensuring human subject protection and the reliability of trial results. Quality management includes the design of efficient clinical trial protocols and tools and procedures for data collection and processing, as well as the collection of information that is essential to decision making.

The methods used to assure and control the quality of the trial should be proportionate to the risks inherent in the trial and the importance of the information collected. The sponsor should ensure that all aspects of the trial are operationally feasible and should avoid unnecessary complexity, procedures, and data collection. Protocols, case report forms, and other operational documents should be clear, concise, and consistent.

The quality management system should use a risk-based approach as described below.

5. 0. 1 *Critical Process and Data Identification*

During protocol development, the sponsor should identify those processes and data that are critical to ensure human subject protection and the reliability of trial results.

5. 0. 2 *Risk Identification*

The sponsor should identify risks to critical trial processes and data. Risks should be considered at both the system level (e. g. , standard operating procedures, computerized systems, personnel) and clinical trial level (e. g. , trial design, data collection, informed consent process) .

5. 0. 3 *Risk Evaluation*

The sponsor should evaluate the identified risks, against existing risk controls by considering:

(a) The likelihood of errors occurring.

(b) The extent to which such errors would be detectable.

(c) The impact of such errors on human subject protection and reliability of trial results.

5. 0. 4 *Risk Control*

The sponsor should decide which risks to reduce and/or which risks to accept. The approach used to reduce risk to an acceptable level should be proportionate to the significance of the risk. Risk reduction activities may be incorporated in protocol design and implementation, monitoring plans, agreements between parties defining roles and responsibilities, systematic safeguards to ensure adherence to standard operating procedures, and training in processes and procedures.

Predefined quality tolerance limits should be established, taking into consideration the medical and statistical characteristics of the variables as well as the statistical design of the trial, to identify systematic issues that can impact subject safety or reliability of trial results. Detection of deviations from the predefined quality tolerance limits should trigger an evaluation to determine if action is needed.

5. 0. 5 *Risk Communication*

The sponsor should document quality management activities. The sponsor should communicate quality management activities to those who are involved in or affected by such activities, to facilitate risk review and continual improvement during clinical trial execution.

5. 0. 6 *Risk Review*

The sponsor should periodically review risk control measures to ascertain whether the implemented quality management activities remain effective and relevant, taking into account emerging knowledge and experience.

5. 0. 7 *Risk Reporting*

The sponsor should describe the quality management approach implemented in the trial and summarize important deviations from the predefined quality tolerance limits and remedial actions taken in the clinical study report (ICH E3, Section 9. 6 Data Quality Assurance) .

## 5. 1 Quality Assurance and Quality Control

5. 1. 1 The sponsor is responsible for implementing and maintaining quality assurance and quality control systems with written SOPs to ensure that trials are conducted and data are generated, documented (recorded), and reported in compliance with the protocol, GCP, and the applicable regulatory requirement(s).

5. 1. 2 The sponsor is responsible for securing agreement from all involved parties to ensure direct access (see 1. 21) to all trial related sites, source data/documents, and reports for the purpose of monitoring and auditing by the sponsor, and inspection by domestic and foreign regulatory authorities.

5. 1. 3 Quality control should be applied to each stage of data handling to ensure that all data are reliable and have been processed correctly.

5. 1. 4 Agreements, made by the sponsor with the investigator/institution and any other parties involved with the clinical trial, should be in writing, as part of the protocol or in a separate agreement.

## 5. 2 Contract Research Organization (CRO)

5. 2. 1 A sponsor may transfer any or all of the sponsor's trial-related duties and functions to a CRO, but the ultimate responsibility for the quality and integrity of the trial data always resides with the sponsor. The CRO should implement quality assurance and quality control.

5. 2. 2 Any trial-related duty and function that is transferred to and assumed by a CRO should be specified in writing.

**Addendum**

The sponsor should ensure oversight of any trial-related duties and functions carried out on its behalf, including trial-related duties and functions that are subcontracted to another party by the sponsor's contracted CRO(s).

5. 2. 3 Any trial-related duties and functions not specifically transferred to and assumed by a CRO are retained by the sponsor.

5. 2. 4 All references to a sponsor in this guideline also apply to a CRO to the extent that a CRO has assumed the trial related duties and functions of a sponsor.

## 5. 3 Medical Expertise

The sponsor should designate appropriately qualified medical personnel who will be readily available to advise on trial related medical questions or problems. If necessary, outside consultant(s) may be appointed for this purpose.

## 5.4 Trial Design

5.4.1 The sponsor should utilize qualified individuals (e.g., biostatisticians, clinical pharmacologists, and physicians) as appropriate, throughout all stages of the trial process, from designing the protocol and CRFs and planning the analyses to analyzing and preparing interim and final clinical trial reports.

5.4.2 For further guidance: Clinical Trial Protocol and Protocol Amendment(s) (see 6.), the ICH Guideline for Structure and Content of Clinical Study Reports, and other appropriate ICH guidance on trial design, protocol and conduct.

## 5.5 Trial Management, Data Handling, and Record Keeping

5.5.1 The sponsor should utilize appropriately qualified individuals to supervise the overall conduct of the trial, to handle the data, to verify the data, to conduct the statistical analyses, and to prepare the trial reports.

5.5.2 The sponsor may consider establishing an independent data-monitoring committee (IDMC) to assess the progress of a clinical trial, including the safety data and the critical efficacy endpoints at intervals, and to recommend to the sponsor whether to continue, modify, or stop a trial. The IDMC should have written operating procedures and maintain written records of all its meetings.

5.5.3 When using electronic trial data handling and/or remote electronic trial data systems, the sponsor should:

(a) Ensure and document that the electronic data processing system(s) conforms to the sponsor's established requirements for completeness, accuracy, reliability, and consistent intended performance (i.e., validation).

**ADDENDUM**

The sponsor should base their approach to validation of such systems on a risk assessment that takes into consideration the intended use of the system and the potential of the system to affect human subject protection and reliability of trial results.

(b) Maintains SOPs for using these systems.

**ADDENDUM**

The SOPs should cover system setup, installation, and use. The SOPs should describe system validation and functionality testing, data collection and handling, system maintenance, system security measures, change control, data backup, recovery, contingency planning, and decommissioning. The responsibilities of the sponsor, investigator, and other parties with respect to the use of these computerized systems should be clear, and the users should be provided with training in their use.

(c) Ensure that the systems are designed to permit data changes in such a way that the data changes are documented and that there is no deletion of entered data (i. e. , maintain an audit trail, data trail, edit trail) .

(d) Maintain a security system that prevents unauthorized access to the data.

(e) Maintain a list of the individuals who are authorized to make data changes (see 4. 1. 5 and 4. 9. 3) .

(f) Maintain adequate backup of the data.

(g) Safeguard the blinding, if any (e. g. , maintain the blinding during data entry and processing) .

**Addendum**

(h) Ensure the integrity of the data including any data that describe the context, content, and structure. This is particularly important when making changes to the computerized systems, such as software upgrades or migration of data.

5. 5. 4 If data are transformed during processing, it should always be possible to compare the original data and observations with the processed data.

5. 5. 5 The sponsor should use an unambiguous subject identification code (see 1. 58) that allows identification of all the data reported for each subject.

5. 5. 6 The sponsor, or other owners of the data, should retain all of the sponsor-specific essential documents pertaining to the trial (see 8. Essential Documents for the Conduct of a Clinical Trial) .

5. 5. 7 The sponsor should retain all sponsor-specific essential documents in conformance with the applicable regulatory requirement (s) of the country (ies) where the product is approved, and/or where the sponsor intends to apply for approval (s).

5. 5. 8 If the sponsor discontinues the clinical development of an investigational product (i. e., for any or all indications, routes of administration, or dosage forms), the sponsor should maintain all sponsor-specific essential documents for at least 2-years after formal discontinuation or in conformance with the applicable regulatory requirement (s).

5. 5. 9 If the sponsor discontinues the clinical development of an investigational product, the sponsor should notify all the trial investigators/institutions and all the regulatory authorities.

5. 5. 10 Any transfer of ownership of the data should be reported to the appropriate authority (ies), as required by the applicable regulatory requirement (s).

5. 5. 11 The sponsor specific essential documents should be retained until at least 2-years after the last approval of a marketing application in an ICH region and until there are no pending or contemplated marketing applications in an ICH region or at least 2-years have elapsed since the formal discontinuation of clinical development of the investigational product. These documents should be retained for a longer period however if required by the applicable regulatory requirement (s) or if needed by the sponsor.

5. 5. 12 The sponsor should inform the investigator (s) /institution (s) in writing of the need for record retention and should notify the investigator (s) /institution (s) in writing when the trial related records are no longer needed.

## 5. 6 Investigator Selection

5. 6. 1 The sponsor is responsible for selecting the investigator (s) /institution (s). Each investigator should be qualified by training and experience and should have adequate resources (see 4. 1, 4. 2) to properly conduct the trial for which the investigator is selected. If organization of a coordinating committee and/or selection of coordinating investigator (s) are to be utilized in multicentre trials, their organization and/or selection are the sponsor's responsibility.

5. 6. 2 Before entering an agreement with an investigator/institution to conduct a trial, the sponsor should provide the investigator (s) /institution (s) with the protocol and an up-to-date Investigator's Brochure, and should provide sufficient time for the investigator/institution to review the protocol and the information provided.

5. 6. 3 The sponsor should obtain the investigator's/institution's agreement:

(a) to conduct the trial in compliance with GCP, with the applicable regulatory requirement (s) (see 4. 1. 3), and with the protocol agreed to by the sponsor and given approval/favourable opinion by the IRB/IEC (see 4. 5. 1);

(b) to comply with procedures for data recording/reporting;

(c) to permit monitoring, auditing and inspection (see 4. 1. 4) and

(d) to retain the trial related essential documents until the sponsor informs the investigator/institution these documents are no longer needed (see 4. 9. 4 and 5. 5. 12).

The sponsor and the investigator/institution should sign the protocol, or an alternative document, to confirm this agreement.

## 5. 7 Allocation of Responsibilities

Prior to initiating a trial, the sponsor should define, establish, and allocate all trial-related duties and functions.

## 5. 8 Compensation to Subjects and Investigators

5. 8. 1 If required by the applicable regulatory requirement (s), the sponsor should provide insurance or should indemnify (legal and financial coverage) the investigator/the institution against claims arising from the trial, except for claims that arise from malpractice and/or negligence.

5. 8. 2 The sponsor's policies and procedures should address the costs of treatment of trial subjects in the event of trial-related injuries in accordance with the applicable regulatory requirement (s).

5. 8. 3 When trial subjects receive compensation, the method and manner of compensation should comply with applicable regulatory requirement (s).

## 5. 9 Financing

The financial aspects of the trial should be documented in an agreement between the sponsor and the investigator/institution.

## 5. 10 Notification/Submission to Regulatory Authority(ies)

Before initiating the clinical trial(s), the sponsor (or the sponsor and the investigator, if required by the applicable regulatory requirement(s)) should submit any required application(s) to the appropriate authority(ies) for review, acceptance, and/or permission (as required by the applicable regulatory requirement(s)) to begin the trial(s). Any notification/submission should be dated and contain sufficient information to identify the protocol.

## 5. 11 Confirmation of Review by IRB/IEC

5. 11. 1 The sponsor should obtain from the investigator/institution:

(a) The name and address of the investigator's/institution's IRB/IEC.

(b) A statement obtained from the IRB/IEC that it is organized and operates according to GCP and the applicable laws and regulations.

(c) Documented IRB/IEC approval/favourable opinion and, if requested by the sponsor, a current copy of protocol, written informed consent form(s) and any other written information to be provided to subjects, subject recruiting procedures, and documents related to payments and compensation available to the subjects, and any other documents that the IRB/IEC may have requested.

5. 11. 2 If the IRB/IEC conditions its approval/favourable opinion upon change(s) in any aspcct of the trial, such as modification(s) of the protocol, written informed consent form and any other written information to be provided to subjects, and/or other procedures, the sponsor should obtain from the investigator/institution a copy of the modification(s) made and the date approval/favourable opinion was given by the IRB/IEC.

5. 11. 3 The sponsor should obtain from the investigator/institution documentation and dates of any IRB/IEC reapprovals/re-evaluations with favourable opinion, and of any withdrawals or suspensions of approval/favourable opinion.

## 5. 12 Information on Investigational Product(s)

5. 12. 1 When planning trials, the sponsor should ensure that sufficient safety and efficacy data from nonclinical studies and/or clinical trials are

available to support human exposure by the route, at the dosages, for the duration, and in the trial population to be studied.

5. 12. 2 The sponsor should update the Investigator's Brochure as significant new information becomes available (see 7. Investigator's Brochure).

## 5. 13 Manufacturing, Packaging, Labelling, and Coding Investigational Product(s)

5. 13. 1 The sponsor should ensure that the investigational product(s) (including active comparator(s) and placebo, if applicable) is characterized as appropriate to the stage of development of the product(s), is manufactured in accordance with any applicable GMP, and is coded and labelled in a manner that protects the blinding, if applicable. In addition, the labelling should comply with applicable regulatory requirement(s).

5. 13. 2 The sponsor should determine, for the investigational product(s), acceptable storage temperatures, storage conditions (e. g., protection from light), storage times, reconstitution fluids and procedures, and devices for product infusion, if any. The sponsor should inform all involved parties (e. g., monitors, investigators, pharmacists, storage managers) of these determinations.

5. 13. 3 The investigational product(s) should be packaged to prevent contamination and unacceptable deterioration during transport and storage.

5. 13. 4 In blinded trials, the coding system for the investigational product(s) should include a mechanism that permits rapid identification of the product(s) in case of a medical emergency, but does not permit undetectable breaks of the blinding.

5. 13. 5 If significant formulation changes are made in the investigational or comparator product(s) during the course of clinical development, the results of any additional studies of the formulated product(s) (e. g., stability, dissolution rate, bioavailability) needed to assess whether these changes would significantly alter the pharmacokinetic profile of the product should be available prior to the use of the new formulation in clinical trials.

## 5. 14 Supplying and Handling Investigational Product(s)

5. 14. 1 The sponsor is responsible for supplying the investigator(s)/in-

stitution(s) with the investigational product(s).

5. 14. 2 The sponsor should not supply an investigator/institution with the investigational product (s) until the sponsor obtains all required documentation (e. g., approval/favourable opinion from IRB/IEC and regulatory authority(ies)).

5. 14. 3 The sponsor should ensure that written procedures include instructions that the investigator/institution should follow for the handling and storage of investigational product (s) for the trial and documentation thereof. The procedures should address adequate and safe receipt, handling, storage, dispensing, retrieval of unused product from subjects, and return of unused investigational product(s) to the sponsor (or alternative disposition if authorized by the sponsor and in compliance with the applicable regulatory requirement(s)).

5. 14. 4 The sponsor should:

(a) Ensure timely delivery of investigational product(s) to the investigator(s).

(b) Maintain records that document shipment, receipt, disposition, return, and destruction of the investigational product(s) (see 8. Essential Documents for the Conduct of a Clinical Trial).

(c) Maintain a system for retrieving investigational products and documenting this retrieval (e. g., for deficient product recall, reclaim after trial completion, expired product reclaim).

(d) Maintain a system for the disposition of unused investigational product(s) and for the documentation of this disposition.

5. 14. 5 The sponsor should:

(a) Take steps to ensure that the investigational product (s) are stable over the period of use.

(b) Maintain sufficient quantities of the investigational product (s) used in the trials to reconfirm specifications, should this become necessary, and maintain records of batch sample analyses and characteristics. To the extent stability permits, samples should be retained either until the analyses of the trial data are complete or as required by the applicable regulatory requirement (s), whichever represents the longer retention period.

## 5. 15 Record Access

5. 15. 1 The sponsor should ensure that it is specified in the protocol or other written agreement that the investigator(s) /institution(s) provide direct access to source data/documents for trial-related monitoring, audits, IRB/IEC review, and regulatory inspection.

5. 15. 2 The sponsor should verify that each subject has consented, in writing, to direct access to his/her original medical records for trial-related monitoring, audit, IRB/IEC review, and regulatory inspection.

## 5. 16 Safety Information

5. 16. 1 The sponsor is responsible for the ongoing safety evaluation of the investigational product(s).

5. 16. 2 The sponsor should promptly notify all concerned investigator(s)/institution(s) and the regulatory authority(ies) of findings that could affect adversely the safety of subjects, impact the conduct of the trial, or alter the IRB/IEC's approval/favourable opinion to continue the trial.

## 5. 17 Adverse Drug Reaction Reporting

5. 17. 1 The sponsor should expedite the reporting to all concerned investigator(s) /institutions(s), to the IRB(s)/IEC(s), where required, and to the regulatory authority(ies) of all adverse drug reactions (ADRs) that are both serious and unexpected.

5. 17. 2 Such expedited reports should comply with the applicable regulatory requirement(s) and with the ICH Guideline for Clinical Safety Data Management: Definitions and Standards for Expedited Reporting.

5. 17. 3 The sponsor should submit to the regulatory authority(ies) all safety updates and periodic reports, as required by applicable regulatory requirement(s).

## 5. 18 Monitoring

5. 18. 1 *Purpose*

The purposes of trial monitoring are to verify that:

(a) The rights and well-being of human subjects are protected.

(b) The reported trial data are accurate, complete, and verifiable from source documents.

(c) The conduct of the trial is in compliance with the currently approved protocol/amendment(s), with GCP, and with the applicable regulatory requirement(s).

5.18.2 *Selection and Qualifications of Monitors*

(a) Monitors should be appointed by the sponsor.

(b) Monitors should be appropriately trained, and should have the scientific and/or clinical knowledge needed to monitor the trial adequately. A monitor's qualifications should be documented.

(c) Monitors should be thoroughly familiar with the investigational product(s), the protocol, written informed consent form and any other written information to be provided to subjects, the sponsor's SOPs, GCP, and the applicable regulatory requirement(s).

5.18.3 *Extent and Nature of Monitoring*

The sponsor should ensure that the trials are adequately monitored. The sponsor should determine the appropriate extent and nature of monitoring. The determination of the extent and nature of monitoring should be based on considerations such as the objective, purpose, design, complexity, blinding, size, and endpoints of the trial. In general there is a need for on-site monitoring, before, during, and after the trial; however in exceptional circumstances the sponsor may determine that central monitoring in conjunction with procedures such as investigators' training and meetings, and extensive written guidance can assure appropriate conduct of the trial in accordance with GCP. Statistically controlled sampling may be an acceptable method for selecting the data to be verified.

**Addendum**

The sponsor should develop a systematic, prioritized, risk-based approach to monitoring clinical trials. The flexibility in the extent and nature of monitoring described in this section is intended to permit varied approaches that improve the effectiveness and efficiency of monitoring. The sponsor may choose on-site monitoring, a combination of on-site and centralized monitoring, or, where justified, centralized monitoring. The sponsor should document the rationale for the chosen monitoring strategy (e.g., in the monitoring plan).

On-site monitoring is performed at the sites at which the clinical trial is being conducted. Centralized monitoring is a remote evaluation of accumulating data, performed in a timely manner, supported by appropriately qualified and trained persons (e.g., data managers, biostatisticians).

Centralized monitoring processes provide additional monitoring capabilities that can complement and reduce the extent and/or frequency of on-site monitoring and help distinguish between reliable data and potentially unreliable data.

Review, that may include statistical analyses, of accumulating data from centralized monitoring can be used to:

(a) identify missing data, inconsistent data, data outliers, unexpected lack of variability and protocol deviations.

(b) examine data trends such as the range, consistency, and variability of data within and across sites.

(c) evaluate for systematic or significant errors in data collection and reporting at a site or across sites; or potential data manipulation or data integrity problems.

(d) analyze site characteristics and performance metrics.

(e) select sites and/or processes for targeted on-site monitoring.

5.18.4 *Monitor's Responsibilities*

The monitor(s) in accordance with the sponsor's requirements should ensure that the trial is conducted and documented properly by carrying out the following activities when relevant and necessary to the trial and the trial site:

(a) Acting as the main line of communication between the sponsor and the investigator.

(b) Verifying that the investigator has adequate qualifications and resources (see 4.1, 4.2, 5.6) and remain adequate throughout the trial period, that facilities, including laboratories, equipment, and staff, are adequate to safely and properly conduct the trial and remain adequate throughout the trial period.

(c) Verifying, for the investigational product(s):

(i) That storage times and conditions are acceptable, and

that supplies are sufficient throughout the trial.

(ii) That the investigational product(s) are supplied only to subjects who are eligible to receive it and at the protocol specified dose(s).

(iii) That subjects are provided with necessary instruction on properly using, handling, storing, and returning the investigational product(s).

(iv) That the receipt, use, and return of the investigational product(s) at the trial sites are controlled and documented adequately.

(v) That the disposition of unused investigational product(s) at the trial sites complies with applicable regulatory requirement(s) and is in accordance with the sponsor.

(d) Verifying that the investigator follows the approved protocol and all approved amendment(s), if any.

(e) Verifying that written informed consent was obtained before each subject's participation in the trial.

(f) Ensuring that the investigator receives the current Investigator's Brochure, all documents, and all trial supplies needed to conduct the trial properly and to comply with the applicable regulatory requirement(s).

(g) Ensuring that the investigator and the investigator's trial staff are adequately informed about the trial.

(h) Verifying that the investigator and the investigator's trial staff are performing the specified trial functions, in accordance with the protocol and any other written agreement between the sponsor and the investigator/institution, and have not delegated these functions to unauthorized individuals.

(i) Verifying that the investigator is enroling only eligible subjects.

(j) Reporting the subject recruitment rate.

(k) Verifying that source documents and other trial records are accurate, complete, kept up-to-date and maintained.

(l) Verifying that the investigator provides all the required reports, notifications, applications, and submissions, and that these documents are accurate, complete, timely, legible, dated, and identify the trial.

(m) Checking the accuracy and completeness of the CRF entries, source documents and other trial-related records against each other. The monitor specifically should verify that:

   (i) The data required by the protocol are reported accurately on the CRFs and are consistent with the source documents.

   (ii) Any dose and/or therapy modifications are well documented for each of the trial subjects.

   (iii) Adverse events, concomitant medications and intercurrent illnesses are reported in accordance with the protocol on the CRFs.

   (iv) Visits that the subjects fail to make, tests that are not conducted, and examinations that are not performed are clearly reported as such on the CRFs.

   (v) All withdrawals and dropouts of enrolled subjects from the trial are reported and explained on the CRFs.

(n) Informing the investigator of any CRF entry error, omission, or illegibility. The monitor should ensure that appropriate corrections, additions, or deletions are made, dated, explained (if necessary), and initialled by the investigator or by a member of the investigator's trial staff who is authorized to initial CRF changes for the investigator. This authorization should be documented.

(o) Determining whether all adverse events (AEs) are appropriately reported within the time periods required by GCP, the protocol, the IRB/IEC, the sponsor, and the applicable regulatory requirement(s).

(p) Determining whether the investigator is maintaining the essential documents (see 8. Essential Documents for the Conduct of a Clinical Trial).

(q) Communicating deviations from the protocol, SOPs, GCP, and the applicable regulatory requirements to the investigator and taking appropriate action designed to prevent recurrence of the detected deviations.

5.18.5 *Monitoring Procedures*

The monitor(s) should follow the sponsor's established written

SOPs as well as those procedures that are specified by the sponsor for monitoring a specific trial.

5. 18. 6 *Monitoring Report*

(a) The monitor should submit a written report to the sponsor after each trial-site visit or trial-related communication.

(b) Reports should include the date, site, name of the monitor, and name of the investigator or other individual(s) contacted.

(c) Reports should include a summary of what the monitor reviewed and the monitor's statements concerning the significant findings/facts, deviations and deficiencies, conclusions, actions taken or to be taken and/or actions recommended to secure compliance.

(d) The review and follow-up of the monitoring report with the sponsor should be documented by the sponsor's designated representative.

**Addendum**

(e) Reports of on-site and/or centralized monitoring should be provided to the sponsor (including appropriate management and staff responsible for trial and site oversight) in a timely manner for review and follow up. Results of monitoring activities should be documented in sufficient detail to allow verification of compliance with the monitoring plan. Reporting of centralized monitoring activities should be regular and may be independent from site visits.

**Addendum**

5. 18. 7 *Monitoring Plan*

The sponsor should develop a monitoring plan that is tailored to the specific human subject protection and data integrity risks of the trial. The plan should describe the monitoring strategy, themonitoring responsibilities of all the parties involved, the various monitoring methods to be used, and the rationale for their use. The plan should also emphasize the monitoring of critical data and processes. Particular attention should be given to those aspects that are not routine clinical practice and that require additional training. The monitoring plan should reference the applicable policies and procedures.

## 5.19 Audit

If or when sponsors perform audits, as part of implementing quality assurance, they should consider:

5.19.1 *Purpose*

The purpose of a sponsor's audit, which is independent of and separate from routine monitoring or quality control functions, should be to evaluate trial conduct and compliance with the protocol, SOPs, GCP, and the applicable regulatory requirements.

5.19.2 *Selection and Qualification of Auditors*

(a) The sponsor should appoint individuals, who are independent of the clinical trials/systems, to conduct audits.

(b) The sponsor should ensure that the auditors are qualified by training and experience to conduct audits properly. An auditor's qualifications should be documented.

5.19.3 *Auditing Procedures*

(a) The sponsor should ensure that the auditing of clinical trials/systems is conducted in accordance with the sponsor's written procedures on what to audit, how to audit, the frequency of audits, and the form and content of audit reports.

(b) The sponsor's audit plan and procedures for a trial audit should be guided by the importance of the trial to submissions to regulatory authorities, the number of subjects in the trial, the type and complexity of the trial, the level of risks to the trial subjects, and any identified problem(s).

(c) The observations and findings of the auditor(s) should be documented.

(d) To preserve the independence and value of the audit function, the regulatory authority(ies) should not routinely request the audit reports. Regulatory authority(ies) may seek access to an audit report on a case by case basis when evidence of serious GCP non-compliance exists, or in the course of legal proceedings.

(e) When required by applicable law or regulation, the sponsor should provide an audit certificate.

## 5.20 Noncompliance

5.20.1 Noncompliance with the protocol, SOPs, GCP, and/or applicable regulatory requirement(s) by an investigator/institution, or by member(s) of the sponsor's staff should lead to prompt action by the sponsor to secure compliance.

**Addendum**

If noncompliance that significantly affects or has the potential to significantly affect human subject protection or reliability of trial results is discovered, the sponsor should perform a root cause analysis and implement appropriate corrective and preventive actions.

5.20.2 If the monitoring and/or auditing identifies serious and/or persistent noncompliance on the part of an investigator/institution, the sponsor should terminate the investigator's/institution's participation in the trial. When an investigator's/institution's participation is terminated because of noncompliance, the sponsor should notify promptly the regulatory authority(ies).

## 5.21 Premature Termination or Suspension of a Trial

If a trial is prematurely terminated or suspended, the sponsor should promptly inform the investigators/institutions, and the regulatory authority(ies) of the termination or suspension and the reason(s) for the termination or suspension. The IRB/IEC should also be informed promptly and provided the reason(s) for the termination or suspension by the sponsor or by the investigator/institution, as specified by the applicable regulatory requirement(s).

## 5.22 Clinical Trial/Study Reports

Whether the trial is completed or prematurely terminated, the sponsor should ensure that the clinical trial reports are prepared and provided to the regulatory agency(ies) as required by the applicable regulatory requirement(s). The sponsor should also ensure that the clinical trial reports in marketing applications meet the standards of the ICH Guideline for Structure and Content of Clinical Study Reports. (NOTE: The ICH Guideline for Structure and Content of Clinical Study Reports specifies that abbreviated study reports may be acceptable in certain cases.)

### 5. 23 Multicentre Trials

For multicentre trials, the sponsor should ensure that:

5. 23. 1 All investigators conduct the trial in strict compliance with the protocol agreed to by the sponsor and, if required, by the regulatory authority(ies), and given approval/favourable opinion by the IRB/IEC.

5. 23. 2 The CRFs are designed to capture the required data at all multicentre trial sites. For those investigators who are collecting additional data, supplemental CRFs should also be provided that are designed to capture the additional data.

5. 23. 3 The responsibilities of coordinating investigator(s) and the other participating investigators are documented prior to the start of the trial.

5. 23. 4 All investigators are given instructions on following the protocol, on complying with a uniform set of standards for the assessment of clinical and laboratory findings, and on completing the CRFs.

5. 23. 5 Communication between investigators is facilitated.

## 6. Clinical Trial Protocol and Protocol Amendment(s)

The contents of a trial protocol should generally include the following topics. However, site specific information may be provided on separate protocol page(s), or addressed in a separate agreement, and some of the information listed below may be contained in other protocol referenced documents, such as an Investigator's Brochure.

### 6. 1 General Information

6. 1. 1 Protocol title, protocol identifying number, and date. Any amendment(s) should also bear the amendment number(s) and date(s).

6. 1. 2 Name and address of the sponsor and monitor (if other than the sponsor).

6. 1. 3 Name and title of the person(s) authorized to sign the protocol and the protocol amendment(s) for the sponsor.

6. 1. 4 Name, title, address, and telephone number(s) of the sponsor's

medical expert (or dentist when appropriate) for the trial.

6.1.5 Name and title of the investigator(s) who is (are) responsible for conducting the trial, and the address and telephone number(s) of the trial site(s).

6.1.6 Name, title, address, and telephone number(s) of the qualified physician (or dentist, if applicable), who is responsible for all trial-site related medical (or dental) decisions (if other than investigator).

6.1.7 Name(s) and address(es) of the clinical laboratory(ies) and other medical and/or technical department(s) and/or institutions involved in the trial.

## 6.2 Background Information

6.2.1 Name and description of the investigational product(s).

6.2.2 A summary of findings from nonclinical studies that potentially have clinical significance and from clinical trials that are relevant to the trial.

6.2.3 Summary of the known and potential risks and benefits, if any, to human subjects.

6.2.4 Description of and justification for the route of administration, dosage, dosage regimen, and treatment period(s).

6.2.5 A statement that the trial will be conducted in compliance with the protocol, GCP and the applicable regulatory requirement(s).

6.2.6 Description of the population to be studied.

6.2.7 References to literature and data that are relevant to the trial, and that provide background for the trial.

## 6.3 Trial Objectives and Purpose

A detailed description of the objectives and the purpose of the trial.

## 6.4 Trial Design

The scientific integrity of the trial and the credibility of the data from the trial depend substantially on the trial design. A description of the trial design, should include:

6.4.1 A specific statement of the primary endpoints and the secondary endpoints, if any, to be measured during the trial.

6.4.2 A description of the type/design of trial to be conducted (e.g., double-blind, placebo-controlled, parallel design) and a schematic diagram of trial design, procedures and stages.

6.4.3 A description of the measures taken to minimize/avoid bias, including:

(a) Randomization.

(b) Blinding.

6.4.4 A description of the trial treatment(s) and the dosage and dosage regimen of the investigational product(s). Also include a description of the dosage form, packaging, and labelling of the investigational product(s).

6.4.5 The expected duration of subject participation, and a description of the sequence and duration of all trial periods, including follow-up, if any.

6.4.6 A description of the "stopping rules" or "discontinuation criteria" for individual subjects, parts of trial and entire trial.

6.4.7 Accountability procedures for the investigational product(s), including the placebo(s) and comparator(s), if any.

6.4.8 Maintenance of trial treatment randomization codes and procedures for breaking codes.

6.4.9 The identification of any data to be recorded directly on the CRFs (i.e., no prior written or electronic record of data), and to be considered to be source data.

## 6.5 Selection and Withdrawal of Subjects

6.5.1 Subject inclusion criteria.

6.5.2 Subject exclusion criteria.

6.5.3 Subject withdrawal criteria (i.e., terminating investigational product treatment/trial treatment) and procedures specifying:

(a) When and how to withdraw subjects from the trial/ investigational product treatment.

(b) The type and timing of the data to be collected for withdrawn subjects.

(c) Whether and how subjects are to be replaced.

(d) The follow-up for subjects withdrawn from investigational product treatment/trial treatment.

## 6.6 Treatment of Subjects

6.6.1 The treatment(s) to be administered, including the name(s) of all the product(s), the dose(s), the dosing schedule(s), the route/

mode(s) of administration, and the treatment period(s), including the follow-up period(s) for subjects for each investigational product treatment/trial treatment group/arm of the trial.

6. 6. 2 Medication(s) /treatment(s) permitted (including rescue medication) and not permitted before and/or during the trial.

6. 6. 3 Procedures for monitoring subject compliance.

## 6. 7 Assessment of Efficacy

6. 7. 1 Specification of the efficacy parameters.

6. 7. 2 Methods and timing for assessing, recording, and analysing of efficacy parameters.

## 6. 8 Assessment of Safety

6. 8. 1 Specification of safety parameters.

6. 8. 2 The methods and timing for assessing, recording, and analysing safety parameters.

6. 8. 3 Procedures for eliciting reports of and for recording and reporting adverse event and intercurrent illnesses.

6. 8. 4 The type and duration of the follow-up of subjects after adverse events.

## 6. 9 Statistics

6. 9. 1 A description of the statistical methods to be employed, including timing of any planned interim analysis(ses).

6. 9. 2 The number of subjects planned to be enrolled. In multicentre trials, the numbers of enrolled subjects projected for each trial site should be specified. Reason for choice of sample size, including reflections on (or calculations of) the power of the trial and clinical justification.

6. 9. 3 The level of significance to be used.

6. 9. 4 Criteria for the termination of the trial.

6. 9. 5 Procedure for accounting for missing, unused, and spurious data.

6. 9. 6 Procedures for reporting any deviation(s) from the original statistical plan (any deviation(s) from the original statistical plan should be described and justified in protocol and/or in the final report, as appropriate).

6. 9. 7 The selection of subjects to be included in the analyses (e. g., all randomized subjects, all dosed subjects, all eligible subjects, evalu-

able subjects).

### 6.10 Direct Access to Source Data/Documents

The sponsor should ensure that it is specified in the protocol or other written agreement that the investigator (s) /institution (s) will permit trial-related monitoring, audits, IRB/IEC review, and regulatory inspection(s), providing direct access to source data/documents.

### 6.11 Quality Control and Quality Assurance

### 6.12 Ethics

Description of ethical considerations relating to the trial.

### 6.13 Data Handling and Record Keeping

### 6.14 Financing and Insurance

Financing and insurance if not addressed in a separate agreement.

### 6.15 Publication Policy

Publication policy, if not addressed in a separate agreement.

### 6.16 Supplements

(NOTE: Since the protocol and the clinical trial/study report are closely related, further relevant information can be found in the ICH Guideline for Structure and Content of Clinical Study Reports.)

## 7. Investigator's Brochure

### 7.1 Introduction

The Investigator's Brochure (IB) is a compilation of the clinical and non-clinical data on the investigational product(s) that are relevant to the study of the product(s) in human subjects. Its purpose is to provide the investigators and others involved in the trial with the information to facilitate their understanding of the rationale for, and their compliance with, many key features of the protocol, such as the dose, dose frequency/interval, methods of administration: and safety monitoring procedures. The IB also provides insight to support the clinical management of the study subjects during the course of the clinical trial. The information should be presented in a concise, simple, objective, balanced, and non-promotional form that enables a clinician, or potential investigator, to understand it and make his/her own unbiased risk-benefit assessment of the appropriateness of the proposed trial. For this reason, a medically qualified person should generally participate in the editing of an IB, but the contents of the IB should be approved by the disciplines that generated the described data.

This guideline delineates the minimum information that should be included in an IB and provides suggestions for its layout. It is expected that the type and extent of information available will vary with the stage of development of the investigational product. If the investigational product is marketed and its pharmacology is widely understood by medical practitioners, an extensive IB may not be necessary. Where permitted by regulatory authorities, a basic product information brochure, package leaflet, or labelling may be an appropriate alternative, provided that it includes current, comprehensive, and detailed information on all aspects of the investigational product that might be of importance to the investigator. If a marketed product is being studied for a new use (i. e. , a new indication) , an IB specific to that new use should be prepared. The IB should be reviewed at least annually and revised as necessary in compliance with a sponsor's written procedures. More frequent revision may be appropriate depending on the stage of development and the generation of relevant new information. However, in accordance with Good Clinical Practice, relevant new information may be so important that it should be communicated to the investigators, and possibly to the Institutional Review Boards (IRBs) /Independent Ethics Committees (IECs) and/or regulatory authorities before it is included in a revised IB. Generally, the sponsor is responsible for ensuring that an up-to-date IB is made available to the investigator(s) and the investigators are responsible for providing the up-to-date IB to the responsible IRBs/IECs. In the case of an investigator sponsored trial, the sponsor-investigator should determine whether a brochure is available from the commercial manufacturer. If the investigational product is provided by the sponsor-investigator, then he or she should provide the necessary information to the trial personnel. In cases where preparation of a formal IB is impractical, the sponsor-investigator should provide, as a substitute, an expanded background information section in the trial protocol that contains the minimum current information described in this guideline.

## 7.2 General Considerations

The IB should include:

7.2.1 *Title Page*

This should provide the sponsor's name, the identity of each investigational product (i. e., research number, chemical or approved generic name, and trade name(s) where legally permissible and desired by the sponsor), and the release date. It is also suggested that an edition number, and a reference to the number and date of the edition it supersedes, be provided. An example is given in Appendix 1.

7.2.2 *Confidentiality Statement*

The sponsor may wish to include a statement instructing the investigator/recipients to treat the IB as a confidential document for the sole information and use of the investigator's team and the IRB/IEC.

## 7.3 Contents of the Investigator's Brochure

The IB should contain the following sections, each with literature references where appropriate:

7.3.1 *Table of Contents*

An example of the Table of Contents is given in Appendix 2.

7.3.2 *Summary*

A brief summary (preferably not exceeding two pages) should be given, highlighting the significant physical, chemical, pharmaceutical, pharmacological, toxicological, pharmacokinetic, metabolic, and clinical information available that is relevant to the stage of clinical development of the investigational product.

7.3.3 *Introduction*

A brief introductory statement should be provided that contains the chemical name (and generic and trade name(s) when approved) of the investigational product(s), all active ingredients, the investigational product(s) pharmacological class and its expected position within this class (e. g., advantages), the rationale for performing research with the investigational product(s), and the anticipated prophylactic, therapeutic, or diagnostic indication(s). Finally, the introductory statement should provide the general approach to be followed in evaluating the investigational product.

7.3.4 *Physical, Chemical, and Pharmaceutical Properties and Formulation*

A description should be provided of the investigational product substance (s)(including the chemical and/or structural formula (e)), and a brief summary should be given of the relevant physical, chemical, and pharmaceutical properties.

To permit appropriate safety measures to be taken in the course of the trial, a description of the formulation (s) to be used, including excipients, should be provided and justified if clinically relevant. Instructions for the storage and handling of the dosage form (s) should also be given.

Any structural similarities to other known compounds should be mentioned.

7.3.5 *Nonclinical Studies*

*Introduction*:

The results of all relevant nonclinical pharmacology, toxicology, pharmacokinetic, and investigational product metabolism studies should be provided in summary form. This summary should address the methodology used, the results, and a discussion of the relevance of the findings to the investigated therapeutic and the possible unfavourable and unintended effects in humans.

The information provided may include the following, as appropriate, if known/available:

- Species tested
- Number and sex of animals in each group
- Unit dose (e. g., milligram/kilogram (mg/kg))
- Dose interval
- Route of administration
- Duration of dosing
- Information on systemic distribution
- Duration of post-exposure follow-up
- Results, including the following aspects:
  - Nature and frequency of pharmacological or toxic effects
  - Severity or intensity of pharmacological or toxic effects
  - Time to onset of effects
  - Reversibility of effects

- Duration of effects
- Dose response

Tabular format/listings should be used whenever possible to enhance the clarity of the presentation.

The following sections should discuss the most important findings from the studies, including the dose response of observed effects, the relevance to humans, and any aspects to be studied in humans. If applicable, the effective and nontoxic dose findings in the same animal species should be compared (i. e., the therapeutic index should be discussed). The relevance of this information to the proposed human dosing should be addressed. Whenever possible, comparisons should be made in terms of blood/tissue levels rather than on a mg/kg basis.

(a) *Nonclinical Pharmacology*

A summary of the pharmacological aspects of the investigational product and, where appropriate, its significant metabolites studied in animals, should be included. Such a summary should incorporate studies that assess potential therapeutic activity (e. g., efficacy models, receptor binding, and specificity) as well as those that assess safety (e. g., special studies to assess pharmacological actions other than the intended therapeutic effect(s)).

(b) *Pharmacokinetics and Product Metabolism in Animals*

A summary of the pharmacokinetics and biological transformation and disposition of the investigational product in all species studied should be given. The discussion of the findings should address the absorption and the local and systemic bioavailability of the investigational product and its metabolites, and their relationship to the pharmacological and toxicological findings in animal species.

(c) *Toxicology*

A summary of the toxicological effects found in relevant studies conducted in different animal species should be described under the following headings where appropriate:

- Single dose
- Repeated dose
- Carcinogenicity

- Special studies (e. g. , irritancy and sensitisation)
- Reproductive toxicity
- Genotoxicity (mutagenicity)

7. 3. 6 *Effects in Humans*

*Introduction*:

A thorough discussion of the known effects of the investigational product(s) in humans should be provided, including information on pharmacokinetics, metabolism, pharmacodynamics, dose response, safety, efficacy, and other pharmacological activities. Where possible, a summary of each completed clinical trial should be provided. Information should also be provided regarding results of any use of the investigational product(s) other than from in clinical trials, such as from experience during marketing.

(a) *Pharmacokinetics and Product Metabolism in Humans*

A summary of information on the pharmacokinetics of the investigational product(s) should be presented, including the following, if available:

- Pharmacokinetics (including metabolism, as appropriate, and absorption, plasma protein binding, distribution, and elimination).
- Bioavailability of the investigational product (absolute, where possible, and/or relative) using a reference dosage form.
- Population subgroups (e. g. , gender, age, and impaired organ function).
- Interactions (e. g. , product-product interactions and effects of food).
- Other pharmacokinetic data (e. g. , results of population studies performed within clinical trial(s).

(b) *Safety and Efficacy*

A summary of information should be provided about the investigational product's/products' (including metabolites, where appropriate) safety, pharmacodynamics, efficacy, and dose response that were obtained from preceding trials in humans (healthy volunteers and/or patients). The implications of this information should be discussed. In cases where a number of clinical trials have been completed, the use of summaries of safety and efficacy across multiple trials by indications in subgroups may provide a clear presentation of the data. Tabular summaries of adverse drug reactions for all the clinical trials (including those for all the studied indications) would be useful. Important differences in adverse drug reaction patterns/incidences across indications or subgroups should be discussed.

The IB should provide a description of the possible risks and adverse drug reactions to be anticipated on the basis of prior experiences with the product under investigation and with related products. A description should also be provided of the precautions or special monitoring to be done as part of the investigational use of the product (s) .

(c) *Marketing Experience*

The IB should identify countries where the investigational product has been marketed or approved. Any significant information arising from the marketed use should be summarised (e. g. , formulations, dosages, routes of administration, and adverse product reactions) . The IB should also identify all the countries where the investigational product did not receive approval/registration for marketing or was withdrawn from marketing/registration.

7. 3. 7 *Summary of Data and Guidance for the Investigator*

This section should provide an overall discussion of the nonclinical and clinical data, and should summarise the information from various sources on different aspects of the investigational product(s), wherever possible. In this way, the investigator can be provided with the most informative interpretation of the available data and with an assessment of the implications of the information for future clinical trials.

Where appropriate, the published reports on related products should be discussed. This could help the investigator to anticipate adverse drug reactions or other problems in clinical trials.

The overall aim of this section is to provide the investigator with a clear understanding of the possible risks and adverse reactions, and of the specific tests, observations, and precautions that may be needed for a clinical trial. This understanding should be based on the available physical, chemical, pharmaceutical, pharmacological, toxicological, and clinical information on the investigational product(s). Guidance should also be provided to the clinical investigator on the recognition and treatment of possible overdose and adverse drug reactions that is based on previous human experience and on the pharmacology of the investigational product.

## 7.4 Appendix 1

**Title Page (Example)**

**SPONSOR'S NAME**

**Product:**

**Research Number:**

**Name (s):** Chemical, Generic (if approved)
Trade Name (s) (if legally permissible and desired by the sponsor)

**INVESTIGATOR'S BROCHURE**

Edition Number:
Release Date:
Replaces Previous Edition Number:
Date:

## 7.5 Appendix 2

**Table of Contents of Investigator's Brochure (Example)**

- Confidentiality Statement (optional)
- Signature Page (optional)



NB: References on 1. Publications 2. Reports

These references should be found at the end of each chapter

Appendices (if any)

# 8. Essential Documents for the Conduct of a Clinical Trial

## 8.1 Introduction

Essential Documents are those documents which individually and collectively permit evaluation of the conduct of a trial and the quality of the data produced. These documents serve to demonstrate the compliance of the investigator, sponsor and monitor with the standards of Good Clinical Practice and with all applicable regulatory requirements.

Essential Documents also serve a number of other important purposes. Filing essential documents at the investigator/institution and sponsor sites in a timely manner can greatly assist in the successful management of a trial by the investigator, sponsor and monitor. These documents are also the ones which are usually audited by the sponsor's independent audit function and inspected by the regulatory authority (ies) as part of the process to confirm the validity of the trial conduct and the integrity of data collected.

The minimum list of essential documents which has been developed follows. The various documents are grouped in three sections according to the stage of the trial during which they will normally be generated: 1) before the clinical phase of the trial commences, 2) during the clinical conduct of the trial, and 3) after completion or termination of the trial. A description is given of the purpose of each document, and whether it should be filed in either the investigator/institution or sponsor files, or both. It is acceptable to combine some of the documents, provided the individual elements are readily identifiable.

Trial master files should be established at the beginning of the trial, both at the investigator/institution's site and at the sponsor's office. A final close-out of a trial can only be done when the monitor has reviewed both investigator/institution and sponsor files and confirmed that all necessary documents are in the appropriate files.

Any or all of the documents addressed in this guideline may be subject to, and should be available for, audit by the sponsor's auditor and inspection by the regulatory authority (ies).

## Addendum

The sponsor and investigator/institution should maintain a record of the location (s) of their respective essential documents including source documents. The storage system used during the trial and for archiving (irrespective of the type of media used) should provide for document identification, version history search, and retrieval.

Essential documents for the trial should be supplemented or may be reduced where justified (in advance of trial initiation) based on the importance and relevance of the specific documents to the trial.

The sponsor should ensure that the investigator has control of and continuous access to the CRF data reported to the sponsor. The sponsor should not have exclusive control of those data.

When a copy is used to replace an original document (e. g. , source documents, CRF) , the copy should fulfill the requirements for certified copies.

The investigator/institution should have control of all essential documents and records generated by the investigator/institution before, during, and after the trial.

## 8. 2 Before the Clinical Phase of the Trial Commences

During this planning stage the following documents should be generated and should be on file before the trial formally starts

**Table 1: Before the Clinical Phase of the Trial Commences**

| | Title of Document | Purpose | Located in Files of | |
|---|---|---|---|---|
| | | | Investigator/ Institution | Sponsor |
| 8. 2. 1 | Investigator's brochure | To document that relevant and current scientific information about the investigational product has been provided to the investigator | × | × |
| 8. 2. 2 | Signed Protocol and Amendments, if any, and sample Case Report Form (CRF) | To document investigator and sponsor agreement to the protocol/amendment(s) and CRF | × | × |

continue

| | Title of Document | Purpose | Located in Files of | |
|---|---|---|---|---|
| | | | Investigator/ Institution | Sponsor |
| 8. 2. 3 | Information given to trial Subject | | | |
| | - Informed Consent Form (including all applicable translations) | To document the informed consent | × | × |
| | - any OTHER WRITTEN information | To document that subjects will be given appropriate written information (content and wording) to support their ability to give fully informed consent | × | × |
| | - Advertisement for Subject Recruitment (if used) | To document that recruitment measures are appropriate and not coercive | × | |
| 8. 2. 4 | FINANCIAL ASPECTS OF THE TRIAL | To document the financial agreement between the investigator/institution and the sponsor for the trial | × | × |
| 8. 2. 5 | Insurance Statement(where required) | To document that compensation to subject(s) for trial-related injury will be available | × | × |
| 8. 2. 6 | Signed Agreement between Involved Parties, e. g. : | To document agreements | | |
| | - investigator/institution and sponsor | | × | × |
| | - investigator/institution and CRO | | × | × (where required) |
| | - sponsor and CRO | | × | × |

continue

| | Title of Document | Purpose | Located in Files of | |
|---|---|---|---|---|
| | | | Investigator/ Institution | Sponsor |
| 8. 2. 6 | - investigator/institution and authority(ies)(where required) | | | × |
| 8. 2. 7 | Dated,Documented Approval/favourable Opinion of Institutional Review Board (irb) /Independent Ethics Committee (IEC) OF THE FOLLOWING: - protocol and any amendments - CRF (if applicable) - informed consent form(s) - any other written information to be provided to the subject(s) - advertisement for subject recruitment (if used) - subject compensation (if any) - any other documents given approval/ favourable opinion | To document that the trial has been subject to IRB/IEC review and given approval/favourable opinion. To identify the version number and date of the document(s) | × | × |
| 8. 2. 8 | Institutional Review Board/Independent Ethics Committee Composition | To document that the IRB/ IEC is constituted in agreement with GCP | × | × (where required) |

continue

| | Title of Document | Purpose | Located in Files of | |
|---|---|---|---|---|
| | | | Investigator/ Institution | Sponsor |
| 8. 2. 9 | Regulatory Authority(ies) authorisation/approval/notification of protocol (where required) | To document appropriate authorisation/approval/notification by the regulatory authority(ies) has been obtained prior to initiation of the trial in compliance with the applicable regulatory requirement(s) | ×<br>(where required) | ×<br>(where required) |
| 8. 2. 10 | Curriculum Vitae and/or other relevant documents evidencing qualifications of investigator(s) and sub-investigator(s) | To document qualifications and eligibility to conduct trial and/or provide medical supervision of subjects | × | × |
| 8. 2. 11 | Normal Value(s)/range(s) for Medical/Laboratory/Technical procedure(s) and/or test(s) included in the protocol | To document normal values and/or ranges of the tests | × | × |
| 8. 2. 12 | Medical/Laboratory/Technical Procedures /tests<br>- certification or<br>- accreditation or<br>- established quality control and/or external quality assessment or<br>-other validation (where required) | To document competence of facility to perform required test(s), and support reliability of results | ×<br>(where required) | × |

continue

| | Title of Document | Purpose | Located in Files of | |
|---|---|---|---|---|
| | | | Investigator/ Institution | Sponsor |
| 8. 2. 13 | Sample of Label(s) attached to investigational product container(s) | To document compliance with applicable labelling regulations and appropriateness of instructions provided to the subjects | | × |
| 8. 2. 14 | Instructions for Handling of Investigational Product(s) and Trial-related Materials (if not included in protocol or Investigator's Brochure) | To document instructions needed to ensure proper storage, packaging, dispensing and disposition of investigational products and trial-related materials | × | × |
| 8. 2. 15 | shipping records for Investigational Product(s) and Trial-Related Materials | To document shipment dates, batch numbers and method of shipment of investigational product(s) and trial-related materials. Allows tracking of product batch, review of shipping conditions, and accountability | × | × |
| 8. 2. 16 | Certificate(s) of Analysis of Investigational Product(s) Shipped | To document identity, purity, and strength of investigational product(s) to be used in the trial | | × |
| 8. 2. 17 | decoding procedures for blinded trials | To document how, in case of an emergency, identity of blinded investigational product can be revealed without breaking the blind for the remaining subjects' treatment | × | × (third party if applicable) |
| 8. 2. 18 | Master Randomisation List | To document method for randomisation of trial population | | × (third party if applicable) |

continue

| | Title of Document | Purpose | Located in Files of | |
|---|---|---|---|---|
| | | | Investigator/ Institution | Sponsor |
| 8. 2. 19 | Pre-Trial Monitoring Report | To document that the site is suitable for the trial (may be combined with 8. 2. 20) | | × |
| 8. 2. 20 | Trial Initiation Monitoring Report | To document that trial procedures were reviewed with the investigator and the investigator's trial staff ( may be combined with 8. 2. 19) | × | × |

## 8. 3 During the Clinical Conduct of the Trial

In addition to having on file the above documents, the following should be added to the files during the trial as evidence that all new relevant information is documented as it becomes available

**Table 2: During the Clinical Conduct of the Trial**

| | Title of Document | Purpose | Located in Files of | |
|---|---|---|---|---|
| | | | Investigator/ Institution | Sponsor |
| 8. 3. 1 | Investigator's brochure updates | To document that investigator is informed in a timely manner of relevant information as it becomes available | × | × |
| 8. 3. 2 | Any Revision to: - protocol/amendment(s) and CRF - informed consent form - any other written information provided to subjects - advertisement for subject recruitment (if used) | To document revisions of these trial related documents that take effect during trial | × | × |

continue

| | Title of Document | Purpose | Located in Files of | |
|---|---|---|---|---|
| | | | Investigator/ Institution | Sponsor |
| 8. 3. 3 | Dated, Documented Approval/favourable Opinion of Institutional Review Board (irb) /Independent Ethics Committee (IEC) OF THE FOLLOWING:<br>- protocol amendment(s)<br>- revision(s) of:<br>- informed consent form<br>- any other written information to be provided to the subject<br>- advertisement for subject recruitment (if used)<br>- any other documents given approval/ favourable opinion<br>- continuing review of trial (where required) | To document that the amendment(s)and/or revision(s) have been subject to IRB/IEC review and were given approval/favourable opinion. To identify the version number and date of the document(s). | × | × |
| 8. 3. 4 | Regulatory Authority (ies) Authorisations/approvals/Notifications where required for:<br>- protocol amendment (s) and other documents | To document compliance with applicable regulatory requirements | × (where required) | × |
| 8. 3. 5 | Curriculum vitae for new Investigator(s)and/ or sub-investigator(s) | (see 8. 2. 10) | × | × |

continue

| | Title of Document | Purpose | Located in Files of | |
|---|---|---|---|---|
| | | | Investigator/ Institution | Sponsor |
| 8. 3. 6 | Updates to normal Value(s)/range(s) for Medical/ Laboratory/ Technical Procedure (s)/test(s)included in the protocol | To document normal values and ranges that are revised during the trial (see 8. 2. 11) | × | × |
| 8. 3. 7 | Updates of Medical/ Laboratory/Technical Procedures/tests<br>- certification or<br>- accreditation or<br>- established quality control and/or external quality assessment or<br>- other validation (where required) | To document that tests remain adequate throughout the trial period (see 8. 2. 12) | × (where required) | × |
| 8. 3. 8 | Documentation of Investigational Product(s)and Trial-Related Materials Shipment | (see 8. 2. 15) | × | × |
| 8. 3. 9 | Certificate (s) of Analysis for new batches of investigational Products | (see 8. 2. 16) | | × |
| 8. 3. 10 | Monitoring visit Reports | To document site visits by, and findings of, the monitor | | × |
| 8. 3. 11 | Relevant Communications other than Site Visits<br>- letters<br>- meeting notes<br>- notes of telephone calls | To document any agreements or significant discussions regarding trial administration, protocol violations, trial conduct, adverse event (AE) reporting | × | × |

continue

| | Title of Document | Purpose | Located in Files of | |
|---|---|---|---|---|
| | | | Investigator/ Institution | Sponsor |
| 8. 3. 12 | Signed Informed Consent Forms | To document that consent is obtained in accordance with GCP and protocol and dated prior to participation of each subject in trial. Also to document direct access permission (see 8. 2. 3) | × | |
| 8. 3. 13 | Source documents | To document the existence of the subject and substantiate integrity of trial data collected. To include original documents related to the trial, to medical treatment, and history of subject | × | |
| 8. 3. 14 | Signed, dated and Completed Case Report Forms (CRF) | To document that the investigator or authorised member of the investigator's staff confirms the observations recorded | × (copy) | × (original) |
| 8. 3. 15 | Documentation of CRF Corrections | To document all changes/additions or corrections made to CRF after initial data were recorded | × (copy) | × (original) |
| 8. 3. 16 | notification by originating investigator to sponsor of serious adverse events and related reports | Notification by originating investigator to sponsor of serious adverse events and related reports in accordance with 4. 11 | × | × |
| 8. 3. 17 | notification by sponsor and/or investigator, where applicable, to regulatory authority(ies) and irb(s)/iec(s) of unexpected serious adverse drug reactions and of other safety information | Notification by sponsor and/or investigator, where applicable, to regulatory authorities and IRB(s)/IEC(s) of unexpected serious adverse drug reactions in accordance with 5. 17 and 4. 11. 1 and of other safety information in accordance with 5. 16. 2 and 4. 11. 2 | × (where required) | × |

continue

| | Title of Document | Purpose | Located in Files of | |
|---|---|---|---|---|
| | | | Investigator/ Institution | Sponsor |
| 8. 3. 18 | Notification by sponsor to investigators of safety information | Notification by sponsor to investigators of safety information in accordance with 5. 16. 2 | × | × |
| 8. 3. 19 | Interim or annual reports to IRb/iec and authority(ies) | Interim or annual reports provided to IRB/IEC in accordance with 4. 10 and to authority(ies) in accordance with 5. 17. 3 | × | × (where required) |
| 8. 3. 20 | subject Screening Log | To document identification of subjects who entered pre-trial screening | × | × (where required) |
| 8. 3. 21 | Subject Identification code List | To document that investigator/institution keeps a confidential list of names of all subjects allocated to trial numbers on enrolling in the trial. Allows investigator/institution to reveal identity of any subject | × | |
| 8. 3. 22 | Subject ENROLMENT Log | To document chronological enrolment of subjects by trial number | × | |
| 8. 3. 23 | Investigational Products Accountability at the site | To document that investigational product(s) have been used according to the protocol | × | × |
| 8. 3. 24 | Signature sheet | To document signatures and initials of all persons authorised to make entries and/ or corrections on CRFs | × | × |
| 8. 3. 25 | Record of Retained Body Fluids/Tissue Samples(if any) | To document location and identification of retained samples if assays need to be repeated | × | × |

## 8.4 After Completion or Termination of the Trial

After completion or termination of the trial, all of the documents identified in Sections 8.2 and 8.3 should be in the file together with the following

**Table 3: After Completion or Termination of the Trial**

| | Title of Document | Purpose | Located in Files of | |
|---|---|---|---|---|
| | | | Investigator/ Institution | Sponsor |
| 8.4.1 | Investigational Product(s) Accountability at site | To document that the investigational product(s) have been used according to the protocol. To documents the final accounting of investigational product(s) received at the site, dispensed to subjects, returned by the subjects, and returned to sponsor | × | × |
| 8.4.2 | Documentation of Investigational Product Destruction | To document destruction of unused investigational products by sponsor or at site | × (if destroyed at site) | × |
| 8.4.3 | Completed Subject Identification code List | To permit identification of all subjects enrolled in the trial in case follow-up is required. List should be kept in a confidential manner and for agreed upon time | × | |
| 8.4.4 | Audit certificate (if available) | To document that audit was performed | | × |
| 8.4.5 | Final Trial Close-out Monitoring Report | To document that all activities required for trial close-out are completed, and copies of essential documents are held in the appropriate files | | × |
| 8.4.6 | treatment allocation and decoding documentation | Returned to sponsor to document any decoding that may have occurred | | × |

continue

| | Title of Document | Purpose | Located in Files of | |
|---|---|---|---|---|
| | | | Investigator/ Institution | Sponsor |
| 8. 4. 7 | final report by investigator to irb/iec where required, and where applicable, to the regulatory authority(ies) | To document completion of the trial | × | |
| 8. 4. 8 | Clinical study Report | To document results and interpretation of trial | × (if applicable) | × |

# Code of Federal Regulations

[Revised as of April 1, 2016]

# 21CFR PART11 ELECTRONIC RECORDS; ELECTRONIC SIGNATURES

## Subpart A - General Provisions

### Sec. 11. 1 Scope.

(a) The regulations in this part set forth the criteria under which the agency considers electronic records, electronic signatures, and handwritten signatures executed to electronic records to be trustworthy, reliable, and generally equivalent to paper records and handwritten signatures executed on paper.

(b) This part applies to records in electronic form that are created, modified, maintained, archived, retrieved, or transmitted, under any records requirements set forth in agency regulations. This part also applies to electronic records submitted to the agency under requirements of the Federal Food, Drug, and Cosmetic Act and the Public Health Service Act, even if such records are not specifically identified in agency regulations. However, this part does not apply to paper records that are, or have been, transmitted by electronic means.

(c) Where electronic signatures and their associated electronic records meet the requirements of this part, the agency will consider the electronic signatures to be equivalent to full handwritten signatures, initials, and other general signings as required by agency regulations, unless specifically excepted by regulation (s) effective on or after August 20, 1997.

(d) Electronic records that meet the requirements of this part may be used in lieu of paper records, in accordance with 11. 2, unless paper records are specifically required.

(e) Computer systems (including hardware and software), controls, and attendant documentation maintained under this part shall be readily available for, and subject to, FDA inspection.

(f)-(o) Omit.

## Sec. 11. 2 Implementation.

(a) For records required to be maintained but not submitted to the agency, persons may use electronic records in lieu of paper records or electronic signatures in lieu of traditional signatures, in whole or in part, provided that the requirements of this part are met.

(b) For records submitted to the agency, persons may use electronic records in lieu of paper records or electronic signatures in lieu of traditional signatures, in whole or in part, provided that:

(1) The requirements of this part are met; and

(2) The document or parts of a document to be submitted have been identified in public docket No. 92S-0251 as being the type of submission the agency accepts in electronic form. This docket will identify specifically what types of documents or parts of documents are acceptable for submission in electronic form without paper records and the agency receiving unit(s) (e. g., specific center, office, division, branch) to which such submissions may be made. Documents to agency receiving unit(s) not specified in the public docket will not be considered as official if they are submitted in electronic form; paper forms of such documents will be considered as official and must accompany any electronic records. Persons are expected to consult with the intended agency receiving unit for details on how (e. g., method of transmission, media, file formats, and technical protocols) and whether to proceed with the electronic submission.

## Sec. 11. 3 Definitions.

(a) The definitions and interpretations of terms contained in section 201 of the act apply to those terms when used in this part.

(b) The following definitions of terms also apply to this part:

(1) *Act* means the Federal Food, Drug, and Cosmetic Act (secs. 201-903 (21 U. S. C. 321-393)).

(2) *Agency* means the Food and Drug Administration.

(3) *Biometrics* means a method of verifying an individual's identity based on measurement of the individual's physical feature (s) or repeatable action (s) where those features and/or actions are both

unique to that individual and measurable.

(4) *Closed system* means an environment in which system access is controlled by persons who are responsible for the content of electronic records that are on the system.

(5) *Digital signature* means an electronic signature based upon cryptographic methods of originator authentication, computed by using a set of rules and a set of parameters such that the identity of the signer and the integrity of the data can be verified.

(6) *Electronic record* means any combination of text, graphics, data, audio, pictorial, or other information representation in digital form that is created, modified, maintained, archived, retrieved, or distributed by a computer system.

(7) *Electronic signature* means a computer data compilation of any symbol or series of symbols executed, adopted, or authorized by an individual to be the legally binding equivalent of the individual's handwritten signature.

(8) *Handwritten signature* means the scripted name or legal mark of an individual handwritten by that individual and executed or adopted with the present intention to authenticate a writing in a permanent form. The act of signing with a writing or marking instrument such as a pen or stylus is preserved. The scripted name or legal mark, while conventionally applied to paper, may also be applied to other devices that capture the name or mark.

(9) *Open system* means an environment in which system access is not controlled by persons who are responsible for the content of electronic records that are on the system.

# Subpart B - Electronic Records

## Sec. 11. 10 Controls for closed systems.

Persons who use closed systems to create, modify, maintain, or transmit electronic records shall employ procedures and controls designed to ensure the authenticity, integrity, and, when appropriate, the confidentiality of electronic records, and to ensure that the signer cannot readily repudiate the signed record as not genuine. Such procedures and controls shall include the following:

(a) Validation of systems to ensure accuracy, reliability, consistent intended performance, and the ability to discern invalid or altered records.

(b) The ability to generate accurate and complete copies of records in both human readable and electronic form suitable for inspection, review, and copying by the agency. Persons should contact the agency if there are any questions regarding the ability of the agency to perform such review and copying of the electronic records.

(c) Protection of records to enable their accurate and ready retrieval throughout the records retention period.

(d) Limiting system access to authorized individuals.

(e) Use of secure, computer-generated, time-stamped audit trails to independently record the date and time of operator entries and actions that create, modify, or delete electronic records. Record changes shall not obscure previously recorded information. Such audit trail documentation shall be retained for a period at least as long as that required for the subject electronic records and shall be available for agency review and copying.

(f) Use of operational system checks to enforce permitted sequencing of steps and events, as appropriate.

(g) Use of authority checks to ensure that only authorized individuals can use the system, electronically sign a record, access the operation or computer system input or output device, alter a record, or perform the operation at hand.

(h) Use of device (e. g. , terminal) checks to determine, as appropriate, the validity of the source of data input or operational instruction.

(i) Determination that persons who develop, maintain, or use electronic record/electronic signature systems have the education, training, and experience to perform their assigned tasks.

(j) The establishment of, and adherence to, written policies that hold individuals accountable and responsible for actions initiated under their electronic signatures, in order to deter record and signature falsification.

(k) Use of appropriate controls over systems documentation including:

  (1) Adequate controls over the distribution of, access to, and use of documentation for system operation and maintenance.

  (2) Revision and change control procedures to maintain an audit trail that documents time-sequenced development and modification of

systems documentation.

### Sec. 11. 30 Controls for open systems.

Persons who use open systems to create, modify, maintain, or transmit electronic records shall employ procedures and controls designed to ensure the authenticity, integrity, and, as appropriate, the confidentiality of electronic records from the point of their creation to the point of their receipt. Such procedures and controls shall include those identified in 11. 10, as appropriate, and additional measures such as document encryption and use of appropriate digital signature standards to ensure, as necessary under the circumstances, record authenticity, integrity, and confidentiality.

### Sec. 11. 50 Signature manifestations.

(a) Signed electronic records shall contain information associated with the signing that clearly indicates all of the following:
  (1) The printed name of the signer;
  (2) The date and time when the signature was executed; and
  (3) The meaning (such as review, approval, responsibility, or authorship) associated with the signature.

(b) The items identified in paragraphs (a)(1), (a)(2), and (a)(3) of this section shall be subject to the same controls as for electronic records and shall be included as part of any human readable form of the electronic record (such as electronic display or printout).

### Sec. 11. 70 Signature/record linking.

Electronic signatures and handwritten signatures executed to electronic records shall be linked to their respective electronic records to ensure that the signatures cannot be excised, copied, or otherwise transferred to falsify an electronic record by ordinary means.

## Subpart C - Electronic Signatures

### Sec. 11. 100 General requirements.

(a) Each electronic signature shall be unique to one individual and shall not be reused by, or reassigned to, anyone else.

(b) Before an organization establishes, assigns, certifies, or otherwise sanctions an individual's electronic signature, or any element of such electronic signature, the organization shall verify the identity of the individual.

(c) Persons using electronic signatures shall, prior to or at the time of such use, certify to the agency that the electronic signatures in their system, used on or after August 20, 1997, are intended to be the legally binding equivalent of traditional handwritten signatures.

  (1) The certification shall be submitted in paper form and signed with a traditional handwritten signature, to the Office of Regional Operations (HFC-100), 5600 Fishers Lane, Rockville, MD 20857.

  (2) Persons using electronic signatures shall, upon agency request, provide additional certification or testimony that a specific electronic signature is the legally binding equivalent of the signer's handwritten signature.

## Sec. 11. 200 Electronic signature components and controls.

(a) Electronic signatures that are not based upon biometrics shall:

  (1) Employ at least two distinct identification components such as an identification code and password.

    (i) When an individual executes a series of signings during a single, continuous period of controlled system access, the first signing shall be executed using all electronic signature components; subsequent signings shall be executed using at least one electronic signature component that is only executable by, and designed to be used only by, the individual.

    (ii) When an individual executes one or more signings not performed during a single, continuous period of controlled system access, each signing shall be executed using all of the electronic signature components.

  (2) Be used only by their genuine owners; and

  (3) Be administered and executed to ensure that attempted use of an individual's electronic signature by anyone other than its genuine owner requires collaboration of two or more individuals.

(b) Electronic signatures based upon biometrics shall be designed to ensure that they cannot be used by anyone other than their genuine owners.

## Sec. 11. 300 Controls for identification codes/passwords.

Persons who use electronic signatures based upon use of identification codes in combination with passwords shall employ controls to ensure their security and integrity. Such controls shall include:

(a) Maintaining the uniqueness of each combined identification code and password, such that no two individuals have the same combination of identification code and password.

(b) Ensuring that identification code and password issuances are periodically checked, recalled, or revised (e. g. , to cover such events as password aging).

(c) Following loss management procedures to electronically deauthorize lost, stolen, missing, or otherwise potentially compromised tokens, cards, and other devices that bear or generate identification code or password information, and to issue temporary or permanent replacements using suitable, rigorous controls.

(d) Use of transaction safeguards to prevent unauthorized use of passwords and/or identification codes, and to detect and report in an immediate and urgent manner any attempts at their unauthorized use to the system security unit, and, as appropriate, to organizational management.

(e) Initial and periodic testing of devices, such as tokens or cards, that bear or generate identification code or password information to ensure that they function properly and have not been altered in an unauthorized manner.

[Revised as of April 1, 2016]

# 21CFR PART50 PROTECTION OF HUMAN SUBJECTS

## Subpart A - General Provisions

### Sec. 50. 1 Scope.

(a) This part applies to all clinical investigations regulated by the Food and Drug Administration under sections 505 (i) and 520 (g) of the Federal Food, Drug, and Cosmetic Act, as well as clinical investigations that support applications for research or marketing permits for products regulated by the Food and Drug Administration, including foods, including dietary supplements, that bear a nutrient content claim or a health claim, infant formulas, food and color additives, drugs for human use, medical devices for human use, biological products for human use, and electronic products. Additional specific obligations and commitments of, and standards of conduct for, persons who sponsor or monitor clinical investigations involving particular test articles may also be found in other parts (e. g. , parts 312 and 812) . Compliance with these parts is intended to protect the rights and safety of subjects involved in investigations filed with the Food and Drug Administration pursuant to sections 403, 406, 409, 412, 413, 502, 503, 505, 510, 513-516, 518-520, 721, and 801 of the Federal Food, Drug, and Cosmetic Act and sections 351 and 354-360F of the Public Health Service Act.

(b) References in this part to regulatory sections of the Code of Federal Regulations are to chapter I of title 21, unless otherwise noted.

### Sec. 50. 3 Definitions.

As used in this part:

(a) *Act* means the Federal Food, Drug, and Cosmetic Act, as amended (secs. 201-902, 52 Stat. 1040 et seq. as amended (21 U. S. C. 321-392) ).

(b) *Application* for research or marketing permit includes:

(1) A color additive petition, described in part 71.

(2) A food additive petition, described in parts 171 and 571.

(3) Data and information about a substance submitted as part of the procedures for establishing that the substance is generally recognized as safe for use that results or may reasonably be expected to result, directly or indirectly, in its becoming a component or otherwise affecting the characteristics of any food, described in 170. 30 and 570. 30.

(4) Data and information about a food additive submitted as part of the procedures for food additives permitted to be used on an interim basis pending additional study, described in 180. 1.

(5) Data and information about a substance submitted as part of the procedures for establishing a tolerance for unavoidable contaminants in food and food-packaging materials, described in section 406 of the act.

(6) An investigational new drug application, described in part 312 of this chapter.

(7) A new drug application, described in part 314.

(8) Data and information about the bioavailability or bioequivalence of drugs for human use submitted as part of the procedures for issuing, amending, or repealing a bioequivalence requirement, described in part 320.

(9) Data and information about an over-the-counter drug for human use submitted as part of the procedures for classifying these drugs as generally recognized as safe and effective and not misbranded, described in part 330.

(10) Data and information about a prescription drug for human use submitted as part of the procedures for classifying these drugs as generally recognized as safe and effective and not misbranded, described in this chapter.

(11) [Reserved]

(12) An application for a biologics license, described in part 601 of this chapter.

(13) Data and information about a biological product submitted as part of the procedures for determining that licensed biological products

are safe and effective and not misbranded, described in part 601.

(14) Data and information about an in vitro diagnostic product submitted as part of the procedures for establishing, amending, or repealing a standard for these products, described in part 809.

(15) An Application for an Investigational Device Exemption, described in part 812.

(16) Data and information about a medical device submitted as part of the procedures for classifying these devices, described in section 513.

(17) Data and information about a medical device submitted as part of the procedures for establishing, amending, or repealing a standard for these devices, described in section 514.

(18) An application for premarket approval of a medical device, described in section 515.

(19) A product development protocol for a medical device, described in section 515.

(20) Data and information about an electronic product submitted as part of the procedures for establishing, amending, or repealing a standard for these products, described in section 358 of the Public Health Service Act.

(21) Data and information about an electronic product submitted as part of the procedures for obtaining a variance from any electronic product performance standard, as described in 1010. 4.

(22) Data and information about an electronic product submitted as part of the procedures for granting, amending, or extending an exemption from a radiation safety performance standard, as described in 1010. 5.

(23) Data and information about a clinical study of an infant formula when submitted as part of an infant formula notification under section 412 (c) of the Federal Food, Drug, and Cosmetic Act.

(24) Data and information submitted in a petition for a nutrient content claim, described in 101. 69 of this chapter, or for a health claim, described in 101. 70 of this chapter.

(25) Data and information from investigations involving children submitted in a new dietary ingredient notification, described in 190. 6 of this chapter.

(c) *Clinical investigation* means any experiment that involves a test article and one or more human subjects and that either is subject to requirements for prior submission to the Food and Drug Administration under section 505 (i) or 520 (g) of the act, or is not subject to requirements for prior submission to the Food and Drug Administration under these sections of the act, but the results of which are intended to be submitted later to, or held for inspection by, the Food and Drug Administration as part of an application for a research or marketing permit. The term does not include experiments that are subject to the provisions of part 58 of this chapter, regarding nonclinical laboratory studies.

(d) *Investigator* means an individual who actually conducts a clinical investigation, i. e. , under whose immediate direction the test article is administered or dispensed to, or used involving, a subject, or, in the event of an investigation conducted by a team of individuals, is the responsible leader of that team.

(e) *Sponsor* means a person who initiates a clinical investigation, but who does not actually conduct the investigation, i. e. , the test article is administered or dispensed to or used involving, a subject under the immediate direction of another individual. A person other than an individual (e. g. , corporation or agency) that uses one or more of its own employees to conduct a clinical investigation it has initiated is considered to be a sponsor (not a sponsor-investigator) , and the employees are considered to be investigators.

(f) *Sponsor-investigator* means an individual who both initiates and actually conducts, alone or with others, a clinical investigation, i. e. , under whose immediate direction the test article is administered or dispensed to, or used involving, a subject. The term does not include any person other than an individual, e. g. , corporation or agency.

(g) *Human subject* means an individual who is or becomes a participant in research, either as a recipient of the test article or as a control. A subject may be either a healthy human or a patient.

(h) *Institution* means any public or private entity or agency (including Federal, State, and other agencies) . The word facility as used in section 520 (g) of the act is deemed to be synonymous with the term institution for purposes of this part.

(i) *Institutional review board* (IRB) means any board, committee, or other group formally designated by an institution to review biomedical research involving humans as subjects, to approve the initiation of and conduct periodic review of such research. The term has the same meaning as the phrase institutional review committee as used in section 520 (g) of the act.

(j) *Test article* means any drug (including a biological product for human use), medical device for human use, human food additive, color additive, electronic product, or any other article subject to regulation under the act or under sections 351 and 354-360F of the Public Health Service Act (42 U. S. C. 262 and 263b-263n).

(k) *Minimal risk* means that the probability and magnitude of harm or discomfort anticipated in the research are not greater in and of themselves than those ordinarily encountered in daily life or during the performance of routine physical or psychological examinations or tests.

(l) *Legally authorized representative* means an individual or judicial or other body authorized under applicable law to consent on behalf of a prospective subject to the subject's particpation in the procedure (s) involved in the research.

(m) *Family member* means any one of the following legally competent persons: Spouse; parents; children (including adopted children); brothers, sisters, and spouses of brothers and sisters; and any individual related by blood or affinity whose close association with the subject is the equivalent of a family relationship.

(n) *Assent* means a child's affirmative agreement to participate in a clinical investigation. Mere failure to object should not, absent affirmative agreement, be construed as assent.

(o) *Children* means persons who have not attained the legal age for consent to treatments or procedures involved in clinical investigations, under the applicable law of the jurisdiction in which the clinical investigation will be conducted.

(p) *Parent* means a child's biological or adoptive parent.

(q) *Ward* means a child who is placed in the legal custody of the State or other agency, institution, or entity, consistent with applicable Federal, State, or local law.

(r) *Permission* means the agreement of parent (s) or guardian to the participation of their child or ward in a clinical investigation.

(s) *Guardian* means an individual who is authorized under applicable

State or local law to consent on behalf of a child to general medical care.

## Subpart B - Informed Consent of Human Subjects

### Sec. 50. 20 General requirements for informed consent.

Except as provided in 50. 23 and 50. 24, no investigator may involve a human being as a subject in research covered by these regulations unless the investigator has obtained the legally effective informed consent of the subject or the subject's legally authorized representative. An investigator shall seek such consent only under circumstances that provide the prospective subject or the representative sufficient opportunity to consider whether or not to participate and that minimize the possibility of coercion or undue influence. The information that is given to the subject or the representative shall be in language understandable to the subject or the representative. No informed consent, whether oral or written, may include any exculpatory language through which the subject or the representative is made to waive or appear to waive any of the subject's legal rights, or releases or appears to release the investigator, the sponsor, the institution, or its agents from liability for negligence.

### Sec. 50. 23 Exception from general requirements.

(a) The obtaining of informed consent shall be deemed feasible unless, before use of the test article (except as provided in paragraph (b) of this section), both the investigator and a physician who is not otherwise participating in the clinical investigation certify in writing all of the following:

(1) The human subject is confronted by a life-threatening situation necessitating the use of the test article.

(2) Informed consent cannot be obtained from the subject because of an inability to communicate with, or obtain legally effective consent from, the subject.

(3) Time is not sufficient to obtain consent from the subject's legal representative.

(4) There is available no alternative method of approved or generally recognized therapy that provides an equal or greater likelihood of

saving the life of the subject.

(b) If immediate use of the test article is, in the investigator's opinion, required to preserve the life of the subject, and time is not sufficient to obtain the independent determination required in paragraph (a) of this section in advance of using the test article, the determinations of the clinical investigator shall be made and, within 5 working days after the use of the article, be reviewed and evaluated in writing by a physician who is not participating in the clinical investigation.

(c) The documentation required in paragraph (a) or (b) of this section shall be submitted to the IRB within 5 working days after the use of the test article.

(d) (1) Under 10 U. S. C. 1107 (f) the President may waive the prior consent requirement for the administration of an investigational new drug to a member of the armed forces in connection with the member's participation in a particular military operation. The statute specifies that only the President may waive informed consent in this connection and the President may grant such a waiver only if the President determines in writing that obtaining consent: Is not feasible; is contrary to the best interests of the military member; or is not in the interests of national security. The statute further provides that in making a determination to waive prior informed consent on the ground that it is not feasible or the ground that it is contrary to the best interests of the military members involved, the President shall apply the standards and criteria that are set forth in the relevant FDA regulations for a waiver of the prior informed consent requirements of section 505(i)(4) of the Federal Food, Drug, and Cosmetic Act (21 U. S. C. 355(i)(4)). Before such a determination may be made that obtaining informed consent from military personnel prior to the use of an investigational drug (including an antibiotic or biological product) in a specific protocol under an investigational new drug application (IND) sponsored by the Department of Defense (DOD) and limited to specific military personnel involved in a particular military operation is not feasible or is contrary to the best interests of the military members involved the Secretary of Defense must first request such a determination from the President, and certify and document to the President that the following standards and criteria contained in paragraphs (d)(1) through (d)(4) of this section have been met.

(i) The extent and strength of evidence of the safety and effectiveness of the investigational new drug in relation to the medical risk that could be encountered during the military operation supports the drug's administration under an IND.

(ii) The military operation presents a substantial risk that military personnel may be subject to a chemical, biological, nuclear, or other exposure likely to produce death or serious or life-threatening injury or illness.

(iii) There is no available satisfactory alternative therapeutic or preventive treatment in relation to the intended use of the investigational new drug.

(iv) Conditioning use of the investigational new drug on the voluntary participation of each member could significantly risk the safety and health of any individual member who would decline its use, the safety of other military personnel, and the accomplishment of the military mission.

(v) A duly constituted institutional review board (IRB) established and operated in accordance with the requirements of paragraphs (d)(2) and (d)(3) of this section, responsible for review of the study, has reviewed and approved the investigational new drug protocol and the administration of the investigational new drug without informed consent. DOD's request is to include the documentation required by 56. 115 (a) (2) of this chapter.

(vi) DOD has explained:

(A) The context in which the investigational drug will be administered, e. g. , the setting or whether it will be self-administered or it will be administered by a health professional;

(B) The nature of the disease or condition for which the preventive or therapeutic treatment is intended; and

(C) To the extent there are existing data or information available, information on conditions that could alter the effects of the investigational drug.

(vii) DOD's recordkeeping system is capable of tracking and will be used to track the proposed treatment from supplier to the individual recipient.

(viii) Each member involved in the military operation will be given, prior to the administration of the investigational new drug, a specific written information sheet (including information required by 10 U. S. C. 1107(d) ) concerning the investigational new drug, the risks and benefits of its use, potential side effects, and other pertinent information about the appropriate use of the product.

(ix) Medical records of members involved in the military operation will accurately document the receipt by members of the notification required by paragraph (d)(1)(viii) of this section.

(x) Medical records of members involved in the military operation will accurately document the receipt by members of any investigational new drugs in accordance with FDA regulations including part 312 of this chapter.

(xi) DOD will provide adequate followup to assess whether there are beneficial or adverse health consequences that result from the use of the investigational product.

(xii) DOD is pursuing drug development, including a time line, and marketing approval with due diligence.

(xiii) FDA has concluded that the investigational new drug protocol may proceed subject to a decision by the President on the informed consent waiver request.

(xiv) DOD will provide training to the appropriate medical personnel and potential recipients on the specific investigational new drug to be administered prior to its use.

(xv) DOD has stated and justified the time period for which the waiver is needed, not to exceed one year, unless separately renewed under these standards and criteria.

(xvi) DOD shall have a continuing obligation to report to the FDA and to the President any changed circumstances relating to these standards and criteria (including the time period referred to in paragraph (d)(1)(xv) of this section) or that otherwise might affect the determination to use an investigational new drug without informed consent.

(xvii) DOD is to provide public notice as soon as practicable and consistent with classification requirements through notice in the Federal Register describing each waiver of informed consent determination, a summary of the most updated scientific information on the products used, and other pertinent information.

(xviii) Use of the investigational drug without informed consent otherwise conforms with applicable law.

(2) The duly constituted institutional review board, described in paragraph (d)(1)(v) of this section, must include at least 3 nonaffiliated members who shall not be employees or officers of the Federal Government (other than for purposes of membership on the IRB) and shall be required to obtain any necessary security clearances. This IRB shall review the proposed IND protocol at a convened meeting at which a majority of the members are present including at least one member whose primary concerns are in nonscientific areas and, if feasible, including a majority of the nonaffiliated members. The information required by 56. 115 (a)(2) of this chapter is to be provided to the Secretary of Defense for further review.

(3) The duly constituted institutional review board, described in paragraph (d)(1)(v) of this section, must review and approve:

(i) The required information sheet;

(ii) The adequacy of the plan to disseminate information, including distribution of the information sheet to potential recipients, on the investigational product (e. g. , in forms other than written) ;

(iii) The adequacy of the information and plans for its dissemination to health care providers, including potential side effects, contraindications, potential interactions, and other pertinent considerations; and

(iv) An informed consent form as required by part 50 of this chapter, in those circumstances in which DOD determines that informed consent may be obtained from some or all personnel involved.

(4) DOD is to submit to FDA summaries of institutional review board meetings at which the proposed protocol has been reviewed.

(5) Nothing in these criteria or standards is intended to preempt or limit FDA's and DOD's authority or obligations under applicable statutes and regulations.

(e) (1) Obtaining informed consent for investigational in vitro diagnostic devices used to identify chemical, biological, radiological, or nuclear agents will be deemed feasible unless, before use of the test article, both the investigator (e. g. , clinical laboratory director or other responsible individual) and a physician who is not otherwise participating in the clinical investigation make the determinations and later certify in writing all of the following:

(i) The human subject is confronted by a life-threatening situation necessitating the use of the investigational in vitro diagnostic device to identify a chemical, biological, radiological, or nuclear agent that would suggest a terrorism event or other public health emergency.

(ii) Informed consent cannot be obtained from the subject because:

(A) There was no reasonable way for the person directing that the specimen be collected to know, at the time the specimen was collected, that there would be a need to use the investigational in vitro diagnostic device on that subject's specimen; and

(B) Time is not sufficient to obtain consent from the subject without risking the life of the subject.

(iii) Time is not sufficient to obtain consent from the subject's legally authorized representative.

(iv) There is no cleared or approved available alternative method of diagnosis, to identify the chemical, biological, radiological, or nuclear agent that provides an equal or greater likelihood of saving the life of the subject.

(2) If use of the investigational device is, in the opinion of the investigator (e. g. , clinical laboratory director or other responsible person) , required to preserve the life of the subject, and time is not sufficient to obtain the independent determination required in para-

graph (e)(1) of this section in advance of using the investigational device, the determinations of the investigator shall be made and, within 5 working days after the use of the device, be reviewed and evaluated in writing by a physician who is not participating in the clinical investigation.

(3) The investigator must submit the written certification of the determinations made by the investigator and an independent physician required in paragraph (e)(1) or (e)(2) of this section to the IRB and FDA within 5 working days after the use of the device.

(4) An investigator must disclose the investigational status of the in vitro diagnostic device and what is known about the performance characteristics of the device in the report to the subject's health care provider and in any report to public health authorities. The investigator must provide the IRB with the information required in 50. 25 (except for the information described in 50. 25(a)(8)) and the procedures that will be used to provide this information to each subject or the subject's legally authorized representative at the time the test results are provided to the subject's health care provider and public health authorities.

(5) The IRB is responsible for ensuring the adequacy of the information required in section 50. 25 (except for the information described in 50. 25 (a)(8) ) and for ensuring that procedures are in place to provide this information to each subject or the subject's legally authorized representative.

(6) No State or political subdivision of a State may establish or continue in effect any law, rule, regulation or other requirement that informed consent be obtained before an investigational in vitro diagnostic device may be used to identify chemical, biological, radiological, or nuclear agent in suspected terrorism events and other potential public health emergencies that is different from, or in addition to, the requirements of this regulation.

## Sec. 50. 24 Exception from informed consent requirements for emergency research.

(a) The IRB responsible for the review, approval, and continuing review of the clinical investigation described in this section may approve that investigation without requiring that informed consent of all research subjects be obtained if the IRB (with the concurrence of a licensed physician who is a member of or consultant to the IRB and who is not otherwise participating in the clinical investigation) finds and documents each of the following:

(1) The human subjects are in a life-threatening situation, available treatments are unproven or unsatisfactory, and the collection of valid scientific evidence, which may include evidence obtained through randomized placebo-controlled investigations, is necessary to determine the safety and effectiveness of particular interventions.

(2) Obtaining informed consent is not feasible because:

(i) The subjects will not be able to give their informed consent as a result of their medical condition;

(ii) The intervention under investigation must be administered before consent from the subjects' legally authorized representatives is feasible; and

(iii) There is no reasonable way to identify prospectively the individuals likely to become eligible for participation in the clinical investigation.

(3) Participation in the research holds out the prospect of direct benefit to the subjects because:

(i) Subjects are facing a life-threatening situation that necessitates intervention;

(ii) Appropriate animal and other preclinical studies have been conducted, and the information derived from those studies and related evidence support the potential for the intervention to provide a direct benefit to the individual subjects; and

(iii) Risks associated with the investigation are reasonable in relation to what is known about the medical condition of the potential class of subjects, the risks and benefits of standard therapy, if any, and what is known about the risks and benefits of the proposed intervention or activity.

(4) The clinical investigation could not practicably be carried out without the waiver.

(5) The proposed investigational plan defines the length of the potential

therapeutic window based on scientific evidence, and the investigator has committed to attempting to contact a legally authorized representative for each subject within that window of time and, if feasible, to asking the legally authorized representative contacted for consent within that window rather than proceeding without consent. The investigator will summarize efforts made to contact legally authorized representatives and make this information available to the IRB at the time of continuing review.

(6) The IRB has reviewed and approved informed consent procedures and an informed consent document consistent with 50. 25. These procedures and the informed consent document are to be used with subjects or their legally authorized representatives in situations where use of such procedures and documents is feasible. The IRB has reviewed and approved procedures and information to be used when providing an opportunity for a family member to object to a subject's participation in the clinical investigation consistent with paragraph (a)(7)(v) of this section.

(7) Additional protections of the rights and welfare of the subjects will be provided, including, at least:

(i) Consultation (including, where appropriate, consultation carried out by the IRB) with representatives of the communities in which the clinical investigation will be conducted and from which the subjects will be drawn;

(ii) Public disclosure to the communities in which the clinical investigation will be conducted and from which the subjects will be drawn, prior to initiation of the clinical investigation, of plans for the investigation and its risks and expected benefits;

(iii) Public disclosure of sufficient information following completion of the clinical investigation to apprise the community and researchers of the study, including the demographic characteristics of the research population, and its results;

(iv) Establishment of an independent data monitoring committee to exercise oversight of the clinical investigation; and

(v) If obtaining informed consent is not feasible and a legally authorized representative is not reasonably available, the investigator has committed, if feasible, to attempting to contact within the therapeutic window the subject's family member who is not a legally authorized representative, and asking whether he or she objects to the subject's participation in the clinical investigation. The investigator will summarize efforts made to contact family members and make this information available to the IRB at the time of continuing review.

(b) The IRB is responsible for ensuring that procedures are in place to inform, at the earliest feasible opportunity, each subject, or if the subject remains incapacitated, a legally authorized representative of the subject, or if such a representative is not reasonably available, a family member, of the subject's inclusion in the clinical investigation, the details of the investigation and other information contained in the informed consent document. The IRB shall also ensure that there is a procedure to inform the subject, or if the subject remains incapacitated, a legally authorized representative of the subject, or if such a representative is not reasonably available, a family member, that he or she may discontinue the subject's participation at any time without penalty or loss of benefits to which the subject is otherwise entitled. If a legally authorized representative or family member is told about the clinical investigation and the subject's condition improves, the subject is also to be informed as soon as feasible. If a subject is entered into a clinical investigation with waived consent and the subject dies before a legally authorized representative or family member can be contacted, information about the clinical investigation is to be provided to the subject's legally authorized representative or family member, if feasible.

(c) The IRB determinations required by paragraph (a) of this section and the documentation required by paragraph (e) of this section are to be retained by the IRB for at least 3 years after completion of the clinical investigation, and the records shall be accessible for inspection and copying by FDA in accordance with 56. 115 (b) of this chapter.

(d) Protocols involving an exception to the informed consent requirement under this section must be performed under a separate investigational new drug application (IND) or investigational device exemption (IDE) that clearly identifies such protocols as protocols that may include subjects who are unable to consent. The submission of those protocols in a separate IND/IDE is required even if an IND for the same drug product or an IDE for the same device already exists. Applications for investigations under this section may not be submitted as amendments under 312. 30 or 812. 35 of this chapter.

(e) If an IRB determines that it cannot approve a clinical investigation because the investigation does not meet the criteria in the exception provided under paragraph (a) of this section or because of other relevant ethical concerns, the IRB must document its findings and provide these findings promptly in writing to the clinical investigator and to the sponsor of the clinical investigation. The sponsor of the clinical investigation must promptly disclose this information to FDA and to the sponsor's clinical investigators who are participating or are asked to participate in this or a substantially equivalent clinical investigation of the sponsor, and to other IRB's that have been, or are, asked to review this or a substantially equivalent investigation by that sponsor.

## Sec. 50. 25 Elements of informed consent.

(a) *Basic elements of informed consent.* In seeking informed consent, the following information shall be provided to each subject:

(1) A statement that the study involves research, an explanation of the purposes of the research and the expected duration of the subject's participation, a description of the procedures to be followed, and identification of any procedures which are experimental.

(2) A description of any reasonably foreseeable risks or discomforts to the subject.

(3) A description of any benefits to the subject or to others which may reasonably be expected from the research.

(4) A disclosure of appropriate alternative procedures or courses of treatment, if any, that might be advantageous to the subject.

(5) A statement describing the extent, if any, to which confidentiality of records identifying the subject will be maintained and that notes the possibility that the Food and Drug Administration may inspect the records.

(6) For research involving more than minimal risk, an explanation as to whether any compensation and an explanation as to whether any medical treatments are available if injury occurs and, if so, what

they consist of, or where further information may be obtained.

(7) An explanation of whom to contact for answers to pertinent questions about the research and research subjects' rights, and whom to contact in the event of a research-related injury to the subject.

(8) A statement that participation is voluntary, that refusal to participate will involve no penalty or loss of benefits to which the subject is otherwise entitled, and that the subject may discontinue participation at any time without penalty or loss of benefits to which the subject is otherwise entitled.

(b) *Additional elements of informed consent.* When appropriate, one or more of the following elements of information shall also be provided to each subject:

(1) A statement that the particular treatment or procedure may involve risks to the subject (or to the embryo or fetus, if the subject is or may become pregnant) which are currently unforeseeable.

(2) Anticipated circumstances under which the subject's participation may be terminated by the investigator without regard to the subject's consent.

(3) Any additional costs to the subject that may result from participation in the research.

(4) The consequences of a subject's decision to withdraw from the research and procedures for orderly termination of participation by the subject.

(5) A statement that significant new findings developed during the course of the research which may relate to the subject's willingness to continue participation will be provided to the subject.

(6) The approximate number of subjects involved in the study.

(c) When seeking informed consent for applicable clinical trials, as defined in 42 U. S. C. 282 (j)(1)(A), the following statement shall be provided to each clinical trial subject in informed consent documents and processes. This will notify the clinical trial subject that clinical trial information has been or will be submitted for inclusion in the clinical trial registry databank under paragraph (j) of section 402 of the Public Health Service Act. The statement is: "A description of this clinical trial will be available onhttp: //www. ClinicalTrials. gov, as required by U. S. Law. This Web site will not include information that can identify you. At most, the Web site will include a summary of the results. You can search this Web site at any time. "

(d) The informed consent requirements in these regulations are not intended to preempt any applicable Federal, State, or local laws which require additional information to be disclosed for informed consent to be legally effective.

(e) Nothing in these regulations is intended to limit the authority of a physician to provide emergency medical care to the extent the physician is permitted to do so under applicable Federal, State, or local law.

## Sec. 50. 27 Documentation of informed consent.

(a) Except as provided in 56. 109 (c) , informed consent shall be documented by the use of a written consent form approved by the IRB and signed and dated by the subject or the subject's legally authorized representative at the time of consent. A copy shall be given to the person signing the form.

(b) Except as provided in 56. 109 (c) , the consent form may be either of the following:

  (1) A written consent document that embodies the elements of informed consent required by 50.25. This form may be read to the subject or the subject's legally authorized representative, but, in any event, the investigator shall give either the subject or the representative adequate opportunity to read it before it is signed.

  (2) A short form written consent document stating that the elements of informed consent required by 50. 25 have been presented orally to the subject or the subject's legally authorized representative. When this method is used, there shall be a witness to the oral presentation. Also, the IRB shall approve a written summary of what is to be said to the subject or the representative. Only the short form itself is to be signed by the subject or the representative. However, the witness shall sign both the short form and a copy of the summary, and the person actually obtaining the consent shall sign a copy of the summary. A copy of the summary shall be given to the subject or the representative in addition to a copy of the short form.

## Subpart C [ Reserved ]

## Subpart D - Additional Safeguards for Children in Clinical Investigations

### Sec. 50. 50 IRB duties.

In addition to other responsibilities assigned to IRBs under this part and part 56 of this chapter, each IRB must review clinical investigations involving children as subjects covered by this subpart D and approve only those clinical investigations that satisfy the criteria described in 50. 51, 50. 52, or 50. 53 and the conditions of all other applicable sections of this subpart D.

### Sec. 50. 51 Clinical investigations not involving greater than minimal risk.

Any clinical investigation within the scope described in 50. 1 and 56. 101 of this chapter in which no greater than minimal risk to children is presented may involve children as subjects only if the IRB finds that:

(a) No greater than minimal risk to children is presented; and

(b) Adequate provisions are made for soliciting the assent of the children and the permission of their parents or guardians as set forth in 50. 55.

### Sec. 50. 52 Clinical investigations involving greater than minimal risk but presenting the prospect of direct benefit to individual subjects.

Any clinical investigation within the scope described in 50. 1 and 56. 101 of this chapter in which more than minimal risk to children is presented by an intervention or procedure that holds out the prospect of direct benefit for the individual subject, or by a monitoring procedure that is likely to contribute to the subject's well-being, may involve children as subjects only if the IRB finds that:

(a) The risk is justified by the anticipated benefit to the subjects;

(b) The relation of the anticipated benefit to the risk is at least as favorable to the subjects as that presented by available alternative approaches; and

(c) Adequate provisions are made for soliciting the assent of the children and permission of their parents or guardians as set forth in 50. 55.

### Sec. 50. 53 Clinical investigations involving greater than minimal risk and no prospect of direct benefit to individual subjects, but likely to yield generalizable knowledge about the subjects' disorder or condition.

Any clinical investigation within the scope described in 50. 1 and 56. 101 of this chapter in which more than minimal risk to children is presented by an intervention or procedure that does not hold out the prospect of direct benefit for the individual subject, or by a monitoring procedure that is not likely to contribute to the well-being of the subject, may involve children as subjects only if the IRB finds that:

(a) The risk represents a minor increase over minimal risk;

(b) The intervention or procedure presents experiences to subjects that are reasonably commensurate with those inherent in their actual or expected medical, dental, psychological, social, or educational situations;

(c) The intervention or procedure is likely to yield generalizable knowledge about the subjects' disorder or condition that is of vital importance for the understanding or amelioration of the subjects' disorder or condition; and

(d) Adequate provisions are made for soliciting the assent of the children and permission of their parents or guardians as set forth in 50. 55.

### Sec. 50. 54 Clinical investigations not otherwise approvable that present an opportunity to understand, prevent, or alleviate a serious problem affecting the health or welfare of children.

If an IRB does not believe that a clinical investigation within the scope described in 50. 1 and 56. 101 of this chapter and involving children as subjects meets the requirements of 50. 51, 50. 52, or 50. 53, the clinical investigation may proceed only if:

(a) The IRB finds that the clinical investigation presents a reasonable opportunity to further the understanding, prevention, or alleviation of a serious problem affecting the health or welfare of children; and

(b) The Commissioner of Food and Drugs, after consultation with a panel of experts in pertinent disciplines (for example: science, medicine, education, ethics, law) and following opportunity for public review and comment, determines either:

(1) That the clinical investigation in fact satisfies the conditions of 50. 51, 50. 52, or 50. 53, as applicable, or

(2) That the following conditions are met:

(i) The clinical investigation presents a reasonable opportunity to further the understanding, prevention, or alleviation of a serious problem affecting the health or welfare of children;

(ii) The clinical investigation will be conducted in accordance with sound ethical principles; and

(iii) Adequate provisions are made for soliciting the assent of children and the permission of their parents or guardians as set forth in 50. 55.

## Sec. 50. 55 Requirements for permission by parents or guardians and for assent by children.

(a) In addition to the determinations required under other applicable sections of this subpart D, the IRB must determine that adequate provisions are made for soliciting the assent of the children when in the judgment of the IRB the children are capable of providing assent.

(b) In determining whether children are capable of providing assent, the IRB must take into account the ages, maturity, and psychological state of the children involved. This judgment may be made for all children to be involved in clinical investigations under a particular protocol, or for each child, as the IRB deems appropriate.

(c) The assent of the children is not a necessary condition for proceeding with the clinical investigation if the IRB determines:

(1) That the capability of some or all of the children is so limited that they cannot reasonably be consulted, or

(2) That the intervention or procedure involved in the clinical investigation holds out a prospect of direct benefit that is important to the health or well-being of the children and is available only in the context of the clinical investigation.

(d) Even where the IRB determines that the subjects are capable of assenting, the IRB may still waive the assent requirement if it finds and documents that:

(1) The clinical investigation involves no more than minimal risk to the

subjects;

(2) The waiver will not adversely affect the rights and welfare of the subjects;

(3) The clinical investigation could not practicably be carried out without the waiver; and

(4) Whenever appropriate, the subjects will be provided with additional pertinent information after participation.

(e) In addition to the determinations required under other applicable sections of this subpart D, the IRB must determine, in accordance with and to the extent that consent is required under part 50, that the permission of each child's parents or guardian is granted.

(1) Where parental permission is to be obtained, the IRB may find that the permission of one parent is sufficient for clinical investigations to be conducted under 50. 51 or 50. 52.

(2) Where clinical investigations are covered by 50. 53 or 50. 54 and permission is to be obtained from parents, both parents must give their permission unless one parent is deceased, unknown, incompetent, or not reasonably available, or when only one parent has legal responsibility for the care and custody of the child.

(f) Permission by parents or guardians must be documented in accordance with and to the extent required by 50. 27.

(g) When the IRB determines that assent is required, it must also determine whether and how assent must be documented.

## Sec. 50. 56 Wards.

(a) Children who are wards of the State or any other agency, institution, or entity can be included in clinical investigations approved under 50. 53 or 50. 54 only if such clinical investigations are:

(1) Related to their status as wards; or

(2) Conducted in schools, camps, hospitals, institutions, or similar settings in which the majority of children involved as subjects are not wards.

(b) If the clinical investigation is approved under paragraph(a) of this section, the IRB must require appointment of an advocate for each child who is a ward.

(1) The advocate will serve in addition to any other individual acting

on behalf of the child as guardian or in loco parentis.

(2) One individual may serve as advocate for more than one child.

(3) The advocate must be an individual who has the background and experience to act in, and agrees to act in, the best interest of the child for the duration of the child's participation in the clinical investigation.

(4) The advocate must not be associated in any way (except in the role as advocate or member of the IRB) with the clinical investigation, the investigator(s), or the guardian organization.

[Revised as of April 1,2016]

# 21CFR PART54 FINANCIAL DISCLOSURE BY CLINICAL INVESTIGATORS

## Sec. 54. 1 Purpose.

(a) The Food and Drug Administration (FDA) evaluates clinical studies submitted in marketing applications, required by law, for new human drugs and biological products and marketing applications and reclassification petitions for medical devices.

(b) The agency reviews data generated in these clinical studies to determine whether the applications are approvable under the statutory requirements. FDA may consider clinical studies inadequate and the data inadequate if, among other things, appropriate steps have not been taken in the design, conduct, reporting, and analysis of the studies to minimize bias. One potential source of bias in clinical studies is a financial interest of the clinical investigator in the outcome of the study because of the way payment is arranged (e. g. , a royalty) or because the investigator has a proprietary interest in the product (e. g. , a patent) or because the investigator has an equity interest in the sponsor of the covered study. This section and conforming regulations require an applicant whose submission relies in part on clinical data to disclose certain financial arrangements between sponsor (s) of the covered studies and the clinical investigators and certain interests of the clinical investigators in the product under study or in the sponsor of the covered studies. FDA will use this information, in conjunction with information about the design and purpose of the study, as well as information obtained through on-site inspections, in the agency's assessment of the reliability of the data.

## Sec. 54. 2 Definitions.

For the purposes of this part:

(a) *Compensation affected by the outcome of clinical studies* means compensation that could be higher for a favorable outcome than for an unfavorable outcome, such as compensation that is explicitly greater for a favorable result or compensation to the investigator in the form of an equity interest in the sponsor of a covered study or in the form of compensation tied to sales of the product, such as a royalty interest.

(b) *Significant equity interest in the sponsor of a covered study* means any ownership interest, stock options, or other financial interest whose value cannot be readily determined through reference to public prices (generally, interests in a nonpublicly traded corporation), or any equity interest in a publicly traded corporation that exceeds $ 50, 000 during the time the clinical investigator is carrying out the study and for 1 year following completion of the study.

(c) *Proprietary interest in the tested product* means property or other financial interest in the product including, but not limited to, a patent, trademark, copyright or licensing agreement.

(d) *Clinical investigator* means only a listed or identified investigator or subinvestigator who is directly involved in the treatment or evaluation of research subjects. The term also includes the spouse and each dependent child of the investigator.

(e) *Covered clinical study* means any study of a drug or device in humans submitted in a marketing application or reclassification petition subject to this part that the applicant or FDA relies on to establish that the product is effective (including studies that show equivalence to an effective product) or any study in which a single investigator makes a significant contribution to the demonstration of safety. This would, in general, not include phase 1 tolerance studies or pharmacokinetic studies, most clinical pharmacology studies (unless they are critical to an efficacy determination), large open safety studies conducted at multiple sites, treatment protocols, and parallel track protocols. An applicant may consult with FDA as to which clinical studies constitute "covered clinical studies" for purposes of complying with financial disclosure requirements.

(f) *Significant payments of other sorts* means payments made by the sponsor of a covered study to the investigator or the institution to support activities of the investigator that have a monetary value of more than $ 25, 000, exclusive of the costs of conducting the clinical study or other clinical studies, (e. g. , a grant to fund ongoing research, compensation in the form of equipment or retainers for ongoing consultation or honoraria) during the time the clinical investigator is carrying out the study and for 1 year following the completion of the study.

(g) *Applicant* means the party who submits a marketing application to FDA for approval of a drug, device, or biologic product. The applicant is responsible for submitting the appropriate certification and disclosure statements required in this part.

(h) *Sponsor of the covered clinical study* means the party supporting a particular study at the time it was carried out.

## Sec. 54. 3 Scope.

The requirements in this part apply to any applicant who submits a marketing application for a human drug, biological product, or device and who submits covered clinical studies. The applicant is responsible for making the appropriate certification or disclosure statement where the applicant either contracted with one or more clinical investigators to conduct the studies or submitted studies conducted by others not under contract to the applicant.

## Sec. 54. 4 Certification and disclosure requirements.

For purposes of this part, an applicant must submit a list of all clinical investigators who conducted covered clinical studies to determine whether the applicant's product meets FDA's marketing requirements, identifying those clinical investigators who are full-time or part-time employees of the sponsor of each covered study. The applicant must also completely and accurately disclose or certify information concerning the financial interests of a clinical investigator who is not a full-time or part-time employee of the sponsor for each covered clinical study. Clinical investigators subject to investigational new drug or investigational device exemption regulations must provide the sponsor of the study with sufficient accurate information needed to allow subsequent disclosure or certification. The applicant is required to submit for each clinical investigator who participates in a covered study, either a certification that none of the financial arrangements described in 54. 2 exist, or disclose the nature of those arrangements to the agency. Where the applicant acts with due diligence to obtain the information required in this section but is unable to do so, the applicant shall certify that despite the applicant's due diligence in attempting to obtain the information, the applicant was unable to obtain the information and shall include the reason.

(a) The applicant (of an application submitted under sections 505, 506, 510 (k), 513, or 515 of the Federal Food, Drug, and Cosmetic Act, or section 351 of the Public Health Service Act) that relies in whole or in part on clinical studies shall submit, for each clinical investigator who participated in a covered clinical study, either a certification described in paragraph (a)(1) of this section or a disclosure statement described in paragraph (a)(3) of this section.

(1) Certification: The applicant covered by this section shall submit for all clinical investigators (as defined in 54. 2 (d)), to whom the certification applies, a completed Form FDA 3454 attesting to the absence of financial interests and arrangements described in paragraph (a)(3) of this section. The form shall be dated and signed by the chief financial officer or other responsible corporate official or representative.

(2) If the certification covers less than all covered clinical data in the application, the applicant shall include in the certification a list of the studies covered by this certification.

(3) Disclosure Statement: For any clinical investigator defined in 54. 2 (d) for whom the applicant does not submit the certification described in paragraph (a)(1) of this section, the applicant shall submit a completed Form FDA 3455 disclosing completely and accurately the following:

  (i) Any financial arrangement entered into between the sponsor of the covered study and the clinical investigator involved in the conduct of a covered clinical trial, whereby the value of the compensation to the clinical investigator for conducting the study could be influenced by the outcome of the study;

  (ii) Any significant payments of other sorts from the sponsor of the covered study, such as a grant to fund ongoing research, compensation in the form of equipment, retainer for ongoing consultation, or honoraria;

  (iii) Any proprietary interest in the tested product held by any clinical investigator involved in a study;

  (iv) Any significant equity interest in the sponsor of the covered study held by any clinical investigator involved in any clinical study; and

  (v) Any steps taken to minimize the potential for bias resulting from any of the disclosed arrangements, interests, or payments.

(b) The clinical investigator shall provide to the sponsor of the covered study sufficient accurate financial information to allow the sponsor to submit complete and accurate certification or disclosure statements as required in paragraph (a) of this section. The investigator shall promptly update this information if any relevant changes occur in the course of the investigation or for 1 year following completion of the study.

(c) Refusal to file application. FDA may refuse to file any marketing application described in paragraph (a) of this section that does not contain the information required by this section or a certification by the applicant that the applicant has acted with due diligence to obtain the information but was unable to do so and stating the reason.

## Sec. 54. 5 Agency evaluation of financial interests.

(a) *Evaluation of disclosure statement*. FDA will evaluate the information disclosed under 54. 4 (a)(2) about each covered clinical study in an application to determine the impact of any disclosed financial interests on the reliability of the study. FDA may consider both the size and nature of a disclosed financial interest (including the potential increase in the value of the interest if the product is approved) and steps that have been taken to minimize the potential for bias.

(b) *Effect of study design*. In assessing the potential of an investigator's financial interests to bias a study, FDA will take into account the design and purpose of the study. Study designs that utilize such approaches as multiple investigators (most of whom do not have a disclosable interest), blinding, objective endpoints, or measurement of endpoints by someone other than the investigator may adequately protect against any bias created by a disclosable financial interest.

(c) *Agency actions to ensure reliability of data*. If FDA determines that the financial interests of any clinical investigator raise a serious question about the integrity of the data, FDA will take any action it deems necessary to ensure the reliability of the data including:

(1) Initiating agency audits of the data derived from the clinical investigator in question;

(2) Requesting that the applicant submit further analyses of data, e. g. ,

to evaluate the effect of the clinical investigator's data on overall study outcome;

(3) Requesting that the applicant conduct additional independent studies to confirm the results of the questioned study; and

(4) Refusing to treat the covered clinical study as providing data that can be the basis for an agency action.

## Sec. 54. 6 Recordkeeping and record retention.

(a) *Financial records of clinical investigators to be retained.* An applicant who has submitted a marketing application containing covered clinical studies shall keep on file certain information pertaining to the financial interests of clinical investigators who conducted studies on which the application relies and who are not full or part-time employees of the applicant, as follows:

(1) Complete records showing any financial interest or arrangement as described in 54. 4 (a)(3)(i) paid to such clinical investigators by the sponsor of the covered study.

(2) Complete records showing significant payments of other sorts, as described in 54. 4 (a)(3)(ii), made by the sponsor of the covered clinical study to the clinical investigator.

(3) Complete records showing any financial interests held by clinical investigators as set forth in 54. 4 (a)(3)(iii) and (a)(3)(iv).

(b) *Requirements for maintenance of clinical investigators' financial records.* (1) For any application submitted for a covered product, an applicant shall retain records as described in paragraph (a) of this section for 2 years after the date of approval of the application.

(2) The person maintaining these records shall, upon request from any properly authorized officer or employee of FDA, at reasonable times, permit such officer or employee to have access to and copy and verify these records.

[Revised as of April 1, 2016]

# 21CFR PART56 INSTITUTIONAL REVIEW BOARDS

## Subpart A-General Provisions

### Sec. 56. 101 Scope.

(a) This part contains the general standards for the composition, operation, and responsibility of an Institutional Review Board (IRB) that reviews clinical investigations regulated by the Food and Drug Administration under sections 505 (i) and 520 (g) of the act, as well as clinical investigations that support applications for research or marketing permits for products regulated by the Food and Drug Administration, including foods, including dietary supplements, that bear a nutrient content claim or a health claim, infant formulas, food and color additives, drugs for human use, medical devices for human use, biological products for human use, and electronic products. Compliance with this part is intended to protect the rights and welfare of human subjects involved in such investigations.

(b) References in this part to regulatory sections of the Code of Federal Regulations are to chapter I of title 21, unless otherwise noted.

### Sec. 56. 102 Definitions.

As used in this part:

(a) *Act* means the Federal Food, Drug, and Cosmetic Act, as amended (secs. 201-902, 52 Stat. 1040 et seq., as amended (21 U. S. C. 321-392)).

(b) *Application for research or marketing permit* includes:

(1) A color additive petition, described in part 71.

(2) Data and information regarding a substance submitted as part of the procedures for establishing that a substance is generally recognized as safe for a use which results or may reasonably be expec-

ted to result, directly or indirectly, in its becoming a component or otherwise affecting the characteristics of any food, described in 170. 35.

(3) A food additive petition, described in part 171.

(4) Data and information regarding a food additive submitted as part of the procedures regarding food additives permitted to be used on an interim basis pending additional study, described in 180. 1.

(5) Data and information regarding a substance submitted as part of the procedures for establishing a tolerance for unavoidable contaminants in food and food-packaging materials, described in section 406 of the act.

(6) An investigational new drug application, described in part 312 of this chapter.

(7) A new drug application, described in part 314.

(8) Data and information regarding the bioavailability or bioequivalence of drugs for human use submitted as part of the procedures for issuing, amending, or repealing a bioequivalence requirement, described in part 320.

(9) Data and information regarding an over-the-counter drug for human use submitted as part of the procedures for classifying such drugs as generally recognized as safe and effective and not misbranded, described in part 330.

(10) An application for a biologics license, described in part 601 of this chapter.

(11) Data and information regarding a biological product submitted as part of the procedures for determining that licensed biological products are safe and effective and not misbranded, as described in part 601 of this chapter.

(12) An Application for an Investigational Device Exemption, described in part 812.

(13) Data and information regarding a medical device for human use submitted as part of the procedures for classifying such devices, described in part 860.

(14) Data and information regarding a medical device for human use submitted as part of the procedures for establishing, amending, or repealing a standard for such device, described in part 861.

(15) An application for premarket approval of a medical device for human use, described in section 515 of the act.

(16) A product development protocol for a medical device for human use, described in section 515 of the act.

(17) Data and information regarding an electronic product submitted as part of the procedures for establishing, amending, or repealing a standard for such products, described in section 358 of the Public Health Service Act.

(18) Data and information regarding an electronic product submitted as part of the procedures for obtaining a variance from any electronic product performance standard, as described in 1010. 4.

(19) Data and information regarding an electronic product submitted as part of the procedures for granting, amending, or extending an exemption from a radiation safety performance standard, as described in 1010. 5.

(20) Data and information regarding an electronic product submitted as part of the procedures for obtaining an exemption from notification of a radiation safety defect or failure of compliance with a radiation safety performance standard, described in subpart D of part 1003.

(21) Data and information about a clinical study of an infant formula when submitted as part of an infant formula notification under section 412 (c) of the Federal Food, Drug, and Cosmetic Act.

(22) Data and information submitted in a petition for a nutrient content claim, described in 101. 69 of this chapter, and for a health claim, described in 101. 70 of this chapter.

(23) Data and information from investigations involving children submitted in a new dietary ingredient notification, described in 190. 6 of this chapter.

(c) *Clinical investigation* means any experiment that involves a test article and one or more human subjects, and that either must meet the requirements for prior submission to the Food and Drug Administration under section 505 (i) or 520 (g) of the act, or need not meet the requirements for prior submission to the Food and Drug Administration under these sections of the act, but the results of which are intended to be later submitted to, or held for inspection by, the Food and Drug Administration as part of an application for a research or marketing permit. The term does not include experiments that must meet the provisions of part 58, regarding nonclinical laboratory studies. The terms research, clinical research, clinical study, study, and clinical investigation are deemed to be synonymous for purposes of this part.

(d) *Emergency use* means the use of a test article on a human subject in a life-threatening situation in which no standard acceptable treatment is available, and in which there is not sufficient time to obtain IRB approval.

(e) *Human subject* means an individual who is or becomes a participant in research, either as a recipient of the test article or as a control. A subject may be either a healthy individual or a patient.

(f) *Institution* means any public or private entity or agency (including Federal, State, and other agencies). The term facility as used in section 520 (g) of the act is deemed to be synonymous with the term institution for purposes of this part.

(g) *Institutional Review Board (IRB)* means any board, committee, or other group formally designated by an institution to review, to approve the initiation of, and to conduct periodic review of, biomedical research involving human subjects. The primary purpose of such review is to assure the protection of the rights and welfare of the human subjects. The term has the same meaning as the phrase institutional review committee as used in section 520 (g) of the act.

(h) *Investigator* means an individual who actually conducts a clinical investigation (i. e. , under whose immediate direction the test article is administered or dispensed to, or used involving, a subject) or, in the event of an investigation conducted by a team of individuals, is the responsible leader of that team.

(i) *Minimal risk* means that the probability and magnitude of harm or discomfort anticipated in the research are not greater in and of themselves than those ordinarily encountered in daily life or during the performance of routine physical or psychological examinations or tests.

(j) *Sponsor* means a person or other entity that initiates a clinical investigation, but that does not actually conduct the investigation, i. e. , the test article is administered or dispensed to, or used involving, a subject under the immediate direction of another individual. A person other than an individual (e. g. , a corporation or agency) that uses one or more of its own employees to conduct an investigation that it has initiated is considered to be a sponsor (not a sponsor-investigator), and the employees are considered to be investigators.

(k) *Sponsor-investigator* means an individual who both initiates and actually conducts, alone or with others, a clinical investigation, i. e. , under whose immediate direction the test article is administered or dispensed to, or used involving, a subject. The term does not include any person other than an individual, e. g. , it does not include a corporation or agency. The obligations of a sponsor-investigator under this part include both those of a sponsor and those of an investigator.

(l) *Test article* means any drug for human use, biological product for human use, medical device for human use, human food additive, color additive, electronic product, or any other article subject to regulation under the act or under sections 351 or 354-360F of the Public Health Service Act.

(m) *IRB approval* means the determination of the IRB that the clinical investigation has been reviewed and may be conducted at an institution within the constraints set forth by the IRB and by other institutional and Federal requirements.

## Sec. 56. 103 Circumstances in which IRB review is required.

(a) Except as provided in 56. 104 and 56. 105, any clinical investigation which must meet the requirements for prior submission (as required in parts 312, 812, and 813) to the Food and Drug Administration shall not be initiated unless that investigation has been reviewed and approved by, and remains subject to continuing review by, an IRB meeting the requirements of this part.

(b) Except as provided in 56. 104 and 56. 105, the Food and Drug Administration may decide not to consider in support of an application for a research or marketing permit any data or information that has been derived from a clinical investigation that has not been approved by, and that was not subject to initial and continuing review by, an IRB meeting the requirements of this part. The determination that a clinical investigation may not be considered in support of an application for a research or marketing permit does not, however, relieve the applicant for such a permit of any obligation under any other applicable regulations to submit the results of the investigation to the Food and Drug Administration.

(c) Compliance with these regulations will in no way render inapplicable pertinent Federal, State, or local laws or regulations.

### Sec. 56. 104 Exemptions from IRB requirement.

The following categories of clinical investigations are exempt from the requirements of this part for IRB review:

(a) Any investigation which commenced before July 27, 1981 and was subject to requirements for IRB review under FDA regulations before that date, provided that the investigation remains subject to review of an IRB which meets the FDA requirements in effect before July 27, 1981.

(b) Any investigation commenced before July 27, 1981 and was not otherwise subject to requirements for IRB review under Food and Drug Administration regulations before that date.

(c) Emergency use of a test article, provided that such emergency use is reported to the IRB within 5 working days. Any subsequent use of the test article at the institution is subject to IRB review.

(d) Taste and food quality evaluations and consumer acceptance studies, if wholesome foods without additives are consumed or if a food is consumed that contains a food ingredient at or below the level and for a use found to be safe, or agricultural, chemical, or environmental contaminant at or below the level found to be safe, by the Food and Drug Administration or approved by the Environmental Protection Agency or the Food Safety and Inspection Service of the U. S. Department of Agriculture.

### Sec. 56. 105 Waiver of IRB requirement.

On the application of a sponsor or sponsor-investigator, the Food and Drug Administration may waive any of the requirements contained in these regulations, including the requirements for IRB review, for specific research activities or for classes of research activities, otherwise covered by these regulations.

## Subpart B-Organization and Personnel

### Sec. 56. 106 Registration.

(a) *Who must register?* Each IRB in the United States that reviews clinical investigations regulated by FDA under sections 505 (i) or 520 (g) of the act and each IRB in the United States that reviews clinical investigations that are intended to support applications for research or marketing permits for FDA-regulated products must register at a site maintained by the Department of Health and Human Services (HHS). (A research permit under section 505 (i) of the act is usually known as an investigational new drug application (IND), while a research permit under section 520 (g) of the act is usually known as an investigational device exemption (IDE).) An individual authorized to act on the IRB's behalf must submit the registration information. All other IRBs may register voluntarily.

(b) *What information must an IRB register?* Each IRB must provide the following information:

(1) The name, mailing address, and street address (if different from the mailing address) of the institution operating the IRB and the name, mailing address, phone number, facsimile number, and electronic mail address of the senior officer of that institution who is responsible for overseeing activities performed by the IRB;

(2) The IRB's name, mailing address, street address (if different from the mailing address), phone number, facsimile number, and electronic mail address; each IRB chairperson's name, phone number, and electronic mail address; and the name, mailing address, phone number, facsimile number, and electronic mail address of the contact person providing the registration information.

(3) The approximate number of active protocols involving FDA-regulated products reviewed. For purposes of this rule, an "active protocol" is any protocol for which an IRB conducted an initial review or a continuing review at a convened meeting or under an expedited review procedure during the preceding 12 months; and

(4) A description of the types of FDA-regulated products (such as biological products, color additives, food additives, human drugs, or medical devices) involved in the protocols that the IRB reviews.

(c) *When must an IRB register?* Each IRB must submit an initial registration. The initial registration must occur before the IRB begins to review a clinical investigation described in paragraph (a) of this section. Each IRB must renew its registration every 3 years. IRB registration becomes effective after review and acceptance by HHS.

(d) *Where can an IRB register?* Each IRB may register electronically through http: //ohrp. cit. nih. gov/efile. If an IRB lacks the ability to register electronically, it must send its registration information, in writing, to the Office of Good Clinical Practice, Office of Special Medical Programs, Food and Drug Administration, 10903 New Hampshire Ave., Bldg. 32, Rm. 5129, Silver Spring, MD 20993.

(e) *How does an IRB revise its registration information?* If an IRB's contact or chair person information changes, the IRB must revise its registration information by submitting any changes in that information within 90 days of the change. An IRB's decision to review new types of FDA-regulated products (such as a decision to review studies pertaining to food additives whereas the IRB previously reviewed studies pertaining to drug products), or to discontinue reviewing clinical investigations regulated by FDA is a change that must be reported within 30 days of the change. An IRB's decision to disband is a change that must be reported within 30 days of permanent cessation of the IRB's review of research. All other information changes may be reported when the IRB renews its registration. The revised information must be sent to FDA either electronically or in writing in accordance with paragraph (d) of this section.

## Sec. 56. 107 IRB membership.

(a) Each IRB shall have at least five members, with varying backgrounds to promote complete and adequate review of research activities commonly conducted by the institution. The IRB shall be sufficiently qualified through the experience and expertise of its members, and the diversity of the members, including consideration of race, gender, cultural backgrounds, and sensitivity to such issues as community attitudes, to promote respect for its advice and counsel in safeguarding the rights and welfare of human subjects. In addition to possessing the professional competence necessary to review the specific research activities, the IRB shall be able to ascertain the acceptability of proposed research in terms of institutional commitments and regulations, applicable law, and standards of professional conduct and practice. The IRB shall therefore include persons knowledgeable in these areas. If an IRB regularly reviews research that involves a vulnerable category of subjects, such as children, prisoners, pregnant women, or handicapped or mentally disabled persons, consideration shall be given to the inclusion of one or more individuals who are knowledgeable about and experienced in working with those subjects.

(b) Every nondiscriminatory effort will be made to ensure that no IRB consists entirely of men or entirely of women, including the instituton's consideration of qualified persons of both sexes, so long as no selection is made to the IRB on the basis of gender. No IRB may consist entirely of members of one profession.

(c) Each IRB shall include at least one member whose primary concerns are in the scientific area and at least one member whose primary concerns are in nonscientific areas.

(d) Each IRB shall include at least one member who is not otherwise affiliated with the institution and who is not part of the immediate family of a person who is affiliated with the institution.

(e) No IRB may have a member participate in the IRB's initial or continuing review of any project in which the member has a conflicting interest, except to provide information requested by the IRB.

(f) An IRB may, in its discretion, invite individuals with competence in special areas to assist in the review of complex issues which require expertise beyond or in addition to that available on the IRB. These individuals may not vote with the IRB.

# Subpart C-IRB Functions and Operations

## Sec. 56. 108 IRB functions and operations.

In order to fulfill the requirements of these regulations, each IRB shall:

(a) Follow written procedures: (1) For conducting its initial and continuing review of research and for reporting its findings and actions to the investigator and the institution; (2) for determining which projects require review more often than annually and which projects need verification from sources other than the investigator that no material changes have occurred since previous IRB review; (3) for ensuring prompt reporting to the IRB of changes in research activity; and (4) for ensuring that changes in approved research, during the period for which IRB approval has already been given, may not be initiated without IRB review and approval except where necessary to eliminate apparent immediate hazards to the human subjects.

(b) Follow written procedures for ensuring prompt reporting to the IRB, appropriate institutional officials, and the Food and Drug Administration of: (1) Any unanticipated problems involving risks to human subjects or others; (2) any instance of serious or continuing noncompliance with these regulations or the requirements or determinations of the IRB; or (3) any suspension or termination of IRB approval.

(c) Except when an expedited review procedure is used (see 56. 110), review proposed research at convened meetings at which a majority of the members of the IRB are present, including at least one member whose primary concerns are in nonscientific areas. In order for the research to be approved, it shall receive the approval of a majority of those members present at the meeting.

## Sec. 56. 109 IRB review of research.

(a) An IRB shall review and have authority to approve, require modifications in (to secure approval), or disapprove all research activities covered by these regulations.

(b) An IRB shall require that information given to subjects as part of informed consent is in accordance with 50. 25. The IRB may require that information, in addition to that specifically mentioned in 50. 25, be given to the subjects when in the IRB's judgment the information would meaningfully add to the protection of the rights and welfare of subjects.

(c) An IRB shall require documentation of informed consent in accordance with 50. 27 of this chapter, except as follows:

  (1) The IRB may, for some or all subjects, waive the requirement that the subject, or the subject's legally authorized representative, sign a written consent form if it finds that the research presents no more than minimal risk of harm to subjects and involves no procedures for which written consent is normally required outside the research context; or

  (2) The IRB may, for some or all subjects, find that the requirements in 50. 24 of this chapter for an exception from informed consent for

emergency research are met.

(d) In cases where the documentation requirement is waived under paragraph (c)(1) of this section, the IRB may require the investigator to provide subjects with a written statement regarding the research.

(e) An IRB shall notify investigators and the institution in writing of its decision to approve or disapprove the proposed research activity, or of modifications required to secure IRB approval of the research activity. If the IRB decides to disapprove a research activity, it shall include in its written notification a statement of the reasons for its decision and give the investigator an opportunity to respond in person or in writing. For investigations involving an exception to informed consent under 50. 24 of this chapter, an IRB shall promptly notify in writing the investigator and the sponsor of the research when an IRB determines that it cannot approve the research because it does not meet the criteria in the exception provided under 50. 24 (a) of this chapter or because of other relevant ethical concerns. The written notification shall include a statement of the reasons for the IRB's determination.

(f) An IRB shall conduct continuing review of research covered by these regulations at intervals appropriate to the degree of risk, but not less than once per year, and shall have authority to observe or have a third party observe the consent process and the research.

(g) An IRB shall provide in writing to the sponsor of research involving an exception to informed consent under 50. 24 of this chapter a copy of information that has been publicly disclosed under 50. 24 (a)(7)(ii) and (a)(7)(iii) of this chapter. The IRB shall provide this information to the sponsor promptly so that the sponsor is aware that such disclosure has occurred. Upon receipt, the sponsor shall provide copies of the information disclosed to FDA.

(h) When some or all of the subjects in a study are children, an IRB must determine that the research study is in compliance with part 50, subpart D of this chapter, at the time of its initial review of the research. When some or all of the subjects in a study that was ongoing on April 30, 2001, are children, an IRB must conduct a review of the research to determine compliance with part 50, subpart D of this chapter, either at the time of continuing review or, at the discretion of the IRB, at an earlier date.

## Sec. 56. 110 Expedited review procedures for certain kinds of research involving no more than minimal risk, and for minor changes in approved research.

(a) The Food and Drug Administration has established, and published in the Federal Register, a list of categories of research that may be reviewed by the IRB through an expedited review procedure. The list will be amended, as appropriate, through periodic republication in the Federal Register.

(b) An IRB may use the expedited review procedure to review either or both of the following: (1) Some or all of the research appearing on the list and found by the reviewer (s) to involve no more than minimal risk, (2) minor changes in previously approved research during the period (of 1 year or less) for which approval is authorized. Under an expedited review procedure, the review may be carried out by the IRB chairperson or by one or more experienced reviewers designated by the IRB chairperson from among the members of the IRB. In reviewing the research, the reviewers may exercise all of the authorities of the IRB except that the reviewers may not disapprove the research. A research activity may be disapproved only after review in accordance with the nonexpedited review procedure set forth in 56. 108 (c).

(c) Each IRB which uses an expedited review procedure shall adopt a method for keeping all members advised of research proposals which have been approved under the procedure.

(d) The Food and Drug Administration may restrict, suspend, or terminate an institution's or IRB's use of the expedited review procedure when necessary to protect the rights or welfare of subjects.

## Sec. 56. 111 Criteria for IRB approval of research.

(a) In order to approve research covered by these regulations the IRB shall determine that all of the following requirements are satisfied:

(1) Risks to subjects are minimized: (i) By using procedures which are consistent with sound research design and which do not unnecessarily expose subjects to risk, and (ii) whenever appropriate, by using procedures already being performed on the subjects for diagnostic or treatment purposes.

(2) Risks to subjects are reasonable in relation to anticipated benefits, if

any, to subjects, and the importance of the knowledge that may be expected to result. In evaluating risks and benefits, the IRB should consider only those risks and benefits that may result from the research (as distinguished from risks and benefits of therapies that subjects would receive even if not participating in the research). The IRB should not consider possible long-range effects of applying knowledge gained in the research (for example, the possible effects of the research on public policy) as among those research risks that fall within the purview of its responsibility.

(3) Selection of subjects is equitable. In making this assessment the IRB should take into account the purposes of the research and the setting in which the research will be conducted and should be particularly cognizant of the special problems of research involving vulnerable populations, such as children, prisoners, pregnant women, handicapped, or mentally disabled persons, or economically or educationally disadvantaged persons.

(4) Informed consent will be sought from each prospective subject or the subject's legally authorized representative, in accordance with and to the extent required by part 50.

(5) Informed consent will be appropriately documented, in accordance with and to the extent required by 50. 27.

(6) Where appropriate, the research plan makes adequate provision for monitoring the data collected to ensure the safety of subjects.

(7) Where appropriate, there are adequate provisions to protect the privacy of subjects and to maintain the confidentiality of data.

(b) When some or all of the subjects, such as children, prisoners, pregnant women, handicapped, or mentally disabled persons, or economically or educationally disadvantaged persons, are likely to be vulnerable to coercion or undue influence additional safeguards have been included in the study to protect the rights and welfare of these subjects.

(c) In order to approve research in which some or all of the subjects are children, an IRB must determine that all research is in compliance with part 50, subpart D of this chapter.

## Sec. 56. 112 Review by institution.

Research covered by these regulations that has been approved by an IRB may be subject to further appropriate review and approval or disapproval by officials of the institution. However, those officials may not approve the research if it has not been approved by an IRB.

### Sec. 56. 113 Suspension or termination of IRB approval of research.

An IRB shall have authority to suspend or terminate approval of research that is not being conducted in accordance with the IRB's requirements or that has been associated with unexpected serious harm to subjects. Any suspension or termination of approval shall include a statement of the reasons for the IRB's action and shall be reported promptly to the investigator, appropriate institutional officials, and the Food and Drug Administration.

### Sec. 56. 114 Cooperative research.

In complying with these regulations, institutions involved in multi-institutional studies may use joint review, reliance upon the review of another qualified IRB, or similar arrangements aimed at avoidance of duplication of effort.

## Subpart D-Records and Reports

### Sec. 56. 115 IRB records.

(a) An institution, or where appropriate an IRB, shall prepare and maintain adequate documentation of IRB activities, including the following：
  (1) Copies of all research proposals reviewed, scientific evaluations, if any, that accompany the proposals, approved sample consent documents, progress reports submitted by investigators, and reports of injuries to subjects.
  (2) Minutes of IRB meetings which shall be in sufficient detail to show attendance at the meetings； actions taken by the IRB； the vote on these actions including the number of members voting for, against, and abstaining； the basis for requiring changes in or disapproving research； and a written summary of the discussion of controverted issues and their resolution.
  (3) Records of continuing review activities.
  (4) Copies of all correspondence between the IRB and the investigators.

(5) A list of IRB members identified by name; earned degrees; representative capacity; indications of experience such as board certifications, licenses, etc. , sufficient to describe each member's chief anticipated contributions to IRB deliberations; and any employment or other relationship between each member and the institution; for example: full-time employee, part-time employee, a member of governing panel or board, stockholder, paid or unpaid consultant.

(6) Written procedures for the IRB as required by 56. 108 (a) and (b) .

(7) Statements of significant new findings provided to subjects, as required by 50. 25.

(b) The records required by this regulation shall be retained for at least 3 years after completion of the research, and the records shall be accessible for inspection and copying by authorized representatives of the Food and Drug Administration at reasonable times and in a reasonable manner.

(c) The Food and Drug Administration may refuse to consider a clinical investigation in support of an application for a research or marketing permit if the institution or the IRB that reviewed the investigation refuses to allow an inspection under this section.

## Subpart E-Administrative Actions for Noncompliance

### Sec. 56. 120 Lesser administrative actions.

(a) If apparent noncompliance with these regulations in the operation of an IRB is observed by an FDA investigator during an inspection, the inspector will present an oral or written summary of observations to an appropriate representative of the IRB. The Food and Drug Administration may subsequently send a letter describing the noncompliance to the IRB and to the parent institution. The agency will require that the IRB or the parent institution respond to this letter within a time period specified by FDA and describe the corrective actions that will be taken by the IRB, the institution, or both to achieve compliance with these regulations.

(b) On the basis of the IRB's or the institution's response, FDA may schedule a reinspection to confirm the adequacy of corrective actions. In addition, until the IRB or the parent institution takes appropriate corrective action, the Agency may require the IRB to:

(1) Withhold approval of new studies subject to the requirements of this part that are conducted at the institution or reviewed by the IRB;

(2) Direct that no new subjects be added to ongoing studies subject to this part; or

(3) Terminate ongoing studies subject to this part when doing so would not endanger the subjects.

(c) When the apparent noncompliance creates a significant threat to the rights and welfare of human subjects, FDA may notify relevant State and Federal regulatory agencies and other parties with a direct interest in the Agency's action of the deficiencies in the operation of the IRB.

(d) The parent institution is presumed to be responsible for the operation of an IRB, and the Food and Drug Administration will ordinarily direct any administrative action under this subpart against the institution. However, depending on the evidence of responsibility for deficiencies, determined during the investigation, the Food and Drug Administration may restrict its administrative actions to the IRB or to a component of the parent institution determined to be responsible for formal designation of the IRB.

## Sec. 56. 121 Disqualification of an IRB or an institution.

(a) Whenever the IRB or the institution has failed to take adequate steps to correct the noncompliance stated in the letter sent by the agency under 56. 120(a), and the Commissioner of Food and Drugs determines that this noncompliance may justify the disqualification of the IRB or of the parent institution, the Commissioner will institute proceedings in accordance with the requirements for a regulatory hearing set forth in part 16.

(b) The Commissioner may disqualify an IRB or the parent institution if the Commissioner determines that:

(1) The IRB has refused or repeatedly failed to comply with any of the regulations set forth in this part, and

(2) The noncompliance adversely affects the rights or welfare of the human subjects in a clinical investigation.

(c) If the Commissioner determines that disqualification is appropriate, the Commissioner will issue an order that explains the basis for the determination and that prescribes any actions to be taken with regard to ongoing clinical research conducted under the review of the IRB. The Food and Drug Administration will send notice of the disqualification to the IRB and the parent institution. Other parties with a direct interest, such as sponsors and clinical investigators, may also be sent a notice of the disqualification. In addition, the agency may elect to publish a notice of its action in the Federal Register.

(d) The Food and Drug Administration will not approve an application for a research permit for a clinical investigation that is to be under the review of a disqualified IRB or that is to be conducted at a disqualified institution, and it may refuse to consider in support of a marketing permit the data from a clinical investigation that was reviewed by a disqualified IRB as conducted at a disqualified institution, unless the IRB or the parent institution is reinstated as provided in 56. 123.

## Sec. 56. 122 Public disclosure of information regarding revocation.

A determination that the Food and Drug Administration has disqualified an institution and the administrative record regarding that determination are disclosable to the public under part 20.

## Sec. 56. 123 Reinstatement of an IRB or an institution.

An IRB or an institution may be reinstated if the Commissioner determines, upon an evaluation of a written submission from the IRB or institution that explains the corrective action that the institution or IRB plans to take, that the IRB or institution has provided adequate assurance that it will operate in compliance with the standards set forth in this part. Notification of reinstatement shall be provided to all persons notified under 56. 121(c).

## Sec. 56. 124 Actions alternative or additional to disqualification.

Disqualification of an IRB or of an institution is independent of, and neither in lieu of nor a precondition to, other proceedings or actions authorized by the act. The Food and Drug Administration may, at any time, through the Department of Justice institute any appropriate judicial proceedings (civil or criminal) and any other appropriate regulatory action, in addition to or in lieu of, and before, at the time of, or after, disqualification. The agency may also refer pertinent matters to another Federal, State, or local government agency for any action that that agency determines to be appropriate.

[Revised as of April 1, 2017]

# 21CFR PART312 INVESTIGATIONAL NEW DRUG APPLICATION

## Subpart A-General Provisions

### Sec. 312. 1 Scope.

(a) This part contains procedures and requirements governing the use of investigational new drugs, including procedures and requirements for the submission to, and review by, the Food and Drug Administration of investigational new drug applications (IND's). An investigational new drug for which an IND is in effect in accordance with this part is exempt from the premarketing approval requirements that are otherwise applicable and may be shipped lawfully for the purpose of conducting clinical investigations of that drug.

(b) References in this part to regulations in the Code of Federal Regulations are to chapter I of title 21, unless otherwise noted.

### Sec. 312. 2 Applicability.

(a) *Applicability*. Except as provided in this section, this part applies to all clinical investigations of products that are subject to section 505 of the Federal Food, Drug, and Cosmetic Act or to the licensing provisions of the Public Health Service Act(58 Stat. 632,as amended(42 U. S. C. 201 et seq. )).

(b) *Exemptions*.

  (1) The clinical investigation of a drug product that is lawfully marketed in the United States is exempt from the requirements of this part if all the following apply:

    (i) The investigation is not intended to be reported to FDA as a well-controlled study in support of a new indication for use nor intended to be used to support any other significant change in the labeling for the drug;

(ii) If the drug that is undergoing investigation is lawfully marketed as a prescription drug product, the investigation is not intended to support a significant change in the advertising for the product;

(iii) The investigation does not involve a route of administration or dosage level or use in a patient population or other factor that significantly increases the risks (or decreases the acceptability of the risks) associated with the use of the drug product;

(iv) The investigation is conducted in compliance with the requirements for institutional review set forth in part 56 and with the requirements for informed consent set forth in part 50; and

(v) The investigation is conducted in compliance with the requirements of 312. 7.

(2) (i) A clinical investigation involving an in vitro diagnostic biological product listed in paragraph (b)(2)(ii) of this section is exempt from the requirements of this part if (a) it is intended to be used in a diagnostic procedure that confirms the diagnosis made by another, medically established, diagnostic product or procedure and (b) it is shipped in compliance with 312. 160.

(ii) In accordance with paragraph (b)(2)(i) of this section, the following products are exempt from the requirements of this part: (a) blood grouping serum; (b) reagent red blood cells; and (c) anti-human globulin.

(3) A drug intended solely for tests in vitro or in laboratory research animals is exempt from the requirements of this part if shipped in accordance with 312. 160.

(4) FDA will not accept an application for an investigation that is exempt under the provisions of paragraph (b)(1) of this section.

(5) A clinical investigation involving use of a placebo is exempt from the requirements of this part if the investigation does not otherwise require submission of an IND.

(6) A clinical investigation involving an exception from informed consent under 50. 24 of this chapter is not exempt from the requirements of this part.

(c) *Bioavailability studies*. The applicability of this part to in vivo bioavailability studies in humans is subject to the provisions of 320. 31.

(d) *Unlabeled indication*. This part does not apply to the use in the practice of medicine for an unlabeled indication of a new drug product approved under part 314 or of a licensed biological product.

(e) *Guidance*. FDA may, on its own initiative, issue guidance on the applicability of this part to particular investigational uses of drugs. On request, FDA will advise on the applicability of this part to a planned clinical investigation.

## Sec. 312. 3 Definitions and interpretations.

(a) The definitions and interpretations of terms contained in section 201 of the Act apply to those terms when used in this part:

(b) The following definitions of terms also apply to this part:

*Act* means the Federal Food, Drug, and Cosmetic Act (secs. 201-902, 52 Stat. 1040 et seq. , as amended (21 U. S. C. 301-392)).

*Clinical investigation* means any experiment in which a drug is administered or dispensed to, or used involving, one or more human subjects. For the purposes of this part, an experiment is any use of a drug except for the use of a marketed drug in the course of medical practice.

*Contract research organization* means a person that assumes, as an independent contractor with the sponsor, one or more of the obligations of a sponsor, e. g. , design of a protocol, selection or monitoring of investigations, evaluation of reports, and preparation of materials to be submitted to the Food and Drug Administration.

*FDA* means the Food and Drug Administration.

*IND* means an investigational new drug application. For purposes of this part, " IND" is synonymous with " Notice of Claimed Investigational Exemption for a New Drug. "

*Independent ethics committee* (*IEC*) means a review panel that is responsible for ensuring the protection of the rights, safety, and well-being of human subjects involved in a clinical investigation and is adequately constituted to provide assurance of that protection. An institutional review board (IRB) , as defined in 56. 102 (g) of this chapter and subject to the requirements of part 56 of this chapter, is one type of IEC.

*Investigational new drug* means a new drug or biological drug that is used in a clinical investigation. The term also includes a biological product that is used in vitro for diagnostic purposes. The terms "investigational drug" and "investigational new drug" are deemed to be synonymous for purposes of this part.

*Investigator* means an individual who actually conducts a clinical investigation (i. e., under whose immediate direction the drug is administered or dispensed to a subject). In the event an investigation is conducted by a team of individuals, the investigator is the responsible leader of the team. "Subinvestigator" includes any other individual member of that team.

*Marketing application* means an application for a new drug submitted under section 505 (b) of the act or a biologics license application for a biological product submitted under the Public Health Service Act.

*Sponsor* means a person who takes responsibility for and initiates a clinical investigation. The sponsor may be an individual or pharmaceutical company, governmental agency, academic institution, private organization, or other organization. The sponsor does not actually conduct the investigation unless the sponsor is a sponsor-investigator. A person other than an individual that uses one or more of its own employees to conduct an investigation that it has initiated is a sponsor, not a sponsor-investigator, and the employees are investigators.

*Sponsor-Investigator* means an individual who both initiates and conducts an investigation, and under whose immediate direction the investigational drug is administered or dispensed. The term does not include any person other than an individual. The requirements applicable to a sponsor-investigator under this part include both those applicable to an investigator and a sponsor.

*Subject* means a human who participates in an investigation, either as a recipient of the investigational new drug or as a control. A subject may be a healthy human or a patient with a disease.

## Sec. 312. 6 Labeling of an investigational new drug.

(a) The immediate package of an investigational new drug intended for human use shall bear a label with the statement "Caution: New Drug—Limited by Federal (or United States) law to investigational use."

(b) The label or labeling of an investigational new drug shall not bear any statement that is false or misleading in any particular and shall not represent that the investigational new drug is safe or effective for the purposes for which it is being investigated.

(c) The appropriate FDA Center Director, according to the procedures set forth in 201. 26 or 610. 68 of this chapter, may grant an exception or alternative to the provision in paragraph (a) of this section, to the extent that this provision is not explicitly required by statute, for specified lots, batches, or other units of a human drug product that is or will be included in the Strategic National Stockpile.

## Sec. 312. 7 Promotion of investigational drugs.

(a) Promotion of an investigational new drug. A sponsor or investigator, or any person acting on behalf of a sponsor or investigator, shall not represent in a promotional context that an investigational new drug is safe or effective for the purposes for which it is under investigation or otherwise promote the drug. This provision is not intended to restrict the full exchange of scientific information concerning the drug, including dissemination of scientific findings in scientific or lay media. Rather, its intent is to restrict promotional claims of safety or effectiveness of the drug for a use for which it is under investigation and to preclude commercialization of the drug before it is approved for commercial distribution.

(b) Commercial distribution of an investigational new drug. A sponsor or investigator shall not commercially distribute or test market an investigational new drug.

(c) Prolonging an investigation. A sponsor shall not unduly prolong an investigation after finding that the results of the investigation appear to establish sufficient data to support a marketing application.

## Sec. 312. 8 Charging for investigational drugs under an IND.

(a) *General criteria for charging*.

(1) A sponsor must meet the applicable requirements in paragraph (b) of this section for charging in a clinical trial or paragraph (c) of this section for charging for expanded access to an investigational drug for treatment use under subpart I of this part, except that sponsors need not fulfill the requirements in this section to charge for an approved drug obtained from another entity not affiliated with the sponsor for use as part of the clinical trial evaluation (e. g. , in a

clinical trial of a new use of the approved drug, for use of the approved drug as an active control).

(2) A sponsor must justify the amount to be charged in accordance with paragraph (d) of this section.

(3) A sponsor must obtain prior written authorization from FDA to charge for an investigational drug.

(4) FDA will withdraw authorization to charge if it determines that charging is interfering with the development of a drug for marketing approval or that the criteria for the authorization are no longer being met.

(b) *Charging in a clinical trial.*

(1) Charging for a sponsor's drug. A sponsor who wishes to charge for its investigational drug, including investigational use of its approved drug, must:

(i) Provide evidence that the drug has a potential clinical benefit that, if demonstrated in the clinical investigations, would provide a significant advantage over available products in the diagnosis, treatment, mitigation, or prevention of a disease or condition;

(ii) Demonstrate that the data to be obtained from the clinical trial would be essential to establishing that the drug is effective or safe for the purpose of obtaining initial approval of a drug, or would support a significant change in the labeling of an approved drug (e. g., new indication, inclusion of comparative safety information); and

(iii) Demonstrate that the clinical trial could not be conducted without charging because the cost of the drug is extraordinary to the sponsor. The cost may be extraordinary due to manufacturing complexity, scarcity of a natural resource, the large quantity of drug needed (e. g., due to the size or duration of the trial), or some combination of these or other extraordinary circumstances (e. g., resources available to a sponsor).

(2) Duration of charging in a clinical trial. Unless FDA specifies a shorter period, charging may continue for the length of the clinical trial.

(c) *Charging for expanded access to investigational drug for treatment use.*

(1) A sponsor who wishes to charge for expanded access to an investigational drug for treatment use under subpart I of this part must provide reasonable assurance that charging will not interfere with developing the drug for marketing approval.

(2) For expanded access under 312. 320 (treatment IND or treatment protocol), such assurance must include:

(i) Evidence of sufficient enrollment in any ongoing clinical trial (s) needed for marketing approval to reasonably assure FDA that the trial (s) will be successfully completed as planned;

(ii) Evidence of adequate progress in the development of the drug for marketing approval; and

(iii) Information submitted under the general investigational plan (312. 23(a)(3)(iv) ) specifying the drug development milestones the sponsor plans to meet in the next year.

(3) The authorization to charge is limited to the number of patients authorized to receive the drug under the treatment use, if there is a limitation.

(4) Unless FDA specifies a shorter period, charging for expanded access to an investigational drug for treatment use under subpart I of this part may continue for 1 year from the time of FDA authorization. A sponsor may request that FDA reauthorize charging for additional periods.

(d) *Costs recoverable when charging for an investigational drug.*

(1) A sponsor may recover only the direct costs of making its investigational drug available.

(i) Direct costs are costs incurred by a sponsor that can be specifically and exclusively attributed to providing the drug for the investigational use for which FDA has authorized cost recovery. Direct costs include costs per unit to manufacture the drug (e. g. , raw materials, labor, and nonreusable supplies and equipment used to manufacture the quantity of drug needed for the use for which charging is authorized) or costs to acquire the drug from another manufacturing source, and direct costs to ship and handle (e. g. , store) the drug.

(ii) Indirect costs include costs incurred primarily to produce the drug for commercial sale (e. g. , costs for facilities and equipment used to manufacture the supply of investigational drug, but that are primarily intended to produce large quantities of drug for eventual commercial sale) and research and development, administrative, labor, or other costs that would be incurred even if the clinical trial or treatment use for which charging is authorized did not occur.

(2) For expanded access to an investigational drug for treatment use under 312. 315 ( intermediate-size patient populations ) and 312. 320 (treatment IND or treatment protocol) , in addition to the direct costs described in paragraph (d)(1)(i) of this section, a sponsor may recover the costs of monitoring the expanded access IND or protocol, complying with IND reporting requirements, and other administrative costs directly associated with the expanded access IND.

(3) To support its calculation for cost recovery, a sponsor must provide supporting documentation to show that the calculation is consistent with the requirements of paragraphs (d)(1) and, if applicable, (d)(2) of this section. The documentation must be accompanied by a statement that an independent certified public accountant has reviewed and approved the calculations.

## Sec. 312. 10 Waivers.

(a) A sponsor may request FDA to waive applicable requirement under this part. A waiver request may be submitted either in an IND or in an information amendment to an IND. In an emergency, a request may be made by telephone or other rapid communication means. A waiver request is required to contain at least one of the following:

(1) An explanation why the sponsor's compliance with the requirement is unnecessary or cannot be achieved;

(2) A description of an alternative submission or course of action that satisfies the purpose of the requirement; or

(3) Other information justifying a waiver.

(b) FDA may grant a waiver if it finds that the sponsor's noncompliance would not pose a significant and unreasonable risk to human subjects of the investigation and that one of the following is met:

(1) The sponsor's compliance with the requirement is unnecessary for the agency to evaluate the application, or compliance cannot be achieved;

(2) The sponsor's proposed alternative satisfies the requirement; or

(3) The applicant's submission otherwise justifies a waiver.

# Subpart B-Investigational New Drug Application (IND)

## Sec. 312. 20 Requirement for an IND.

(a) A sponsor shall submit an IND to FDA if the sponsor intends to conduct a clinical investigation with an investigational new drug that is subject to 312. 2 (a).

(b) A sponsor shall not begin a clinical investigation subject to 312. 2 (a) until the investigation is subject to an IND which is in effect in accordance with 312. 40.

(c) A sponsor shall submit a separate IND for any clinical investigation involving an exception from informed consent under 50. 24 of this chapter. Such a clinical investigation is not permitted to proceed without the prior written authorization from FDA. FDA shall provide a written determination 30 days after FDA receives the IND or earlier.

## Sec. 312. 21 Phases of an investigation.

An IND may be submitted for one or more phases of an investigation. The clinical investigation of a previously untested drug is generally divided into three phases. Although in general the phases are conducted sequentially, they may overlap. These three phases of an investigation are a follows:

(a) *Phase* 1.

(1) Phase 1 includes the initial introduction of an investigational new drug into humans. Phase 1 studies are typically closely monitored and may be conducted in patients or normal volunteer subjects. These studies are designed to determine the metabolism and pharmacologic actions of the drug in humans, the side effects associated with increasing doses, and, if possible, to gain early evidence on effectiveness. During Phase 1, sufficient information about the

drug's pharmacokinetics and pharmacological effects should be obtained to permit the design of well-controlled, scientifically valid, Phase 2 studies. The total number of subjects and patients included in Phase 1 studies varies with the drug, but is generally in the range of 20 to 80.

(2) Phase 1 studies also include studies of drug metabolism, structure-activity relationships, and mechanism of action in humans, as well as studies in which investigational drugs are used as research tools to explore biological phenomena or disease processes.

(b) *Phase* 2. Phase 2 includes the controlled clinical studies conducted to evaluate the effectiveness of the drug for a particular indication or indications in patients with the disease or condition under study and to determine the common short-term side effects and risks associated with the drug. Phase 2 studies are typically well controlled, closely monitored, and conducted in a relatively small number of patients, usually involving no more than several hundred subjects.

(c) *Phase* 3. Phase 3 studies are expanded controlled and uncontrolled trials. They are performed after preliminary evidence suggesting effectiveness of the drug has been obtained, and are intended to gather the additional information about effectiveness and safety that is needed to evaluate the overall benefit-risk relationship of the drug and to provide an adequate basis for physician labeling. Phase 3 studies usually include from several hundred to several thousand subjects.

## Sec. 312. 22 General principles of the IND submission.

(a) FDA's primary objectives in reviewing an IND are, in all phases of the investigation, to assure the safety and rights of subjects, and, in Phase 2 and 3, to help assure that the quality of the scientific evaluation of drugs is adequate to permit an evaluation of the drug's effectiveness and safety. Therefore, although FDA's review of Phase 1 submissions will focus on assessing the safety of Phase 1 investigations, FDA's review of Phases 2 and 3 submissions will also include an assessment of the scientific quality of the clinical investigations and the likelihood that the investigations will yield data capable of meeting statutory standards for marketing approval.

(b) The amount of information on a particular drug that must be submitted in an IND to assure the accomplishment of the objectives described in paragraph (a) of this section depends upon such factors as the novelty of the drug, the extent to which it has been studied previously, the known or suspected risks, and the developmental phase of the drug.

(c) The central focus of the initial IND submission should be on the general investigational plan and the protocols for specific human studies. Subsequent amendments to the IND that contain new or revised protocols should build logically on previous submissions and should be supported by additional information, including the results of animal toxicology studies or other human studies as appropriate. Annual reports to the IND should serve as the focus for reporting the status of studies being conducted under the IND and should update the general investigational plan for the coming year.

(d) The IND format set forth in 312. 23 should be followed routinely by sponsors in the interest of fostering an efficient review of applications. Sponsors are expected to exercise considerable discretion, however, regarding the content of information submitted in each section, depending upon the kind of drug being studied and the nature of the available information. Section 312. 23 outlines the information needed for a commercially sponsored IND for a new molecular entity. A sponsor-investigator who uses, as a research tool, an investigational new drug that is already subject to a manufacturer's IND or marketing application should follow the same general format, but ordinarily may, if authorized by the manufacturer, refer to the manufacturer's IND or marketing application in providing the technical information supporting the proposed clinical investigation. A sponsor-investigator who uses an investigational drug not subject to a manufacturer's IND or marketing application is ordinarily required to submit all technical information supporting the IND, unless such information may be referenced from the scientific literature.

## Sec. 312. 23 IND content and format.

(a) A sponsor who intends to conduct a clinical investigation subject to this part shall submit an "Investigational New Drug Application" (IND) including, in the following order:

(1) *Cover sheet* (*Form FDA-1571*). A cover sheet for the application containing the following:

(i) The name, address, and telephone number of the sponsor, the date of the application, and the name of the investigational new drug.

(ii) Identification of the phase or phases of the clinical investigation to be conducted.

(iii) A commitment not to begin clinical investigations until an IND covering the investigations is in effect.

(iv) A commitment that an Institutional Review Board (IRB) that complies with the requirements set forth in part 56 will be responsible for the initial and continuing review and approval of each of the studies in the proposed clinical investigation and that the investigator will report to the IRB proposed changes in the research activity in accordance with the requirements of part 56.

(v) A commitment to conduct the investigation in accordance with all other applicable regulatory requirements.

(vi) The name and title of the person responsible for monitoring the conduct and progress of the clinical investigations.

(vii) The name (s) and title (s) of the person (s) responsible under 312. 32 for review and evaluation of information relevant to the safety of the drug.

(viii) If a sponsor has transferred any obligations for the conduct of any clinical study to a contract research organization, a statement containing the name and address of the contract research organization, identification of the clinical study, and a listing of the obligations transferred. If all obligations governing the conduct of the study have been transferred, a general statement of this transfer—in lieu of a listing of the specific obligations transferred—may be submitted.

(ix) The signature of the sponsor or the sponsor's authorized representative. If the person signing the application does not reside or have a place of business within the United States, the IND is required to contain the name and address of, and be countersigned by, an attorney, agent, or other authorized official who resides or maintains a place of business within the United States.

(2) *A table of contents.*

(3) *Introductory statement and general investigational plan.*

(i) A brief introductory statement giving the name of the drug and all active ingredients, the drug's pharmacological class, the structural formula of the drug (if known), the formulation of the dosage form (s) to be used, the route of administration, and the broad objectives and planned duration of the proposed clinical investigation (s).

(ii) A brief summary of previous human experience with the drug, with reference to other IND's if pertinent, and to investigational or marketing experience in other countries that may be relevant to the safety of the proposed clinical investigation (s).

(iii) If the drug has been withdrawn from investigation or marketing in any country for any reason related to safety or effectiveness, identification of the country (ies) where the drug was withdrawn and the reasons for the withdrawal.

(iv) A brief description of the overall plan for investigating the drug product for the following year. The plan should include the following: (a) The rationale for the drug or the research study; (b) the indication (s) to be studied; (c) the general approach to be followed in evaluating the drug; (d) the kinds of clinical trials to be conducted in the first year following the submission (if plans are not developed for the entire year, the sponsor should so indicate); (e) the estimated number of patients to be given the drug in those studies; and (f) any risks of particular severity or seriousness anticipated on the basis of the toxicological data in animals or prior studies in humans with the drug or related drugs.

(4) [Reserved]

(5) *Investigator's brochure.* If required under 312. 55, a copy of the investigator's brochure, containing the following information:

(i) A brief description of the drug substance and the formulation, including the structural formula, if known.

(ii) A summary of the pharmacological and toxicological effects of the drug in animals and, to the extent known, in humans.

(iii) A summary of the pharmacokinetics and biological disposition of the drug in animals and, if known, in humans.

(iv) A summary of information relating to safety and effectiveness in humans obtained from prior clinical studies. (Reprints of published articles on such studies may be appended when useful. )

(v) A description of possible risks and side effects to be anticipated on the basis of prior experience with the drug under investigation or with related drugs, and of precautions or special monitoring to be done as part of the investigational use of the drug.

(6) *Protocols.*

(i) A protocol for each planned study. (Protocols for studies not submitted initially in the IND should be submitted in accordance with 312. 30 (a) . ) In general, protocols for Phase 1 studies may be less detailed and more flexible than protocols for Phase 2 and 3 studies. Phase 1 protocols should be directed primarily at providing an outline of the investigation—an estimate of the number of patients to be involved, a description of safety exclusions, and a description of the dosing plan including duration, dose, or method to be used in determining dose—and should specify in detail only those elements of the study that are critical to safety, such as necessary monitoring of vital signs and blood chemistries. Modifications of the experimental design of Phase 1 studies that do not affect critical safety assessments are required to be reported to FDA only in the annual report.

(ii) In Phases 2 and 3, detailed protocols describing all aspects of the study should be submitted. A protocol for a Phase 2 or 3 investigation should be designed in such a way that, if the sponsor anticipates that some deviation from the study design may become necessary as the investigation progresses, alternatives or contingencies to provide for such deviation are built into the protocols at the outset. For example, a protocol for a controlled short-term study might include a plan for an early crossover of nonresponders to an alternative therapy.

(iii) A protocol is required to contain the following, with the specific elements and detail of the protocol reflecting the above distinctions depending on the phase of study:

(A) A statement of the objectives and purpose of the study.

(B) The name and address and a statement of the qualifications (curriculum vitae or other statement of qualifications) of each investigator, and the name of each subinvestigator (e. g., research fellow, resident) working under the supervision of the investigator; the name and address of the research facilities to be used; and the name and address of each reviewing Institutional Review Board.

(C) The criteria for patient selection and for exclusion of patients and an estimate of the number of patients to be studied.

(D) A description of the design of the study, including the kind of control group to be used, if any, and a description of methods to be used to minimize bias on the part of subjects, investigators, and analysts.

(E) The method for determining the dose (s) to be administered, the planned maximum dosage, and the duration of individual patient exposure to the drug.

(F) A description of the observations and measurements to be made to fulfill the objectives of the study.

(G) A description of clinical procedures, laboratory tests, or other measures to be taken to monitor the effects of the drug in human subjects and to minimize risk.

(7) *Chemistry, manufacturing, and control information.*

(i) As appropriate for the particular investigations covered by the IND, a section describing the composition, manufacture, and control of the drug substance and the drug product. Although in each phase of the investigation sufficient information is required to be submitted to assure the proper identification, quality, purity, and strength of the investigational drug, the amount of information needed to make that assurance will vary with the phase of the investigation, the proposed duration of the investigation, the dosage form, and the amount of information otherwise available. FDA recognizes that modifications to the method of preparation of the new drug substance and dosage form and changes in the dosage form itself are likely as the investigation progresses. Therefore, the emphasis in an initial Phase 1 submission should generally be placed on the identification and control of the raw materials and the new drug substance. Final specifications for the drug substance and drug product are not expected until the end of the investigational process.

(ii) It should be emphasized that the amount of information to be submitted depends upon the scope of the proposed clinical investigation. For example, although stability data are required in all phases of the IND to demonstrate that the new drug substance and drug product are within acceptable chemical and physical limits for the planned duration of the proposed clinical investigation, if very short-term tests are proposed, the supporting stability data can be correspondingly limited.

(iii) As drug development proceeds and as the scale or production is changed from the pilot-scale production appropriate for the limited initial clinical investigations to the larger-scale production needed for expanded clinical trials, the sponsor should submit information amendments to supplement the initial information submitted on the chemistry, manufacturing, and control processes with information appropriate to the expanded scope of the investigation.

(iv) Reflecting the distinctions described in this paragraph (a)(7), and based on the phase (s) to be studied, the submission is required to contain the following:

(A) *Drug substance*. A description of the drug substance, including its physical, chemical, or biological characteristics; the name and address of its manufacturer; the general method of preparation of the drug substance; the acceptable limits and analytical methods used to assure the identity, strength, quality, and purity of the drug substance; and information sufficient to support stability of the drug substance during the toxicological studies and the planned clinical studies. Reference to the current edition of the United States Pharmacopeia—National Formulary may satisfy relevant requirements in this paragraph.

(B) *Drug product*. A list of all components, which may include reasonable alternatives for inactive compounds, used in the manufacture of the investigational drug product, including both those components intended to appear in the drug product and those which may not appear but which are used in the manufacturing process, and, where applicable, the quantitative composition of the investigational drug product, including any reasonable variations that may be expected during the investigational stage; the name and address of the drug product manufacturer; a brief general description of the manufacturing and packaging procedure as appropriate for the product; the acceptable limits and analytical methods used to assure the identity, strength, quality, and purity of the drug product; and information sufficient to assure the product's stability during the planned clinical studies. Reference to the current edition of the United States Pharmacopeia—National Formulary may satisfy certain requirements in this paragraph.

(C) A brief general description of the composition, manufacture, and control of any placebo used in a controlled clinical trial.

(D) *Labeling*. A copy of all labels and labeling to be provided to each investigator.

(E) *Environmental analysis requirements*. A claim for categorical exclusion under 25. 30 or 25. 31 or an environmental assessment under 25. 40.

(8) *Pharmacology and toxicology information*. Adequate information about pharmacological and toxicological studies of the drug involving laboratory animals or in vitro, on the basis of which the sponsor has concluded that it is reasonably safe to conduct the proposed clinical investigations. The kind, duration, and scope of ani-

mal and other tests required varies with the duration and nature of the proposed clinical investigations. Guidance documents are available from FDA that describe ways in which these requirements may be met. Such information is required to include the identification and qualifications of the individuals who evaluated the results of such studies and concluded that it is reasonably safe to begin the proposed investigations and a statement of where the investigations were conducted and where the records are available for inspection. As drug development proceeds, the sponsor is required to submit informational amendments, as appropriate, with additional information pertinent to safety.

(i) *Pharmacology and drug disposition*. A section describing the pharmacological effects and mechanism (s) of action of the drug in animals, and information on the absorption, distribution, metabolism, and excretion of the drug, if known.

(ii) *Toxicology*.

(A) An integrated summary of the toxicological effects of the drug in animals and in vitro. Depending on the nature of the drug and the phase of the investigation, the description is to include the results of acute, subacute, and chronic toxicity tests; tests of the drug's effects on reproduction and the developing fetus; any special toxicity test related to the drug's particular mode of administration or conditions of use (e. g. , inhalation, dermal, or ocular toxicology) ; and any in vitro studies intended to evaluate drug toxicity.

(B) For each toxicology study that is intended primarily to support the safety of the proposed clinical investigation, a full tabulation of data suitable for detailed review.

(iii) For each nonclinical laboratory study subject to the good laboratory practice regulations under part 58, a statement that the study was conducted in compliance with the good laboratory practice regulations in part 58, or, if the study was not conducted in compliance with those regulations, a brief statement of the reason for the noncompliance.

(9) *Previous human experience with the investigational drug*. A

summary of previous human experience known to the applicant, if any, with the investigational drug. The information is required to include the following:

(i) If the investigational drug has been investigated or marketed previously, either in the United States or other countries, detailed information about such experience that is relevant to the safety of the proposed investigation or to the investigation's rationale. If the drug has been the subject of controlled trials, detailed information on such trials that is relevant to an assessment of the drug's effectiveness for the proposed investigational use (s) should also be provided. Any published material that is relevant to the safety of the proposed investigation or to an assessment of the drug's effectiveness for its proposed investigational use should be provided in full. Published material that is less directly relevant may be supplied by a bibliography.

(ii) If the drug is a combination of drugs previously investigated or marketed, the information required under paragraph (a)(9)(i) of this section should be provided for each active drug component. However, if any component in such combination is subject to an approved marketing application or is otherwise lawfully marketed in the United States, the sponsor is not required to submit published material concerning that active drug component unless such material relates directly to the proposed investigational use (including publications relevant to component-component interaction).

(iii) If the drug has been marketed outside the United States, a list of the countries in which the drug has been marketed and a list of the countries in which the drug has been withdrawn from marketing for reasons potentially related to safety or effectiveness.

(10) *Additional information*. In certain applications, as described below, information on special topics may be needed. Such information shall be submitted in this section as follows:

(i) *Drug dependence and abuse potential*. If the drug is a psychotropic substance or otherwise has abuse potential, a section describing relevant clinical studies and experience and studies in test animals.

(ii) *Radioactive drugs*. If the drug is a radioactive drug, sufficient data from animal or human studies to allow a reasonable calculation of radiation-absorbed dose to the whole body and critical organs upon administration to a human subject. Phase 1 studies of radioactive drugs must include studies which will obtain sufficient data for dosimetry calculations.

(iii) *Pediatric studies*. Plans for assessing pediatric safety and effectiveness.

(iv) *Other information*. A brief statement of any other information that would aid evaluation of the proposed clinical investigations with respect to their safety or their design and potential as controlled clinical trials to support marketing of the drug.

(11) *Relevant information*. If requested by FDA, any other relevant information needed for review of the application.

(b) *Information previously submitted*. The sponsor ordinarily is not required to resubmit information previously submitted, but may incorporate the information by reference. A reference to information submitted previously must identify the file by name, reference number, volume, and page number where the information can be found. A reference to information submitted to the agency by a person other than the sponsor is required to contain a written statement that authorizes the reference and that is signed by the person who submitted the information.

(c) *Material in a foreign language*. The sponsor shall submit an accurate and complete English translation of each part of the IND that is not in English. The sponsor shall also submit a copy of each original literature publication for which an English translation is submitted.

(d) *Number of copies*. The sponsor shall submit an original and two copies of all submissions to the IND file, including the original submission and all amendments and reports.

(e) *Numbering of IND submissions*. Each submission relating to an IND is required to be numbered serially using a single, three-digit serial number. The initial IND is required to be numbered 000; each subsequent submission (e. g. , amendment, report, or correspondence) is required to be numbered chronologically in sequence.

(f) *Identification of exception from informed consent*. If the investigation involves an exception from informed consent under 50. 24 of this chapter, the sponsor shall prominently identify on the cover sheet that the investigation is subject to the requirements in 50. 24 of this chapter.

## Sec. 312. 30 Protocol amendments.

Once an IND is in effect, a sponsor shall amend it as needed to ensure that the clinical investigations are conducted according to protocols included in the application. This section sets forth the provisions under which new protocols may be submitted and changes in previously submitted protocols may be made. Whenever a sponsor intends to conduct a clinical investigation with an exception from informed consent for emergency research as set forth in 50. 24 of this chapter, the sponsor shall submit a separate IND for such investigation.

(a) *New protocol*. Whenever a sponsor intends to conduct a study that is not covered by a protocol already contained in the IND, the sponsor shall submit to FDA a protocol amendment containing the protocol for the study. Such study may begin provided two conditions are met: (1) The sponsor has submitted the protocol to FDA for its review; and (2) the protocol has been approved by the Institutional Review Board (IRB) with responsibility for review and approval of the study in accordance with the requirements of part 56. The sponsor may comply with these two conditions in either order.

(b) *Changes in a protocol*.

(1) A sponsor shall submit a protocol amendment describing any change in a Phase 1 protocol that significantly affects the safety of subjects or any change in a Phase 2 or 3 protocol that significantly affects the safety of subjects, the scope of the investigation, or the scientific quality of the study. Examples of changes requiring an amendment under this paragraph include:

(i) Any increase in drug dosage or duration of exposure of individual subjects to the drug beyond that in the current protocol, or any significant increase in the number of subjects under study.

(ii) Any significant change in the design of a protocol (such as the addition or dropping of a control group).

(iii) The addition of a new test or procedure that is intended to improve monitoring for, or reduce the risk of, a side effect or adverse event; or the dropping of a test intended to monitor safety.

(2) (i) A protocol change under paragraph (b)(1) of this section may be made provided two conditions are met:

(A) The sponsor has submitted the change to FDA for its review; and

(B) The change has been approved by the IRB with responsibility for review and approval of the study. The sponsor may comply with these two conditions in either order.

(ii) Notwithstanding paragraph (b)(2)(i) of this section, a protocol change intended to eliminate an apparent immediate hazard to subjects may be implemented immediately provided FDA is subsequently notified by protocol amendment and the reviewing IRB is notified in accordance with 56. 104 (c).

(c) *New investigator*. A sponsor shall submit a protocol amendment when a new investigator is added to carry out a previously submitted protocol, except that a protocol amendment is not required when a licensed practitioner is added in the case of a treatment protocol under 312. 315 or 312. 320. Once the investigator is added to the study, the investigational drug may be shipped to the investigator and the investigator may begin participating in the study. The sponsor shall notify FDA of the new investigator within 30 days of the investigator being added.

(d) *Content and format*. A protocol amendment is required to be prominently identified as such (i. e., "Protocol Amendment: New Protocol", "Protocol Amendment: Change in Protocol", or "Protocol Amendment: New Investigator"), and to contain the following:

(1) (i) In the case of a new protocol, a copy of the new protocol and a brief description of the most clinically significant differences between it and previous protocols.

(ii) In the case of a change in protocol, a brief description of the change and reference (date and number) to the submission that contained the protocol.

(iii) In the case of a new investigator, the investigator's name, the qualifications to conduct the investigation, reference to the previously submitted protocol, and all additional information about the investigator's study as is required under 312. 23 (a) (6)(iii)(b) .

(2) Reference, if necessary, to specific technical information in the IND or in a concurrently submitted information amendment to the IND that the sponsor relies on to support any clinically significant change in the new or amended protocol. If the reference is made to supporting information already in the IND, the sponsor shall identify by name, reference number, volume, and page number the location of the information.

(3) If the sponsor desires FDA to comment on the submission, a request for such comment and the specific questions FDA's response should address.

(e) *When submitted*. A sponsor shall submit a protocol amendment for a new protocol or a change in protocol before its implementation. Protocol amendments to add a new investigator or to provide additional information about investigators may be grouped and submitted at 30-day intervals. When several submissions of new protocols or protocol changes are anticipated during a short period, the sponsor is encouraged, to the extent feasible, to include these all in a single submission.

## Sec. 312. 31 Information amendments.

(a) *Requirement for information amendment*. A sponsor shall report in an information amendment essential information on the IND that is not within the scope of a protocol amendment, IND safety reports, or annual report. Examples of information requiring an information amendment include:

(1) New toxicology, chemistry, or other technical information; or

(2) A report regarding the discontinuance of a clinical investigation.

(b) *Content and format of an information amendment*. An information amendment is required to bear prominent identification of its contents (e. g. , "Information Amendment: Chemistry, Manufacturing, and Control" , "Information Amendment: Pharmacology-Toxicology" , "Information Amendment: Clinical" ) , and to contain the following:

(1) A statement of the nature and purpose of the amendment.

(2) An organized submission of the data in a format appropriate for sci-

entific review.

(3) If the sponsor desires FDA to comment on an information amendment, a request for such comment.

(c) *When submitted*. Information amendments to the IND should be submitted as necessary but, to the extent feasible, not more than every 30 days.

## Sec. 312. 32 IND safety reporting.

(a) *Definitions*. The following definitions of terms apply to this section:

*Adverse event* means any untoward medical occurrence associated with the use of a drug in humans, whether or not considered drug related.

*Life-threatening adverse event or life-threatening suspected adverse reaction*. An adverse event or suspected adverse reaction is considered "life-threatening" if, in the view of either the investigator or sponsor, its occurrence places the patient or subject at immediate risk of death. It does not include an adverse event or suspected adverse reaction that, had it occurred in a more severe form, might have caused death.

*Serious adverse event or serious suspected adverse reaction*. An adverse event or suspected adverse reaction is considered "serious" if, in the view of either the investigator or sponsor, it results in any of the following outcomes: Death, a life-threatening adverse event, inpatient hospitalization or prolongation of existing hospitalization, a persistent or significant incapacity or substantial disruption of the ability to conduct normal life functions, or a congenital anomaly/birth defect. Important medical events that may not result in death, be life-threatening, or require hospitalization may be considered serious when, based upon appropriate medical judgment, they may jeopardize the patient or subject and may require medical or surgical intervention to prevent one of the outcomes listed in this definition. Examples of such medical events include allergic bronchospasm requiring intensive treatment in an emergency room or at home, blood dyscrasias or convulsions that do not result in inpatient hospitalization, or the development of drug dependency or drug abuse.

*Suspected adverse reaction* means any adverse event for which there is a reasonable possibility that the drug caused the adverse event. For the purposes of IND safety reporting, "reasonable possibility" means there is evidence to suggest a causal relationship between the drug and the adverse event. Suspected adverse reaction implies a lesser degree of certainty about causality than adverse reaction, which means any adverse event caused by a drug.

*Unexpected adverse event or unexpected suspected adverse reaction*. An adverse event or suspected adverse reaction is considered "unexpected" if it is not listed in the investigator brochure or is not listed at the specificity or severity that has been observed; or, if an investigator brochure is not required or available, is not consistent with the risk information described in the general investigational plan or elsewhere in the current application, as amended. For example, under this definition, hepatic necrosis would be unexpected (by virtue of greater severity) if the investigator brochure referred only to elevated hepatic enzymes or hepatitis. Similarly, cerebral thromboembolism and cerebral vasculitis would be unexpected (by virtue of greater specificity) if the investigator brochure listed only cerebral vascular accidents. "Unexpected" as used in this definition, also refers to adverse events or suspected adverse reactions that are mentioned in the investigator brochure as occurring with a class of drugs or as anticipated from the pharmacological properties of the drug, but are not specifically mentioned as occurring with the particular drug under investigation.

(b) *Review of safety information*. The sponsor must promptly review all information relevant to the safety of the drug obtained or otherwise received by the sponsor from foreign or domestic sources, including information derived from any clinical or epidemiological investigations, animal or in vitro studies, reports in the scientific literature, and unpublished scientific papers, as well as reports from foreign regulatory authorities and reports of foreign commercial marketing experience for drugs that are not marketed in the United States.

(c) (1) *IND safety reports*. The sponsor must notify FDA and all participating investigators (i. e., all investigators to whom the sponsor is providing drug under its INDs or under any investigator's IND) in an IND safety report of potential serious risks, from clinical trials or any other source, as soon as possible, but in no case later than 15 calendar days after the sponsor determines that the information qualifies for reporting under paragraph (c)(1)(i), (c)(1)(ii), (c)(1)(iii), or (c)(1)(iv) of this section. In each IND safety report, the sponsor must identify all IND safety reports previously submitted to FDA concerning a similar suspected adverse reaction, and must analyze the significance of the suspected adverse reaction in light of previous, similar reports or any other relevant information.

(i) *Serious and unexpected suspected adverse reaction*. The sponsor must report any suspected adverse reaction that is both serious and unexpected. The sponsor must report an adverse event as a suspected adverse reaction only if there is evidence to suggest a causal relationship between the drug and the adverse event, such as:

(A) A single occurrence of an event that is uncommon and known to be strongly associated with drug exposure (e. g., angioedema, hepatic injury, Stevens-Johnson Syndrome);

(B) One or more occurrences of an event that is not commonly associated with drug exposure, but is otherwise uncommon in the population exposed to the drug (e. g., tendon rupture);

(C) An aggregate analysis of specific events observed in a clinical trial (such as known consequences of the underlying disease or condition under investigation or other events that commonly occur in the study population independent of drug therapy) that indicates those events occur more frequently in the drug treatment group than in a concurrent or historical control group.

(ii) *Findings from other studies*. The sponsor must report any findings from epidemiological studies, pooled analysis of multiple studies, or clinical studies (other than those reported under paragraph (c)(1)(i) of this section), whether or not conducted under an IND, and whether or not conducted by the sponsor, that suggest a significant risk in humans exposed to the drug. Ordinarily, such a finding would result in a safety-related change in the protocol, informed consent, investigator brochure (excluding routine updates of these documents), or other aspects of the overall conduct of the clinical investigation.

(iii) *Findings from animal or in vitro testing.* The sponsor must report any findings from animal or in vitro testing, whether or not conducted by the sponsor, that suggest a significant risk in humans exposed to the drug, such as reports of mutagenicity, teratogenicity, or carcinogenicity, or reports of significant organ toxicity at or near the expected human exposure. Ordinarily, any such findings would result in a safety-related change in the protocol, informed consent, investigator brochure (excluding routine updates of these documents), or other aspects of the overall conduct of the clinical investigation.

(iv) *Increased rate of occurrence of serious suspected adverse reactions.* The sponsor must report any clinically important increase in the rate of a serious suspected adverse reaction over that listed in the protocol or investigator brochure.

(v) *Submission of IND safety reports.* The sponsor must submit each IND safety report in a narrative format or on FDA Form 3500A or in an electronic format that FDA can process, review, and archive. FDA will periodically issue guidance on how to provide the electronic submission (e. g., method of transmission, media, file formats, preparation and organization of files). The sponsor may submit foreign suspected adverse reactions on a Council for International Organizations of Medical Sciences (CIOMS) I Form instead of a FDA Form 3500A. Reports of overall findings or pooled analyses from published and unpublished in vitro, animal, epidemiological, or clinical studies must be submitted in a narrative format. Each notification to FDA must bear prominent identification of its contents, i. e., "IND Safety Report," and must be transmitted to the review division in the Center for Drug Evaluation and Research or in the Center for Biologics Evaluation and Research that has responsibility for review of the IND. Upon request from FDA, the sponsor must submit to FDA any additional data or information that the agency deems necessary, as soon as possible, but in no case later than 15 calendar days after receiving the request.

(2) *Unexpected fatal or life-threatening suspected adverse reaction reports*. The sponsor must also notify FDA of any unexpected fatal or life-threatening suspected adverse reaction as soon as possible but in no case later than 7 calendar days after the sponsor's initial receipt of the information.

(3) *Reporting format or frequency*. FDA may require a sponsor to submit IND safety reports in a format or at a frequency different than that required under this paragraph. The sponsor may also propose and adopt a different reporting format or frequency if the change is agreed to in advance by the director of the FDA review division that has responsibility for review of the IND.

(4) *Investigations of marketed drugs*. A sponsor of a clinical study of a drug marketed or approved in the United States that is conducted under an IND is required to submit IND safety reports for suspected adverse reactions that are observed in the clinical study, at domestic or foreign study sites. The sponsor must also submit safety information from the clinical study as prescribed by the postmarketing safety reporting requirements (e. g. , 310. 305, 314. 80, and 600. 80 of this chapter) .

(5) *Reporting study endpoints*. Study endpoints (e. g. , mortality or major morbidity) must be reported to FDA by the sponsor as described in the protocol and ordinarily would not be reported under paragraph (c) of this section. However, if a serious and unexpected adverse event occurs for which there is evidence suggesting a causal relationship between the drug and the event (e. g. , death from anaphylaxis) , the event must be reported under 312. 32 (c)(1)(i) as a serious and unexpected suspected adverse reaction even if it is a component of the study endpoint (e. g. , all-cause mortality) .

(d) *Follow up*.

(1) The sponsor must promptly investigate all safety information it receives.

(2) Relevant followup information to an IND safety report must be submitted as soon as the information is available and must be identified as such, i. e. , "Followup IND Safety Report. "

(3) If the results of a sponsor's investigation show that an adverse event not initially determined to be reportable under paragraph (c) of

this section is so reportable, the sponsor must report such suspected adverse reaction in an IND safety report as soon as possible, but in no case later than 15 calendar days after the determination is made.

(e) *Disclaimer*. A safety report or other information submitted by a sponsor under this part (and any release by FDA of that report or information) does not necessarily reflect a conclusion by the sponsor or FDA that the report or information constitutes an admission that the drug caused or contributed to an adverse event. A sponsor need not admit, and may deny, that the report or information submitted by the sponsor constitutes an admission that the drug caused or contributed to an adverse event.

## Sec. 312. 33 Annual reports.

A sponsor shall within 60 days of the anniversary date that the IND went into effect, submit a brief report of the progress of the investigation that includes:

(a) *Individual study information*. A brief summary of the status of each study in progress and each study completed during the previous year. The summary is required to include the following information for each study:

(1) The title of the study (with any appropriate study identifiers such as protocol number), its purpose, a brief statement identifying the patient population, and a statement as to whether the study is completed.

(2) The total number of subjects initially planned for inclusion in the study; the number entered into the study to date, tabulated by age group, gender, and race; the number whose participation in the study was completed as planned; and the number who dropped out of the study for any reason.

(3) If the study has been completed, or if interim results are known, a brief description of any available study results.

(b) *Summary information*. Information obtained during the previous year's clinical and nonclinical investigations, including:

(1) A narrative or tabular summary showing the most frequent and most serious adverse experiences by body system.

(2) A summary of all IND safety reports submitted during the past year.

(3) A list of subjects who died during participation in the investigation, with the cause of death for each subject.

(4) A list of subjects who dropped out during the course of the investi-

gation in association with any adverse experience, whether or not thought to be drug related.

(5) A brief description of what, if anything, was obtained that is pertinent to an understanding of the drug's actions, including, for example, information about dose response, information from controlled trials, and information about bioavailability.

(6) A list of the preclinical studies (including animal studies) completed or in progress during the past year and a summary of the major preclinical findings.

(7) A summary of any significant manufacturing or microbiological changes made during the past year.

(c) A description of the general investigational plan for the coming year to replace that submitted 1 year earlier. The general investigational plan shall contain the information required under 312. 23 (a)(3)(iv) .

(d) If the investigator brochure has been revised, a description of the revision and a copy of the new brochure.

(e) A description of any significant Phase 1 protocol modifications made during the previous year and not previously reported to the IND in a protocol amendment.

(f) A brief summary of significant foreign marketing developments with the drug during the past year, such as approval of marketing in any country or withdrawal or suspension from marketing in any country.

(g) If desired by the sponsor, a log of any outstanding business with respect to the IND for which the sponsor requests or expects a reply, comment, or meeting.

## Sec. 312. 38 Withdrawal of an IND.

(a) At any time a sponsor may withdraw an effective IND without prejudice.

(b) If an IND is withdrawn, FDA shall be so notified, all clinical investigations conducted under the IND shall be ended, all current investigators notified, and all stocks of the drug returned to the sponsor or otherwise disposed of at the request of the sponsor in accordance with 312. 59.

(c) If an IND is withdrawn because of a safety reason, the sponsor shall promptly so inform FDA, all participating investigators, and all reviewing Institutional Review Boards, together with the reasons for such withdrawal.

## Subpart C-Administrative Actions

### Sec. 312. 40 General requirements for use of an investigational new drug in a clinical investigation.

(a) An investigational new drug may be used in a clinical investigation if the following conditions are met:

(1) The sponsor of the investigation submits an IND for the drug to FDA; the IND is in effect under paragraph (b) of this section; and the sponsor complies with all applicable requirements in this part and parts 50 and 56 with respect to the conduct of the clinical investigations; and

(2) Each participating investigator conducts his or her investigation in compliance with the requirements of this part and parts 50 and 56.

(b) An IND goes into effect:

(1) Thirty days after FDA receives the IND, unless FDA notifies the sponsor that the investigations described in the IND are subject to a clinical hold under 312. 42; or

(2) On earlier notification by FDA that the clinical investigations in the IND may begin. FDA will notify the sponsor in writing of the date it receives the IND.

(c) A sponsor may ship an investigational new drug to investigators named in the IND:

(1) Thirty days after FDA receives the IND; or

(2) On earlier FDA authorization to ship the drug.

(d) An investigator may not administer an investigational new drug to human subjects until the IND goes into effect under paragraph (b) of this section.

### Sec. 312. 41 Comment and advice on an IND.

(a) FDA may at any time during the course of the investigation communicate with the sponsor orally or in writing about deficiencies in the IND or about FDA's need for more data or information.

(b) On the sponsor's request, FDA will provide advice on specific matters relating to an IND. Examples of such advice may include advice on the adequacy of technical data to support an investigational plan, on the design of a clinical trial, and on whether proposed investigations are likely to produce the data and information that is needed to meet requirements for a marketing application.

(c) Unless the communication is accompanied by a clinical hold order under 312. 42, FDA communications with a sponsor under this section are solely advisory and do not require any modification in the planned or ongoing clinical investigations or response to the agency.

### Sec. 312. 42 Clinical holds and requests for modification.

(a) *General*. A clinical hold is an order issued by FDA to the sponsor to delay a proposed clinical investigation or to suspend an ongoing investigation. The clinical hold order may apply to one or more of the investigations covered by an IND. When a proposed study is placed on clinical hold, subjects may not be given the investigational drug. When an ongoing study is placed on clinical hold, no new subjects may be recruited to the study and placed on the investigational drug; patients already in the study should be taken off therapy involving the investigational drug unless specifically permitted by FDA in the interest of patient safety.

(b) *Grounds for imposition of clinical hold.*

(1) *Clinical hold of a Phase 1 study under an IND.* FDA may place a proposed or ongoing Phase 1 investigation on clinical hold if it finds that:

(i) Human subjects are or would be exposed to an unreasonable and significant risk of illness or injury;

(ii) The clinical investigators named in the IND are not qualified by reason of their scientific training and experience to conduct the investigation described in the IND;

(iii) The investigator brochure is misleading, erroneous, or materially incomplete; or

(iv) The IND does not contain sufficient information required under 312. 23 to assess the risks to subjects of the proposed studies.

(v) The IND is for the study of an investigational drug intended to treat a life-threatening disease or condition that affects both genders, and men or women with reproductive potential who have the disease or condition being studied are excluded from eligibility because of a risk or potential risk from use of the investigational drug of reproductive toxicity (i. e. , affecting reproductive organs) or developmental toxicity (i. e. , affecting potential offspring) . The phrase "women with reproductive potentia" does not include pregnant women. For purposes of this paragraph, "life-threatening illnesses or diseases" are defined as "diseases or conditions where the likelihood of death is high unless the course of the disease is interrupted. " The clinical hold would not apply under this paragraph to clinical studies conducted:

(A) Under special circumstances, such as studies pertinent only to one gender (e. g. , studies evaluating the excretion of a drug in semen or the effects on menstrual function) ;

(B) Only in men or women, as long as a study that does not exclude members of the other gender with reproductive potential is being conducted concurrently, has been conducted, or will take place within a reasonable time agreed upon by the agency; or

(C) Only in subjects who do not suffer from the disease or condition for which the drug is being studied.

(2) *Clinical hold of a Phase 2 or 3 study under an IND.* FDA may place a proposed or ongoing Phase 2 or 3 investigation on clinical hold if it finds that:

(i) Any of the conditions in paragraphs (b)(1)(i) through(b)(1)(v) of this section apply; or

(ii) The plan or protocol for the investigation is clearly deficient in design to meet its stated objectives.

(3) *Clinical hold of an expanded access IND or expanded access protocol*. FDA may place an expanded access IND or expanded access protocol on clinical hold under the following conditions:

(i) Final use. FDA may place a proposed expanded access IND or treatment use protocol on clinical hold if it is determined that:

(A) The pertinent criteria in subpart I of this part for permitting the expanded access use to begin are not satisfied; or

(B) The expanded access IND or expanded access protocol does not comply with the requirements for expanded access submissions in subpart I of this part.

(ii) Ongoing use. FDA may place an ongoing expanded access IND or expanded access protocol on clinical hold if it is determined that the pertinent criteria in subpart I of this part for permitting the expanded access are no longer satisfied.

(4) *Clinical hold of any study that is not designed to be adequate and well-controlled*. FDA may place a proposed or ongoing investigation that is not designed to be adequate and well-controlled on clinical hold if it finds that:

(i) Any of the conditions in paragraph (b)(1) or (b)(2) of this section apply; or

(ii) There is reasonable evidence the investigation that is not designed to be adequate and well-controlled is impeding enrollment in, or otherwise interfering with the conduct or completion of, a study that is designed to be an adequate and well-controlled investigation of the same or another investigational drug; or

(iii) Insufficient quantities of the investigational drug exist to adequately conduct both the investigation that is not designed to be adequate and well-controlled and the investigations that are designed to be adequate and well-controlled; or

(iv) The drug has been studied in one or more adequate and well-controlled investigations that strongly suggest lack of effectiveness; or

(v) Another drug under investigation or approved for the same indication and available to the same patient population has demonstrated a better potential benefit/risk balance; or

(vi) The drug has received marketing approval for the same indication in the same patient population; or

(vii) The sponsor of the study that is designed to be an adequate and well-controlled investigation is not actively pursuing marketing approval of the investigational drug with due diligence; or

(viii) The Commissioner determines that it would not be in the public interest for the study to be conducted or continued. FDA ordinarily intends that clinical holds under paragraphs(b)(4)(ii), (b)(4)(iii) and (b)(4)(v) of this section would only apply to additional enrollment in nonconcurrently controlled trials rather than eliminating continued access to individuals already receiving the investigational drug.

(5) *Clinical hold of any investigation involving an exception from informed consent under 50. 24 of this chapter.* FDA may place a proposed or ongoing investigation involving an exception from informed consent under 50. 24 of this chapter on clinical hold if it is determined that:

(i) Any of the conditions in paragraphs (b)(1) or (b)(2) of this section apply; or

(ii) The pertinent criteria in 50. 24 of this chapter for such an investigation to begin or continue are not submitted or not satisfied.

(6) Clinical hold of any investigation involving an exception from informed consent under 50. 23 (d) of this chapter. FDA may place a proposed or ongoing investigation involving an exception from informed consent under 50. 23 (d) of this chapter on clinical hold if it is determined that:

(i) Any of the conditions in paragraphs (b)(1) or (b)(2) of this section apply; or

(ii) A determination by the President to waive the prior consent requirement for the administration of an investigational new drug has not been made.

(c) *Discussion of deficiency.* Whenever FDA concludes that a deficiency exists in a clinical investigation that may be grounds for the imposition of clinical hold FDA will, unless patients are exposed to immediate and serious risk, attempt to discuss and satisfactorily resolve the matter with the sponsor before issuing the clinical hold order.

(d) *Imposition of clinical hold.* The clinical hold order may be made by telephone or other means of rapid communication or in writing. The clinical hold order will identify the studies under the IND to which the hold applies, and will briefly explain the basis for the action. The clinical hold order will be made by or on behalf of the Division Director with responsibility for review of the IND. As soon as possible, and no more than 30 days after imposition of the clinical hold, the Division Director will provide the sponsor a written explanation of the basis for the hold.

(e) *Resumption of clinical investigations*. An investigation may only resume after FDA (usually the Division Director, or the Director's designee, with responsibility for review of the IND) has notified the sponsor that the investigation may proceed. Resumption of the affected investigation(s) will be authorized when the sponsor corrects the deficiency(ies) previously cited or otherwise satisfies the agency that the investigation(s) can proceed. FDA may notify a sponsor of its determination regarding the clinical hold by telephone or other means of rapid communication. If a sponsor of an IND that has been placed on clinical hold requests in writing that the clinical hold be removed and submits a complete response to the issue(s) identified in the clinical hold order, FDA shall respond in writing to the sponsor within 30-calendar days of receipt of the request and the complete response. FDA's response will either remove or maintain the clinical hold, and will state the reasons for such determination. Notwithstanding the 30-calendar day response time, a sponsor may not proceed with a clinical trial on which a clinical hold has been imposed until the sponsor has been notified by FDA that the hold has been lifted.

(f) *Appeal*. If the sponsor disagrees with the reasons cited for the clinical hold, the sponsor may request reconsideration of the decision in accordance with 312. 48.

(g) *Conversion of IND on clinical hold to inactive status*. If all investigations covered by an IND remain on clinical hold for 1 year or more, the IND may be placed on inactive status by FDA under 312. 45.

## Sec. 312. 44 Termination.

(a) *General*. This section describes the procedures under which FDA may terminate an IND. If an IND is terminated, the sponsor shall end all clinical investigations conducted under the IND and recall or otherwise provide for the disposition of all unused supplies of the drug. A termination action may be based on deficiencies in the IND or in the conduct of an investigation under an IND. Except as provided in paragraph (d) of this section, a termination shall be preceded by a proposal to terminate by FDA and an opportunity for the sponsor to respond. FDA will, in general, only initiate an action under this section after first attempting to resolve differences informally or, when appropriate, through the clinical hold procedures described in 312. 42.

(b) *Grounds for termination*.

(1) *Phase* 1. FDA may propose to terminate an IND during Phase 1 if it finds that:

(i) Human subjects would be exposed to an unreasonable and significant risk of illness or unjury.

(ii) The IND does not contain sufficient information required under 312. 23 to assess the safety to subjects of the clinical investigations.

(iii) The methods, facilities, and controls used for the manufacturing, processing, and packing of the investigational drug are inadequate to establish and maintain appropriate standards of identity, strength, quality, and purity as needed for subject safety.

(iv) The clinical investigations are being conducted in a manner substantially different than that described in the protocols submitted in the IND.

(v) The drug is being promoted or distributed for commercial purposes not justified by the requirements of the investigation or permitted by 312. 7.

(vi) The IND, or any amendment or report to the IND, contains an untrue statement of a material fact or omits material information required by this part.

(vii) The sponsor fails promptly to investigate and inform the Food and Drug Administration and all investigators of serious and unexpected adverse experiences in accordance with 312. 32 or fails to make any other report required under this part.

(viii) The sponsor fails to submit an accurate annual report of the investigations in accordance with 312. 33.

(ix) The sponsor fails to comply with any other applicable requirement of this part, part 50, or part 56.

(x) The IND has remained on inactive status for 5 years or more.

(xi) The sponsor fails to delay a proposed investigation under the IND or to suspend an ongoing investigation that has been placed on clinical hold under 312. 42(b)(4).

(2) *Phase 2 or 3*. FDA may propose to terminate an IND during Phase 2 or Phase 3 if FDA finds that:

(i) Any of the conditions in paragraphs (b)(1)(i) through (b)(1)(xi) of this section apply; or

(ii) The investigational plan or protocol(s) is not reasonable as a bona fide scientific plan to determine whether or not the drug is safe and effective for use; or

(iii) There is convincing evidence that the drug is not effective for the purpose for which it is being investigated.

(3) FDA may propose to terminate a treatment IND if it finds that:

(i) Any of the conditions in paragraphs (b)(1)(i) through (x) of this section apply; or

(ii) Any of the conditions in 312. 42(b)(3) apply.

(c) *Opportunity for sponsor response*. (1) If FDA proposes to terminate an IND, FDA will notify the sponsor in writing, and invite correction or explanation within a period of 30 days.

(2) On such notification, the sponsor may provide a written explanation or correction or may request a conference with FDA to provide the requested explanation or correction. If the sponsor does not respond to the notification within the allocated time, the IND shall be terminated.

(3) If the sponsor responds but FDA does not accept the explanation or correction submitted, FDA shall inform the sponsor in writing of the reason for the nonacceptance and provide the sponsor with an opportunity for a regulatory hearing before FDA under part 16 on the question of whether the IND should be terminated. The sponsor's request for a regulatory hearing must be made within 10 days of the sponsor's receipt of FDA's notification of nonacceptance.

(d) *Immediate termination of IND*. Notwithstanding paragraphs (a) through (c) of this section, if at any time FDA concludes that continuation of the investigation presents an immediate and substantial danger to the health of individuals, the agency shall immediately, by written notice to the sponsor from the Director of the Center for Drug Evaluation and Research or the Director of the Center for Biologics Evaluation and Research, terminate the IND. An IND so terminated is subject to reinstatement by the Director on the basis of additional submissions that eliminate such danger. If an IND is terminated under this paragraph, the agency will afford the sponsor an opportunity for a regulatory hearing under part 16 on the question of whether the IND should be reinstated.

### Sec. 312. 45 Inactive status.

(a) If no subjects are entered into clinical studies for a period of 2 years or more under an IND, or if all investigations under an IND remain on clinical hold for 1 year or more, the IND may be placed by FDA on inactive status. This action may be taken by FDA either on request of the sponsor or on FDA's own initiative. If FDA seeks to act on its own initiative under this section, it shall first notify the sponsor in writing of the proposed inactive status. Upon receipt of such notification, the sponsor shall have 30 days to respond as to why the IND should continue to remain active.

(b) If an IND is placed on inactive status, all investigators shall be so notified and all stocks of the drug shall be returned or otherwise disposed of in accordance with 312. 59.

(c) A sponsor is not required to submit annual reports to an IND on inactive status. An inactive IND is, however, still in effect for purposes of the public disclosure of data and information under 312. 130.

(d) A sponsor who intends to resume clinical investigation under an IND placed on inactive status shall submit a protocol amendment under 312. 30 containing the proposed general investigational plan for the coming year and appropriate protocols. If the protocol amendment relies on information previously submitted, the plan shall reference such information. Additional information supporting the proposed investigation, if any, shall be submitted in an information amendment. Notwithstanding the provisions of 312. 30, clinical investigations under an IND on inactive status may only resume (1) 30 days after FDA receives the protocol amendment, unless FDA notifies the sponsor that the investigations described in the amendment are subject to a clinical hold under 312. 42, or (2) on earlier notification by FDA that the clinical investigations described in the protocol amendment may begin.

(e) An IND that remains on inactive status for 5 years or more may be terminated under 312. 44.

## Sec. 312. 47 Meetings.

(a) *General*. Meetings between a sponsor and the agency are frequently useful in resolving questions and issues raised during the course of a clinical investigation. FDA encourages such meetings to the extent that they aid in the evaluation of the drug and in the solution of scientific problems concerning the drug, to the extent that FDA's resources permit. The general principle underlying the conduct of such meetings is that there should be free, full, and open communication about any scientific or medical question that may arise during the clinical investigation. These meetings shall be conducted and documented in accordance with part 10.

(b) "*End-of-Phase 2*" meetings and meetings held before submission of a marketing application. At specific times during the drug investigation process, meetings between FDA and a sponsor can be especially helpful in minimizing wasteful expenditures of time and money and thus in speeding the drug development and evaluation process. In particular, FDA has found that meetings at the end of Phase 2 of an investigation (end-of-Phase 2 meetings) are of considerable assistance in planning later studies and that meetings held near completion of Phase 3 and before submission of a marketing application ("pre-NDA" meetings) are helpful in developing methods of presentation and submission of data in the marketing application that facilitate review and allow timely FDA response.

(1) *End-of-Phase 2 meetings*.

(i) *Purpose*. The purpose of an end-of-phase 2 meeting is to determine the safety of proceeding to Phase 3, to evaluate the Phase 3 plan and protocols and the adequacy of current studies and plans to assess pediatric safety and effectiveness, and to identify any additional information necessary to support a marketing application for the uses under investigation.

(ii) *Eligibility for meeting*. While the end-of-Phase 2 meeting is designed primarily for IND's involving new molecular entities or major new uses of marketed drugs, a sponsor of any IND may request and obtain an end-of-Phase 2 meeting.

(iii) *Timing*. To be most useful to the sponsor, end-of-Phase 2 meetings should be held before major commitments of effort and resources to specific Phase 3 tests are made. The scheduling of an end-of-Phase 2 meeting is not, however, intended to delay the transition of an investigation from Phase 2 to Phase 3.

(iv) *Advance information*. At least 1 month in advance of an end-of-Phase 2 meeting, the sponsor should submit background information on the sponsor's plan for Phase 3, including summaries of the Phase 1 and 2 investigations, the specific protocols for Phase 3 clinical studies, plans for any additional nonclinical studies, plans for pediatric studies, including a time line for protocol finalization, enrollment, completion, and data analysis, or information to support any planned request for waiver or deferral of pediatric studies, and, if available, tentative labeling for the drug. The recommended contents of such a submission are described more fully in FDA Staff Manual Guide 4850. 7 that is publicly available under FDA's public information regulations in part 20.

(v) *Conduct of meeting*. Arrangements for an end-of-Phase 2 meeting are to be made with the division in FDA's Center for Drug Evaluation and Research or the Center for Biologics Evaluation and Research which is responsible for review of the IND. The meeting will be scheduled by FDA at a time convenient to both FDA and the sponsor. Both the sponsor and FDA may bring consultants to the meeting. The meeting should be directed primarily at establishing agreement between FDA and the sponsor of the overall plan for Phase 3 and the objectives and design of particular studies. The adequacy of the technical information to support Phase 3 studies and/or a marketing application may also be discussed. FDA will also provide its best judgment, at that time, of the pediatric studies that will be required for the drug product and whether their submission will be deferred until after approval. Agreements reached at the meeting on these matters will be recorded in minutes of the conference that will be taken by FDA in accordance with 10. 65 and provided to the sponsor. The minutes along with any other written material provided to the sponsor will serve as a permanent record of any agreements reached. Barring a significant scientific development that requires otherwise, studies conducted in accordance with the agreement shall be presumed to be sufficient in objective and design for the purpose of obtaining marketing approval for the drug.

(2) *"Pre-NDA" and "pre-BLA" meetings*. FDA has found that delays associated with the initial review of a marketing application may be reduced by exchanges of information about a proposed marketing application. The primary purpose of this kind of exchange is to uncover any major unresolved problems, to identify those studies that the sponsor is relying on as adequate and well-controlled to establish the drug's effectiveness, to identify the status of ongoing or needed studies adequate to assess pediatric safety and effectiveness, to acquaint FDA reviewers with the general information to be submitted in the marketing application (including technical information), to discuss appropriate methods for statistical analysis of the data, and to discuss the best approach to the presentation and formatting of data in the marketing application. Arrangements for such a meeting are to be initiated by the sponsor with the division responsible for review of the IND. To permit FDA to provide the sponsor with the most useful advice on preparing a marketing application, the sponsor should submit to FDA's reviewing division at least 1 month in advance of the meeting the following information:

(i) A brief summary of the clinical studies to be submitted in the application.

(ii) A proposed format for organizing the submission, including methods for presenting the data.

(iii) Information on the status of needed or ongoing pediatric studies.

(iv) Any other information for discussion at the meeting.

### Sec. 312. 48 Dispute resolution.

(a) *General*. The Food and Drug Administration is committed to resolving differences between sponsors and FDA reviewing divisions with respect to requirements for IND's as quickly and amicably as possible through the cooperative exchange of information and views.

(b) *Administrative and procedural issues*. When administrative or procedural disputes arise, the sponsor should first attempt to resolve the matter with the division in FDA's Center for Drug Evaluation and Research or Center for Biologics Evaluation and Research which is responsible for review of the IND, beginning with the consumer safety officer assigned to the application. If the dispute is not resolved, the sponsor may raise the matter with the person designated as ombudsman, whose function shall be to investigate what has happened and to facilitate a timely and equitable resolution. Appropriate issues to raise with the ombudsman include resolving difficulties in scheduling meetings and obtaining timely replies to inquiries. Further details on this procedure are contained in FDA Staff Manual Guide 4820. 7 that is publicly available under FDA's public information regulations in part 20.

(c) *Scientific and medical disputes*.

(1) When scientific or medical disputes arise during the drug investigation process, sponsors should discuss the matter directly with the responsible reviewing officials. If necessary, sponsors may request a meeting with the appropriate reviewing officials and management representatives in order to seek a resolution. Requests for such meetings shall be directed to the director of the division in FDA's Center for Drug Evaluation and Research or Center for Biologics Evaluation and Research which is responsible for review of the IND. FDA will make every attempt to grant requests for meetings that involve important issues and that can be scheduled at mutually convenient times.

(2) The "end-of-Phase 2" and "pre-NDA" meetings described in 312. 47 (b) will also provide a timely forum for discussing and resolving scientific and medical issues on which the sponsor disagrees with the agency.

(3) In requesting a meeting designed to resolve a scientific or medical dispute, applicants may suggest that FDA seek the advice of outside experts, in which case FDA may, in its discretion, invite to the meeting one or more of its advisory committee members or other consultants, as designated by the agency. Applicants may rely on, and may bring to any meeting, their own consultants. For major scientific and medical policy issues not resolved by informal meetings, FDA may refer the matter to one of its standing advisory committees for its consideration and recommendations.

## Subpart D-Responsibilities of Sponsors and Investigators

### Sec. 312. 50 General responsibilities of sponsors.

Sponsors are responsible for selecting qualified investigators, providing them with the information they need to conduct an investigation properly, ensuring proper monitoring of the investigation (s) , ensuring that the investigation (s) is conducted in accordance with the general investigational plan and protocols contained in the IND, maintaining an effective IND with respect to the investigations, and ensuring that FDA and all participating investigators are promptly informed of significant new adverse effects or risks with respect to the drug. Additional specific responsibilities of sponsors are described elsewhere in this part.

### Sec. 312. 52 Transfer of obligations to a contract research organization.

(a) A sponsor may transfer responsibility for any or all of the obligations set forth in this part to a contract research organization. Any such transfer shall be described in writing. If not all obligations are transferred, the writing is required to describe each of the obligations being assumed by the contract research organization. If all obligations are transferred, a general statement that all obligations have been transferred is acceptable. Any obligation not covered by the written description shall be deemed not to have been transferred.

(b) A contract research organization that assumes any obligation of a sponsor shall comply with the specific regulations in this chapter applicable to this obligation and shall be subject to the same regulatory action as a sponsor for failure to comply with any obligation assumed under these regulations. Thus, all references to "sponsor" in this part apply to a contract research organization to the extent that it assumes one or more obligations of the sponsor.

## Sec. 312. 53 Selecting investigators and monitors.

(a) *Selecting investigators.* A sponsor shall select only investigators qualified by training and experience as appropriate experts to investigate the drug.

(b) *Control of drug.* A sponsor shall ship investigational new drugs only to investigators participating in the investigation.

(c) *Obtaining information from the investigator.* Before permitting an investigator to begin participation in an investigation, the sponsor shall obtain the following:

(1) A signed investigator statement (Form FDA-1572) containing:

(i) The name and address of the investigator;

(ii) The name and code number, if any, of the protocol(s) in the IND identifying the study(ies) to be conducted by the investigator;

(iii) The name and address of any medical school, hospital, or other research facility where the clinical investigation(s) will be conducted;

(iv) The name and address of any clinical laboratory facilities to be used in the study;

(v) The name and address of the IRB that is responsible for review and approval of the study(ies);

(vi) A commitment by the investigator that he or she:

(A) Will conduct the study (ies) in accordance with the relevant, current protocol (s) and will only make changes in a protocol after notifying the sponsor, except when necessary to protect the safety, the rights, or welfare of subjects;

(B) Will comply with all requirements regarding the obligations of clinical investigators and all other pertinent requirements in this part;

(C) Will personally conduct or supervise the described investigation(s);

(D) Will inform any potential subjects that the drugs are being used for investigational purposes and will ensure that the requirements relating to obtaining informed consent (21 CFR part 50) and institutional review board review and approval (21 CFR part 56) are met;

(E) Will report to the sponsor adverse experiences that occur in the course of the investigation(s) in accordance with 312. 64;

(F) Has read and understands the information in the investigator's brochure, including the potential risks and side effects of the drug; and

(G) Will ensure that all associates, colleagues, and employees assisting in the conduct of the study(ies) are informed about their obligations in meeting the above commitments.

(vii) A commitment by the investigator that, for an investigation subject to an institutional review requirement under part 56, an IRB that complies with the requirements of that part will be responsible for the initial and continuing review and approval of the clinical investigation and that the investigator will promptly report to the IRB all changes in the research activity and all unanticipated problems involving risks to human subjects or others, and will not make any changes in the research without IRB approval, except where necessary to eliminate apparent immediate hazards to the human subjects.

(viii) A list of the names of the subinvestigators (e. g., research fellows, residents) who will be assisting the investigator in the conduct of the investigation(s).

(2) *Curriculum vitae*. A curriculum vitae or other statement of qualifications of the investigator showing the education, training, and experience that qualifies the investigator as an expert in the clinical investigation of the drug for the use under investigation.

(3) *Clinical protocol.*

(i) For Phase 1 investigations, a general outline of the planned investigation including the estimated duration of the study and the maximum number of subjects that will be involved.

(ii) For Phase 2 or 3 investigations, an outline of the study protocol including an approximation of the number of subjects to be treated with the drug and the number to be employed as controls, if any; the clinical uses to be investigated; characteristics of subjects by age, sex, and condition; the kind of clinical observations and laboratory tests to be conducted; the estimated duration of the study; and copies or a description of case report forms to be used.

(4) *Financial disclosure information.* Sufficient accurate financial information to allow the sponsor to submit complete and accurate certification or disclosure statements required under part 54 of this chapter. The sponsor shall obtain a commitment from the clinical investigator to promptly update this information if any relevant changes occur during the course of the investigation and for 1 year following the completion of the study.

(d) *Selecting monitors.* A sponsor shall select a monitor qualified by training and experience to monitor the progress of the investigation.

## Sec. 312. 54 Emergency research under 50. 24 of this chapter.

(a) The sponsor shall monitor the progress of all investigations involving an exception from informed consent under 50. 24 of this chapter. When the sponsor receives from the IRB information concerning the public disclosures required by 50. 24 (a)(7)(ii) and (a)(7)(iii) of this chapter, the sponsor promptly shall submit to the IND file and to Docket Number 95S-0158 in the Division of Dockets Management (HFA-305) , Food and Drug Administration, 5630 Fishers Lane, rm. 1061, Rockville, MD 20852, copies of the information that was disclosed, identified by the IND number.

(b) The sponsor also shall monitor such investigations to identify when an IRB determines that it cannot approve the research because it does not meet the criteria in the exception in 50. 24 (a) of this chapter or because of other relevant ethical concerns. The sponsor promptly shall provide this information in writing to FDA, investigators who are asked to participate in this or a substantially equivalent clinical investigation, and other IRB's that are asked to review this or a substantially equivalent investigation.

## Sec. 312. 55 Informing investigators.

(a) Before the investigation begins, a sponsor (other than a sponsor-investigator) shall give each participating clinical investigator an investigator brochure containing the information described in 312. 23 (a)(5).

(b) The sponsor shall, as the overall investigation proceeds, keep each participating investigator informed of new observations discovered by or reported to the sponsor on the drug, particularly with respect to adverse effects and safe use. Such information may be distributed to investigators by means of periodically revised investigator brochures, reprints or published studies, reports or letters to clinical investigators, or other appropriate means. Important safety information is required to be relayed to investigators in accordance with 312. 32.

## Sec. 312. 56 Review of ongoing investigations.

(a) The sponsor shall monitor the progress of all clinical investigations being conducted under its IND.

(b) A sponsor who discovers that an investigator is not complying with the signed agreement (Form FDA-1572) , the general investigational plan, or the requirements of this part or other applicable parts shall promptly either secure compliance or discontinue shipments of the investigational new drug to the investigator and end the investigator's participation in the investigation. If the investigator's participation in the investigation is ended, the sponsor shall require that the investigator dispose of or return the investigational drug in accordance with the requirements of 312. 59 and shall notify FDA.

(c) The sponsor shall review and evaluate the evidence relating to the safety and effectiveness of the drug as it is obtained from the investigator. The sponsors shall make such reports to FDA regarding information relevant to the safety of the drug as are required under 312. 32. The sponsor shall make annual reports on the progress of the investigation in accordance with 312. 33.

(d) A sponsor who determines that its investigational drug presents an unreasonable and significant risk to subjects shall discontinue those investigations that present the risk, notify FDA, all institutional review boards, and all investigators who have at any time participated in the investigation of the discontinuance, assure the disposition of all stocks of the drug outstanding as required by 312. 59, and furnish FDA with a full report of the sponsor's actions. The sponsor shall discontinue the investigation as soon as possible, and in no event later than 5 working days after making the determination that the investigation should be discontinued. Upon request, FDA will confer with a sponsor on the need to discontinue an investigation.

## Sec. 312. 57 Recordkeeping and record retention.

(a) A sponsor shall maintain adequate records showing the receipt, shipment, or other disposition of the investigational drug. These records are required to include, as appropriate, the name of the investigator to whom the drug is shipped, and the date, quantity, and batch or code mark of each such shipment.

(b) A sponsor shall maintain complete and accurate records showing any financial interest in 54. 4 (a)(3)(i) , (a)(3)(ii) , (a)(3)(iii) , and (a)(3)(iv) of this chapter paid to clinical investigators by the sponsor of the covered study. A sponsor shall also maintain complete and accurate records concerning all other financial interests of investigators subject to part 54 of this chapter.

(c) A sponsor shall retain the records and reports required by this part for 2 years after a marketing application is approved for the drug; or, if an application is not approved for the drug, until 2 years after shipment and delivery of the drug for investigational use is discontinued and FDA has been so notified.

(d) A sponsor shall retain reserve samples of any test article and reference standard identified in, and used in any of the bioequivalence or bioavailability studies described in, 320. 38 or 320. 63 of this chapter, and release the reserve samples to FDA upon request, in accordance with, and for the period specified in 320. 38.

## Sec. 312. 58 Inspection of sponsor's records and reports.

(a) *FDA inspection*. A sponsor shall upon request from any properly authorized officer or employee of the Food and Drug Administration, at reasonable times, permit such officer or employee to have access to and copy and verify any records and reports relating to a clinical investigation conducted under this part. Upon written request by FDA, the sponsor shall submit the records or reports (or copies of them) to FDA. The sponsor shall discontinue shipments of the drug to any investigator who has failed to maintain or make available records or reports of the investigation as required by this part.

(b) *Controlled substances*. If an investigational new drug is a substance listed in any schedule of the Controlled Substances Act (21 U. S. C. 801; 21 CFR part 1308), records concerning shipment, delivery, receipt, and disposition of the drug, which are required to be kept under this part or other applicable parts of this chapter shall, upon the request of a properly authorized employee of the Drug Enforcement Administration of the U. S. Department of Justice, be made available by the investigator or sponsor to whom the request is made, for inspection and copying. In addition, the sponsor shall assure that adequate precautions are taken, including storage of the investigational drug in a securely locked, substantially constructed cabinet, or other securely locked, substantially constructed enclosure, access to which is limited, to prevent theft or diversion of the substance into illegal channels of distribution.

## Sec. 312. 59 Disposition of unused supply of investigational drug.

The sponsor shall assure the return of all unused supplies of the investigational drug from each individual investigator whose participation in the investigation is discontinued or terminated. The sponsor may authorize alternative disposition of unused supplies of the investigational drug provided this alternative disposition does not expose humans to risks from the drug. The sponsor shall maintain written records of any disposition of the drug in accordance with 312. 57.

## Sec. 312. 60 General responsibilities of investigators.

An investigator is responsible for ensuring that an investigation is conducted according to the signed investigator statement, the investigational plan, and applicable regulations; for protecting the rights, safety, and welfare of subjects under the investigator's care; and for the control of drugs under investigation. An investigator shall, in accordance with the provisions of part 50 of this chapter, obtain the informed consent of each human subject to whom the drug is administered, except as provided in 50. 23 or 50. 24 of this chapter. Additional specific responsibilities of clinical investigators are set forth in this part and in parts 50 and 56 of this chapter.

## Sec. 312. 61 Control of the investigational drug.

An investigator shall administer the drug only to subjects under the investigator's personal supervision or under the supervision of a subinvestigator responsible to the investigator. The investigator shall not supply the investigational drug to any person not authorized under this part to receive it.

## Sec. 312. 62 Investigator recordkeeping and record retention.

(a) *Disposition of drug*. An investigator is required to maintain adequate records of the disposition of the drug, including dates, quantity, and use by subjects. If the investigation is terminated, suspended, discontinued, or completed, the investigator shall return the unused supplies of the drug to the sponsor, or otherwise provide for disposition of the unused supplies of the drug under 312. 59.

(b) *Case histories*. An investigator is required to prepare and maintain adequate and accurate case histories that record all observations and other data pertinent to the investigation on each individual administered the investigational drug or employed as a control in the investigation. Case histories include the case report forms and supporting data including, for example, signed and dated consent forms and medical records including, for example, progress notes of the physician, the individual's hospital chart (s) , and the nurses' notes. The case history for each individual shall document that informed consent was obtained prior to participation in the study.

(c) *Record retention*. An investigator shall retain records required to be maintained under this part for a period of 2 years following the date a marketing application is approved for the drug for the indication for which it is being investigated; or, if no application is to be filed or if the application is not approved for such indication, until 2 years after the investigation is discontinued and FDA is notified.

## Sec. 312. 64 Investigator reports.

(a) *Progress reports*. The investigator shall furnish all reports to the sponsor of the drug who is responsible for collecting and evaluating the results obtained. The sponsor is required under 312. 33 to submit annual reports to FDA on the progress of the clinical investigations.

(b) *Safety reports*. An investigator must immediately report to the sponsor any serious adverse event, whether or not considered drug related, including those listed in the protocol or investigator brochure and must include an assessment of whether there is a reasonable possibility that the drug caused the event. Study endpoints that are serious adverse events (e. g. , all-cause mortality) must be reported in accordance with the protocol unless there is evidence suggesting a causal relationship between the drug and the event (e. g. , death from anaphylaxis) . In that case, the investigator must immediately report the event to the sponsor. The investigator must record nonserious adverse events and report them to the sponsor according to the timetable for reporting specified in the protocol.

(c) *Final report*. An investigator shall provide the sponsor with an adequate report shortly after completion of the investigator's participation in the investigation.

(d) *Financial disclosure reports*. The clinical investigator shall provide the sponsor with sufficient accurate financial information to allow an applicant to submit complete and accurate certification or disclosure statements as required under part 54 of this chapter. The clinical investigator shall promptly update this information if any relevant changes occur during the course of the investigation and for 1 year following the completion of the study.

## Sec. 312. 66 Assurance of IRB review.

An investigator shall assure that an IRB that complies with the requirements set forth in part 56 will be responsible for the initial and continuing review and approval of the proposed clinical study. The investigator shall also assure that he or she will promptly report to the IRB all changes in the research activity and all unanticipated problems involving risk to human subjects or others, and that he or she will not make any changes in the research without IRB approval, except where necessary to eliminate apparent immediate hazards to human subjects.

## Sec. 312. 68 Inspection of investigator's records and reports.

An investigator shall upon request from any properly authorized officer or employee of FDA, at reasonable times, permit such officer or employee to have access to, and copy and verify any records or reports made by the investigator pursuant to 312. 62. The investigator is not required to divulge subject names unless the records of particular individuals require a more detailed study of the cases, or unless there is reason to believe that the records do not represent actual case studies, or do not represent actual results obtained.

## Sec. 312. 69 Handling of controlled substances.

If the investigational drug is subject to the Controlled Substances Act, the investigator shall take adequate precautions, including storage of the investigational drug in a securely locked, substantially constructed cabinet, or other securely locked, substantially constructed enclosure, access to which is limited, to prevent theft or diversion of the substance into illegal channels of distribution.

## Sec. 312. 70 Disqualification of a clinical investigator.

(a) If FDA has information indicating that an investigator (including a sponsor-investigator) has repeatedly or deliberately failed to comply with the requirements of this part, part 50 or part 56 of this chapter, or has repeatedly or deliberately submitted to FDA or to the sponsor false information in any required report, the Center for Drug Evaluation and Research or the Center for Biologics Evaluation and Research will furnish the investigator written notice of the matter complained of and offer the investigator an opportunity to explain the matter in writing, or, at the option of the investigator, in an informal conference. If an explanation is offered and accepted by the applicable Center, the Center will discontinue the disqualification proceeding. If an explanation is offered but not accepted by the applicable Center, the investigator will be given an opportunity for a regulatory hearing under part 16 of this chapter on the question of whether the investigator is eligible to receive test articles under this part and eligible to conduct any clinical investigation that supports an application for a research or marketing permit for products regulated by FDA.

(b) After evaluating all available information, including any explanation presented by the investigator, if the Commissioner determines that the investigator has repeatedly or deliberately failed to comply with the requirements of this part, part 50 or part 56 of this chapter, or has repeatedly or deliberately submitted to FDA or to the sponsor false information in any required report, the Commissioner will notify the investigator, the sponsor of any investigation in which the investigator has been named as a participant, and the reviewing institutional review boards (IRBs) that the investigator is not eligible to receive test articles under this part. The notification to the investigator, sponsor, and IRBs will provide a statement of the basis for such determination. The notification also will explain that an investigator determined to be ineligible to receive test articles under this part will be ineligible to conduct any clinical investigation that supports an application for a research or marketing permit for products regulated by FDA, including drugs, biologics, devices, new animal drugs, foods, including dietary supplements, that bear a nutrient content claim or a health claim, infant formulas, food and color additives, and tobacco products.

(c) Each application or submission to FDA under the provisions of this chapter containing data reported by an investigator who has been determined to be ineligible to receive FDA-regulated test articles is subject to examination to determine whether the investigator has submitted unreliable data that are essential to the continuation of an investigation or essential to the approval of a marketing application, or essential to the continued marketing of an FDA-regulated product.

(d) If the Commissioner determines, after the unreliable data submitted by the investigator are eliminated from consideration, that the data remaining are inadequate to support a conclusion that it is reasonably safe to continue the investigation, the Commissioner will notify the sponsor, who shall have an opportunity for a regulatory hearing under part 16 of this chapter. If a danger to the public health exists, however, the Commissioner shall terminate the IND immediately and notify the sponsor and the reviewing IRBs of the termination. In such case, the sponsor shall have an opportunity for a regulatory hearing before FDA under part 16 on the question of whether the IND should be reinstated. The determination that an investigation may not be considered in support of a research or marketing application or a notification or petition submission does not, however, relieve the sponsor of any obligation under any other applicable regulation to submit to FDA the results of the investigation.

(e) If the Commissioner determines, after the unreliable data submitted by the investigator are eliminated from consideration, that the continued approval of the product for which the data were submitted cannot be justified, the Commissioner will proceed to withdraw approval of the product in accordance with the applicable provisions of the relevant statutes.

(f) An investigator who has been determined to be ineligible under paragraph (b) of this section may be reinstated as eligible when the Commissioner determines that the investigator has presented adequate assurances that the investigator will employ all test articles, and will conduct any clinical investigation that supports an application for a research or marketing permit for products regulated by FDA, solely in compliance with the applicable provisions of this chapter.

## Subpart E-Drugs Intended to Treat Life-threatening and Severely-debilitating Illnesses

### Sec. 312. 80 Purpose.

The purpose of this section is to establish procedures designed to expedite the development, evaluation, and marketing of new therapies intended to treat persons with life-threatening and severely-debilitating illnesses, especially where no satisfactory alternative therapy exists. As stated 314. 105 (c) of this chapter, while the statutory standards of safety and effectiveness apply to all drugs, the many kinds of drugs that are subject to them, and the wide range of uses for those drugs, demand flexibility in applying the standards. The Food and Drug Administration (FDA) has determined that it is appropriate to exercise the broadest flexibility in applying the statutory standards, while preserving appropriate guarantees for safety and effectiveness. These procedures reflect the recognition that physicians and patients are generally willing to accept greater risks or side effects from products that treat life-threatening and severely-debilitating illnesses, than they would accept from products that treat less serious illnesses. These procedures also reflect the recognition that the benefits of the drug need to be evaluated in light of the severity of the disease being treated. The procedure outlined in this section should be interpreted consistent with that purpose.

### Sec. 312. 81 Scope.

This section applies to new drug and biological products that are being studied for their safety and effectiveness in treating life-threatening or severely-debilitating diseases.

(a) For purposes of this section, the term "life-threatening" means:

(1) Diseases or conditions where the likelihood of death is high unless the course of the disease is interrupted; and

(2) Diseases or conditions with potentially fatal outcomes, where the end point of clinical trial analysis is survival.

(b) For purposes of this section, the term "severely debilitating" means diseases or conditions that cause major irreversible morbidity.

(c) Sponsors are encouraged to consult with FDA on the applicability of these procedures to specific products.

## Sec. 312. 82 Early consultation.

For products intended to treat life-threatening or severely-debilitating illnesses, sponsors may request to meet with FDA-reviewing officials early in the drug development process to review and reach agreement on the design of necessary preclinical and clinical studies. Where appropriate, FDA will invite to such meetings one or more outside expert scientific consultants or advisory committee members. To the extent FDA resources permit, agency reviewing officials will honor requests for such meetings

(a) *Pre-investigational new drug (IND) meetings.* Prior to the submission of the initial IND, the sponsor may request a meeting with FDA-reviewing officials. The primary purpose of this meeting is to review and reach agreement on the design of animal studies needed to initiate human testing. The meeting may also provide an opportunity for discussing the scope and design of phase 1 testing, plans for studying the drug product in pediatric populations, and the best approach for presentation and formatting of data in the IND.

(b) *End-of-phase 1 meetings.* When data from phase 1 clinical testing are available, the sponsor may again request a meeting with FDA-reviewing officials. The primary purpose of this meeting is to review and reach agreement on the design of phase 2 controlled clinical trials, with the goal that such testing will be adequate to provide sufficient data on the drug's safety and effectiveness to support a decision on its approvability for marketing, and to discuss the need for, as well as the design and timing of, studies of the drug in pediatric patients. For drugs for life-threatening diseases, FDA will provide its best judgment, at that time, whether pediatric studies will be required and whether their submission will be deferred until after approval. The procedures outlined in 312. 47 (b) (1) with respect to end-of-phase 2 conferences, including documentation of agreements reached, would also be used for end-of-phase 1 meetings.

### Sec. 312. 83 Treatment protocols.

If the preliminary analysis of phase 2 test results appears promising, FDA may ask the sponsor to submit a treatment protocol to be reviewed under the procedures and criteria listed in 312. 305 and 312. 320. Such a treatment protocol, if requested and granted, would normally remain in effect while the complete data necessary for a marketing application are being assembled by the sponsor and reviewed by FDA (unless grounds exist for clinical hold of ongoing protocols, as provided in 312. 42 (b)(3)(ii)) .

### Sec. 312. 84 Risk-benefit analysis in review of marketing applications for drugs to treat life-threatening and severely-debilitating illnesses.

(a) FDA's application of the statutory standards for marketing approval shall recognize the need for a medical risk-benefit judgment in making the final decision on approvability. As part of this evaluation, consistent with the statement of purpose in 312. 80, FDA will consider whether the benefits of the drug outweigh the known and potential risks of the drug and the need to answer remaining questions about risks and benefits of the drug, taking into consideration the severity of the disease and the absence of satisfactory alternative therapy.

(b) In making decisions on whether to grant marketing approval for products that have been the subject of an end-of-phase 1 meeting under 312. 82, FDA will usually seek the advice of outside expert scientific consultants or advisory committees. Upon the filing of such a marketing application under 314. 101 or part 601 of this chapter, FDA will notify the members of the relevant standing advisory committee of the application's filing and its availability for review.

(c) If FDA concludes that the data presented are not sufficient for marketing approval, FDA will issue a complete response letter under 314. 110 of this chapter or the biological product licensing procedures. Such letter, in describing the deficiencies in the application, will address why the results of the research design agreed to under 312. 82, or in subsequent meetings, have not provided sufficient evidence for marketing approval. Such letter will also describe any recommendations made by the advisory committee regarding the application.

(d) Marketing applications submitted under the procedures contained in this section will be subject to the requirements and procedures contained in part 314 or part 600 of this chapter, as well as those in this subpart.

## Sec. 312. 85 Phase 4 studies.

Concurrent with marketing approval, FDA may seek agreement from the sponsor to conduct certain postmarketing (phase 4) studies to delineate additional information about the drug's risks, benefits, and optimal use. These studies could include, but would not be limited to, studying different doses or schedules of administration than were used in phase 2 studies, use of the drug in other patient populations or other stages of the disease, or use of the drug over a longer period of time.

## Sec. 312. 86 Focused FDA regulatory research.

At the discretion of the agency, FDA may undertake focused regulatory research on critical rate-limiting aspects of the preclinical, chemical/manufacturing, and clinical phases of drug development and evaluation. When initiated, FDA will undertake such research efforts as a means for meeting a public health need in facilitating the development of therapies to treat life-threatening or severely debilitating illnesses.

## Sec. 312. 87 Active monitoring of conduct and evaluation of clinical trials.

For drugs covered under this section, the Commissioner and other agency officials will monitor the progress of the conduct and evaluation of clinical trials and be involved in facilitating their appropriate progress.

## Sec. 312. 88 Safeguards for patient safety.

All of the safeguards incorporated within parts 50, 56, 312, 314, and 600 of this chapter designed to ensure the safety of clinical testing and the safety of products following marketing approval apply to drugs covered by this section. This includes the requirements for informed consent (part 50 of this chapter) and institutional review boards (part 56 of this chapter). These safeguards further include the review of animal studies prior to initial human testing (312. 23) , and the monitoring of adverse drug experiences through the requirements of IND safety reports (312. 32) , safety update reports during agency review of a marketing application (314. 50 of this chapter) , and post-marketing adverse reaction reporting (314. 80 of this chapter) .

## Subpart F-Miscellaneous

### Sec. 312. 110 Import and export requirements.

(a) *Imports*. An investigational new drug offered for import into the United States complies with the requirements of this part if it is subject to an IND that is in effect for it under 312. 40 and: (1) The consignee in the United States is the sponsor of the IND; (2) the consignee is a qualified investigator named in the IND; or (3) the consignee is the domestic agent of a foreign sponsor, is responsible for the control and distribution of the investigational drug, and the IND identifies the consignee and describes what, if any, actions the consignee will take with respect to the investigational drug.

(b) *Exports*. An investigational new drug may be exported from the United States for use in a clinical investigation under any of the following conditions:

  (1) An IND is in effect for the drug under 312. 40, the drug complies with the laws of the country to which it is being exported, and each person who receives the drug is an investigator in a study submitted to and allowed to proceed under the IND; or

  (2) The drug has valid marketing authorization in Australia, Canada, Israel, Japan, New Zealand, Switzerland, South Africa, or in any country in the European Union or the European Economic Area, and complies with the laws of the country to which it is being exported, section 802 (b)(1)(A), (f) , and (g) of the act, and 1. 101 of this chapter; or

  (3) The drug is being exported to Australia, Canada, Israel, Japan, New Zealand, Switzerland, South Africa, or to any country in the European Union or the European Economic Area, and complies with the laws of the country to which it is being exported, the applicable provisions of section 802 (c) , (f) , and (g) of the act, and 1. 101 of

this chapter. Drugs exported under this paragraph that are not the subject of an IND are exempt from the label requirement in 312. 6 (a) ; or

(4) Except as provided in paragraph (b)(5) of this section, the person exporting the drug sends a written certification to the Office of International Programs (HFG-1), Food and Drug Administration, 5600 Fishers Lane, Rockville, MD 20857, at the time the drug is first exported and maintains records documenting compliance with this paragraph. The certification shall describe the drug that is to be exported (i. e., trade name (if any), generic name, and dosage form), identify the country or countries to which the drug is to be exported, and affirm that:

(i) The drug is intended for export;

(ii) The drug is intended for investigational use in a foreign country;

(iii) The drug meets the foreign purchaser's or consignee's specifications;

(iv) The drug is not in conflict with the importing country's laws;

(v) The outer shipping package is labeled to show that the package is intended for export from the United States;

(vi) The drug is not sold or offered for sale in the United States;

(vii) The clinical investigation will be conducted in accordance with 312. 120;

(viii) The drug is manufactured, processed, packaged, and held in substantial conformity with current good manufacturing practices;

(ix) The drug is not adulterated within the meaning of section 501 (a)(1), (a)(2)(A), (a)(3), (c), or (d) of the act;

(x) The drug does not present an imminent hazard to public health, either in the United States, if the drug were to be reimported, or in the foreign country; and

(xi) The drug is labeled in accordance with the foreign country's laws.

(5) In the event of a national emergency in a foreign country, where the national emergency necessitates exportation of an investigational new drug, the requirements in paragraph (b)(4) of this section ap-

ply as follows:

(i) *Situations where the investigational new drug is to be stockpiled in anticipation of a national emergency*. There may be instances where exportation of an investigational new drug is needed so that the drug may be stockpiled and made available for use by the importing country if and when a national emergency arises. In such cases:

(A) A person may export an investigational new drug under paragraph (b)(4) of this section without making an affirmation with respect to any one or more of paragraphs (b)(4)(i), (b)(4)(iv), (b)(4)(vi), (b)(4)(vii), (b)(4)(viii), and/or (b)(4)(ix) of this section, provided that he or she:

① Provides a written statement explaining why compliance with each such paragraph is not feasible or is contrary to the best interests of the individuals who may receive the investigational new drug;

② Provides a written statement from an authorized official of the importing country's government. The statement must attest that the official agrees with the exporter's statement made under paragraph (b)(5)(i)(A)① of this section; explain that the drug is to be stockpiled solely for use of the importing country in a national emergency; and describe the potential national emergency that warrants exportation of the investigational new drug under this provision; and

③ Provides a written statement showing that the Secretary of Health and Human Services (the Secretary), or his or her designee, agrees with the findings of the authorized official of the importing country's government. Persons who wish to obtain a written statement from the Secretary should direct their requests to Secretary's Operations Center, Office of Emergency Operations and Security Programs, Office of Public Health Emergency Preparedness, Office of the Secretary, Department of Health and Human Services, 200 Independence Ave. SW., Washington, DC 20201.

Requests may be also be sent by FAX: 202-619-7870 or by e-mail: HHS. SOC@hhs. gov.

(B) Exportation may not proceed until FDA has authorized exportation of the investigational new drug. FDA may deny authorization if the statements provided under paragraphs (b)(5)(i)(A)①or (b)(5)(i)(A)②of this section are inadequate or if exportation is contrary to public health.

(ii) *Situations where the investigational new drug is to be used for a sudden and immediate national emergency*. There may be instances where exportation of an investigational new drug is needed so that the drug may be used in a sudden and immediate national emergency that has developed or is developing. In such cases:

(A) A person may export an investigational new drug under paragraph (b)(4) of this section without making an affirmation with respect to any one or more of paragraphs (b)(4)(i), (b)(4)(iv), (b)(4)(v), (b)(4)(vi), (b)(4)(vii), (b)(4)(viii), (b)(4)(ix), and/or (b)(4)(xi), provided that he or she:

① Provides a written statement explaining why compliance with each such paragraph is not feasible or is contrary to the best interests of the individuals who are expected to receive the investigational new drug and

② Provides sufficient information from an authorized official of the importing country's government to enable the Secretary, or his or her designee, to decide whether a national emergency has developed or is developing in the importing country, whether the investigational new drug will be used solely for that national emergency, and whether prompt exportation of the investigational new drug is necessary. Persons who wish to obtain a determination from the Secretary should direct their requests to Secretary's Operations Center, Office of Emergency Operations and Security Programs, Office of Public Health Emergency

Preparedness, Office of the Secretary, Department of Health and Human Services, 200 Independence Ave. SW., Washington, DC 20201. Requests may be also be sent by FAX: 202-619-7870 or by e-mail: HHS. SOC@hhs. gov.

(B) Exportation may proceed without prior FDA authorization.

(c) *Limitations*. Exportation under paragraph (b) of this section may not occur if:

(1) For drugs exported under paragraph (b)(1) of this section, the IND pertaining to the clinical investigation is no longer in effect;

(2) For drugs exported under paragraph (b)(2) of this section, the requirements in section 802 (b)(1), (f), or (g) of the act are no longer met;

(3) For drugs exported under paragraph (b)(3) of this section, the requirements in section 802 (c), (f), or (g) of the act are no longer met;

(4) For drugs exported under paragraph (b)(4) of this section, the conditions underlying the certification or the statements submitted under paragraph (b)(5) of this section are no longer met; or

(5) For any investigational new drugs under this section, the drug no longer complies with the laws of the importing country.

(d) *Insulin and antibiotics*. New insulin and antibiotic drug products may be exported for investigational use in accordance with section 801(e)(1) of the act without complying with this section.

## Sec. 312. 120 Foreign clinical studies not conducted under an IND.

(a) *Acceptance of studies*.

(1) FDA will accept as support for an IND or application for marketing approval (an application under section 505 of the act or section 351 of the Public Health Service Act (the PHS Act) (42 U. S. C. 262)) a well-designed and well-conducted foreign clinical study not conducted under an IND, if the following conditions are met:

(i) The study was conducted in accordance with good clinical practice (GCP). For the purposes of this section, GCP is defined as a standard for the design, conduct, performance, monitoring, auditing, recording, analysis, and reporting of clinical trials in a way that provides assurance that the data and reported results are credible and accurate and that the rights, safety, and well-being of trial subjects are protected. GCP includes review and approval (or provision of a favorable opinion) by an independent ethics committee (IEC) before initiating a study, continuing review of an ongoing study by an IEC, and obtaining and documenting the freely given informed consent of the subject (or a subject's legally authorized representative, if the subject is unable to provide informed consent) before initiating a study. GCP does not require informed consent in life-threatening situations when the IEC reviewing the study finds, before initiation of the study, that informed consent is not feasible and either that the conditions present are consistent with those described in 50. 23 or 50. 24 (a) of this chapter, or that the measures described in the study protocol or elsewhere will protect the rights, safety, and well-being of subjects; and

(ii) FDA is able to validate the data from the study through an on-site inspection if the agency deems it necessary.

(2) Although FDA will not accept as support for an IND or application for marketing approval a study that does not meet the conditions of paragraph (a)(1) of this section, FDA will examine data from such a study.

(3) Marketing approval of a new drug based solely on foreign clinical data is governed by 314. 106 of this chapter.

(b) *Supporting information.* A sponsor or applicant who submits data from a foreign clinical study not conducted under an IND as support for an IND or application for marketing approval must submit to FDA, in addition to information required elsewhere in parts 312, 314, or 601 of this chapter, a description of the actions the sponsor or applicant took to ensure that the research conformed to GCP as described in paragraph (a)(1)(i) of this section. The description is not required to duplicate information already submitted in the IND or application for marketing approval. Instead, the description must provide either the following information or a cross-reference to another section of the submission where the information is located:

(1) The investigator's qualifications;

(2) A description of the research facilities;

(3) A detailed summary of the protocol and results of the study and, should FDA request, case records maintained by the investigator or additional background data such as hospital or other institutional records;

(4) A description of the drug substance and drug product used in the study, including a description of the components, formulation, specifications, and, if available, bioavailability of the specific drug product used in the clinical study;

(5) If the study is intended to support the effectiveness of a drug product, information showing that the study is adequate and well controlled under 314. 126 of this chapter;

(6) The name and address of the IEC that reviewed the study and a statement that the IEC meets the definition in 312. 3 of this chapter. The sponsor or applicant must maintain records supporting such statement, including records of the names and qualifications of IEC members, and make these records available for agency review upon request;

(7) A summary of the IEC's decision to approve or modify and approve the study, or to provide a favorable opinion;

(8) A description of how informed consent was obtained;

(9) A description of what incentives, if any, were provided to subjects to participate in the study;

(10) A description of how the sponsor(s) monitored the study and ensured that the study was carried out consistently with the study protocol; and

(11) A description of how investigators were trained to comply with GCP (as described in paragraph (a)(1)(i) of this section) and to conduct the study in accordance with the study protocol, and a statement on whether written commitments by investigators to comply with GCP and the protocol were obtained. Any signed written commitments by investigators must be maintained by the sponsor or applicant and made available for agency review upon request.

(c) *Waivers.*

(1) A sponsor or applicant may ask FDA to waive any applicable requirements under paragraphs (a)(1) and (b) of this section. A waiver request may be submitted in an IND or in an information amendment to an IND, or in an application or in an amendment or supplement to an application submitted under part 314 or 601 of this chapter. A waiver request is required to contain at least one of the following:

(i) An explanation why the sponsor's or applicant's compliance with the requirement is unnecessary or cannot be achieved;

(ii) A description of an alternative submission or course of action that satisfies the purpose of the requirement; or

(iii) Other information justifying a waiver.

(2) FDA may grant a waiver if it finds that doing so would be in the interest of the public health.

(d) *Records.* A sponsor or applicant must retain the records required by this section for a foreign clinical study not conducted under an IND as follows:

(1) If the study is submitted in support of an application for marketing approval, for 2 years after an agency decision on that application;

(2) If the study is submitted in support of an IND but not an application for marketing approval, for 2 years after the submission of the IND.

## Sec. 312. 130 Availability for public disclosure of data and information in an IND.

(a) The existence of an investigational new drug application will not be disclosed by FDA unless it has previously been publicly disclosed or acknowledged.

(b) The availability for public disclosure of all data and information in an investigational new drug application for a new drug will be handled in accordance with the provisions established in 314. 430 for the confidentiality of data and information in applications submitted in part 314. The availability for public disclosure of all data and information in an investigational new drug application for a biological product will be governed by the provisions of 601. 50 and 601. 51.

(c) Notwithstanding the provisions of 314. 430, FDA shall disclose upon request to an individual to whom an investigational new drug has been given a copy of any IND safety report relating to the use in the individual.

(d) The availability of information required to be publicly disclosed for investigations involving an exception from informed consent under 50. 24 of this chapter will be handled as follows: Persons wishing to request the publicly disclosable information in the IND that was required to be filed in Docket Number 95S-0158 in the Division of Dockets Management (HFA-305), Food and Drug Administration, 5630 Fishers Lane, rm. 1061, Rockville, MD 20852, shall submit a request under the Freedom of Information Act.

## Sec. 312. 140 Address for correspondence.

(a) *A sponsor must send an initial IND submission to the Center for Drug Evaluation and Research (CDER) or to the Center for Biologics Evaluation and Research (CBER), depending on the Center responsible for regulating the product as follows:*

(1) *For drug products regulated by CDER.* Send the IND submission to the Central Document Room, Center for Drug Evaluation and Research, Food and Drug Administration, 5901-B Ammendale Rd., Beltsville, MD 20705-1266; except send an IND submission for an in vivo bioavailability or bioequivalence study in humans to support an abbreviated new drug application to the Office of Generic Drugs (HFD-600), Center for Drug Evaluation and Research, Food and Drug Administration, Metro Park North VII, 7620 Standish Pl., Rockville, MD 20855.

(2) *For biological products regulated by CDER.* Send the IND submission to the Central Document Room, Center for Drug Evaluation and Research, Food and Drug Administration, 5901-B Ammendale Rd., Beltsville, MD 20705-1266.

(3) *For biological products regulated by CBER.* Send the IND submission to the Food and Drug Administration, Center for Biologics Evaluation and Research, Document Control Center, 10903 New Hampshire Ave., Bldg. 71, Rm. G112, Silver Spring, MD 20993-0002.

(b) On receiving the IND, the responsible Center will inform the sponsor which one of the divisions in CDER or CBER is responsible for the IND. Amendments, reports, and other correspondence relating to matters covered by the IND should be sent to the appropriate center at the address indicated in this section and marked to the attention of the responsible division. The outside wrapper of each submission shall state what is contained in the submission, for example, "IND Application" , "Protocol Amendment" , etc.

(c) All correspondence relating to export of an investigational drug under 312. 110 (b)(2) shall be submitted to the International Affairs Staff (HFY-50) , Office of Health Affairs, Food and Drug Administration, 5600 Fishers Lane, Rockville, MD 20857.

### Sec. 312. 145 Guidance documents.

(a) FDA has made available guidance documents under 10. 115 of this chapter to help you to comply with certain requirements of this part.

(b) The Center for Drug Evaluation and Research (CDER) and the Center for Biologics Evaluation and Research (CBER) maintain lists of guidance documents that apply to the centers' regulations. The lists are maintained on the Internet and are published annually in the Federal Register. A request for a copy of the CDER list should be directed to the Office of Training and Communications, Division of Drug Information, Center for Drug Evaluation and Research, Food and Drug Administration, 10903 New Hampshire Ave. , Silver Spring, MD 20993-0002. A request for a copy of the CBER list should be directed to the Food and Drug Administration, Center for Biologics Evaluation and Research, Office of Communication, Outreach and Development, 10903 New Hampshire Ave. , Bldg. 71, Rm. 3103, Silver Spring, MD 20993-0002.

## Subpart G-Drugs for Investigational Use in Laboratory Research Animals or In Vitro Tests

### Sec. 312. 160 Drugs for investigational use in laboratory research animals or in vitro tests.

(a) *Authorization to ship.*

(1) (i) A person may ship a drug intended solely for tests in vitro or in animals used only for laboratory research purposes if it is labeled as follows:

CAUTION: Contains a new drug for investigational use only in laboratory research animals, or for tests in vitro. Not for use in humans.

(ii) A person may ship a biological product for investigational in vitro diagnostic use that is listed in 312. 2 (b)(2)(ii) if it is labeled as follows:

CAUTION: Contains a biological product for investigational in vitro diagnostic tests only.

(2) A person shipping a drug under paragraph (a) of this section shall use due diligence to assure that the consignee is regularly engaged in conducting such tests and that the shipment of the new drug will actually be used for tests in vitro or in animals used only for laboratory research.

(3) A person who ships a drug under paragraph (a) of this section shall maintain adequate records showing the name and post office address of the expert to whom the drug is shipped and the date, quantity, and batch or code mark of each shipment and delivery. Records of shipments under paragraph (a)(1)(i) of this section are to be maintained for a period of 2 years after the shipment. Records and reports of data and shipments under paragraph (a)(1)(ii) of this section are to be maintained in accordance with 312. 57 (b) . The person who ships the drug shall upon request from any properly authorized officer or employee of the Food and Drug Administration, at reasonable times, permit such officer or employee to have access to and copy and verify records required to be maintained under this section.

(b) *Termination of authorization to ship*. FDA may terminate authorization to ship a drug under this section if it finds that:

(1) The sponsor of the investigation has failed to comply with any of the conditions for shipment established under this section; or

(2) The continuance of the investigation is unsafe or otherwise contrary to the public interest or the drug is used for purposes other than bo-

na fide scientific investigation. FDA will notify the person shipping the drug of its finding and invite immediate correction. If correction is not immediately made, the person shall have an opportunity for a regulatory hearing before FDA pursuant to part 16.

(c) *Disposition of unused drug*. The person who ships the drug under paragraph (a) of this section shall assure the return of all unused supplies of the drug from individual investigators whenever the investigation discontinues or the investigation is terminated. The person who ships the drug may authorize in writing alternative disposition of unused supplies of the drug provided this alternative disposition does not expose humans to risks from the drug, either directly or indirectly (e. g, through food-producing animals) . The shipper shall maintain records of any alternative disposition.

## Subpart H [Reserved]

## Subpart I-Expanded Access to Investigational Drugs for Treatment Use

### Sec. 312. 300 General.

(a) *Scope*. This subpart contains the requirements for the use of investigational new drugs and approved drugs where availability is limited by a risk evaluation and mitigation strategy (REMS) when the primary purpose is to diagnose, monitor, or treat a patient's disease or condition. The aim of this subpart is to facilitate the availability of such drugs to patients with serious diseases or conditions when there is no comparable or satisfactory alternative therapy to diagnose, monitor, or treat the patient's disease or condition.

(b) *Definitions*. The following definitions of terms apply to this subpart:

*Immediately life-threatening disease or condition* means a stage of disease in which there is reasonable likelihood that death will occur within a matter of months or in which premature death is likely without early treatment.

*Serious disease or condition* means a disease or condition associated with morbidity that has substantial impact on day-to-day functioning. Short-lived and self-limiting morbidity will usually not be sufficient, but the morbidity need not be irreversible, provided it is persistent or recurrent. Whether a disease or condition is serious is a matter of clinical judgment, based on its impact on such factors as survival, day-to-day functioning, or the likelihood that the disease, if left untreated, will progress from a less severe condition to a more serious one.

## Sec. 312. 305 Requirements for all expanded access uses.

The criteria, submission requirements, safeguards, and beginning treatment information set out in this section apply to all expanded access uses described in this subpart. Additional criteria, submission requirements, and safeguards that apply to specific types of expanded access are described in 312. 310 through 312. 320.

(a) *Criteria*. FDA must determine that:

(1) The patient or patients to be treated have a serious or immediately life-threatening disease or condition, and there is no comparable or satisfactory alternative therapy to diagnose, monitor, or treat the disease or condition;

(2) The potential patient benefit justifies the potential risks of the treatment use and those potential risks are not unreasonable in the context of the disease or condition to be treated; and

(3) Providing the investigational drug for the requested use will not interfere with the initiation, conduct, or completion of clinical investigations that could support marketing approval of the expanded access use or otherwise compromise the potential development of the expanded access use.

(b) *Submission*.

(1) An expanded access submission is required for each type of expanded access described in this subpart. The submission may be a new IND or a protocol amendment to an existing IND. Information required for a submission may be supplied by referring to pertinent information contained in an existing IND if the sponsor of the existing IND grants a right of reference to the IND.

(2) The expanded access submission must include:

(i) A cover sheet (Form FDA 1571) meeting the requirements of

312. 23 (a) ;

(ii) The rationale for the intended use of the drug, including a list of available therapeutic options that would ordinarily be tried before resorting to the investigational drug or an explanation of why the use of the investigational drug is preferable to the use of available therapeutic options;

(iii) The criteria for patient selection or, for an individual patient, a description of the patient's disease or condition, including recent medical history and previous treatments of the disease or condition;

(iv) The method of administration of the drug, dose, and duration of therapy;

(v) A description of the facility where the drug will be manufactured;

(vi) Chemistry, manufacturing, and controls information adequate to ensure the proper identification, quality, purity, and strength of the investigational drug;

(vii) Pharmacology and toxicology information adequate to conclude that the drug is reasonably safe at the dose and duration proposed for expanded access use (ordinarily, information that would be adequate to permit clinical testing of the drug in a population of the size expected to be treated) ; and

(viii) A description of clinical procedures, laboratory tests, or other monitoring necessary to evaluate the effects of the drug and minimize its risks.

(3) The expanded access submission and its mailing cover must be plainly marked "EXPANDED ACCESS SUBMISSION." If the expanded access submission is for a treatment IND or treatment protocol, the applicable box on Form FDA 1571 must be checked.

(c) *Safeguards*. The responsibilities of sponsors and investigators set forth in subpart D of this part are applicable to expanded access use under this subpart as described in this paragraph.

(1) A licensed physician under whose immediate direction an investigational drug is administered or dispensed for an expanded access use under this subpart is considered aninvestigator, for purposes of

this part, and must comply with the responsibilities for investigators set forth in subpart D of this part to the extent they are applicable to the expanded access use.

(2) An individual or entity that submits an expanded access IND or protocol under this subpart is considered a sponsor , for purposes of this part, and must comply with the responsibilities for sponsors set forth in subpart D of this part to the extent they are applicable to the expanded access use.

(3) A licensed physician under whose immediate direction an investigational drug is administered or dispensed, and who submits an IND for expanded access use under this subpart is considered a sponsor-investigator , for purposes of this part, and must comply with the responsibilities for sponsors and investigators set forth in subpart D of this part to the extent they are applicable to the expanded access use.

(4) *Investigators*. In all cases of expanded access, investigators are responsible for reporting adverse drug events to the sponsor, ensuring that the informed consent requirements of part 50 of this chapter are met, ensuring that IRB review of the expanded access use is obtained in a manner consistent with the requirements of part 56 of this chapter, and maintaining accurate case histories and drug disposition records and retaining records in a manner consistent with the requirements of 312. 62. Depending on the type of expanded access, other investigator responsibilities under subpart D may also apply.

(5) *Sponsors*. In all cases of expanded access, sponsors are responsible for submitting IND safety reports and annual reports (when the IND or protocol continues for 1 year or longer) to FDA as required by 312. 32 and 312. 33, ensuring that licensed physicians are qualified to administer the investigational drug for the expanded access use, providing licensed physicians with the information needed to minimize the risk and maximize the potential benefits of the investigational drug (the investigator's brochure must be provided if one exists for the drug) , maintaining an effective IND for the expanded access use, and maintaining adequate drug disposition records and

retaining records in a manner consistent with the requirements of 312. 57. Depending on the type of expanded access, other sponsor responsibilities under subpart D may also apply.

(d) *Beginning treatment.*

(1) *INDs.* An expanded access IND goes into effect 30 days after FDA receives the IND or on earlier notification by FDA that the expanded access use may begin.

(2) *Protocols.* With the following exceptions, expanded access use under a protocol submitted under an existing IND may begin as described in 312. 30 (a) .

(i) Expanded access use under the emergency procedures described in 312. 310 (d) may begin when the use is authorized by the FDA reviewing official.

(ii) Expanded access use under 312. 320 may begin 30 days after FDA receives the protocol or upon earlier notification by FDA that use may begin.

(3) *Clinical holds.* FDA may place any expanded access IND or protocol on clinical hold as described in 312. 42.

## Sec. 312. 310 Individual patients, including for emergency use.

Under this section, FDA may permit an investigational drug to be used for the treatment of an individual patient by a licensed physician.

(a) *Criteria.* The criteria in 312. 305 (a) must be met; and the following determinations must be made:

(1) The physician must determine that the probable risk to the person from the investigational drug is not greater than the probable risk from the disease or condition; and

(2) FDA must determine that the patient cannot obtain the drug under another IND or protocol.

(b) *Submission.* The expanded access submission must include information adequate to demonstrate that the criteria in 312. 305 (a) and paragraph (a) of this section have been met. The expanded access submission must meet the requirements of 312. 305 (b) .

(1) If the drug is the subject of an existing IND, the expanded access submission may be made by the sponsor or by a licensed physician.

(2) A sponsor may satisfy the submission requirements by amending its existing IND to include a protocol for individual patient expanded access.

(3) A licensed physician may satisfy the submission requirements by obtaining from the sponsor permission for FDA to refer to any information in the IND that would be needed to support the expanded access request (right of reference) and by providing any other required information not contained in the IND (usually only the information specific to the individual patient).

(c) *Safeguards*.

(1) Treatment is generally limited to a single course of therapy for a specified duration unless FDA expressly authorizes multiple courses or chronic therapy.

(2) At the conclusion of treatment, the licensed physician or sponsor must provide FDA with a written summary of the results of the expanded access use, including adverse effects.

(3) FDA may require sponsors to monitor an individual patient expanded access use if the use is for an extended duration.

(4) When a significant number of similar individual patient expanded access requests have been submitted, FDA may ask the sponsor to submit an IND or protocol for the use under 312. 315 or 312. 320.

(d) *Emergency procedures*. If there is an emergency that requires the patient to be treated before a written submission can be made, FDA may authorize the expanded access use to begin without a written submission. The FDA reviewing official may authorize the emergency use by telephone.

(1) Emergency expanded access use may be requested by telephone, facsimile, or other means of electronic communications. For investigational biological drug products regulated by the Center for Biologics Evaluation and Research, the request should be directed to the Office of Communication, Outreach and Development, Center for Biologics Evaluation and Research, 240-402-8010 or 1-800-835-4709, e-mail: ocod @ fda. hhs. gov. For all other investigational drugs, the request for authorization should be directed to the Division of Drug Information, Center for Drug Evaluation and Re-

search, 301-796-3400, e-mail: druginfo@fda.hhs.gov. After normal working hours (8 a.m. to 4:30 p.m.), the request should be directed to the FDA Emergency Call Center, 866-300-4374, e-mail: emergency.operations@fda.hhs.gov.

(2) The licensed physician or sponsor must explain how the expanded access use will meet the requirements of 312.305 and 312.310 and must agree to submit an expanded access submission within 15 working days of FDA's authorization of the use.

## Sec. 312.315 Intermediate-size patient populations.

Under this section, FDA may permit an investigational drug to be used for the treatment of a patient population smaller than that typical of a treatment IND or treatment protocol. FDA may ask a sponsor to consolidate expanded access under this section when the agency has received a significant number of requests for individual patient expanded access to an investigational drug for the same use.

(a) *Need for expanded access.* Expanded access under this section may be needed in the following situations:

(1) *Drug not being developed.* The drug is not being developed, for example, because the disease or condition is so rare that the sponsor is unable to recruit patients for a clinical trial.

(2) *Drug being developed.* The drug is being studied in a clinical trial, but patients requesting the drug for expanded access use are unable to participate in the trial. For example, patients may not be able to participate in the trial because they have a different disease or stage of disease than the one being studied or otherwise do not meet the enrollment criteria, because enrollment in the trial is closed, or because the trial site is not geographically accessible.

(3) *Approved or related drug.*

(i) The drug is an approved drug product that is no longer marketed for safety reasons or is unavailable through marketing due to failure to meet the conditions of the approved application, or

(ii) The drug contains the same active moiety as an approved drug product that is unavailable through marketing due to failure to meet the conditions of the approved application or a drug shortage.

(b) *Criteria*. The criteria in 312. 305 (a) must be met; and FDA must determine that:

(1) There is enough evidence that the drug is safe at the dose and duration proposed for expanded access use to justify a clinical trial of the drug in the approximate number of patients expected to receive the drug under expanded access; and

(2) There is at least preliminary clinical evidence of effectiveness of the drug, or of a plausible pharmacologic effect of the drug to make expanded access use a reasonable therapeutic option in the anticipated patient population.

(c) *Submission*. The expanded access submission must include information adequate to satisfy FDA that the criteria in 312. 305 (a) and paragraph (b) of this section have been met. The expanded access submission must meet the requirements of 312. 305 (b) . In addition:

(1) The expanded access submission must state whether the drug is being developed or is not being developed and describe the patient population to be treated.

(2) If the drug is not being actively developed, the sponsor must explain why the drug cannot currently be developed for the expanded access use and under what circumstances the drug could be developed.

(3) If the drug is being studied in a clinical trial, the sponsor must explain why the patients to be treated cannot be enrolled in the clinical trial and under what circumstances the sponsor would conduct a clinical trial in these patients.

(d) *Safeguards*.

(1) Upon review of the IND annual report, FDA will determine whether it is appropriate for the expanded access to continue under this section.

(i) If the drug is not being actively developed or if the expanded access use is not being developed (but another use is being developed) , FDA will consider whether it is possible to conduct a clinical study of the expanded access use.

(ii) If the drug is being actively developed, FDA will consider whether providing the investigational drug for expanded access use is interfering with the clinical development of the drug.

(iii) As the number of patients enrolled increases, FDA may ask the sponsor to submit an IND or protocol for the use under 312. 320.

(2) The sponsor is responsible for monitoring the expanded access protocol to ensure that licensed physicians comply with the protocol and the regulations applicable to investigators.

## Sec. 312. 320 Treatment IND or treatment protocol.

Under this section, FDA may permit an investigational drug to be used for widespread treatment use.

(a) *Criteria*. The criteria in 312. 305 (a) must be met, and FDA must determine that:

(1) *Trial status*.

(i) The drug is being investigated in a controlled clinical trial under an IND designed to support a marketing application for the expanded access use, or

(ii) All clinical trials of the drug have been completed; and

(2) *Marketing status*. The sponsor is actively pursuing marketing approval of the drug for the expanded access use with due diligence; and

(3) *Evidence*.

(i) When the expanded access use is for a serious disease or condition, there is sufficient clinical evidence of safety and effectiveness to support the expanded access use. Such evidence would ordinarily consist of data from phase 3 trials, but could consist of compelling data from completed phase 2 trials; or

(ii) When the expanded access use is for an immediately life-threatening disease or condition, the available scientific evidence, taken as a whole, provides a reasonable basis to conclude that the investigational drug may be effective for the expanded access use and would not expose patients to an unreasonable and significant risk of illness or injury. This evidence would ordinarily consist of clinical data from phase 3 or phase 2 trials, but could be based on more preliminary clinical evidence.

(b) *Submission*. The expanded access submission must include information adequate to satisfy FDA that the criteria in 312. 305 (a) and paragraph (a) of this section have been met. The expanded access submission must meet the requirements of 312. 305 (b) .

(c) *Safeguard*. The sponsor is responsible for monitoring the treatment protocol to ensure that licensed physicians comply with the protocol and the regulations applicable to investigators.

[e-CFR data is current as of June 30,2017]

# 21CFR PART812 INVESTIGATIONAL DEVICE EXEMPTIONS

## Subpart A-General Provisions

### 812. 1 Scope.

(a) The purpose of this part is to encourage, to the extent consistent with the protection of public health and safety and with ethical standards, the discovery and development of useful devices intended for human use, and to that end to maintain optimum freedom for scientific investigators in their pursuit of this purpose. This part provides procedures for the conduct of clinical investigations of devices. An approved investigational device exemption (IDE) permits a device that otherwise would be required to comply with a performance standard or to have premarket approval to be shipped lawfully for the purpose of conducting investigations of that device. An IDE approved under 812. 30 or considered approved under 812. 2(b) exempts a device from the requirements of the following sections of the Federal Food, Drug, and Cosmetic Act (the act) and regulations issued thereunder: Misbranding under section 502 of the act, registration, listing, and premarket notification under section 510, performance standards under section 514, premarket approval under section 515, a banned device regulation under section 516, records and reports under section 519, restricted device requirements under section 520 (e), good manufacturing practice requirements under section 520 (f) except for the requirements found in 820. 30, if applicable (unless the sponsor states an intention to comply with these requirements under 812. 20(b)(3) or 812. 140(b)(4)(v)) and color additive requirements under section 721.

(b) References in this part to regulatory sections of the Code of Federal

Regulations are to chapter I of title 21, unless otherwise noted.

## 812. 2 Applicability.

(a) *General.* This part applies to all clinical investigations of devices to determine safety and effectiveness, except as provided in paragraph (c) of this section.

(b) *Abbreviated requirements.* The following categories of investigations are considered to have approved applications for IDE's, unless FDA has notified a sponsor under 812. 20 (a) that approval of an application is required:

(1) An investigation of a device other than a significant risk device, if the device is not a banned device and the sponsor:

(i) Labels the device in accordance with 812. 5;

(ii) Obtains IRB approval of the investigation after presenting the reviewing IRB with a brief explanation of why the device is not a significant risk device, and maintains such approval;

(iii) Ensures that each investigator participating in an investigation of the device obtains from each subject under the investigator's care, informed consent under part 50 and documents it, unless documentation is waived by an IRB under 56. 109 (c).

(iv) Complies with the requirements of 812. 46 with respect to monitoring investigations;

(v) Maintains the records required under 812. 140 (b)(4) and (5) and makes the reports required under 812. 150 (b)(1) through (3) and (5) through (10);

(vi) Ensures that participating investigators maintain the records required by 812. 140 (a)(3)(i) and make the reports required under 812. 150 (a)(1), (2), (5), and (7); and

(vii) Complies with the prohibitions in 812. 7 against promotion and other practices.

(2) An investigation of a device other than one subject to paragraph (e) of this section, if the investigation was begun on or before July 16, 1980, and to be completed, and is completed, on or before January 19, 1981.

(c) *Exempted investigations.* This part, with the exception of 812. 119, does not apply to investigations of the following categories of devices:

(1) A device, other than a transitional device, in commercial distribution immediately before May 28, 1976, when used or investigated in accordance with the indications in labeling in effect at that time.

(2) A device, other than a transitional device, introduced into commercial distribution on or after May 28, 1976, that FDA has determined to be substantially equivalent to a device in commercial distribution immediately before May 28, 1976, and that is used or investigated in accordance with the indications in the labeling FDA reviewed under subpart E of part 807 in determining substantial equivalence.

(3) A diagnostic device, if the sponsor complies with applicable requirements in 809. 10 (c) and if the testing:

  (i) Is noninvasive,

  (ii) Does not require an invasive sampling procedure that presents significant risk,

  (iii) Does not by design or intention introduce energy into a subject, and

  (iv) Is not used as a diagnostic procedure without confirmation of the diagnosis by another, medically established diagnostic product or procedure.

(4) A device undergoing consumer preference testing, testing of a modification, or testing of a combination of two or more devices in commercial distribution, if the testing is not for the purpose of determining safety or effectiveness and does not put subjects at risk.

(5) A device intended solely for veterinary use.

(6) A device shipped solely for research on or with laboratory animals and labeled in accordance with 812. 5 (c) .

(7) A custom device as defined in 812. 3 (b) , unless the device is being used to determine safety or effectiveness for commercial distribution.

(d) *Limit on certain exemptions*. In the case of class Ⅱ or class Ⅲ device described in paragraph (c)(1) or (2) of this section, this part applies beginning on the date stipulated in an FDA regulation or order that calls for the submission of premarket approval applications for an unapproved class Ⅲ device, or establishes a performance standard for a class

Ⅱ device.

(e) *Investigations subject to IND's*. A sponsor that, on July 16, 1980, has an effective investigational new drug application (IND) for an investigation of a device shall continue to comply with the requirements of part 312 until 90 days after that date. To continue the investigation after that date, a sponsor shall comply with paragraph (b) (1) of this section, if the device is not a significant risk device, or shall have obtained FDA approval under 812. 30 of an IDE application for the investigation of the device.

## 812. 3 Definitions.

(a) *Act* means the Federal Food, Drug, and Cosmetic Act (sections 201-901, 52 Stat. 1040 et seq. , as amended (21 U. S. C. 301-392)) .

(b) *A custom device* means a device within the meaning of section 520 (b) of the Federal Food, Drug, and Cosmetic Act.

(c) *FDA* means the Food and Drug Administration.

(d) *Implant* means a device that is placed into a surgically or naturally formed cavity of the human body if it is intended to remain there for a period of 30 days or more. FDA may, in order to protect public health, determine that devices placed in subjects for shorter periods are also "implants" for purposes of this part.

(e) *Institution* means a person, other than an individual, who engages in the conduct of research on subjects or in the delivery of medical services to individuals as a primary activity or as an adjunct to providing residential or custodial care to humans. The term includes, for example, a hospital, retirement home, confinement facility, academic establishment, and device manufacturer. The term has the same meaning as "facility" in section 520 (g) of the act.

(f) *Institutional review board* (*IRB*) means any board, committee, or other group formally designated by an institution to review biomedical research involving subjects and established, operated, and functioning in conformance with part 56. The term has the same meaning as "institutional review committee" in section 520 (g) of the act.

(g) *Investigational device* means a device, including a transitional device, that is the object of an investigation.

(h) *Investigation* means a clinical investigation or research involving one or more subjects to determine the safety or effectiveness of a device.

(i) *Investigator* means an individual who actually conducts a clinical investigation, i. e. , under whose immediate direction the test article is administered or dispensed to, or used involving, a subject, or, in the event of an investigation conducted by a team of individuals, is the responsible leader of that team.

(j) *Monitor* ,when used as a noun, means an individual designated by a sponsor or contract research organization to oversee the progress of an investigation. The monitor may be an employee of a sponsor or a consultant to the sponsor, or an employee of or consultant to a contract research organization. Monitor, when used as a verb, means to oversee an investigation.

(k) *Noninvasive* ,when applied to a diagnostic device or procedure, means one that does not by design or intention: (1) Penetrate or pierce the skin or mucous membranes of the body, the ocular cavity, or the urethra, or (2) enter the ear beyond the external auditory canal, the nose beyond the nares, the mouth beyond the pharynx, the anal canal beyond the rectum, or the vagina beyond the cervical os. For purposes of this part, blood sampling that involves simple venipuncture is considered noninvasive, and the use of surplus samples of body fluids or tissues that are left over from samples taken for noninvestigational purposes is also considered noninvasive.

(l) *Person* includes any individual, partnership, corporation, association, scientific or academic establishment, Government agency or organizational unit of a Government agency, and any other legal entity.

(m) *Significant risk* device means an investigational device that:

(1) Is intended as an implant and presents a potential for serious risk to the health, safety, or welfare of a subject;

(2) Is purported or represented to be for a use in supporting or sustaining human life and presents a potential for serious risk to the health, safety, or welfare of a subject;

(3) Is for a use of substantial importance in diagnosing, curing, mitigating, or treating disease, or otherwise preventing impairment of human health and presents a potential for serious risk to the health, safety, or welfare of a subject; or

## 812. 10 Waivers.

(a) *Request.* A sponsor may request FDA to waive any requirement of this part. A waiver request, with supporting documentation, may be submitted separately or as part of an application to the address in 812. 19.

(b) *FDA action.* FDA may by letter grant a waiver of any requirement that FDA finds is not required by the act and is unnecessary to protect the rights, safety, or welfare of human subjects.

(c) *Effect of request.* Any requirement shall continue to apply unless and until FDA waives it.

## 812. 18 Import and export requirements.

(a) *Imports.* In addition to complying with other requirements of this part, a person who imports or offers for importation an investigational device subject to this part shall be the agent of the foreign exporter with respect to investigations of the device and shall act as the sponsor of the clinical investigation, or ensure that another person acts as the agent of the foreign exporter and the sponsor of the investigation.

(b) *Exports.* A person exporting an investigational device subject to this part shall obtain FDA's prior approval, as required by section 801 (e) of the act or comply with section 802 of the act.

## 812. 19 Address for IDE correspondence.

(a) If you are sending an application, supplemental application, report, request for waiver, request for import or export approval, or other correspondence relating to matters covered by this part, you must send the submission to the appropriate address as follows:

(1) For devices regulated by the Center for Devices and Radiological Health, send it to Food and Drug Administration, Center for Devices and Radiological Health, Document Mail Center, 10903 New Hampshire Ave, Bldg. 66, rm. G609, Silver Spring, MD 20993-0002.

(2) For devices regulated by the Center for Biologics Evaluation and Research, send it to the Food and Drug Administration, Center for Biologics Evaluation and Research, Document Control Center, 10903 New Hampshire Ave. , Bldg. 71, Rm. G112, Silver Spring, MD 20993-0002.

(3) For devices regulated by the Center for Drug Evaluation and Research, send it to Central Document Control Room, Center for Drug

Evaluation and Research, Food and Drug Administration, 5901-B Ammendale Rd. , Beltsville, MD 20705-1266.

(b) You must state on the outside wrapper of each submission what the submission is, for example, an "IDE application," a "supplemental IDE application," or a "correspondence concerning an IDE (or an IDE application)."

# Subpart B-Application and Administrative Action

## 812. 20 Application.

(a) *Submission.*

(1) A sponsor shall submit an application to FDA if the sponsor intends to use a significant risk device in an investigation, intends to conduct an investigation that involves an exception from informed consent under 50. 24 of this chapter, or if FDA notifies the sponsor that an application is required for an investigation.

(2) A sponsor shall not begin an investigation for which FDA's approval of an application is required until FDA has approved the application.

(3) A sponsor shall submit three copies of a signed "Application for an Investigational Device Exemption" (IDE application) , together with accompanying materials, by registered mail or by hand to the address in 812. 19. Subsequent correspondence concerning an application or a supplemental application shall be submitted by registered mail or by hand.

(4) (i) A sponsor shall submit a separate IDE for any clinical investigation involving an exception from informed consent under 50. 24 of this chapter. Such a clinical investigation is not permitted to proceed without the prior written authorization of FDA. FDA shall provide a written determination 30 days after FDA receives the IDE or earlier.

(ii) If the investigation involves an exception from informed consent under 50. 24 of this chapter, the sponsor shall prominently identify on the cover sheet that the investigation is subject to the requirements in 50. 24 of this chapter.

(b) *Contents*. An IDE application shall include, in the following order:

(1) The name and address of the sponsor.

(2) A complete report of prior investigations of the device and an accurate summary of those sections of the investigational plan described in 812. 25 (a) through(e) or, in lieu of the summary, the complete plan. The sponsor shall submit to FDA a complete investigational plan and a complete report of prior investigations of the device if no IRB has reviewed them, if FDA has found an IRB's review inadequate, or if FDA requests them.

(3) A description of the methods, facilities, and controls used for the manufacture, processing, packing, storage, and, where appropriate, installation of the device, in sufficient detail so that a person generally familiar with good manufacturing practices can make a knowledgeable judgment about the quality control used in the manufacture of the device.

(4) An example of the agreements to be entered into by all investigators to comply with investigator obligations under this part, and a list of the names and addresses of all investigators who have signed the agreement.

(5) A certification that all investigators who will participate in the investigation have signed the agreement, that the list of investigators includes all the investigators participating in the investigation, and that no investigators will be added to the investigation until they have signed the agreement.

(6) A list of the name, address, and chairperson of each IRB that has been or will be asked to review the investigation and a certification of the action concerning the investigation taken by each such IRB.

(7) The name and address of any institution at which a part of the investigation may be conducted that has not been identified in accordance with paragraph (b)(6) of this section.

(8) If the device is to be sold, the amount to be charged and an explanation of why sale does not constitute commercialization of the device.

(9) A claim for categorical exclusion under 25. 30 or 25. 34 or an environmental assessment under 25. 40.

(10) Copies of all labeling for the device.

(11) Copies of all forms and informational materials to be provided to subjects to obtain informed consent.

(12) Any other relevant information FDA requests for review of the application.

(c) *Additional information.* FDA may request additional information concerning an investigation or revision in the investigational plan. The sponsor may treat such a request as a disapproval of the application for purposes of requesting a hearing under part 16.

(d) *Information previously submitted.* Information previously submitted to the Center for Devices and Radiological Health, the Center for Biologics Evaluation and Research, or the Center for Drug Evaluation and Research, as applicable, in accordance with this chapter ordinarily need not be resubmitted, but may be incorporated by reference.

## 812.25 Investigational plan.

The investigational plan shall include, in the following order:

(a) *Purpose.* The name and intended use of the device and the objectives and duration of the investigation.

(b) *Protocol.* A written protocol describing the methodology to be used and an analysis of the protocol demonstrating that the investigation is scientifically sound.

(c) *Risk analysis.* A description and analysis of all increased risks to which subjects will be exposed by the investigation; the manner in which these risks will be minimized; a justification for the investigation; and a description of the patient population, including the number, age, sex, and condition.

(d) *Description of device.* A description of each important component, ingredient, property, and principle of operation of the device and of each anticipated change in the device during the course of the investigation.

(e) *Monitoring procedures.* The sponsor's written procedures for monitoring the investigation and the name and address of any monitor.

(f) *Labeling.* Copies of all labeling for the device.

(g) *Consent materials.* Copies of all forms and informational materials to be provided to subjects to obtain informed consent.

(h) *IRB information*. A list of the names, locations, and chairpersons of all IRB's that have been or will be asked to review the investigation, and a certification of any action taken by any of those IRB's with respect to the investigation.

(i) *Other institutions*. The name and address of each institution at which a part of the investigation may be conducted that has not been identified in paragraph (h) of this section.

(j) *Additional records and reports*. A description of records and reports that will be maintained on the investigation in addition to those prescribed in subpart G.

## 812. 27 Report of prior investigations.

(a) *General*. The report of prior investigations shall include reports of all prior clinical, animal, and laboratory testing of the device and shall be comprehensive and adequate to justify the proposed investigation.

(b) *Specific contents*. The report also shall include:

(1) A bibliography of all publications, whether adverse or supportive, that are relevant to an evaluation of the safety or effectiveness of the device, copies of all published and unpublished adverse information, and, if requested by an IRB or FDA, copies of other significant publications.

(2) A summary of all other unpublished information (whether adverse or supportive) in the possession of, or reasonably obtainable by, the sponsor that is relevant to an evaluation of the safety or effectiveness of the device.

(3) If information on nonclinical laboratory studies is provided, a statement that all such studies have been conducted in compliance with applicable requirements in the good laboratory practice regulations in part 58, or if any such study was not conducted in compliance with such regulations, a brief statement of the reason for the noncompliance. Failure or inability to comply with this requirement does not justify failure to provide information on a relevant nonclinical test study.

## 812. 30 FDA action on applications.

(a) *Approval or disapproval*. FDA will notify the sponsor in writing of the date it receives an application. FDA may approve an investigation as proposed, approve it with modifications, or disapprove it. An investigation may not begin until:

(1) Thirty days after FDA receives the application at the address in 812. 19 for the investigation of a device other than a banned device, unless FDA notifies the sponsor that the investigation may not begin; or

(2) FDA approves, by order, an IDE for the investigation.

(b) *Grounds for disapproval or withdrawal*. FDA may disapprove or withdraw approval of an application if FDA finds that:

(1) There has been a failure to comply with any requirement of this part or the act, any other applicable regulation or statute, or any condition of approval imposed by an IRB or FDA.

(2) The application or a report contains an untrue statement of a material fact, or omits material information required by this part.

(3) The sponsor fails to respond to a request for additional information within the time prescribed by FDA.

(4) There is reason to believe that the risks to the subjects are not outweighed by the anticipated benefits to the subjects and the importance of the knowledge to be gained, or informed consent is inadequate, or the investigation is scientifically unsound, or there is reason to believe that the device as used is ineffective.

(5) It is otherwise unreasonable to begin or to continue the investigation owing to the way in which the device is used or the inadequacy of:

(i) The report of prior investigations or the investigational plan;

(ii) The methods, facilities, and controls used for the manufacturing, processing, packaging, storage, and, where appropriate, installation of the device; or

(iii) Monitoring and review of the investigation.

(c) *Notice of disapproval or withdrawal*. If FDA disapproves an application or proposes to withdraw approval of an application, FDA will notify the sponsor in writing.

(1) A disapproval order will contain a complete statement of the reasons for disapproval and a statement that the sponsor has an opportunity to request a hearing under part 16.

(2) A notice of a proposed withdrawal of approval will contain a complete statement of the reasons for withdrawal and a statement that the sponsor has an opportunity to request a hearing under part 16. FDA will provide the opportunity for hearing before withdrawal of approval, unless FDA determines in the notice that continuation of testing under the exemption will result in an unreasonble risk to the public health and orders withdrawal of approval before any hearing.

## 812. 35 Supplemental applications.

(a) *Changes in investigational plan.*

(1) *Changes requiring prior approval.* Except as described in paragraphs (a)(2) through (a)(4) of this section, a sponsor must obtain approval of a supplemental application under 812. 30 (a), and IRB approval when appropriate (see 56. 110 and 56. 111 of this chapter), prior to implementing a change to an investigational plan. If a sponsor intends to conduct an investigation that involves an exception to informed consent under 50. 24 of this chapter, the sponsor shall submit a separate investigational device exemption (IDE) application in accordance with 812. 20 (a) .

(2) *Changes effected for emergency use.* The requirements of paragraph (a)(1) of this section regarding FDA approval of a supplement do not apply in the case of a deviation from the investigational plan to protect the life or physical well-being of a subject in an emergency. Such deviation shall be reported to FDA within 5-working days after the sponsor learns of it (see 812. 150 (a)(4)).

(3) *Changes effected with notice to FDA within 5 days.* A sponsor may make certain changes without prior approval of a supplemental application under paragraph (a)(1) of this section if the sponsor determines that these changes meet the criteria described in paragraphs (a)(3)(i) and (a)(3)(ii) of this section, on the basis of credible information defined in paragraph (a)(3)(iii) of this section, and the sponsor provides notice to FDA within 5-working days of making these changes.

(i) *Developmental changes.* The requirements in paragraph (a) (1) of this section regarding FDA approval of a supplement do not apply to developmental changes in the device (including manufacturing changes) that do not constitute a significant change in design or basic principles of operation and that are made in response to information gathered during the course of an investigation.

(ii) *Changes to clinical protocol.* The requirements in paragraph (a)(1) of this section regarding FDA approval of a supplement do not apply to changes to clinical protocols that do not affect:

(A) The validity of the data or information resulting from the completion of the approved protocol, or the relationship of likely patient risk to benefit relied upon to approve the protocol;

(B) The scientific soundness of the investigational plan; or

(C) The rights, safety, or welfare of the human subjects involved in the investigation.

(iii) *Definition of credible information.* (A) Credible information to support developmental changes in the device (including manufacturing changes) includes data generated under the design control procedures of 820. 30, preclinical/animal testing, peer reviewed published literature, or other reliable information such as clinical information gathered during a trial or marketing.

(B) Credible information to support changes to clinical protocols is defined as the sponsor's documentation supporting the conclusion that a change does not have a significant impact on the study design or planned statistical analysis, and that the change does not affect the rights, safety, or welfare of the subjects. Documentation shall include information such as peer reviewed published literature, the recommendation of the clinical investigator(s) , and/or the data gathered during the clinical trial or marketing.

(iv) *Notice of IDE change.* Changes meeting the criteria in paragraphs (a)(3)(i) and (a)(3)(ii) of this section that are supported by credible information as defined in paragraph (a)(3)(iii) of this section may be made without prior FDA approval if the sponsor submits a notice of the change to the IDE not later than 5-working days after making the change. Changes to devices are deemed to occur on the date the device, manufactured incorporating the design or manufacturing change, is distributed to the investigator(s). Changes to a clinical protocol are deemed to occur when a clinical investigator is notified by thc sponsor that the change should be implemented in the protocol or, for sponsor-investigator studies, when a sponsor-investigator incorporates the change in the protocol. Such notices shall be identified as a "notice of IDE change."

(A) For a developmental or manufacturing change to the device, the notice shall include a summary of the relevant information gathered during the course of the investigation upon which the change was based; a description of the change to the device or manufacturing process (cross-referenced to the appropriate sections of the original device description or manufacturing process); and, if design controls were used to assess the change, a statement that no new risks were identified by appropriate risk analysis and that the verification and validation testing, as appropriate, demonstrated that the design outputs met the design input requirements. If another method of assessment was used, the notice shall include a summary of the information which served as the credible information supporting the change.

(B) For a protocol change, the notice shall include a description of the change (cross-referenced to the appropriate sections of the original protocol); an assessment supporting the conclusion that the change does not have a significant impact on the study design or planned statistical analysis; and a summary of the information that served as the credible information supporting the sponsor's determination that the change does not affect the rights, safety, or welfare of the subjects.

(4) *Changes submitted in annual report.* The requirements of paragraph (a)(1) of this section do not apply to minor changes to the

purpose of the study, risk analysis, monitoring procedures, labeling, informed consent materials, and IRB information that do not affect:

(i) The validity of the data or information resulting from the completion of the approved protocol, or the relationship of likely patient risk to benefit relied upon to approve the protocol;

(ii) The scientific soundness of the investigational plan; or

(iii) The rights, safety, or welfare of the human subjects involved in the investigation. Such changes shall be reported in the annual progress report for the IDE, under 812. 150 (b)(5) .

(b) *IRB approval for new facilities.* A sponsor shall submit to FDA a certification of any IRB approval of an investigation or a part of an investigation not included in the IDE application. If the investigation is otherwise unchanged, the supplemental application shall consist of an updating of the information required by 812. 20 (b) and (c) and a description of any modifications in the investigational plan required by the IRB as a condition of approval. A certification of IRB approval need not be included in the initial submission of the supplemental application, and such certification is not a precondition for agency consideration of the application. Nevertheless, a sponsor may not begin a part of an investigation at a facility until the IRB has approved the investigation, FDA has received the certification of IRB approval, and FDA, under 812. 30 (a) , has approved the supplemental application relating to that part of the investigation (see 56. 103 (a) ) .

## 812. 36 Treatment use of an investigational device.

(a) *General.* A device that is not approved for marketing may be under clinical investigation for a serious or immediately life-threatening disease or condition in patients for whom no comparable or satisfactory alternative device or other therapy is available. During the clinical trial or prior to final action on the marketing application, it may be appropriate to use the device in the treatment of patients not in the trial under the provisions of a treatment investigational device exemption (IDE) . The purpose of this section is to facilitate the availability of promising new devices to desperately ill patients as early in the device development process as possible, before general marketing begins, and to obtain additional data on the device's safety and effectiveness. In the case of a serious disease, a device ordinarily may be made available for treatment use under this section after all clinical trials have been completed. In the case of an immediately life-threatening disease, a device may be made available for treatment use under this section prior to the completion of all clinical trials. For the purpose of this section, an "immediately life-threatening" disease means a stage of a disease in which there is a reasonable likelihood that death will occur within a matter of months or in which premature death is likely without early treatment. For purposes of this section, "treatment use" of a device includes the use of a device for diagnostic purposes.

(b) *Criteria*. FDA shall consider the use of an investigational device under a treatment IDE if:

  (1) The device is intended to treat or diagnose a serious or immediately life-threatening disease or condition;

  (2) There is no comparable or satisfactory alternative device or other therapy available to treat or diagnose that stage of the disease or condition in the intended patient population;

  (3) The device is under investigation in a controlled clinical trial for the same use under an approved IDE, or such clinical trials have been completed; and

  (4) The sponsor of the investigation is actively pursuing marketing approval/clearance of the investigational device with due diligence.

(c) *Applications for treatment use*.

  (1) A treatment IDE application shall include, in the following order:

    (i) The name, address, and telephone number of the sponsor of the treatment IDE;

    (ii) The intended use of the device, the criteria for patient selection, and a written protocol describing the treatment use;

    (iii) An explanation of the rationale for use of the device, including, as appropriate, either a list of the available regimens that ordinarily should be tried before using the investigational device or an explanation of why the use of the investigational device is preferable to the use of available marketed treatments;

(iv) A description of clinical procedures, laboratory tests, or other measures that will be used to evaluate the effects of the device and to minimize risk;

(v) Written procedures for monitoring the treatment use and the name and address of the monitor;

(vi) Instructions for use for the device and all other labeling as required under 812. 5 (a) and (b) ;

(vii) Information that is relevant to the safety and effectiveness of the device for the intended treatment use. Information from other IDE's may be incorporated by reference to support the treatment use;

(viii) A statement of the sponsor's commitment to meet all applicable responsibilities under this part and part 56 of this chapter and to ensure compliance of all participating investigators with the informed consent requirements of part 50 of this chapter;

(ix) An example of the agreement to be signed by all investigators participating in the treatment IDE and certification that no investigator will be added to the treatment IDE before the agreement is signed; and

(x) If the device is to be sold, the price to be charged and a statement indicating that the price is based on manufacturing and handling costs only.

(2) A licensed practitioner who receives an investigational device for treatment use under a treatment IDE is an " investigator" under the IDE and is responsible for meeting all applicable investigator responsibilities under this part and parts 50 and 56 of this chapter.

(d) *FDA action on treatment IDE applications.*

(1) *Approval of treatment IDE's.* Treatment use may begin 30 days after FDA receives the treatment IDE submission at the address specified in 812. 19, unless FDA notifies the sponsor in writing earlier than the 30 days that the treatment use may or may not begin. FDA may approve the treatment use as proposed or approve it with modifications.

(2) *Disapproval or withdrawal of approval of treatment*

*IDE's*. FDA may disapprove or withdraw approval of a treatment IDE if:

(i) The criteria specified in 812. 36 (b) are not met or the treatment IDE does not contain the information required in 812. 36 (c);

(ii) FDA determines that any of the grounds for disapproval or withdrawal of approval listed in 812. 30 (b)(1) through (b)(5) apply;

(iii) The device is intended for a serious disease or condition and there is insufficient evidence of safety and effectiveness to support such use;

(iv) The device is intended for an immediately life-threatening disease or condition and the available scientific evidence, taken as a whole, fails to provide a reasonable basis for concluding that the device:

 (A) May be effective for its intended use in its intended population; or

 (B) Would not expose the patients to whom the device is to be administered to an unreasonable and significant additional risk of illness or injury;

(v) There is reasonable evidence that the treatment use is impeding enrollment in, or otherwise interfering with the conduct or completion of, a controlled investigation of the same or another investigational device;

(vi) The device has received marketing approval/clearance or a comparable device or therapy becomes available to treat or diagnose the same indication in the same patient population for which the investigational device is being used;

(vii) The sponsor of the controlled clinical trial is not pursuing marketing approval/clearance with due diligence;

(viii) Approval of the IDE for the controlled clinical investigation of the device has been withdrawn; or

(ix) The clinical investigator(s) named in the treatment IDE are not qualified by reason of their scientific training and/or experience to use the investigational device for the intended treatment use.

(3) *Notice of disapproval or withdrawal.* If FDA disapproves or proposes to withdraw approval of a treatment IDE, FDA will follow the procedures set forth in 812. 30 (c) .

(e) *Safeguards.* Treatment use of an investigational device is conditioned upon the sponsor and investigators complying with the safeguards of the IDE process and the regulations governing informed consent (part 50 of this chapter) and institutional review boards (part 56 of this chapter) .

(f) *Reporting requirements.* The sponsor of a treatment IDE shall submit progress reports on a semi-annual basis to all reviewing IRB's and FDA until the filing of a marketing application. These reports shall be based on the period of time since initial approval of the treatment IDE and shall include the number of patients treated with the device under the treatment IDE, the names of the investigators participating in the treatment IDE, and a brief description of the sponsor's efforts to pursue marketing approval/clearance of the device. Upon filing of a marketing application, progress reports shall be submitted annually in accordance with 812. 150 (b)(5) . The sponsor of a treatment IDE is responsible for submitting all other reports required under 812. 150.

## 812. 38 Confidentiality of data and information.

(a) *Existence of IDE.* FDA will not disclose the existence of an IDE unless its existence has previously been publicly disclosed or acknowledged, until FDA approves an application for premarket approval of the device subject to the IDE; or a notice of completion of a product development protocol for the device has become effective.

(b) *Availability of summaries or data.*

(1) FDA will make publicly available, upon request, a detailed summary of information concerning the safety and effectiveness of the device that was the basis for an order approving, disapproving, or withdrawing approval of an application for an IDE for a banned device. The summary shall include information on any adverse effect on health caused by the device.

(2) If a device is a banned device or if the existence of an IDE has been publicly disclosed or acknowledged, data or information contained in the file is not available for public disclosure before approval of an application for premarket approval or the effective

date of a notice of completion of a product development protocol except as provided in this section. FDA may, in its discretion, disclose a summary of selected portions of the safety and effectiveness data, that is, clinical, animal, or laboratory studies and tests of the device, for public consideration of a specific pending issue.

(3) If the existence of an IDE file has not been publicly disclosed or acknowledged, no data or information in the file are available for public disclosure except as provided in paragraphs (b)(1) and (c) of this section.

(4) Notwithstanding paragraph (b)(2) of this section, FDA will make available to the public, upon request, the information in the IDE that was required to be filed in Docket Number 95S-0158 in the Division of Dockets Management (HFA-305) , Food and Drug Administration, 5630 Fishers Lane, rm. 1061, Rockville, MD 20852, for investigations involving an exception from informed consent under 50. 24 of this chapter. Persons wishing to request this information shall submit a request under the Freedom of Information Act.

(c) *Reports of adverse effects*. Upon request or on its own initiative, FDA shall disclose to an individual on whom an investigational device has been used a copy of a report of adverse device effects relating to that use.

(d) *Other rules*. Except as otherwise provided in this section, the availability for public disclosure of data and information in an IDE file shall be handled in accordance with 814. 9.

# Subpart C-Responsibilities of Sponsors

## 812. 40 General responsibilities of sponsors.

Sponsors are responsible for selecting qualified investigators and providing them with the information they need to conduct the investigation properly, ensuring proper monitoring of the investigation, ensuring that IRB review and approval are obtained, submitting an IDE application to FDA, and ensuring that any reviewing IRB and FDA are promptly informed of significant new information about an investigation. Additional responsibilities of sponsors are described in subparts B and G.

## 812. 42 FDA and IRB approval.

A sponsor shall not begin an investigation or part of an investigation until an IRB and FDA have both approved the application or supplemental application relating to the investigation or part of an investigation.

## 812. 43 Selecting investigators and monitors.

(a) *Selecting investigators*. A sponsor shall select investigators qualified by training and experience to investigate the device.

(b) *Control of device*. A sponsor shall ship investigational devices only to qualified investigators participating in the investigation.

(c) *Obtaining agreements*. A sponsor shall obtain from each participating investigator a signed agreement that includes:

(1) The investigator's curriculum vitae.

(2) Where applicable, a statement of the investigator's relevant experience, including the dates, location, extent, and type of experience.

(3) If the investigator was involved in an investigation or other research that was terminated, an explanation of the circumstances that led to termination.

(4) A statement of the investigator's commitment to:

(i) Conduct the investigation in accordance with the agreement, the investigational plan, this part and other applicable FDA regulations, and conditions of approval imposed by the reviewing IRB or FDA;

(ii) Supervise all testing of the device involving human subjects; and

(iii) Ensure that the requirements for obtaining informed consent are met.

(5) Sufficient accurate financial disclosure information to allow the sponsor to submit a complete and accurate certification or disclosure statement as required under part 54 of this chapter. The sponsor shall obtain a commitment from the clinical investigator to promptly update this information if any relevant changes occur during the course of the investigation and for 1 year following completion of the study. This information shall not be submitted in an investigational device exemption application, but

shall be submitted in any marketing application involving the device.

(d) *Selecting monitors.* A sponsor shall select monitors qualified by training and experience to monitor the investigational study in accordance with this part and other applicable FDA regulations.

## 812. 45 Informing investigators.

A sponsor shall supply all investigators participating in the investigation with copies of the investigational plan and the report of prior investigations of the device.

## 812. 46 Monitoring investigations.

(a) *Securing compliance.* A sponsor who discovers that an investigator is not complying with the signed agreement, the investigational plan, the requirements of this part or other applicable FDA regulations, or any conditions of approval imposed by the reviewing IRB or FDA shall promptly either secure compliance, or discontinue shipments of the device to the investigator and terminate the investigator's participation in the investigation. A sponsor shall also require such an investigator to dispose of or return the device, unless this action would jeopardize the rights, safety, or welfare of a subject.

(b) *Unanticipated adverse device effects.*

(1) A sponsor shall immediately conduct an evaluation of any unanticipated adverse device effect.

(2) A sponsor who determines that an unanticipated adverse device effect presents an unreasonable risk to subjects shall terminate all investigations or parts of investigations presenting that risk as soon as possible. Termination shall occur not later than 5 working days after the sponsor makes this determination and not later than 15 working days after the sponsor first received notice of the effect.

(c) *Resumption of terminated studies.* If the device is a significant risk device, a sponsor may not resume a terminated investigation without IRB and FDA approval. If the device is not a significant risk device, a sponsor may not resume a terminated investigation without IRB approval and, if the investigation was terminated under paragraph (b)(2) of this section, FDA approval.

### 812. 47 Emergency research under 50. 24 of this chapter.

(a) The sponsor shall monitor the progress of all investigations involving an exception from informed consent under 50. 24 of this chapter. When the sponsor receives from the IRB information concerning the public disclosures under 50. 24 (a)(7)(ii) and (a)(7)(iii) of this chapter, the sponsor shall promptly submit to the IDE file and to Docket Number 95S-0158 in the Division of Dockets Management (HFA-305) , Food and Drug Administration, 5630 Fishers Lane, rm. 1061, Rockville, MD 20852, copies of the information that was disclosed, identified by the IDE number.

(b) The sponsor also shall monitor such investigations to determine when an IRB determines that it cannot approve the research because it does not meet the criteria in the exception in 50. 24 (a) of this chapter or because of other relevant ethical concerns. The sponsor promptly shall provide this information in writing to FDA, investigators who are asked to participate in this or a substantially equivalent clinical investigation, and other IRB's that are asked to review this or a substantially equivalent investigation.

## Subpart D-IRB Review and Approval

### 812. 60 IRB composition, duties, and functions.

An IRB reviewing and approving investigations under this part shall comply with the requirements of part 56 in all respects, including its composition, duties, and functions.

### 812. 62 IRB approval.

(a) An IRB shall review and have authority to approve, require modifications in (to secure approval) , or disapprove all investigations covered by this part.

(b) If no IRB exists or if FDA finds that an IRB's review is inadequate, a sponsor may submit an application to FDA.

### 812. 64 IRB's continuing review.

The IRB shall conduct its continuing review of an investigation in accordance with part 56.

### 812. 65 [Reserved]

### 812. 66 Significant risk device determinations.

If an IRB determines that an investigation, presented for approval under 812. 2 (b)(1)(ii) , involves a significant risk device, it shall so notify the investigator and, where appropriate, the sponsor. A sponsor may not begin the investigation except as provided in 812. 30 (a) .

## Subpart E-Responsibilities of Investigators

### 812. 100 General responsibilities of investigators.

An investigator is responsible for ensuring that an investigation is conducted according to the signed agreement, the investigational plan and applicable FDA regulations, for protecting the rights, safety, and welfare of subjects under the investigator's care, and for the control of devices under investigation. An investigator also is responsible for ensuring that informed consent is obtained in accordance with part 50 of this chapter. Additional responsibilities of investigators are described in subpart G.

### 812. 110 Specific responsibilities of investigators.

(a) *Awaiting approval.* An investigator may determine whether potential subjects would be interested in participating in an investigation, but shall not request the written informed consent of any subject to participate, and shall not allow any subject to participate before obtaining IRB and FDA approval.

(b) *Compliance.* An investigator shall conduct an investigation in accordance with the signed agreement with the sponsor, the investigational plan, this part and other applicable FDA regulations, and any conditions of approval imposed by an IRB or FDA.

(c) *Supervising device use.* An investigator shall permit an investigational device to be used only with subjects under the investigator's supervision. An investigator shall not supply an investigational device to any person not authorized under this part to receive it.

(d) *Financial disclosure.* A clinical investigator shall disclose to the sponsor sufficient accurate financial information to allow the applicant to submit complete and accurate certification or disclosure statements required under part 54 of this chapter. The investigator shall promptly update this information if any relevant changes occur during the course of the investigation and for 1 year following completion of the study.

(e) *Disposing of device.* Upon completion or termination of a clinical investigation or the investigator's part of an investigation, or at the sponsor's request, an investigator shall return to the sponsor any remaining supply of the device or otherwise dispose of the device as the sponsor directs.

## 812.119 Disqualification of a clinical investigator.

(a) If FDA has information indicating that an investigator (including a sponsor-investigator) has repeatedly or deliberately failed to comply with the requirements of this part, part 50, or part 56 of this chapter, or has repeatedly or deliberately submitted to FDA or to the sponsor false information in any required report, the Center for Devices and Radiological Health, the Center for Biologics Evaluation and Research, or the Center for Drug Evaluation and Research will furnish the investigator written notice of the matter complained of and offer the investigator an opportunity to explain the matter in writing, or, at the option of the investigator, in an informal conference. If an explanation is offered and accepted by the applicable Center, the Center will discontinue the disqualification proceeding. If an explanation is offered but not accepted by the applicable Center, the investigator will be given an opportunity for a regulatory hearing under part 16 of this chapter on the question of whether the investigator is eligible to receive test articles under this part and eligible to conduct any clinical investigation that supports an application for a research or marketing permit for products regulated by FDA.

(b) After evaluating all available information, including any explanation presented by the investigator, if the Commissioner determines that the investigator has repeatedly or deliberately failed to comply with the requirements of this part, part 50, or part 56 of this chapter, or has repeatedly or deliberately submitted to FDA or to the sponsor false information in any required report, the Commissioner will notify the investigator, the sponsor of any investigation in which the investigator has been named as a participant, and the reviewing investigational review boards (IRBs) that the investigator is not eligible to receive test articles under this part. The notification to the investigator, sponsor and IRBs will provide a statement of the basis for such determination. The notification also will explain that an investigator determined to be ineligible to receive test articles under this part will be ineligible to conduct any clinical investigation that supports an application for a research or marketing permit for products regulated by FDA, including drugs, biologics, devices, new animal drugs, foods, including dietary supplements, that bear a nutrient content claim or a health claim, infant formulas, food and color additives, and tobacco products.

(c) Each application or submission to FDA under the provisions of this chapter containing data reported by an investigator who has been determined to be ineligible to receive FDA-regulated test articles is subject to examination to determine whether the investigator has submitted unreliable data that are essential to the continuation of an investigation or essential to the clearance or approval of a marketing application, or essential to the continued marketing of an FDA-regulated product.

(d) If the Commissioner determines, after the unreliable data submitted by the investigator are eliminated from consideration, that the data remaining are inadequate to support a conclusion that it is reasonably safe to continue the investigation, the Commissioner will notify the sponsor, who shall have an opportunity for a regulatory hearing under part 16 of this chapter. If a danger to the public health exists, however, the Commissioner shall terminate the investigational device exemption (IDE) immediately and notify the sponsor and the reviewing IRBs of the termination. In such case, the sponsor shall have an opportunity for a regulatory hearing before FDA under part 16 of this chapter on the question of whether the IDE should be reinstated. The determination that an investigation may not be considered in support of a research or marketing application or a notification or petition submission does not, however, relieve the sponsor of any obligation under any other applicable regulation to submit to FDA the results of the investigation.

(e) If the Commissioner determines, after the unreliable data submitted by the investigator are eliminated from consideration, that the continued clearance or approval of the product for which the data were submitted cannot be justified, the Commissioner will proceed to rescind clearance or withdraw approval of the product in accordance with the applicable provisions of the relevant statutes.

(f) An investigator who has been determined to be ineligible under paragraph (b) of this section may be reinstated as eligible when the Commissioner determines that the investigator has presented adequate assurances that the investigator will employ all test articles, and will conduct any clinical investigation that supports an application for a research or marketing permit for products regulated by FDA, solely in compliance with the applicable provisions of this chapter.

# Subpart F [Reserved]

# Subpart G-Records and Reports

## 812. 140 Records.

(a) *Investigator records*. A participating investigator shall maintain the following accurate, complete, and current records relating to the investigator's participation in an investigation:

(1) All correspondence with another investigator, an IRB, the sponsor, a monitor, or FDA, including required reports.

(2) Records of receipt, use or disposition of a device that relate to:

(i) The type and quantity of the device, the dates of its receipt, and the batch number or code mark.

(ii) The names of all persons who received, used, or disposed of each device.

(iii) Why and how many units of the device have been returned to the sponsor, repaired, or otherwise disposed of.

(3) Records of each subject's case history and exposure to the device. Case histories include the case report forms and supporting data including, for example, signed and dated consent forms and

medical records including, for example, progress notes of the physician, the individual's hospital chart ( s ) , and the nurses' notes. Such records shall include:

(i) Documents evidencing informed consent and, for any use of a device by the investigator without informed consent, any written concurrence of a licensed physician and a brief description of the circumstances justifying the failure to obtain informed consent. The case history for each individual shall document that informed consent was obtained prior to participation in the study.

(ii) All relevant observations, including records concerning adverse device effects (whether anticipated or unanticipated) , information and data on the condition of each subject upon entering, and during the course of, the investigation, including information about relevant previous medical history and the results of all diagnostic tests.

(iii) A record of the exposure of each subject to the investigational device, including the date and time of each use, and any other therapy.

(4) The protocol, with documents showing the dates of and reasons for each deviation from the protocol.

(5) Any other records that FDA requires to be maintained by regulation or by specific requirement for a category of investigations or a particular investigation.

(b) *Sponsor records*. A sponsor shall maintain the following accurate, complete, and current records relating to an investigation:

(1) All correspondence with another sponsor, a monitor, an investigator, an IRB, or FDA, including required reports.

(2) Records of shipment and disposition. Records of shipment shall include the name and address of the consignee, type and quantity of device, date of shipment, and batch number or code mark. Records of disposition shall describe the batch number or code marks of any devices returned to the sponsor, repaired, or disposed of in other ways by the investigator or another person, and the reasons for and method of disposal.

(3) Signed investigator agreements including the financial disclosure

information required to be collected under 812. 43 (c)(5) in accordance with part 54 of this chapter.

(4) For each investigation subject to 812. 2 (b)(1) of a device other than a significant risk device, the records described in paragraph (b)(5) of this section and the following records, consolidated in one location and available for FDA inspection and copying:

(i) The name and intended use of the device and the objectives of the investigation;

(ii) A brief explanation of why the device is not a significant risk device:

(iii) The name and address of each investigator:

(iv) The name and address of each IRB that has reviewed the investigation:

(v) A statement of the extent to which the good manufacturing practice regulation in part 820 will be followed in manufacturing the device; and

(vi) Any other information required by FDA.

(5) Records concerning adverse device effects (whether anticipated or unanticipated) and complaints and

(6) Any other records that FDA requires to be maintained by regulation or by specific requirement for a category of investigation or a particular investigation.

(c) *IRB records*. An IRB shall maintain records in accordance with part 56 of this chapter.

(d) *Retention period*. An investigator or sponsor shall maintain the records required by this subpart during the investigation and for a period of 2 years after the latter of the following two dates: The date on which the investigation is terminated or completed, or the date that the records are no longer required for purposes of supporting a premarket approval application or a notice of completion of a product development protocol.

(e) *Records custody*. An investigator or sponsor may withdraw from the responsibility to maintain records for the period required in paragraph (d) of this section and transfer custody of the records to any other person who will accept responsibility for them under this part, including the requirements of 812. 145. Notice of a transfer shall be given to FDA not later than 10 working days after transfer occurs.

## 812. 145 Inspections.

(a) *Entry and inspection.* A sponsor or an investigator who has authority to grant access shall permit authorized FDA employees, at reasonable times and in a reasonable manner, to enter and inspect any establishment where devices are held (including any establishment where devices are manufactured, processed, packed, installed, used, or implanted or where records of results from use of devices are kept) .

(b) *Records inspection.* A sponsor, IRB, or investigator, or any other person acting on behalf of such a person with respect to an investigation, shall permit authorized FDA employees, at reasonable times and in a reasonable manner, to inspect and copy all records relating to an investigation.

(c) *Records identifying subjects.* An investigator shall permit authorized FDA employees to inspect and copy records that identify subjects, upon notice that FDA has reason to suspect that adequate informed consent was not obtained, or that reports required to be submitted by the investigator to the sponsor or IRB have not been submitted or are incomplete, inaccurate, false, or misleading.

## 812. 150 Reports.

(a) *Investigator reports.* An investigator shall prepare and submit the following complete, accurate, and timely reports:

(1) *Unanticipated adverse device effects.* An investigator shall submit to the sponsor and to the reviewing IRB a report of any unanticipated adverse device effect occurring during an investigation as soon as possible, but in no event later than 10 working days after the investigator first learns of the effect.

(2) *Withdrawal of IRB approval.* An investigator shall report to the sponsor, within 5 working days, a withdrawal of approval by the reviewing IRB of the investigator's part of an investigation.

(3) *Progress.* An investigator shall submit progress reports on the investigation to the sponsor, the monitor, and the reviewing IRB at regular intervals, but in no event less often than yearly.

(4) *Deviations from the investigational plan.* An investigator shall notify the sponsor and the reviewing IRB (see 56. 108 (a)(3) and (4)) of any deviation from the investigational plan to protect the life or physical well-being of a subject in an emergency. Such notice shall be given as soon as possible, but in no event later than 5 working days after the emergency occurred. Except in such an emergency, prior approval by the sponsor is required for changes in or deviations from a plan, and if these changes or deviations may affect the scientific soundness of the plan or the rights, safety, or welfare of human subjects, FDA and IRB in accordance with 812. 35 (a) also is required.

(5) *Informed consent.* If an investigator uses a device without obtaining informed consent, the investigator shall report such use to the sponsor and the reviewing IRB within 5 working days after the use occurs.

(6) *Final report.* An investigator shall, within 3 months after termination or completion of the investigation or the investigator's part of the investigation, submit a final report to the sponsor and the reviewing IRB.

(7) *Other.* An investigator shall, upon request by a reviewing IRB or FDA, provide accurate, complete, and current information about any aspect of the investigation.

(b) *Sponsor reports.* A sponsor shall prepare and submit the following complete, accurate, and timely reports:

(1) *Unanticipated adverse device effects.* A sponsor who conducts an evaluation of an unanticipated adverse device effect under 812. 46 (b) shall report the results of such evaluation to FDA and to all reviewing IRB's and participating investigators within 10 working days after the sponsor first receives notice of the effect. Thereafter the sponsor shall submit such additional reports concerning the effect as FDA requests.

(2) *Withdrawal of IRB approval.* A sponsor shall notify FDA and all reviewing IRB's and participating investigators of any withdrawal of approval of an investigation or a part of an investigation by a reviewing IRB within 5 working days after receipt of the withdrawal of approval.

(3) *Withdrawal of FDA approval.* A sponsor shall notify all reviewing IRB's and participating investigators of any withdrawal of FDA approval of the investigation, and shall do so within 5 working days after receipt of notice of the withdrawal of approval.

(4) *Current investigator list.* A sponsor shall submit to FDA, at 6-month intervals, a current list of the names and addresses of all investigators participating in the investigation. The sponsor shall submit the first such list 6 months after FDA approval.

(5) *Progress reports.* At regular intervals, and at least yearly, a sponsor shall submit progress reports to all reviewing IRB's. In the case of a significant risk device, a sponsor shall also submit progress reports to FDA. A sponsor of a treatment IDE shall submit semi-annual progress reports to all reviewing IRB's and FDA in accordance with 812. 36 (f) and annual reports in accordance with this section.

(6) *Recall and device disposition.* A sponsor shall notify FDA and all reviewing IRB's of any request that an investigator return, repair, or otherwise dispose of any units of a device. Such notice shall occur within 30 working days after the request is made and shall state why the request was made.

(7) *Final report.* In the case of a significant risk device, the sponsor shall notify FDA within 30 working days of the completion or termination of the investigation and shall submit a final report to FDA and all reviewing the IRB's and participating investigators within 6 months after completion or termination. In the case of a device that is not a significant risk device, the sponsor shall submit a final report to all reviewing IRB's within 6 months after termination or completion.

(8) *Informed consent.* A sponsor shall submit to FDA a copy of any report by an investigator under paragraph (a)(5) of this section of use of a device without obtaining informed consent, within 5 working days of receipt of notice of such use.

(9) *Significant risk device determinations.* If an IRB determines that a device is a significant risk device, and the sponsor had proposed that the IRB consider the device not to be a significant risk

device, the sponsor shall submit to FDA a report of the IRB's determination within 5 working days after the sponsor first learns of the IRB's determination.

(10) *Other*. A sponsor shall, upon request by a reviewing IRB or FDA, provide accurate, complete, and current information about any aspect of the investigation.

[Effective July 14,2009]

# 45CFR PART46 PROTECTION OF HUMAN SUBJECTS

## Subpart A-Basic HHS Policy for Protection of Human Research Subjects

### 46. 101 To what does this policy apply? (Omit)

### 46. 102 Definitions.

(a) *Department or agency head* means the head of any federal department or agency and any other officer or employee of any department or agency to whom authority has been delegated.

(b) *Institution* means any public or private entity or agency (including federal, state, and other agencies).

(c) *Legally* authorized representative means an individual or judicial or other body authorized under applicable law to consent on behalf of a prospective subject to the subject's participation in the procedure(s) involved in the research.

(d) *Research* means a systematic investigation, including research development, testing and evaluation, designed to develop or contribute to generalizable knowledge. Activities which meet this definition constitute research for purposes of this policy, whether or not they are conducted or supported under a program which is considered research for other purposes. For example, some demonstration and service programs may include research activities.

(e) *Research subject to regulation*, and similar terms are intended to encompass those research activities for which a federal department or agency has specific responsibility for regulating as a research activity, (for example, Investigational New Drug requirements administered by the Food and Drug Administration). It does not include research activities which are incidentally regulated by a federal department or agency solely as part of the department's or agency's broader responsibility to regulate certain types of activities whether research or non-research in nature (for example, Wage and Hour requirements administered by the Department of Labor) .

(f) *Human subject* means a living individual about whom an investigator (whether professional or student) conducting research obtains

(1) Data through intervention or interaction with the individual, or

(2) Identifiable private information.

Interventionincludes both physical procedures by which data are gathered (for example, venipuncture) and manipulations of the subject or the subject's environment that are performed for research purposes. Interaction includes communication or interpersonal contact between investigator and subject. Private information includes information about behavior that occurs in a context in which an individual can reasonably expect that no observation or recording is taking place, and information which has been provided for specific purposes by an individual and which the individual can reasonably expect will not be made public (for example, a medical record) . Private information must be individually identifiable (i. e. , the identity of the subject is or may readily be ascertained by the investigator or associated with the information) in order for obtaining the information to constitute research involving human subjects.

(g) *IRB* means an institutional review board established in accord with and for the purposes expressed in this policy.

(h) *IRB approval* means the determination of the IRB that the research has been reviewed and may be conducted at an institution within the constraints set forth by the IRB and by other institutional and federal requirements.

(i) *Minimal risk* means that the probability and magnitude of harm or discomfort anticipated in the research are not greater in and of themselves than those ordinarily encountered in daily life or during the performance of routine physical or psychological examinations or tests.

(j) *Certification* means the official notification by the institution to the supporting department or agency, in accordance with the requirements of this policy, that a research project or activity involving human subjects has been reviewed and approved by an IRB in accordance with an approved assurance.

## 46. 103 Assuring compliance with this policy—research conducted or supported by any Federal Department or Agency.

(a) Each institution engaged in research which is covered by this policy and which is conducted or supported by a federal department or agency shall provide written assurance satisfactory to the department or agency head that it will comply with the requirements set forth in this policy. In lieu of requiring submission of an assurance, individual department or agency heads shall accept the existence of a current assurance, appropriate for the research in question, on file with the Office for Human Research Protections, HHS, or any successor office, and approved for federalwide use by that office. When the existence of an HHS-approved assurance is accepted in lieu of requiring submission of an assurance, reports (except certification) required by this policy to be made to department and agency heads shall also be made to the Office for Human Research Protections, HHS, or any successor office.

(b) Departments and agencies will conduct or support research covered by this policy only if the institution has an assurance approved as provided in this section, and only if the institution has certified to the department or agency head that the research has been reviewed and approved by an IRB provided for in the assurance, and will be subject to continuing review by the IRB. Assurances applicable to federally supported or conducted research shall at a minimum include:

(1) A statement of principles governing the institution in the discharge of its responsibilities for protecting the rights and welfare of human subjects of research conducted at or sponsored by the institution, regardless of whether the research is subject to Federal regulation. This may include an appropriate existing code, declaration, or statement of ethical principles, or a statement formulated by the institution itself. This requirement does not preempt provisions of this policy applicable to department- or agency-supported or regulated research and need not be applicable to any research exempted or waived under 46. 101 (b) or (i) .

(2) Designation of one or more IRBs established in accordance with the requirements of this policy, and for which provisions are made for meeting space and sufficient staff to support the IRB's review and recordkeeping duties.

(3) A list of IRB members identified by name; earned degrees; representative capacity; indications of experience such as board certifications, licenses, etc., sufficient to describe each member's chief anticipated contributions to IRB deliberations; and any employment or other relationship between each member and the institution; for example: full-time employee, part-time employee, member of governing panel or board, stockholder, paid or unpaid consultant. Changes in IRB membership shall be reported to the department or agency head, unless in accord with 46. 103 (a) of this policy, the existence of an HHS-approved assurance is accepted. In this case, change in IRB membership shall be reported to the Office for Human Research Protections, HHS, or any successor office.

(4) Written procedures which the IRB will follow (i) for conducting its initial and continuing review of research and for reporting its findings and actions to the investigator and the institution; (ii) for determining which projects require review more often than annually and which projects need verification from sources other than the investigators that no material changes have occurred since previous IRB review; and (iii) for ensuring prompt reporting to the IRB of proposed changes in a research activity, and for ensuring that such changes in approved research, during the period for which IRB approval has already been given, may not be initiated without IRB review and approval except when necessary to eliminate apparent immediate hazards to the subject.

(5) Written procedures for ensuring prompt reporting to the IRB, appropriate institutional officials, and the department or agency head of (i) any unanticipated problems involving risks to subjects or others or any serious or continuing noncompliance with this policy or the requirements or determinations of the IRB; and (ii) any suspension or termination of IRB approval.

(c) The assurance shall be executed by an individual authorized to act for the institution and to assume on behalf of the institution the obligations imposed by this policy and shall be filed in such form and manner as the department or agency head prescribes.

(d) The department or agency head will evaluate all assurances submitted in accordance with this policy through such officers and employees of the department or agency and such experts or consultants engaged for this purpose as the department or agency head determines to be appropriate. The department or agency head's evaluation will take into consideration the adequacy of the proposed IRB in light of the anticipated scope of the institution's research activities and the types of subject populations likely to be involved, the appropriateness of the proposed initial and continuing review procedures in light of the probable risks, and the size and complexity of the institution.

(e) On the basis of this evaluation, the department or agency head may approve or disapprove the assurance, or enter into negotiations to develop an approvable one. The department or agency head may limit the period during which any particular approved assurance or class of approved assurances shall remain effective or otherwise condition or restrict approval.

(f) Certification is required when the research is supported by a federal department or agency and not otherwise exempted or waived under 46. 101 (b) or (i) . An institution with an approved assurance shall certify that each application or proposal for research covered by the assurance and by 46. 103 of this Policy has been reviewed and approved by the IRB. Such certification must be submitted with the application or proposal or by such later date as may be prescribed by the department or agency to which the application or proposal is submitted. Under no condition shall research covered by46. 103 of the Policy be supported prior to receipt of the certification that the research has been reviewed and approved by the IRB. Institutions without an approved assurance covering the research shall certify within 30 days after receipt of a request for such a certification from the department or agency, that the application or proposal has been approved by the IRB. If the certification is not submitted within these time limits, the application or proposal may be returned to the institution.

## 46. 104—46. 106 [Reserved]

## 46. 107 IRB membership.

(a) Each IRB shall have at least five members, with varying backgrounds to promote complete and adequate review of research activities commonly conducted by the institution. The IRB shall be sufficiently qualified through the experience and expertise of its members, and the diversity of the members, including consideration of race, gender, and cultural backgrounds and sensitivity to such issues as community attitudes, to promote respect for its advice and counsel in safeguarding the rights and welfare of human subjects. In addition to possessing the professional competence necessary to review specific research activities, the IRB shall be able to ascertain the acceptability of proposed research in terms of institutional commitments and regulations, applicable law, and standards of professional conduct and practice. The IRB shall therefore include persons knowledgeable in these areas. If an IRB regularly reviews research that involves a vulnerable category of subjects, such as children, prisoners, pregnant women, or handicapped or mentally disabled persons, consideration shall be given to the inclusion of one or more individuals who are knowledgeable about and experienced in working with these subjects.

(b) Every nondiscriminatory effort will be made to ensure that no IRB consists entirely of men or entirely of women, including the institution's consideration of qualified persons of both sexes, so long as no selection is made to the IRB on the basis of gender. No IRB may consist entirely of members of one profession.

(c) Each IRB shall include at least one member whose primary concerns are in scientific areas and at least one member whose primary concerns are in nonscientific areas.

(d) Each IRB shall include at least one member who is not otherwise affiliated with the institution and who is not part of the immediate family of a person who is affiliated with the institution.

(e) No IRB may have a member participate in the IRB's initial or continuing review of any project in which the member has a conflicting interest, except to provide information requested by the IRB.

(f) An IRB may, in its discretion, invite individuals with competence in special areas to assist in the review of issues which require expertise beyond or in addition to that available on the IRB. These individuals may not vote with the IRB.

## 46. 108 IRB functions and operations.

In order to fulfill the requirements of this policy each IRB shall:

(a) Follow written procedures in the same detail as described in 46. 103 (b) (4) and, to the extent required by, 46. 103 (b)(5) .

(b) Except when an expedited review procedure is used (see 46. 110) , review proposed research at convened meetings at which a majority of the members of the IRB are present, including at least one member whose primary concerns are in nonscientific areas. In order for the research to be approved, it shall receive the approval of a majority of those members present at the meeting.

## 46. 109 IRB review of research.

(a) An IRB shall review and have authority to approve, require modifications in (to secure approval) , or disapprove all research activities covered by this policy.

(b) An IRB shall require that information given to subjects as part of informed consent is in accordance with 46. 116. The IRB may require that information, in addition to that specifically mentioned in 46. 116, be given to the subjects when in the IRB's judgment the information would meaningfully add to the protection of the rights and welfare of subjects.

(c) An IRB shall require documentation of informed consent or may waive documentation in accordance with 46. 117.

(d) An IRB shall notify investigators and the institution in writing of its decision to approve or disapprove the proposed research activity, or of modifications required to secure IRB approval of the research activity. If the IRB decides to disapprove a research activity, it shall include in its written notification a statement of the reasons for its decision and give the investigator an opportunity to respond in person or in writing.

(e) An IRB shall conduct continuing review of research covered by this policy at intervals appropriate to the degree of risk, but not less than once per year, and shall have authority to observe or have a third party observe the consent process and the research.

## 46. 110 Expedited review procedures for certain kinds of research involving no more than minimal risk, and for minor changes in approved research.

(a) The Secretary, HHS, has established, and published as a Notice in the FEDERAL REGISTER, alist of categories of research that may be reviewed by the IRB through an expedited review procedure. The list will be amended, as appropriate, after consultation with other departments and agencies, through periodic republication by the Secretary, HHS, in the FEDERAL REGISTER. A copy of the list is available from the Office for Human Research Protections, HHS, or any successor office.

(b) An IRB may use the expedited review procedure to review either or both of the following:

  (1) some or all of the research appearing on the list and found by the reviewer(s) to involve no more than minimal risk,

  (2) minor changes in previously approved research during the period (of one year or less) for which approval is authorized.

  Under an expedited review procedure, the review may be carried out by the IRB chairperson or by one or more experienced reviewers designated by the chairperson from among members of the IRB. In reviewing the research, the reviewers may exercise all of the authorities of the IRB except that the reviewers may not disapprove the research. A research activity may be disapproved only after review in accordance with the non-expedited procedure set forth in 46. 108 (b) .

(c) Each IRB which uses an expedited review procedure shall adopt a method for keeping all members advised of research proposals which have been approved under the procedure.

(d) The department or agency head may restrict, suspend, terminate, or choose not to authorize an institution's or IRB's use of the expedited review procedure.

## 46. 111 Criteria for IRB approval of research.

(a) In order to approve research covered by this policy the IRB shall determine that all of the following requirements are satisfied:

  (1) Risks to subjects are minimized:(i) By using procedures which are consistent with sound research design and which do not unnecessarily expose subjects to risk, and (ii) whenever appropriate, by using procedures already being performed on the subjects for diagnostic or treatment purposes.

  (2) Risks to subjects are reasonable in relation to anticipated benefits, if any, to subjects, and the importance of the knowledge that may reasonably be expected to result. In evaluating risks and benefits, the IRB should consider only those risks and benefits that may result from the research (as distinguished from risks and benefits of therapies subjects would receive even if not participating in the re-

search) . The IRB should not consider possible long-range effects of applying knowledge gained in the research (for example, the possible effects of the research on public policy) as among those research risks that fall within the purview of its responsibility.

(3) Selection of subjects is equitable. In making this assessment the IRB should take into account the purposes of the research and the setting in which the research will be conducted and should be particularly cognizant of the special problems of research involving vulnerable populations, such as children, prisoners, pregnant women, mentally disabled persons, or economically or educationally disadvantaged persons.

(4) Informed consent will be sought from each prospective subject or the subject's legally authorized representative, in accordance with, and to the extent required by 46. 116.

(5) Informed consent will be appropriately documented, in accordance with, and to the extent required by 46. 117.

(6) When appropriate, the research plan makes adequate provision for monitoring the data collected to ensure the safety of subjects.

(7) When appropriate, there are adequate provisions to protect the privacy of subjects and to maintain the confidentiality of data.

(b) When some or all of the subjects are likely to be vulnerable to coercion or undue influence, such as children, prisoners, pregnant women, mentally disabled persons, or economically or educationally disadvantaged persons, additional safeguards have been included in the study to protect the rights and welfare of these subjects.

## 46. 112 Review by institution.

Research covered by this policy that has been approved by an IRB may be subject to further appropriate review and approval or disapproval by officials of the institution. However, those officials may not approve the research if it has not been approved by an IRB.

## 46. 113 Suspension or termination of IRB approval of research.

An IRB shall have authority to suspend or terminate approval of research that is not being conducted in accordance with the IRB's requirements or that has been associated with unexpected serious harm to subjects. Any suspension or termination of approval shall include a statement of the reasons for the IRB's action and shall be reported promptly to the investigator, appropriate institutional officials, and the department or agency head.

## 46. 114 Cooperative research.

Cooperative research projects are those projects covered by this policy which involve more than one institution. In the conduct of cooperative research projects, each institution is responsible for safeguarding the rights and welfare of human subjects and for complying with this policy. With the approval of the department or agency head, an institution participating in a cooperative project may enter into a joint review arrangement, rely upon the review of another qualified IRB, or make similar arrangements for avoiding duplication of effort.

## 46. 115 IRB records.

(a) An institution, or when appropriate an IRB, shall prepare and maintain adequate documentation of IRB activities, including the following:

(1) Copies of all research proposals reviewed, scientific evaluations, if any, that accompany the proposals, approved sample consent documents, progress reports submitted by investigators, and reports of injuries to subjects.

(2) Minutes of IRB meetings which shall be in sufficient detail to show attendance at the meetings; actions taken by the IRB; the vote on these actions including the number of members voting for, against, and abstaining; the basis for requiring changes in or disapproving research; and a written summary of the discussion of controverted issues and their resolution.

(3) Records of continuing review activities.

(4) Copies of all correspondence between the IRB and the investigators.

(5) A list of IRB members in the same detail as described in 46. 103 (b)(3) .

(6) Written procedures for the IRB in the same detail as described in 46. 103 (b)(4) and46. 103 (b)(5) .

(7) Statements of significant new findings provided to subjects, as required by 46. 116 (b)(5) .

(b) The records required by this policy shall be retained for at least 3 years, and records relating to research which is conducted shall be retained for at least 3 years after completion of the research. All records shall be accessible for inspection and copying by authorized representatives of the department or agency at reasonable times and in a reasonable manner.

## 46. 116 General requirements for informed consent.

Except as provided elsewhere in this policy, no investigator may involve a human being as a subject in research covered by this policy unless the investigator has obtained the legally effective informed consent of the subject or the subject's legally authorized representative. An investigator shall seek such consent only under circumstances that provide the prospective subject or the representative sufficient opportunity to consider whether or not to participate and that minimize the possibility of coercion or undue influence. The information that is given to the subject or the representative shall be in language understandable to the subject or the representative. No informed consent, whether oral or written, may include any exculpatory language through which the subject or the representative is made to waive or appear to waive any of the subject's legal rights, or releases or appears to release the investigator, the sponsor, thc institution or its agents from liability for negligence.

(a) Basic elements of informed consent. Except as provided in paragraph (c) or (d) of this section, in seeking informed consent the following information shall be provided to each subject:

(1) A statement that the study involves research, an explanation of the purposes of the research and the expected duration of the subject's participation, a description of the procedures to be followed, and identification of any procedures which are experimental;

(2) A description of any reasonably foreseeable risks or discomforts to the subject;

(3) A description of any benefits to the subject or to others which may reasonably be expected from the research;

(4) A disclosure of appropriate alternative procedures or courses of treatment, if any, that might be advantageous to the subject;

(5) A statement describing the extent, if any, to which confidentiality of records identifying the subject will be maintained;

(6) For research involving more than minimal risk, an explanation as to whether any compensation and an explanation as to whether any medical treatments are available if injury occurs and, if so, what they consist of, or where further information may be obtained;

(7) An explanation of whom to contact for answers to pertinent questions about the research and research subjects' rights, and whom to contact in the event of a research-related injury to the subject; and

(8) A statement that participation is voluntary, refusal to participate will involve no penalty or loss of benefits to which the subject is otherwise entitled, and the subject may discontinue participation at any time without penalty or loss of benefits to which the subject is otherwise entitled.

(b) Additional elements of informed consent. When appropriate, one or more of the following elements of information shall also be provided to each subject:

(1) A statement that the particular treatment or procedure may involve risks to the subject (or to the embryo or fetus, if the subject is or may become pregnant) which are currently unforeseeable;

(2) Anticipated circumstances under which the subject's participation may be terminated by the investigator without regard to the subject's consent;

(3) Any additional costs to the subject that may result from participation in the research;

(4) The consequences of a subject's decision to withdraw from the research and procedures for orderly termination of participation by the subject;

(5) A statement that significant new findings developed during the course of the research which may relate to the subject's willingness to continue participation will be provided to the subject; and

(6) The approximate number of subjects involved in the study.

(c) An IRB may approve a consent procedure which does not include, or which alters, some or all of the elements of informed consent set forth above, or waive the requirement to obtain informed consent provided the IRB finds and documents that:

(1) The research or demonstration project is to be conducted by or subject to the approval of state or local government officials and is designed to study, evaluate, or otherwise examine: (i) public benefit or service programs; (ii) procedures for obtaining benefits or services under those programs; (iii) possible changes in or alternatives to those programs or procedures; or (iv) possible changes in meth-

ods or levels of payment for benefits or services under those programs; and

(2) The research could not practicably be carried out without the waiver or alteration.

(d) An IRB may approve a consent procedure which does not include, or which alters, some or all of the elements of informed consent set forth in this section, or waive the requirements to obtain informed consent provided the IRB finds and documents that:

(1) The research involves no more than minimal risk to the subjects;

(2) The waiver or alteration will not adversely affect the rights and welfare of the subjects;

(3) The research could not practicably be carried out without the waiver or alteration; and

(4) Whenever appropriate, the subjects will be provided with additional pertinent information after participation.

(e) The informed consent requirements in this policy are not intended to preempt any applicable federal, state, or local laws which require additional information to be disclosed in order for informed consent to be legally effective.

(f) Nothing in this policy is intended to limit the authority of a physician to provide emergency medical care, to the extent the physician is permitted to do so under applicable federal, state, or local law.

## 46. 117 Documentation of informed consent.

(a) Except as provided in paragraph (c) of this section, informed consent shall be documented by the use of a written consent form approved by the IRB and signed by the subject or the subject's legally authorized representative. A copy shall be given to the person signing the form.

(b) Except as provided in paragraph (c) of this section, the consent form may be either of the following:

(1) A written consent document that embodies the elements of informed consent required by46. 116. This form may be read to the subject or the subject's legally authorized representative, but in any event, the investigator shall give either the subject or the representative adequate opportunity to read it before it is signed; or

(2) A short form written consent document stating that the elements of informed consent required by 46. 116 have been presented orally to the subject or the subject's legally authorized representative. When this

method is used, there shall be a witness to the oral presentation. Also, the IRB shall approve a written summary of what is to be said to the subject or the representative. Only the short form itself is to be signed by the subject or the representative. However, the witness shall sign both the short form and a copy of the summary, and the person actually obtaining consent shall sign a copy of the summary. A copy of the summary shall be given to the subject or the representative, in addition to a copy of the short form.

(c) An IRB may waive the requirement for the investigator to obtain a signed consent form for some or all subjects if it finds either:

(1) That the only record linking the subject and the research would be the consent document and the principal risk would be potential harm resulting from a breach of confidentiality. Each subject will be asked whether the subject wants documentation linking the subject with the research, and the subject's wishes will govern; or

(2) That the research presents no more than minimal risk of harm to subjects and involves no procedures for which written consent is normally required outside of the research context.

In cases in which the documentation requirement is waived, the IRB may require the investigator to provide subjects with a written statement regarding the research.

## 46. 118 Applications and proposals lacking definite plans for involvement of human subjects.

Certain types of applications for grants, cooperative agreements, or contracts are submitted to departments or agencies with the knowledge that subjects may be involved within the period of support, but definite plans would not normally be set forth in the application or proposal. These include activities such as institutional type grants when selection of specific projects is the institution's responsibility; research training grants in which the activities involving subjects remain to be selected; and projects in which human subjects' involvement will depend upon completion of instruments, prior animal studies, or purification of compounds. These applications need not be reviewed by an IRB before an award may be made. However, except for research exempted or waived under 46. 101 (b) or (i) , no human subjects may be involved in any project supported by these awards until the project has been reviewed and approved by the IRB, as provided in this policy, and certification submitted, by the institution, to the department or agency.

### 46. 119 Research undertaken without the intention of involving human subjects.

In the event research is undertaken without the intention of involving human subjects, but it is later proposed to involve human subjects in the research, the research shall first be reviewed and approved by an IRB, as provided in this policy, a certification submitted, by the institution, to the department or agency, and final approval given to the proposed change by the department or agency.

### 46. 120 Evaluation and disposition of applications and proposals for research to be conducted or supported by a Federal Department or Agency.

(a) The department or agency head will evaluate all applications and proposals involving human subjects submitted to the department or agency through such officers and employees of the department or agency and such experts and consultants as the department or agency head determines to be appropriate. This evaluation will take into consideration the risks to the subjects, the adequacy of protection against these risks, the potential benefits of the research to the subjects and others, and the importance of the knowledge gained or to be gained.

(b) On the basis of this evaluation, the department or agency head may approve or disapprove the application or proposal, or enter into negotiations to develop an approvable one.

### 46. 121 [Reserved]

### 46. 122 Use of Federal funds.

Federal funds administered by a department or agency may not be expended for research involving human subjects unless the requirements of this policy have been satisfied.

### 46. 123 Early termination of research support: Evaluation of applications and proposals.

(a) The department or agency head may require that department or agency support for any project be terminated or suspended in the manner prescribed in applicable program requirements, when the department or agency head finds an institution has materially failed to comply with the terms of this policy.

(b) In making decisions about supporting or approving applications or proposals covered by this policy the department or agency head may take into account, in addition to all other eligibility requirements and program criteria, factors such as whether the applicant has been subject to a termination or suspension under paragraph (a) of this section and whether the applicant or the person or persons who would direct or has/have directed the scientific and technical aspects of an activity has/have, in the judgment of the department or agency head, materially failed to discharge responsibility for the protection of the rights and welfare of human subjects (whether or not the research was subject to federal regulation).

### 46. 124 Conditions.

With respect to any research project or any class of research projects the department or agency head may impose additional conditions prior to or at the time of approval when in the judgment of the department or agency head additional conditions are necessary for the protection of human subjects.

## Subpart B-Additional Protections for Pregnant Women, Human Fetuses and Neonates Involved in Research

### 46. 201 To what do these regulations apply? (Omit)

### 46. 202 Definitions.

The definitions in 46. 102 shall be applicable to this subpart as well. In addition, as used in this subpart:

(a) *Dead fetus* means a fetus that exhibits neither heartbeat, spontaneous respiratory activity, spontaneous movement of voluntary muscles, nor pulsation of the umbilical cord.

(b) *Delivery* means complete separation of the fetus from the woman by expulsion or extraction or any other means.

(c) *Fetus* means the product of conception from implantation until delivery.

(d) *Neonate* means a newborn.

(e) *Nonviable neonate* means a neonate after delivery that, although living, is not viable.

(f) *Pregnancy* encompasses the period of time from implantation until delivery. A woman shall be assumed to be pregnant if she exhibits any of the pertinent presumptive signs of pregnancy, such as missed menses, until the results of a pregnancy test are negative or until delivery.

(g) *Secretary* means the Secretary of Health and Human Services and any other officer or employee of the Department of Health and Human Services to whom authority has been delegated.

(h) *Viable*, as it pertains to the neonate, means being able, after delivery, to survive (given the benefit of available medical therapy) to the point of independently maintaining heartbeat and respiration. The Secretary may from time to time, taking into account medical advances, publish in the FEDERAL REGISTER guidelines to assist in determining whether a neonate is viable for purposes of this subpart. If a neonate is viable then it may be included in research only to the extent permitted and in accordance with the requirements of subparts A and D of this part.

## 46. 203 Duties of IRBs in connection with research involving pregnant women, fetuses, and neonates.

In addition to other responsibilities assigned to IRBs under this part, each IRB shall review research covered by this subpart and approve only research which satisfies the conditions of all applicable sections of this subpart and the other subparts of this part.

## 46. 204 Research involving pregnant women or fetuses.

Pregnant women or fetuses may be involved in research if all of the following conditions are met:

(a) Where scientifically appropriate, preclinical studies, including studies on pregnant animals, and clinical studies, including studies on nonpregnant women, have been conducted and provide data for assessing potential risks to pregnant women and fetuses;

(b) The risk to the fetus is caused solely by interventions or procedures that hold out the prospect of direct benefit for the woman or the fetus; or, if there is no such prospect of benefit, the risk to the fetus is not greater than minimal and the purpose of the research is the development of important biomedical knowledge which cannot be obtained by any other means;

(c) Any risk is the least possible for achieving the objectives of the research;

(d) If the research holds out the prospect of direct benefit to the pregnant woman, the prospect of a direct benefit both to the pregnant woman and the fetus, or no prospect of benefit for the woman nor the fetus when risk to the fetus is not greater than minimal and the purpose of the research is the development of important biomedical knowledge that cannot be obtained by any other means, her consent is obtained in accord with the informed consent provisions of subpart A of this part;

(e) If the research holds out the prospect of direct benefit solely to the fetus then the consent of the pregnant woman and the father is obtained in accord with the informed consent provisions of subpart A of this part, except that the father's consent need not be obtained if he is unable to consent because of unavailability, incompetence, or temporary incapacity or the pregnancy resulted from rape or incest.

(f) Each individual providing consent under paragraph (d) or (e) of this section is fully informed regarding the reasonably foreseeable impact of the research on the fetus or neonate;

(g) For children as defined in 46. 402 (a) who are pregnant, assent and permission are obtained in accord with the provisions of subpart D of this part;

(h) No inducements, monetary or otherwise, will be offered to terminate a pregnancy;

(i) Individuals engaged in the research will have no part in any decisions as to the timing, method, or procedures used to terminate a pregnancy; and

(j) Individuals engaged in the research will have no part in determining the viability of a neonate.

## 46. 205 Research involving neonates.

(a) Neonates of uncertain viability and nonviable neonates may be involved in research if all of the following conditions are met:

(1) Where scientifically appropriate, preclinical and clinical studies have been conducted and provide data for assessing potential risks to neonates.

(2) Each individual providing consent under paragraph (b)(2) or (c)(5) of this section is fully informed regarding the reasonably foreseeable impact of the research on the neonate.

(3) Individuals engaged in the research will have no part in determining the viability of a neonate.

(4) The requirements of paragraph (b) or (c) of this section have been met as applicable.

(b) Neonates of uncertain viability. Until it has been ascertained whether or not a neonate is viable, a neonate may not be involved in research covered by this subpart unless the following additional conditions have been met:

(1) The IRB determines that:

(i) The research holds out the prospect of enhancing the probability of survival of the neonate to the point of viability, and any risk is the least possible for achieving that objective, or

(ii) The purpose of the research is the development of important biomedical knowledge which cannot be obtained by other means and there will be no added risk to the neonate resulting from the research; and

(2) The legally effective informed consent of either parent of the neonate or, if neither parent is able to consent because of unavailability, incompetence, or temporary incapacity, the legally effective informed consent of either parent's legally authorized representative is obtained in accord with subpart A of this part, except that the consent of the father or his legally authorized representative need not be obtained if the pregnancy resulted from rape or incest.

(c) Nonviable neonates. After delivery nonviable neonate may not be involved in research covered by this subpart unless all of the following additional conditions are met:

(1) Vital functions of the neonate will not be artificially maintained;

(2) The research will not terminate the heartbeat or respiration of the neonate;

(3) There will be no added risk to the neonate resulting from the research;

(4) The purpose of the research is the development of important biomedical knowledge that cannot be obtained by other means; and

(5) The legally effective informed consent of both parents of the neonate is obtained in accord with subpart A of this part, except that the waiver and alteration provisions of 46. 116 (c) and (d) do not apply. However, if either parent is unable to consent because of

unavailability, incompetence, or temporary incapacity, the informed consent of one parent of a nonviable neonate will suffice to meet the requirements of this paragraph (c)(5), except that the consent of the father need not be obtained if the pregnancy resulted from rape or incest. The consent of a legally authorized representative of either or both of the parents of a nonviable neonate will not suffice to meet the requirements of this paragraph (c)(5).

(d) Viable neonates. A neonate, after delivery, that has been determined to be viable may be included in research only to the extent permitted by and in accord with the requirements of subparts A and D of this part.

## 46. 206 Research involving, after delivery, the placenta, the dead fetus or fetal material.

(a) Research involving, after delivery, the placenta; the dead fetus; macerated fetal material; or cells, tissue, or organs excised from a dead fetus, shall be conducted only in accord with any applicable federal, state, or local laws and regulations regarding such activities.

(b) If information associated with material described in paragraph (a) of this section is recorded for research purposes in a manner that living individuals can be identified, directly or through identifiers linked to those individuals, those individuals are research subjects and all pertinent subparts of this part are applicable.

## 46. 207 Research not otherwise approvable which presents an opportunity to understand, prevent, or alleviate a serious problem affecting the health or welfare of pregnant women, fetuses, or neonates.

The Secretary will conduct or fund research that the IRB does not believe meets the requirements of 46. 204 or 46. 205 only if:

(a) The IRB finds that the research presents a reasonable opportunity to further the understanding, prevention, or alleviation of a serious problem affecting the health or welfare of pregnant women, fetuses or neonates; and

(b) The Secretary, after consultation with a panel of experts in pertinent disciplines (for example: science, medicine, ethics, law) and following opportunity for public review and comment, including a public meeting announced in the FEDERAL REGISTER, has determined either:

(1) That the research in fact satisfies the conditions of 46. 204, as

applicable; or

(2) The following:

(i) The research presents a reasonable opportunity to further the understanding, prevention, or alleviation of a serious problem affecting the health or welfare of pregnant women, fetuses or neonates;

(ii) The research will be conducted in accord with sound ethical principles; and

(iii) Informed consent will be obtained in accord with the informed consent provisions of subpart A and other applicable subparts of this part.

## Subpart C-Additional Protections Pertaining to Biomedical and Behavioral Research Involving Prisoners as Subjects

### 46. 301 Applicability (Omit) .

### 46. 302 Purpose.

Inasmuch as prisoners may be under constraints because of their incarceration which could affect their ability to make a truly voluntary and uncoerced decision whether or not to participate as subjects in research, it is the purpose of this subpart to provide additional safeguards for the protection of prisoners involved in activities to which this subpart is applicable.

### 46. 303 Definitions.

As used in this subpart:

(a) *Secretary* means the Secretary of Health and Human Services and any other officer or employee of the Department of Health and Human Services to whom authority has been delegated.

(b) *DHHS* means the Department of Health and Human Services.

(c) *Prisoner* means any individual involuntarily confined or detained in a penal institution. The term is intended to encompass individuals sentenced to such an institution under a criminal or civil statute, individuals detained in other facilities by virtue of statutes or commitment procedures which provide alternatives to criminal prosecution or incarceration in a penal institution, and individuals detained pending arraignment, trial, or sentencing.

(d) *Minimal risk* is the probability and magnitude of physical or psychological harm that is normally encountered in the daily lives, or in the routine medical, dental, or psychological examination of healthy persons.

## 46. 304 Composition of Institutional Review Boards where prisoners are involved.

In addition to satisfying the requirements in 46. 107 of this part, an Institutional Review Board, carrying out responsibilities under this part with respect to research covered by this subpart, shall also meet the following specific requirements:

(a) A majority of the Board (exclusive of prisoner members) shall have no association with the prison(s) involved, apart from their membership on the Board.

(b) At least one member of the Board shall be a prisoner, or a prisoner representative with appropriate background and experience to serve in that capacity, except that where a particular research project is reviewed by more than one Board only one Board need satisfy this requirement.

## 46. 305 Additional duties of the Institutional Review Boards where prisoners are involved.

(a) In addition to all other responsibilities prescribed for Institutional Review Boards under this part, the Board shall review research covered by this subpart and approve such research only if it finds that:

  (1) The research under review represents one of the categories of research permissible under46. 306 (a)(2) ;

  (2) Any possible advantages accruing to the prisoner through his or her participation in the research, when compared to the general living conditions, medical care, quality of food, amenities and opportunity for earnings in the prison, are not of such a magnitude that his or her ability to weigh the risks of the research against the value of such advantages in the limited choice environment of the prison is impaired;

  (3) The risks involved in the research are commensurate with risks that would be accepted by nonprisoner volunteers;

  (4) Procedures for the selection of subjects within the prison are fair to

all prisoners and immune from arbitrary intervention by prison authorities or prisoners. Unless the principal investigator provides to the Board justification in writing for following some other procedures, control subjects must be selected randomly from the group of available prisoners who meet the characteristics needed for that particular research project;

(5) The information is presented in language which is understandable to the subject population;

(6) Adequate assurance exists that parole boards will not take into account a prisoner's participation in the research in making decisions regarding parole, and each prisoner is clearly informed in advance that participation in the research will have no effect on his or her parole; and

(7) Where the Board finds there may be a need for follow-up examination or care of participants after the end of their participation, adequate provision has been made for such examination or care, taking into account the varying lengths of individual prisoners' sentences, and for informing participants of this fact.

(b) The Board shall carry out such other duties as may be assigned by the Secretary.

(c) The institution shall certify to the Secretary, in such form and manner as the Secretary may require, that the duties of the Board under this section have been fulfilled.

## 46. 306 Permitted research involving prisoners.

(a) Biomedical or behavioral research conducted or supported by DHHS may involve prisoners as subjects only if:

(1) The institution responsible for the conduct of the research has certified to the Secretary that the Institutional Review Board has approved the research under 46. 305 of this subpart; and

(2) In the judgment of the Secretary the proposed research involves solely the following:

(i) Study of the possible causes, effects, and processes of incarceration, and of criminal behavior, provided that the study presents no more than minimal risk and no more than inconvenience to the subjects;

(ii) Study of prisons as institutional structures or of prisoners as incarcerated persons, provided that the study presents no more than minimal risk and no more than inconvenience to the subjects;

(iii) Research on conditions particularly affecting prisoners as a class (for example, vaccine trials and other research on hepatitis which is much more prevalent in prisons than elsewhere; and research on social and psychological problems such as alcoholism, drug addiction, and sexual assaults) provided that the study may proceed only after the Secretary has consulted with appropriate experts including experts in penology, medicine, and ethics, and published notice, in the FEDERAL REGISTER, of his intent to approve such research; or

(iv) Research on practices, both innovative and accepted, which have the intent and reasonable probability of improving the health or well-being of the subject. In cases in which those studies require the assignment of prisoners in a manner consistent with protocols approved by the IRB to control groups which may not benefit from the research, the study may proceed only after the Secretary has consulted with appropriate experts, including experts in penology, medicine, and ethics, and published notice, in the FEDERAL REGISTER, of the intent to approve such research.

(b) Except as provided in paragraph (a) of this section, biomedical or behavioral research conducted or supported by DHHS shall not involve prisoners as subjects.

## Subpart D-Additional Protections for Children Involved as Subjects in Research

### 46. 401 To what do these regulations apply? (Omit)

### 46. 402 Definitions.

The definitions in 46. 102 of subpart A shall be applicable to this subpart as well. In addition, as used in this subpart:

(a) *Children* are persons who have not attained the legal age for consent to treatments or procedures involved in the research, under the applicable law of the jurisdiction in which the research will be conducted.

(b) *Assent* means a child's affirmative agreement to participate in research. Mere failure to object should not, absent affirmative agreement, be construed as assent.

(c) *Permission* means the agreement of parent(s) or guardian to the participation of their child or ward in research.

(d) *Parent* means a child's biological or adoptive parent.

(e) *Guardian* means an individual who is authorized under applicable State or local law to consent on behalf of a child to general medical care.

## 46. 403 IRB duties.

In addition to other responsibilities assigned to IRBs under this part, each IRB shall review research covered by this subpart and approve only research which satisfies the conditions of all applicable sections of this subpart.

## 46. 404 Research not involving greater than minimal risk.

HHS will conduct or fund research in which the IRB finds that no greater than minimal risk to children is presented, only if the IRB finds that adequate provisions are made for soliciting the assent of the children and the permission of their parents or guardians, as set forth in 46. 408.

## 46. 405 Research involving greater than minimal risk but presenting the prospect of direct benefit to the individual subjects.

HHS will conduct or fund research in which the IRB finds that more than minimal risk to children is presented by an intervention or procedure that holds out the prospect of direct benefit for the individual subject, or by a monitoring procedure that is likely to contribute to the subject's well-being, only if the IRB finds that:

(a) The risk is justified by the anticipated benefit to the subjects;

(b) The relation of the anticipated benefit to the risk is at least as favorable to the subjects as that presented by available alternative approaches; and

(c) Adequate provisions are made for soliciting the assent of the children and permission of their parents or guardians, as set forth in 46. 408.

## 46. 406 Research involving greater than minimal risk and no prospect of direct benefit to individual subjects, but likely to yield generalizable knowledge about the subject's disorder or condition.

HHS will conduct or fund research in which the IRB finds that more than minimal risk to children is presented by an intervention or procedure that does not hold out the prospect of direct benefit for the individual subject, or by a monitoring procedure which is not likely to contribute to the well-being of the subject, only if the IRB finds that:

(a) The risk represents a minor increase over minimal risk;

(b) The intervention or procedure presents experiences to subjects that are reasonably commensurate with those inherent in their actual or expected medical, dental, psychological, social, or educational situations;

(c) The intervention or procedure is likely to yield generalizable knowledge about the subjects' disorder or condition which is of vital importance for the understanding or amelioration of the subjects' disorder or condition; and

(d) Adequate provisions are made for soliciting assent of the children and permission of their parents or guardians, as set forth in 46. 408.

## 46. 407 Research not otherwise approvable which presents an opportunity to understand, prevent, or alleviate a serious problem affecting the health or welfare of children.

HHS will conduct or fund research that the IRB does not believe meets the requirements of 46. 404, 46. 405, or 46. 406only if:

(a) The IRB finds that the research presents a reasonable opportunity to further the understanding, prevention, or alleviation of a serious problem affecting the health or welfare of children; and

(b) The Secretary, after consultation with a panel of experts in pertinent disciplines (for example: science, medicine, education, ethics, law) and following opportunity for public review and comment, has determined either:

(1) That the research in fact satisfies the conditions of 46. 404, 46. 405, or 46. 406, as applicable, or

(2) the following:

(i) The research presents a reasonable opportunity to further the understanding, prevention, or alleviation of a serious problem affecting the health or welfare of children;

(ii) The research will be conducted in accordance with sound ethical principles;

(iii) Adequate provisions are made for soliciting the assent of children and the permission of their parents or guardians, as set forth in 46. 408.

## 46. 408 Requirements for permission by parents or guardians and for assent by children.

(a) In addition to the determinations required under other applicable sections of this subpart, the IRB shall determine that adequate provisions are made for soliciting the assent of the children, when in the judgment of the IRB the children are capable of providing assent. In determining whether children are capable of assenting, the IRB shall take into account the ages, maturity, and psychological state of the children involved. This judgment may be made for all children to be involved in research under a particular protocol, or for each child, as the IRB deems appropriate. If the IRB determines that the capability of some or all of the children is so limited that they cannot reasonably be consulted or that the intervention or procedure involved in the research holds out a prospect of direct benefit that is important to the health or well-being of the children and is available only in the context of the research, the assent of the children is not a necessary condition for proceeding with the research. Even where the IRB determines that the subjects are capable of assenting, the IRB may still waive the assent requirement under circumstances in which consent may be waived in accord with 46. 116 of Subpart A.

(b) In addition to the determinations required under other applicable sections of this subpart, the IRB shall determine, in accordance with and to the extent that consent is required by 46. 116 of Subpart A, that adequate provisions are made for soliciting the permission of each child's parents or guardian. Where parental permission is to be obtained, the IRB may find that the permission of one parent is sufficient for research to be conducted under 46. 404 or 46. 405. Where research is covered by46. 406

and 46. 407 and permission is to be obtained from parents, both parents must give their permission unless one parent is deceased, tunknown, incompetent, or not reasonably available, or when only one parent has legal responsibility for the care and custody of the child.

(c) In addition to the provisions for waiver contained in 46. 116 of subpart A, if the IRB determines that a research protocol is designed for conditions or for a subject population for which parental or guardian permission is not a reasonable requirement to protect the subjects (for example, neglected or abused children) , it may waive the consent requirements in Subpart A of this part and paragraph (b) of this section, provided an appropriate mechanism for protecting the children who will participate as subjects in the research is substituted, and provided further that the waiver is not inconsistent with federal, state, or local law. The choice of an appropriate mechanism would depend upon the nature and purpose of the activities described in the protocol, the risk and anticipated benefit to the research subjects, and their age, maturity, status, and condition.

(d) Permission by parents or guardians shall be documented in accordance with and to the extent required by 46. 117 of subpart A.

(e) When the IRB determines that assent is required, it shall also determine whether and how assent must be documented.

## 46. 409 Wards.

(a) Children who are wards of the state or any other agency, institution, or entity can be included in research approved under 46. 406 or 46. 407 only if such research is:

  (1) Related to their status as wards; or

  (2) Conducted in schools, camps, hospitals, institutions, or similar settings in which the majority of children involved as subjects are not wards.

(b) If the research is approved under paragraph (a) of this section, the IRB shall require appointment of an advocate for each child who is a ward, in addition to any other individual acting on behalf of the child as guardian or in loco parentis. One individual may serve as advocate for more than one child. The advocate shall be an individual who has the background and experience to act in, and agrees to act in, the best interests of the child for the duration of the child's participation in the research and who is not associated in any way (except in the role as advocate or member of the IRB) with the research, the investigator(s), or the guardian organization.

# Subpart E-Registration of Institutional Review Boards (Omit)